The Beethoven Reader

The BEETHOVEN Reader

Edited by
DENIS ARNOLD
and
NIGEL FORTUNE

W. W. NORTON & COMPANY, INC.
New York

THE CONTRIBUTORS

PHILIP BARFORD
Senior Lecturer in Music, Institute of Extension Studies, University of Liverpool; has published numerous articles on Beethoven and a book on C. P. E. Bach

DEREK MELVILLE
Composer and pianist; currently working on a study of Chopin and the Pleyel piano

HAROLD TRUSCOTT
Composer, and Senior Lecturer in Music, Huddersfield Polytechnic; has published many articles on early nineteenth-century music

NIGEL FORTUNE
Reader in Music, University of Birmingham; Text Editor, sixth edition of *Grove's dictionary of music and musicians* (in preparation)

ROBERT SIMPSON
Has published studies of, among other subjects, Bruckner, Nielsen and Beethoven's symphonies

BASIL DEANE
Rossiter Hoyle Professor of Music in the University of Sheffield; author of monographs on Cherubini and Roussel

The Contributors

WINTON DEAN
Author of *Handel's dramatic oratorios and masques* and of the recent study *Handel and the opera seria*

DENIS McCALDIN
Lecturer in Music, University of Liverpool

LESLIE ORREY
Lately Head of the Music Department, Goldsmiths' College, University of London; author of a recent study of Bellini

ALAN TYSON
Fellow of All Souls College, Oxford; Visiting Professor of Music, Columbia University, New York, 1969; author of a number of books and articles on Beethoven and his contemporaries

ELSIE ARNOLD
Editorial Assistant, eleventh edition of *The Oxford companion to music* (in preparation)

DENIS ARNOLD
Professor of Music in the University of Nottingham; author of a monograph on Monteverdi

CONTENTS

9

Contents

IV. The Orchestral Music

V. The Operatic and Vocal Music

VI. Practical Matters

VII. The View of Posterity

ILLUSTRATIONS

between pp. 64 and 65

ACKNOWLEDGEMENTS

THE EDITORS WOULD LIKE TO RECORD their gratitude to the following for help in the preparation of this book: Mr. John M. Thomson, for assistance in its general planning; Mr. Anthony D. Ford, for reading the entire book in proof; Mrs. Diane Ford and Mrs. Elsie Arnold for help with the proofs; Mrs. Mary Whittall for helping with translations from German; and Contessa Loredana da Schio for checking translations from Italian.

For help in connection with the illustrations we are grateful to the following: Dr. Kurt Wegerer of the Kunsthistorisches Museum, Vienna, for permission to reproduce plates 2 and 3; Mr. C. F. Colt, for permission to reproduce plate 4(*b*); Dr. Hans Schmidt of the Beethoven-Archiv, Bonn, for permission to reproduce plates 5, 6 and 8; and Mr. Mark Rumary, for taking photographs for plate 5.

Extracts in Chapter 14 have been taken from the following books:

Hector Berlioz, trans. Edwin Evans, 'A critical study of Beethoven's nine symphonies', from *A travers chants*, Reeves, 1913 reprint 1958.

Felix Mendelssohn, *Letters*, ed. G. Selden-Goth, Paul Elek, 1946.

L. B. Plantinga, *Schumann as critic*, Yale University Press, 1967.

Jacques Barzun, *Pleasures of Music*, Michael Joseph, 1952.

Acknowledgements

Walter Riezler, *Beethoven*, Atlantis Verlag, Zürich, 1936, reprint 1966.

Romain Rolland, *Beethoven*, trans, B. Constance Hull, Kegan Paul, 1924.

G. B. Shaw, *London Music in 1888–89 as heard by Corno di Bassetto (later known as Bernard Shaw)*, Constable, 1937.

Edward J. Dent, *Ferruccio Busoni*, Oxford University Press, 1933.

Ferruccio Busoni, *The Essence of Music and other papers*, trans. Rosamund Ley, Rockliff, 1957.

Cecil Gray, *The History of Music*, Kegan Paul, 1928.

Murray Schafer, *British composers in interview*, Faber, 1963.

Ernest Newman, *The Unconscious Beethoven*, revised ed., Gollancz, 1968.

Igor Stravinsky and Robert Craft, *Dialogues and a Diary*, Faber, 1968.

Maxim Gorky, *Days with Lenin*, New York International Publishers, 1932.

PREFACE

MODERN STATISTICAL METHODS could no doubt calculate whether more words have been written about Beethoven than any other composer; they are scarcely necessary to realize that he has provoked more varied comment of all shades and kinds than anyone else (though Mozart must be a close competitor). The list only begins with the musicologist and music critic: novelists and politicians, philosophers and poets have all added to the riot of words, using a sometimes mythical figure for their own ends. In spite of a literature which already presents a formidable challenge to the bibliographer, it is safe to say that there will be no halt to its growth.

It therefore comes as a surprise, if not a shock, to find how much remains to be done if a complete picture of the musician is to emerge. Though it is difficult to believe that Beethoven's day-by-day existence can provide many surprises for the researcher, and the continuing publication and analysis of the sketchbooks clearly give us a considerable insight into his methods of work, the accuracy of the published texts of his music still needs to be investigated (a recent edition of the Violin Concerto has shown how much we are inclined to accept as eccentricity when in another composer we should suspect corrupt sources); and we also need a much expanded knowledge of the musical background of the early decades of the nineteenth century, which still await the thorough treatment that we take for granted in the study of early epochs. And to this we should add a study of the methods of performance current in Beethoven's time; in this respect, tradition is still a bad master, and the clearing away of its varnish might well yield surprises.

This process will take time and labour and is certainly beyond the scope of a centennial tribute. Even so, we hope that the essays in this *Beethoven Reader* will add some facets of interest to both scholar and music-lover. There has been no attempt to discuss every work of Beethoven, nor to achieve a balance based on the relative importance of each genre: for example, there are no chapters devoted to the chamber music for wind instruments (except that with piano, too), nor to the non-operatic stage music; and the piano music is treated at greater length than music for other media. Nevertheless we have attempted to cover at reasonable length some aspect of every major field in which he worked; to remind an age that is ready to accept new sonorities that Beethoven's own first study, the piano, was an instrument far different from that which we may too readily assume he knew; and finally, to accept with humility that our views on Beethoven's significance and intentions are by no means sacrosanct and are not likely to be particularly novel. Though there are new facts to be found and new attitudes to be awakened, one essential truth of which the study of Beethoven's œuvre continually reminds us is that music is too important to be left to the musician. He, like every great composer, is beyond the coterie and for humanity.

DENIS ARNOLD
NIGEL FORTUNE

September 1969

ABBREVIATIONS

AMZ   *Allgemeine Musikalische Zeitung*

HV   Willy Hess, *Verzeichnis der nicht in der Gesamtausgabe veröffentlichten Werke Ludwig van Beethovens* (Wiesbaden, 1957)

KH   Georg Kinsky (ed. Hans Halm), *Das Werk Beethovens: thematisch-bibliographisches Verzeichnis* (Munich and Duisburg, 1955)

LA   *The Letters of Beethoven*, coll., trans., and ed. with an introduction, appendixes, notes and indexes by Emily Anderson, 3 vols. (London, 1961)

NB   Gustav Nottebohm, *Beethoveniana: Aufsätze und Mittheilungen* (Leipzig, 1872)

NZB   idem, *Zweite Beethoveniana: nachgelassene Aufsätze* (Leipzig, 1887)

SB   Anton Felix Schindler, *Beethoven as I knew him*, ed. Donald W. MacArdle, trans. Constance S. Jolly (London, 1966)

TF   *Thayer's Life of Beethoven*, rev. and ed. Elliot Forbes, 2 vols. (Princeton, 1967)

WoO   denotes a work by Beethoven without an opus number (= Werk ohne Opuszahl, in *KH* above)

I
The Man and Artist

ONE

Beethoven as Man and Artist

PHILIP BARFORD

THE MUSIC-LOVER whose image of Beethoven is conditioned as much by the Bourdelle[1] head as by the music often arrives at a romantic conception which may have little connection with reality. A visit to the Beethovenhaus in Bonn brings one no nearer the truth. Unlike old parish churches, which deepen their atmosphere and impact through the devotions of those who use them, composers' shrines, with their pathetic relics, idealized portraits, lofty guides and commercial gimmickry, seem to deteriorate into empty shells. The spirit has fled the place of its earthly incarnation. Today, hordes of tourists descend upon Bonn, Salzburg or Vienna, moved not always by love or a sense of pilgrimage but often simply to be able to say they have been. The birthplace can be melancholy, dispiriting, filled less with the invisible presence of the master than with the shuffling ineptitude of the tripper hungry for souvenirs. It is true that the little pictures, busts and miniature scores often available at famous places of musical pilgrimage are usually tasteful mementoes of a holiday visit; the houses themselves are generally excellently arranged by their curators. The point that often strikes home is that music is such an abstract, idealized art that the actual places where composers were born or lived and worked seem curiously irrelevant to the nature of their achievement. No doubt some materialistic craving for tangible evidence of life and love and tragedy makes us wax sentimental

---

[1] In Musée Bourdelle, Paris. It can be seen reproduced in, for example, Burnett James, *Beethoven and human destiny* (London, 1960), frontispiece.

over ear-trumpets, or spectacles, or fragments of letters and so on. One wonders, sometimes, precisely what kind of image of the composer is privately entertained by some of those who stand in silent awe before the glass cases. How would Beethoven himself have reacted to the horn-rimmed female who dissolved in tears at the sight of his ear-trumpet, sobbing: 'You poor guy . . .'? And wouldn't he be furiously affronted by the visitor who shook his head sadly in front of a relic and said, in genuine mystification: 'Some kind of a nut, I guess!'

In respect of his own person, we should strive to grant Beethoven a discriminating approach to the truth. Sometimes, in correcting romantic delusions, it is necessary to swing to the other extreme to establish a balance, and in our own day there is no shortage of information which reveals that Beethoven, whatever his musical achievement, was always difficult and frequently unpleasant.

Totally opposed to the romantic image of Beethoven the Creator and Conqueror is the psychological, psychiatric, even clinical view. Beethoven was a genius with the characteristic marks of genius—neurotic without a doubt, unstable, oscillating between moody introspection and depression on the one hand and backslapping exaltation and enthusiasm on the other, with his own view of himself enlarged by solid convictions of his own worth and tainted by excursions into self-pity. He was aggressive, oversensitive, restless, undisciplined in his way of life, gross and crude with an 'unbuttoned' sense of humour, devious, intolerant and sometimes hypocritical. He suffered a great deal of ill-health.[1]

The attempt to know or 'possess' Beethoven through scientific data, images of his material form and circumstances, must always be misleading, at best absurd. One is often tempted to lump all the physical data together—the romantic portraits, the busts, the bronze statues, the ear-trumpets, spectacles and grand pianos—and hurl them impatiently into the Rhine. Beethoven's enduring monument is his music. There, in the notes, are his intellectual functions revealed. Beethoven *is* the music. The symphonies, quartets, sonatas

[1] Cf. Edward Larkin, 'Beethoven's medical history', in Martin Cooper, *Beethoven: the last decade, 1817–1827* (London, 1970), p. 439.

—these are the very structure of his consciousness, the framework of his being enshrined in symbols which reveal the truth to us in the only language that matters. Why look further? Where is the gain in doing so, except to our craving for the tangible and the visual, or our sentimental love of a picture? If you want to feel the physical power of Beethoven, thrust your hands into the C minor chord which opens the *Sonate Pathétique*! If you want to make contact with the visionary tone-poet, play through the *Arietta* of Op. 111!

And yet the traditional romantic images must be given their due. A bust, an engraving or a painting that is a true work of art brings something through which is true to its subject, something discerned intuitively by the artist who has made, however fleetingly, living contact with the inner life behind the appearances. From this point of view, images projected in idealized busts and portraits by artists who never even saw Beethoven could be allowed their measure of truth. For what, after all, is a bust? It is a representation which exalts the head. And why is the head exalted? Because it is the noblest part, the vessel of the thinking principle, the projection of consciousness itself, the summit of a man's being. In exalting the head the romantic principle reveals its enduring concern with the intellectual consciousness, with the sanctity of thought, inspiration and truth.

Yet when we look at Lyser's[1] sketches we feel intuitively the pull of a more rounded perception. Beethoven emerges in later life as a rather scrubby figure with a bristly chin and a thick, powerful, rather short body. There is a distinct feeling that the cravat wound round his neck would not be distinguished by sparkling cleanliness. Speculation runs on to consider his personal hygiene in general. In the heyday of his youthful association with the Breunings, Beethoven had set himself fashionable standards. And he could always smarten himself up under the influence of a new passion. At one time he even rode out like a city gentleman on a horse. But this phase did not long survive the onset of deafness in his thirty-first year. With the affliction came self-imposed social

[1] Johann Peter Theodor Lyser (1803–70), a writer, painter and musician, who became deaf at the age of sixteen.

withdrawal, introspection, increasing bouts of depression, and to some extent diminishing control over his own aggressive instincts, which led on many occasions to offensive behaviour against his best friends.

And there was his fundamental restlessness. In Vienna he was always changing his lodgings after quarrels with landladies. He consistently failed to find a harmonious pattern of day-to-day existence. His relations with publishers were marked by suspicion and double-dealing arising from a fundamental conviction that anyone who owed him money was a knave (it is only fair to add that he was quite justified in being on his guard against unscrupulous publishers). He was intolerable to his brother's wife, whom he called 'Queen of the Night'. To his nephew Karl he set himself in the exaggerated image of a father-figure, driving the boy to despair and a near-successful suicide. His private domestic circumstances descended to the lowest standards of undisciplined bachelordom— his favourite dish being a mess of eggs hashed up in a large bowl. It is impossible to imagine Beethoven married, and surrounded by children. He would have demanded total attention, and while pouring out devotion upon his suffering wife would yet have annihilated her nerves with outbursts of temper and sarcasm.

It is easier to attribute this to the subject of Lyser's sketches than to the inspired head painted in 1818–19 by Schimon (pl. 1);[1] but Schimon surely caught something of Beethoven's essentially solitary nature, a matter of inward spiritual independence rather than social seclusion. The simple fact that we have these two visual images—so fantastically unlike one another that it is difficult to believe they are of the same person—means that the fundamental question remains unsolved: what was Beethoven *really* like? What did Lyser draw that Schimon missed? What did Schimon see? He certainly saw something that was there, because Decker[2] in 1824 caught something of the same depth and quality, an aura of profound intellectual abstraction. Decker's pastel drawing is a

---

[1] Ferdinand Schimon (1797–1852), court singer and painter, friend of Schubert.

[2] Stephan Decker's crayon sketch was subsequently lithographed by Engelmann and is reproduced in this form in *LA*, facing p. 1008.

deeply convincing projection of the Beethoven of the third period. It is the portrait of a man of tremendous inwardness; the eyes, the lines of the face, the set of the head, symbolize a mind which has grappled with its own substance. Lyser drew the Beethoven of the country walks, the man who was thoroughly at home in wind, rain or sun, or swilling wine in a tavern.

To ask what Beethoven was really like is also to ask: what is the nature of man? And such a question cannot be answered without some recourse to introspection. All the external data are in Thayer's biography (*TF*) and in the collected letters (*LA*). More interesting than the impact of all that information upon modern readers is the fact that Thayer started out with an ideal view of his hero and finally had to leave his life's work unfinished. In the end he could not even think about the biography without being afflicted by headaches. The truth he uncovered shattered his illusions. This may well indicate the error of prejudging a character in the absence of full information. What we have now to do is to discover the true key, the psychological formula which unites the extremes of Beethoven's character in one complex being, so that we know how Lyser, Schimon and Decker really depicted the same man. It is not enough to dismiss the ideal image and exalt the real. What, in the last resort, do 'ideal' and 'real' mean? When we know a person well, our idea of his inner nature is threaded involuntarily into our perception of the external image, so that perception itself is an idealizing act of consciousness.

It is a commonplace of introspection that our lives are lived at different levels. Unreflective man identifies his selfhood with his physical body, his feelings and emotions, his reactions to immediate circumstances. Conventional religion teaches a spiritual 'soul' which leaves the body at death for some heavenly realm, and this puts the true centre of a man's being in a spiritual world, not a physical one. Psychology speaks of the 'persona' through which consciousness interacts with its environment. Mysticism generally attributes the centre of consciousness to the immaterial centre of the universe, or even beyond and above it. Some hold that there are growth and development in consciousness and creative function according to the measure of our intuition of our real spiritual nature and destiny. This is a view that Beethoven himself appeared to hold. An unauthenticated letter of his[1] contains the statement that he cared nothing for the world because he aimed at something higher. He appeared to relate his own creative powers to a divine centre and in general to regard this world and its sufferings as a vale of soul-making. A merely naïve materialism will see all this as illusion and fantasy, and account for the genius and creativity as accidents of brain function, physical heredity, glands and cells.

In solving the puzzle of Beethoven we have to bear in mind a necessary distinction between *levels of function*. Such a distinction applies to us all, and that is why introspection can help us in assessing the true significance of historical data. True, history is about verifiable facts, and once a person is dead the precise nature of his character can scarcely be verifiable by any known methods of historical research; but the important facts of musical history are facts relating to the *musical* consciousness. Music itself only exists as a function of consciousness. The history of music is really the history of musical functions; and this goes also for the mentalism and therefore the distinctive character of a composer long dead.

So in analysing the character of a creative musical genius we must distinguish between his physical being, his 'earth-orientated' consciousness, and the ideal level at which he expresses his characteristic function. 'Ideal', for a musician, implies a level of conscious awareness expressed in idealized tonal perceptions and the relations between them. A perception of sound is musically idealized by abstracting the idea or image of the sound (the words 'idea' and 'image' are here correlative) from its sensuous apprehension, the percept. In the imagination of a composer, the tonal idea or image is the essential datum. In his musical intellect, thought is the force which binds tonal images together in structural and formal relationships. The wholeness of the process of musical thinking at once fuses images of the concrete sounds and evolves an abstract pattern of pure relations between them. The creative musician discovers universal relations in the basic material

---

[1] To Bettina von Arnim, dated August 1812; in *LA*, p. 1357. Even if the letter is not genuine its contents may yet be based on reminiscences of conversations between Beethoven and Bettina von Arnim.

and then works quite logically within the formal frame of reference that the material implies. Composition is thus both the fusion of images by formal synthesis and the analysis of universal relations implicit in these idealized tonal elements. To compose is to discover the order in an initial tonal complex, whether this complex is the outcome of conscious invention or inspiration. If it is inspirational it comes in some sense spontaneously from other levels of being, from the so-called 'subconscious' or, what many would not allow because they only think from below upwards, from the 'super-conscious'. In this connection we might consider the possibility that as there is a level below consciousness, so there could well be one above it; in which case the general word 'unconscious' would subsume both what emerges from below and what is given from above. Very loosely, the term 'above' would signify what most people call God. Our relationship to it, if we believe it is 'there', is aspirational. It is the realm of the future of our own individual being, the level of the 'something higher' to which Beethoven aspired.

The important point is that, in working out the structural and formal implications of tonal images, the composer brings *universal* principles of relationship to bear upon the material. For example, every composer contemporary with Beethoven thought in the universal musical concepts of diatonic intervals, scale passages, triads, classical key-schemes and so on; it was precisely a collection of these that Diabelli offered to the composers of his day for variation. Each composer brought the same universal principles of musical thought to bear upon the basic material—in Schubert's case quite charmingly; but Beethoven alone revealed tremendous possibilities in the rudimentary elements assembled by Diabelli. Why is this? All the others knew the rules of the classical game. The answer can only be that in Beethoven's mind imagination and conceptual energy—that is, the form aspect of musical thinking, the musical equivalent of thinking with abstract concepts—were a single tremendous power. It is this fusion of imagination and thought which is important. One often comes across music students who can invent good thematic material, tonal images pregnant with structural dynamism, who lack the power of mental abstraction

27

which enables them to draw out the hidden form. Similarly, one meets the opposite type—the student who can write a good examination fugue on someone else's subject, but who never produces a single original idea worth writing down. The thrill of discovering a *Grundgestalt*[1] in a great work of art is that of making contact with the universal principle from which particular tonal images have evolved and which disciplines and orders their creative use. The key to successful composition lies in this important function: namely, being able to elevate the emotional energy generated by the particular tonal image to the universal principles of formal thinking which govern its use.

Now to live in the physical world with a physical body in which all the senses are fully alive is one thing. It is quite another to live

[1] Literally 'basic whole'—a group of tones from which different themes are derived and to which they relate as 'moments' or 'aspects' of a unity. Such a 'basic whole' can be explicit in a composition, in which case it will appear complete in original, inverted or retrograde forms, etc. Alternatively, and this seems to be more the case in Beethoven, it is a nascent complex, an overall *nisus* to a certain characteristic thematic order detectable in many quite different figures which can be heard in subtle interconnections. The method of analysis to which the apprehension of basic wholeness gives rise was looked upon unfavourably by Tovey, who insisted in his *A Companion to Beethoven's pianoforte sonatas* (London, 1943), p. 3, that analysis is about what we hear, not about what we can only see in the notation. Tovey, whose analytical methods have been considered infallible for many a long year, gives the impression of being a little naïve and ambivalent in this matter. The point about functional analysis directed to the basic wholeness is that it helps the ear to recognize consciously what might otherwise be missed. It presumes awareness of the totality of a work as a non-temporal fact experienced in the temporal flow. In so far as Tovey recognized (op. cit., p. 4) the need to identify groups and sections in the abstract, i.e. out of their strict time-sequence, he really granted by implication the basic principle of functional analysis, which is to grasp the entire structure of the being of a work in the flow of its becoming.

The bearing of this upon an understanding of Beethoven's mind is crucial. Like other creative geniuses he apprehended the form in the process, the fact in the flow, the shape in the series. And to do this he had to have that quality of mind which sees the metaphysical wholeness above and yet through every functional detail. The position implied here is a kind of 'meta-musical realism'. The Tovey type of analysis, in hands less skilled than his, and in the understanding of minds less perceptive than his, leads only to an arid 'naming of parts', and at worst to an idle numbering of bars.

28

inwardly as an artist in the ideal world of tonal images, with the power to fuse and unfold the formal potentiality of those images by a creative force which at once dignifies their intrinsic nature and elevates this to the abstract level of pure thinking; it is also something achieved by very few. It may well be that Beethoven's deafness was after all a relevant factor here, and not something to be swept aside as of no ultimate consequence. Not only was it a challenge that Beethoven accepted. Paradoxically, by limiting and finally almost totally denying physical tonal sensation, except in moments of aural lucidity which occasionally returned, it exalted the ideal value of tonal images to the nth degree. It must have done. In such a purely inward and ideal world of tonal imagination Beethoven lived during the second half of his life; and this ideal world was deepened and explored by a powerful intellect which had completely mastered the structural energies of classical musical terminology.

It would seem that there are levels of our human being which correspond with the different levels of function here indicated, and they cannot all be subsumed in the concept of human personality. Personality is an ephemeral thing, quite largely determined by the physical body, heredity and the circumstances of birth. In Buddhism, for instance, it is not considered to be more than an illusion, to be transcended as quickly as possible, the outward effect of a temporary association, in a certain proportion, of universal constituents which everyone has in common.

Beethoven's personality was rough, powerful, emotional, overreactive, gross, uninhibited and crude—all these aspects being joined together in a matching physical body which evidently took great satisfaction in physical nature. He was by instinct earthy, elemental and untamed.[1] Someone once remarked that his handwriting was like an elemental force.

But expressed through this personality was a powerful mind, a wonderful tonal imagination and a most exalted and delicate sensi-

[1] After meeting Beethoven at Teplitz, Goethe wrote to Zelter: 'his talent amazed me; unfortunately he is an utterly untamed personality, who is not altogether in the wrong in holding the world to be detestable but surely does not make it any the more enjoyable either for himself or others by his attitude . . .' Quoted in *TF*, p. 537.

bility. These factors all relate to that in him which elevated the impatient, appetitive physical man to a level of consciousness where his musical mind could function in a purely ideal world in complete abstraction from physical considerations. Because this level of function individualizes forms of experience by fusing tonal images in structures of thought, let us call it the level of Individuality. This term also carries the implication that, precisely in this kind of creative function, that in a man which is universal and personality-transcending *individualizes itself*.

Through this analysis something of the mystery of Beethoven lies revealed. Lyser's bristly profile and Decker's visionary pastel begin, so to speak, to flow together. In Beethoven the Individuality and the Personality are one; but there are two quite clearly perceptible levels of function. One is the level of the physical-based personality. The other is the level of the mind-based individuality in which the composer recognized his own reality in the mastery of tonal images by thought. The bull-like tenacity, aggressiveness and above all *will* to surmount obstacles were an overflowing energy in the physical personality, the effect of the self-recognition of the individuality. *The physical personality was the necessary vehicle in the substance of earth for a musical mind of that quality and power*, and its earthly energies were taken up into the creative world of the composer's imagination.[1]

It is interesting that those women who were attracted to Beethoven were able to see beyond the more obvious deficiencies of his personality and the chaos he made of his social and personal life. Nor could there have been friendships with rich and cultured patrons if the overwhelming force and magnetism of the inner fire had not been clearly apparent. In general, it is the female of the species and the feminine in man who first respond to the impact of a powerful artistic nature, and it is thus easier for an artist to communicate with women or artistically sensitive men than with those whose energies revolve around material possessions and ambitions. Possibly Beethoven sensed this, because he showed women a gentler side of his nature.

Beethoven's relations with women suggest the same idealizing

[1] See Philip Barford, 'Beethoven', *Music Review*, XXVI (1965), p. 192.

tendency that he brought to bear upon the sensuous world of tone. It seems fairly obvious that each woman in the long series of love affairs represented for him a projection of the ideal feminine, and that whether he realized it or not—and he was spiritually intuitive enough to do so—his overall experience was somewhat analogous to that described by Dante in *La Vita nuova*. It also seems obvious, and wholly characteristic, that Beethoven's innermost secret love-affair was with Leonore, the ideal wife in his only opera, the liberator and champion of freedom. Did he, as Jung might have said, confront in *Fidelio* his own contra-sexual image in this ideal woman? And did the recognition release the profounder energies of the last creative period? 'When this image is recognized and revealed', writes Jolande Jacobi,[1] 'then it ceases to work from out of the unconscious and allows us finally to differentiate this contra-sexual component and to incorporate it into our conscious orientation, through which an extraordinary enrichment of the contents belonging to our consciousness and therewith a broadening of our personality is attained.'

To distinguish between the individuality and personality of Beethoven is to see the impact of a universal force upon its chosen vessel. But this is no final explanation, even though the analysis is largely vindicated by the relationship between Beethoven's life and music. His own words are deeply significant and should not be ignored if we are to attempt a comprehensive character-study.

Beethoven believed in Freedom and in God, and like many others in his day and ours saw no reason to waste time saying what he meant by these terms. Like many he had felt the impact of the French Revolution. Unlike most his notion of freedom rose quite above political considerations and the local circumstances of his life, although he was interested in politics and freely criticized politicians and the police during a period of Viennese history when it was unwise to do so. His cavalier treatment of sonata conventions reveals a mind which, of its own creative momentum, had broken through previously accepted limitations. A wider background to this is his spontaneous assumption of freedom as a spiritual principle beyond all orthodox religious formulations. For Beethoven,

[1] Jolande Jacobi, *The Psychology of Jung* (London, 1942), p. 142.

experience of the free spirit which 'bloweth where it listeth' is man's natural, God-given estate, with correlative implications for the conditions of our life here on earth. There are few moments in *Fidelio* more moving than the emergence of the prisoners into the open air for a brief glimpse of daylight. This is symbolic of a general attitude which permeated his entire way of life.

Freedom from theological restraints is clearly indicated in Beethoven's credo, which he adopted from an inscription on a temple in Jean-François Champollion's *Pictures of Egypt*. 'I am that which is. I am everything that is, that was, and that will be. No mortal man has raised my veil. He is of himself alone, and it is to this aloneness that all things owe their being.' Beethoven copied out these words, framed them, and kept them on his desk.[1] Schindler reports that he venerated them highly. Such a formulation of the nature of God should be considered in relation to Beethoven's views about himself. Highly significant is a remark to Johann Nepomuk Kanka in 1814, to the effect that he loved the 'empire of the mind . . . as the highest of all spiritual and worldly monarchies'.[2] This bears out what has already been suggested in connection with the principle of individuality. To put it colloquially, Beethoven was a highly mental type, drawn to the notion of a universal medium of mind-stuff within which the nature of God is expressed without conceptual limitation. Beethoven recognized his own true being in the realm of mind in which, though as a musician and not as a philosopher, he was superbly equipped. In spirit he blended well into the background of idealism which characterized the philosophy of his day. This tended to place the world, and human experience of it, in the all-embracing, all-permeating *milieu* of a single Absolute, universal spirit. Beethoven's love of 'the realm of mind' implied his recognition of the reality of this concept, his sense of unity with the universal *Geist* or world-spirit. On one occasion he explicitly rejected all claim

[1] Cf. *SB*, pp. 365–6 and 390. Beethoven also noted down mystical formulations from a variety of other sources. See the section 'God' in Friedrich Kerst, *Beethoven: the man and the artist as revealed in his own words*, trans. and ed. Henry Edward Krehbiel (London, 1906), pp. 101 ff.

[2] *LA*, letter 502. The word here translated as 'mind' would be better understood as 'spirit'.

upon his own ego-nature, taking the near-oriental view that his own personality was nothing. Writing to the Countess Erdödy in 1815 he said: 'No news from me—that is to say, *nothing from nothing . . .*'[1] The remark takes on deeper overtones in connection with the notion of death. There is an oft-quoted statement to the effect that Beethoven had known how to die since he was fifteen years old. It was vindicated by the actual manner in which he passed through death. By all reasonable standards he suffered a physically degrading exit from this life. The fact remains that amid all the dirt and pain and squalor he impressed everyone who came to him with the manner of his dying. Such a bearing, at such a time and in such appalling conditions, can only mean that his words about God and the realm of mind were no idle hypocrisy.

It is also suggestive that in a letter of 1810 to Therese Malfatti[2] he should have quoted thus from Goethe's *Egmont*: 'People are united not only when they are together; even the distant one, the absent one too is present with us.' At the very least it suggests a community of consciousness in a universal mind transcending the limitations of time and space. Again, in spirit if not in form, his words fit into the prevailing philosophical idealism of his time. It has always been maintained, in systems which uphold monism as a way of mystical life and not merely as a body of ideas, that the condition of participating consciously in universal being is the absolute transcendence of the delusion of narrow egohood—that is, the belief that 'I' am my personality. Along these lines Beethoven once prayed: 'O God, give me strength to overcome myself, nothing must hold me to this life.'[3] He had surely glimpsed heights beyond the limits of the personality, a realm of freedom beyond finite limitation. But there was no escapism in all this, no dropping out, no retreat into a mystical quietude. To the end he wrestled with notes, and in wrestling with notes he struggled with the substance of his own being.

To the twofold distinction of personality and individuality already proposed, perhaps a third term should be added. It could

[1] Ibid., letter 563.
[2] Ibid., letter 258.
[3] Cf. Kerst, op. cit., p. 85.

best be symbolized by a question mark, to indicate the ineffable centre of the universe, Which or Whom Beethoven knew as God. Around this centre flows the limitless ocean of mind, the level of being wherein his own consciousness individualized itself in the construction of musical forms.

Anyone who has seriously introspected his own character and consciousness in this way will know something of the struggle that is involved. Once an ideal centre has been postulated, the unconscious never lets go, and a battle is joined between the different levels of being. Some may avoid the conflict by shrinking from the initial credo or by retreating into a kind of non-committal scepticism which forgets the involvement of the subjective consciousness as a growing point of life. In that case the whole matter slides underground, perhaps to re-emerge in some troublesome neurosis the true cause of which is then hard to identify—although it could well be wise to heed Jung's confession that throughout his long psychological practice he had found no patient whose fundamental problem was not at root a religious one.

Beethoven had made the central affirmation, however, and ratified it at Heiligenstadt. Psychologically the famous Testament is a spectacular document uncannily vindicating Hegel's analysis of consciousness in his *Phenomenology of Spirit*, where a fundamental conflict between two levels of the self is analysed in considerable depth and with tremendous acuity. The *Phenomenology* was completed the night before the Battle of Jena in 1807. Beethoven went through his own great crisis in 1802, the time of the Heiligenstadt Testament. As Beethoven and Hegel were the same age it is highly likely that Hegel, whose entire world-view is based upon the idea of opposition and transcendence through synthesis of the opposing factors, was formulating his theme of the dual nature of the self when Beethoven was actually struggling with it, although it is impossible to believe that Hegel's profound psychological insights were based upon nothing more personal than an idea of Heraclitus 2,000 years earlier, or a happy logical trick. The *Phenomenology* is autobiographical in the deepest possible sense, as the testimony of a mind coming to understand its own nature and functions.

A significant phase of the development of mind through the consciousness of an individual is when consciousness begins to introspect its own substance. To do this it must for a time turn aside from the immediate claims of the external world. Having done this, it discovers itself to be divided, to be two selves—one perfect, ideal, inspirational, the other imperfect, materialized, aspirational. This phase of duality is characteristic of mind as universal world-essence, where it is marked by the confrontation of being and becoming; but it has to be relived by each evolving soul. There is thus a time when the latent dialectic of the 'unhappy' or 'divided' nature will erupt into self-consciousness and disturb the unreflective flow of a mind which has not yet begun to individualize itself. When this time is reached, we might add, something will happen in the life to produce the necessary awakening—a religious crisis, a tragic love-affair, the death of a loved one, even, perhaps, a serious physical affliction.

Be that as it may, the 'unhappy consciousness' is the as yet 'unwon unity of the two selves'.[1] In terms of our analysis, Beethoven was at one and the same time the imperfect, imprisoned consciousness of the personality, aspirational towards a far-off divine perfection, and the awakened individuality, functioning in the purely ideal world of musical thought, attributing inspiration and goodness to God and never deviating from a sense of destiny in and creative duty towards that world and to God. In 1815 he wrote in his diary: 'All things flowed clear and pure out of God. Though often darkly led to evil by passion, I returned, through penance and purification, to the pure fountain—to God—and to your art. In this I was never impelled by selfishness; may it always be

[1] From Josiah Royce's translation of the *Phenomenology* quoted in *Hegel: Selections*, ed. Jacob Loewenberg (New York, 1929). These excerpts include Royce's translation of the section of the *Phenomenology* dealing with '*das Unglückliche Bewusstsein*', unhappily translated as 'the unhappy or contrite consciousness'. For a full English translation see that of J. B. Baillie (London, 1910); repr., ed. George Lichtheim (New York, 1967). All commentaries in English on Hegel's life and thought, especially with reference to the cultural background of Beethoven's day, have been superseded by Walter Kaufmann, *Hegel: a reinterpretation* (New York, 1965).

so. . . .'[1] And to Archduke Rudolph in 1823: 'There is nothing higher than to approach the Godhead more nearly than other mortals and by means of that contact to spread the rays of the Godhead through the human race.'[2]

Now, it is always possible that these and similar remarks, scattered through letters or found on odd bits of paper amongst manuscripts, do represent the self-deceptions of a hypocritical idealist whose fine words were countermanded by an inveterately irascible and deceitful personality. On the whole, however, the evidence of contemporaries seemed to be against this view. Many remarked upon the largeness of heart beneath the tempestuous and tormented temperament. Others, such as Julius Benedict,[3] noted the rapt look that characterized the composer's features during the years of the last great compositions, the quality of powerful interior abstraction and the visionary expression in the eyes which were caught in Decker's pastel drawing.

To overlook Beethoven's faults would be absurd. Equally misleading would be to serve up once again the old romantic image which has for so long obscured the whole truth of his personality. On the other hand, precisely because this is a sceptical, scientized age, we should guard against attempts to dismiss Beethoven's religion as either irrelevant or a sad delusion from which behaviourism or any other materialistic system has saved us. One of the most depressing experiences offered by the modern world is the spectacle of philosophers, psychologists and social scientists trying to prove that people who think like Beethoven are fooling themselves and that the satisfaction derived from his music arises only from his skill in manipulating sensations and deflecting anticipated resolutions. The 'nothing-but' attitude to life, when applied to music, creates a spiritual vacuum which strips it of all significance.

In the present writer's view, Beethoven, and others in the

---

[1] Cf. Kerst, op. cit., p. 105. The portion of this extract to '— to God —' seems to be a quotation, after which Beethoven continues in his own words and with a change of person.

[2] *LA*, letter 1248.

[3] Cf. *TF*, p. 873. Benedict wrote of 'an expression (in Beethoven's eyes) which no painter could render . . . a feeling of sublimity and melancholy combined . . .'

history of music, literature, philosophy, religion and exploration of both the inner and outer worlds who have undertaken the hardest fight of all, the struggle with the self, are the spearhead of human evolution. This evolution is something we now have to conduct upon ourselves. It is a matter of vision, faith in something more than the machinery of matter, and the will to apply the energies of our own being in the struggle of self-transcendence. In the case of art, this struggle is paradoxically a struggle with the material substance of things; but the real battlefield is the mind.

Beethoven is still very much before us, not only as a musical genius but as a challenge to the further growth of humanity, the symbol of man's eternal rejection of negative attitudes to life, and all narrow cleaving to petty ambitions of the finite self. The forces of his personality, which overflowed into unrefined excesses and offensive behaviour, were reflections of forces transmuted at a higher level of his being—the level of his better self, his individuality—into music. Indeed, they may well have been the involution of these same forces in a physical mould, taken over by the fusion of imagination and thought, endlessly refined, and lifted up. In all this there was a mighty centralizing force which led the individuality out upon a higher arc far beyond the claims of the finite personality. Beethoven himself explicitly related this centralizing force to the intuition of a universal centre in art, in nature, in the human soul, towards which human consciousness must evolve under its own direction and will, content to suffer in the purgation of its deviations until the battle of the 'unhappy consciousness' is transcended—if necessary in death itself. If this is anything like a true picture of what went on in the complex inwardness of Beethoven, then the detritus of Beethoven's physical personality, the squalor, the financial shiftiness, even the open profession of a belief in values which appearances seemed to deny—all this is now no less than a symbol of the unregenerate and unredeemed nature of humankind. To set against it, in Beethoven's case, there is the mighty achievement. Beethoven's music has always resisted the attitude of detached connoisseurship. It is an involvement, a challenge to the very substance of the mind, a perpetual assault upon our complacency, a symbol of the victory of consciousness over itself.

Have we, then, embraced the romantic view? Only, perhaps, in so far as the creative struggle of the mind with itself and with matter must always seem to offer itself for our contemplation in romantic images. To that extent Hegel's philosophy, which directed the struggle of thought to its ideal goal, is inherently romantic. Yet one of the most penetrating observations ever made about Hegel was that his dialectical system projected the true spirit of *comedy*.[1] Did Beethoven, in his deepest insights, see life in the same terms?

'Plaudite, amici, comoedia finita est!'

[1] See Loewenberg's introduction to *Hegel: Selections*, pp. xl ff. 'Grave is the life of the mind as human history displays and unfolds it. What could be graver than the vision of life as comic? What more tragic than the view that human folly is universal and ineradicable? . . . The march of the world, which is the march of the Absolute itself, is through Hell and Purgatory. This divine comedy . . . is too sublime for laughter.'

II
The Pianos and the Piano Music

TWO

Beethoven's Pianos

DEREK MELVILLE

PERHAPS THE MOST IMPORTANT contribution that a study of
Beethoven's pianos can make is to provide a fresh outlook on the
interpretation of his piano music, particularly in the fields of style
and dynamics.

Beethoven lived during a period of rapid development of the
piano, so that he was familiar with several different types, each with
its own distinctive characteristics. It is important to remember that
as a young man he had pianos similar to those that Haydn and
Mozart were using. There is, of course, a great difference between
these early pianos and those we use today. During his later years
Beethoven had early nineteenth-century English and Viennese
pianos. These may appear more like ours; they are nevertheless
very different instruments. Inevitably Beethoven's pianos will be
compared with and judged against the modern piano as if this were
the ultimate yardstick, but it needs little thought to realize the
folly of judging early instruments in such a way. They must be
allowed to speak for themselves in their own right, as they did
originally, and without reference to what has developed since. It
should be remembered that piano tone as we know it has existed
for only eighty or ninety years and that in Beethoven's day it could
vary quite considerably from maker to maker and also in different
countries. This fact was accepted, and no doubt enjoyed as a virtue.

The most important way in which pianos of Beethoven's day
differ from ours is that they were made entirely of wood and were,
by comparison, lightly constructed. Because of this, there was a

limit to the amount of string-tension that could be employed. The strings were not overstrung, nor were they as thick and heavy as those in our modern pianos, which need an iron frame capable of taking a strain of over thirty tons. As the strings were so much thinner, the leather-covered hammers[1] were correspondingly smaller; moreover, the instrument had a thin and flexible sound-board. The compass of the keyboard was smaller, too. A piano of 1785 by the Viennese maker Anton Walter (pl. 2) has five octaves and two notes, from the third F below middle C to the third G above. The Erard that Beethoven had in 1803 (pl. 3) goes a perfect fourth higher than that; the Broadwood of 1817 (pl. 4a) has six octaves; and the Graf of 1825 (pl. 5) six octaves and a fourth, from the third C below middle C to the fourth F above. These graceful and beautifully-made instruments were all far more elegant than their modern counterparts; sometimes they were decorated with inlaid brasswork, and often a simple cross-banding was used as a distinctive feature of the case-work.

Because of the notable differences between Beethoven's early and later pianos we ought to make more distinction than we normally do now between interpretations of the early and the late works. The dynamics used today in an early Beethoven sonata, if, for example, there is a *sfz*, *f*, or *ff*, are much the same as those employed in any of his last sonatas. This is quite incorrect, as becomes apparent immediately the different pianos are played, for instance a Stein of 1770 and a Graf of 1824 (to leave out of account for the moment the intervening makes and types).

It is but a step from realizing this fact to understanding that it is

[1] Ernst Pauer wrote in the second edition of *Grove's dictionary of music and musicians* (London, 1899), II, p. 744: 'Whilst the Viennese hammer of the time of Beethoven and Hummel (1815–1830) was covered with four or five layers of buckskin of varying thicknesses, the present hammer is covered with only one piece of felt, and produces a tone which, though larger and stronger, is undoubtedly less elastic; the action of the Viennese piano was very simple and it lacked many improvements which enable the present piano, with its almost perfect mechanism, to do a considerable part of the work for the performer. Thus we find that while formerly tone, with its different gradations, touch, the position of the fingers, etc., had to be matters of special study, the present piano with its accomplishments saves this labour.'

absurd to employ the enormous force which is so often used on modern pianos. The fact that none of the pianos—whether a Stein, Streicher, Walter, Schanz, Erard, Broadwood or Graf—would stand up to anything like this treatment is obvious proof that the contrasts between *ppp* and *ff* have been stretched beyond any sensible limit. It is only *contrast* that Beethoven wanted, not sheer volume of sound or exploitation of the instrument for its own sake (*ppp* is much the same on all pianos—rather better on some of Beethoven's, though of a different quality). In the sixty-two piano sonatas of Haydn, there are only two markings of *ff*. Beethoven has one in the seventh bar of his very first Piano Sonata, in F minor, Op. 2, No. 1; but Tovey is right to suggest that in the early works a *fortissimo* might be merely melodic and not percussive.[1]

There is no doubt that of all instruments the piano has undergone the greatest evolution. Strings and woodwind have not altered in anything like the same way during a similar period of time. The greatest change in string-playing is in the technical sphere, stemming from Paganini, who gave his first concert in Vienna on 29 March 1828, just one year and three days after Beethoven's death. Nevertheless, a Beethoven string quartet is still played on the same instruments for which it was written. Sometimes in a piano trio a pianist may be 'kept in order' by the other players, who do not wish to be 'drowned'. Possibly in Beethoven's day it was the other way round.

In performing Beethoven's piano music it is the range of expression that is the important point, not great volume of sound. No one would dream of saying that a miniature by Nicholas Hilliard or a small seventeenth-century Dutch landscape was too small and should be enlarged, or made similar in size to a Titian! There is a curious difference between the eyes and the ears. The eye accepts reproductions of large paintings scaled down to a convenient size; unfortunately the ear seems to crave the maximum volume of sound.

Recently a pianist wrote that he was surprised that 'Beethoven's music sounded more genuine and had a fresher impact' on an old

[1] Cf. Associated Board edition of Beethoven's piano sonatas, ed. Donald Francis Tovey and Harold Craxton (London, n.d.), I, p. [11].

Broadwood of 1806 than on a modern piano. The piano music of the eighteenth and nineteenth centuries is our priceless heritage; does it not owe its distinctive character to the type of instruments that the composers had at their disposal? And who are we to say that we can 'improve' it by transferring it to what is virtually a different instrument? The lesson that the old pianos can teach us is that we should treat our modern instruments more in accordance with an earlier style of playing.

There are fundamental differences of timbre between Beethoven's pianos and ours. A wooden-framed piano has a bright, crystal-clear resonance, which modern heavy, iron-framed, overstrung pianos do not possess. In years to come piano manufacturers may start making wooden-framed pianos again. In the meantime we must make the best of what we have: a magnificent and very beautiful-sounding instrument, which, however, is entirely different from anything Beethoven or his contemporaries ever heard.

Many people have considered it reasonable to suppose that Beethoven would have approved the development of the piano into the instrument we have today. I would add 'to some extent', as I think it possible that he would regret the replacing of the clarity due to the wooden frame by the duller timbre produced by the heavy cast-iron frame and thicker strings. Be that as it may, there is surely an enormous disparity between present-day dynamics and those that Beethoven would have envisaged. While he might have rejoiced in the full tone and reliability of the modern piano, I doubt if he would have approved some of the violent attacks that are made upon it in the interpretation of some of his most forceful music.

Certainly, no early piano can compare in tonal output to the maximum level that can be achieved on the modern piano, but it should be remembered that by the 1820s piano manufacturers all over Europe had achieved a volume of sound from their instruments quite sufficient for moderately large concert-halls. They were, in fact, loud enough for all normal requirements. It cannot be stressed too strongly that the dynamic range available from these pianos (that is, the difference between *pp* and *ff*) was very great, and a good player could achieve an extreme *pianissimo* without fear of the hammers failing to strike the strings, and also a *fortissimo* of great brilliance while still remaining within what can be regarded as a genuinely musical tone-quality.

Beethoven's early pianos were nearly all Viennese; they are rather different in character from their English counterparts and from the Erard which he had in 1803. This piano is very similar in design and construction to a Broadwood of that date. In spite of Beethoven's criticisms,[1] it is still possible to make a beautiful sound on it now that it has been restored; but it is necessary to use great finger-control and an exceedingly sensitive touch. It is in the Kunsthistorisches Museum, Vienna, where there is a most remarkable collection of pianos: it is very instructive to be able to compare the Erard with a piano made by Walter in 1785. Beethoven would certainly have used such an instrument. It has an outstandingly beautiful tone, far superior to that of the Erard, although it is a smaller instrument: it is instruments such as this that persuade some discerning people that pianos of this type and period represent the highest peak that the piano has ever reached.

In the same collection there is a piano with four strings to each key by Konrad Graf, who presented Beethoven with a similar model, now at the birthplace in Bonn and reproduced as plate 5. Unfortunately, the condition of that instrument when I saw it made it impossible to assess its qualities, but the one in Vienna was in perfect order and is a very disappointing instrument, not comparable with the normal three-stringed piano by the same maker. In spite of the four strings the tone is poor, especially in the treble. This probably accounts for the fact that there is not a single reference to the Graf in any of Beethoven's letters. It is possible that because of his deafness he could not hear it very well, but according to contemporary accounts it was fitted, on the advice of Johann Nepomuk Mälzel, who had constructed hearing-aids for Beethoven, with an extra sounding- or resonance-board over the strings to which could be connected a hearing-aid, shaped like a shell and made of very thin wood, not unlike a prompter's box. Both these items have been lost. Having four strings to each key

[1] Cf. *LA*, letters 275 and 283, quoted below, pp. 59–60.

was not a success. The wire had to be thinner to avoid an increase in tension that the wooden frame would not stand; and so it produced a smaller volume of sound than the normal three-stringed instrument, particularly in the higher octaves. It does not appear to have been made specifically for Beethoven, but was simply an experiment of the period. Its one advantage was that the strings were less likely to break with rough treatment, and this may have been the reason why Graf lent it to Beethoven in 1825, as by this time he was liable to employ too much force in order to try to hear himself play.

In the typical English piano of Beethoven's time, and its derivatives, the action is deep and heavy compared with the Viennese piano, while the tone of any note comes to maximum fullness slowly after the moment of impact. A comparatively prolonged period of time is necessary to allow full development of tone in the instrument. Similarly, the damping (especially in the bass) is slow, there being no very sharp decline of tone after the damper has returned to the string. In the typical Viennese piano the action is light and shallow, speech is extremely rapid and the full tone of the strings is achieved with no discernible delay after the blow of the hammer. In these instruments, too, the damping is exceedingly precise—a result of the design of the mechanism which made use of leather-covered wedges and split-wedges. These factors have a great effect on the clarity that can be achieved. The fullness of the English tone combined with the gradual development and decay of sound may detract a little from great clarity, but it encourages the use of broadly contrasted tonal effects and an almost impressionistic use of tone-colour. On the other hand, the clear precision of typical Viennese piano-tone allows for the utmost clarity and possibly more rapid tempi. Also it has a more neutral tone-colour, but with distinctive timbres in the bass, middle and treble registers, while the English piano has a full and colourful tone evenly distributed throughout the compass.

It is possible that as Beethoven had the Broadwood piano in 1818 and had thus for seven years (even though deaf) become accustomed to the distinctive English tone-quality, he did not find the clarity of the Graf that he had in 1825 of any assistance to him or particularly congenial, especially as it was unfortunately softer. In the last sonatas he does use the piano in an 'impressionistic' way; possibly this was due in part to the tonal characteristics of the Broadwood.

Many writers in the past have speculated as to how, when it was later extended, Beethoven might have written certain passages that lie at either extreme of the keyboard. There seems little point in this, which is, after all, only idle speculation. He never attempted to alter any of his earlier works when the compass of the piano had been extended. Some editors have been foolish enough to do this for him; and Tovey, oddly enough, decided that the compass of the piano hampered Beethoven in all his works for it and even suggested that he was not sure what was available to him in his last years.[1]

What is interesting is that he must have been composing the 'Hammerklavier' Sonata when he received the Broadwood, but he continued to use the piano that Streicher made for him with six and a half octaves, for this sonata extends beyond the compass of the Broadwood. None of the last three sonatas (1820–2), nor the Diabelli Variations (1819–23), nor the Bagatelles, Op. 126 (1823–4), have such a wide compass as Op. 106, which surely points to the fact that Beethoven was then using his Broadwood.

The fact that Beethoven was first really troubled with deafness in 1801, at the age of thirty-one, has sometimes been overlooked, and in other quarters misunderstood and exaggerated, as regards the effect on his own playing and on the state of his pianos during his lifetime and at his death. The condition of his Broadwood at his death was illustrated in a contemporary picture, and imaginary portraits of Beethoven, battered pianos and ear-trumpets, have appeared in this century. It cannot be too strongly emphasized that the obvious cause for the partial destruction of his pianos towards the end of his life was that he was trying to make himself *hear* the music he was writing. If he had not been afflicted with deafness, he would never have maltreated his pianos to the extent of breaking the strings. It proves that he desperately wanted to hear and judge what he was composing. The broken strings should never con-

[1] Cf. op. cit., preface (printed in all three volumes of the edition).

sciously (or unconsciously) be connected with his more forceful dynamic markings. It is true that he had a very forceful and explosive personality, but this one aspect of him should not be used as a reason or excuse for violent attacks on the piano (or in his orchestral works) and for rough playing of *f* or *ff*. There ought to be as much opportunity for subtlety in playing Beethoven as there is in playing Chopin. As has already been suggested, he was the first composer consistently to use the dynamic marking *ff*, but he never used *fff* in any of his piano music; however, he frequently used *pp*, and in the last sonatas quite often *ppp*, too. His *ff* in his Op. 2, written in 1794–5, has an entirely different meaning from that of Chopin's in *his* Op. 2, written in 1827. Both markings are often hopelessly misinterpreted today.

The idea that Beethoven was always dissatisfied with his pianos is not correct; his letters confirm this, and he would never have written so much for the instrument had this been the case. Out of some 140 opus numbers, forty-two denote works for solo piano, which includes the piano concertos (there are, of course, sometimes more than one work to a number); and there are twenty-six original chamber-works with piano: a total of seventy works, quite apart from songs with piano accompaniment and many lesser pieces without opus numbers.

Another erroneous idea is that he was always a very heavy-handed pianist. It may be that as a young man his playing was, as his friend Franz Wegeler reported, 'rude and hard'.[1] But in the early 1790s Beethoven heard the famous pianist Johann Franz Xaver Sterkel, who was admired for his light and graceful playing; as Thayer puts it,[2] 'this grace and delicacy, if not power of execution, which he now heard were a new revelation to him'.

Beethoven's injunction to Carl Czerny later on, 'Do as I say, don't do as I do', is linked to his great admiration for Johann Baptist Cramer's playing—to quote Ernst Pauer:[3] 'Beethoven preferred Cramer's touch to all others; the quietness, smoothness, the pliability of the movements of his hands and fingers, the excep-

[1] Quoted in *TF*, p. 103.
[2] Loc. cit.
[3] Cf. Edith Hipkins, *How Chopin played* (London, 1937), p. 22.

tional clearness and correctness of his style, rendered his performances unique. All who had the good fortune to hear Cramer play, speak of his legato and adagio playing with rapture, and describe the finish and delicacy of his touch as something exquisite.' This is ample proof of Beethoven's fundamental feelings towards the instrument and how it should be treated. It can be reinforced by a description of Beethoven's playing by Willibrord Joseph Mähler in 1803, which is almost interchangeable with that of Cramer's: 'Beethoven played with his hands so very still; wonderful as his execution was, there was no tossing of them to and fro, up and down; they seemed to glide right and left over the keys, the fingers alone doing the work'.[1] This is confirmed by Beethoven's own words when he said that some pieces should be as smooth as if they were being played with a violin bow. And Czerny reported: 'His bearing while playing was masterfully quiet, noble and beautiful, without the slightest grimace (only bent forward low, as his deafness grew upon him) . . . In teaching he laid great stress on a correct position of the fingers (after the school of Emanuel Bach, which he used in teaching me) . . .'[2]

The technical side of Beethoven's playing had its foundation in clavichord technique. Christian Gottlieb Neefe (1748–98), Beethoven's first teacher, from the age of twelve, undoubtedly played the clavichord, as he was a great disciple of C. P. E. Bach. He was responsible for the building of Beethoven's piano technique, and it is possible that Beethoven's early clavichord-playing influenced his piano writing in the slow movement of the A flat Sonata, Op. 110. Certainly Beethoven was grateful to Neefe, as is clear from a letter of 1793:'. . . I thank you for the advice you have very often given me about making progress in my divine art. Should I ever become a great man, you too will have a share in my success . . .'[3] In Germany the clavichord had long been the principal practice instrument. It was the natural vehicle for the new music that grew up in Neefe's lifetime and was only superseded when the piano was sufficiently developed. The English fortepiano was basically

[1] Quoted in *TF*, p. 337.
[2] Quoted in *TF*, p. 368.
[3] *LA*, letter 6.

an expressive *harpsichord*, while the Viennese school regarded the instrument as a more powerful *clavichord*.

It is important to mention one or two of the special effects that were possible on Beethoven's pianos and that were used primarily to vary the timbre and extend the dynamic range of these instruments. The *una corda* was fitted to both English and Viennese pianos in the earliest phase of their respective developments, but only in the English instrument was a true *una corda* possible. In the Viennese pianos the hammers could never strike fewer than two strings but made up for this by being fitted with various muting devices. One of these was called a *sordino*, or *sourdine*. This was a long thin piece of felt that came between the strings and the hammer, giving a muted effect, quite different from, and in addition to, the *una corda* or soft pedal. Mechanisms such as these were often controlled by hand-stops in the earlier Viennese pianos. The dampers, too, were not operated by pedals, but by knee-levers.

The dampers that are controlled by the right-hand pedal on modern pianos are called *sordini*. At this point one can quote A. J. Hipkins, who was connected with Broadwoods for sixty-three years; he is referring to the square pianos made by Zumpe *c.* 1760–5: 'The dampers (*Sordini*), collectively divided into two halves, bass and treble, were taken off by hand-stops placed within the case of the instrument; another stop brought a long strip of leather [or, later on, felt] called a "sourdine" (*Sordino*), into contact with the strings to produce a *pizzicato*. The direction for the dampers being raised thus became "senza sordini", and the resumption of their use "con sordini". To use the sourdine or muting stop was "con sordino", to remove it "senza sordino".'[1] Confusion has arisen because in the early editions of his works Beethoven made no distinction between '*sordini*' and '*sordino*'. '*Sordini*' is the plural of '*sordino*', but it appears that he designated *both* types of entirely different mechanism by the singular, '*sordino*'.

He gave some special instructions at the beginning of the first movement of the Sonata in C sharp minor, Op. 27, No. 2 (the 'Moonlight'), published by Giovanni Cappi in Vienna in 1802.

[1] A. J. Hipkins, *A Description and history of the pianoforte . . .* (London and New York, 1896), p. 102.

Above the treble stave is printed '*Si deve suonare tutto questo pezzo delicatissimamente e senza sordino*', and above the bass stave '*sempre pianissimo e senza sordino*'. For at least the last hundred years most editions of this work have altered '*sordino*' into the plural '*sordini*', which has complicated matters still further.

There are two schools of thought regarding the correct interpretation of Beethoven's instructions. One is that it means 'without dampers' (*sordini*), i.e. with the sustaining pedal held down, and this includes the people who do not know that '*sordino*' has been changed subsequently to '*sordini*'. This school confuses the issue still further by taking the instructions absolutely literally, which is unfortunate. To quote Tovey: 'as for *senza sordini*, this simply means "with raised dampers"; and on the feeble instruments of 1802 there was no reason for changing the pedal at all in this movement, for the sound of the undamped strings did not out-last its slow changes of harmony'.[1] This last remark is patently untrue, and one can only assume that Tovey never heard an early piano. It is just possible to play the movement with raised dampers very slowly indeed on a square piano of this date, as it is smaller and has much less power and resonance; even so, it is very difficult to manage and is not really satisfactory.

It is true that in order to play this work correctly the dampers must be raised from the strings, or the right-hand pedal held down all the time, except for the split-second damping that is necessary at changes of harmony. I myself have played this work on two of Beethoven's own pianos and also on other pianos of his period; and it is possible to state quite categorically that Beethoven would never have tolerated the frightful dissonances which result if the sustaining pedal were held down and not moved throughout the piece. To distort such a work as this, or the second movement of the Third Piano Concerto,[2] would be unthinkable, and it is highly unlikely that Beethoven ever did. The reason for the coming into existence (through Czerny) of this idea that Beethoven held the pedal down throughout an entire movement or theme is that

[1] Op. cit., II, p. 50.
[2] Czerny reported one occasion when Beethoven played the whole of the main theme of the slow movement with dampers raised throughout.

probably no one at that time would have realized that he made the very quick changes of knee-lever or pedal that are necessary.

The other school of thought takes the instruction '*senza sordino*' at its face-value and does not use the *sourdine* pedal on an early piano if there is one. The *sourdine* pedal is not found any more on the modern grand piano—occasionally it appears on inferior upright pianos as the soft or left-hand pedal and called a celeste—but both Beethoven's Erard and Graf pianos had the *sourdine*. Apart from not using the *sourdine* the second school would play the movement using both the soft and sustaining pedals on a modern piano or on a piano of Beethoven's time.

In giving the instructions 'The whole of this piece should be played as delicately as possible . . .' Beethoven wanted to make sure that pianists did not simply try to obtain the effect of a delicate touch by using a *sourdine* or mute-stop, and by not troubling to exercise sufficient finger-control. He wanted the darker and richer sound of the freely vibrating strings.

Beethoven's Erard piano of 1803 may well have been the first instrument he possessed to have pedals instead of knee-levers. It was certainly the first time he had a piano with a true *una corda* and a *sourdine*, both of which he could control with pedals. The Erard had four pedals: from left to right, lute-stop, sustaining pedal, *sourdine* and *una corda*. The Third Piano Concerto was composed in 1800, but it was not published until 1804, so it is reasonable to suppose that Beethoven introduced into the score the new effects he could produce on this piano. (He had a marked preference for quiet and soft effects, as we can tell from a letter of 1802[1] and the extremely soft dynamic markings in the last sonatas.)

In the original edition of the concerto the slow movement presents in places a strange sight (see plate 7). It is frequently marked '*con sordino*' and '*senza sordino*', and these markings do not make so much sense if interpreted as 'with' and 'without the sustaining pedal' as they do if they are taken to refer to the *sourdine* pedal; then they not only make sense but can produce a magical effect. It is possible to obtain great contrasts with the *sourdine* not only by playing *piano*, but *forte* too, and by using the sustaining pedal as

[1] *LA*, letter 66.

well in the normal way. The perplexing thing is that in the first and last movements of this concerto the very few times that '*con sordino*' and '*senza sordino*' are marked they would seem, at least in some cases, to refer to the sustaining pedal only. It is impossible to be dogmatic about this interpretation of '*con sordino*' and '*senza sordino*', but it is important to try to dismiss the idea that Beethoven's pianos were so lacking in resonance that they did not need damping when a change of harmony occurred.

Tovey is by no means the only writer to have fostered erroneous ideas about the true qualities and assets of Beethoven's pianos. It is true that Beethoven made one disparaging remark about the piano late in life, but it is surely very unwise to imply that he was dissatisfied with it, without taking several very important facts into consideration, e.g. the state of his health, his deafness, his domestic affairs, his pecuniary circumstances, the demands of his publishers, and, last and by no means least, his relations with his nephew Karl.

Recordings of some Beethoven sonatas and bagatelles have been made on pianos of Beethoven's time—two Broadwood grands, one of 1806, the other of 1819, and a Graf of about 1830, all from the Colt Clavier Collection at Bethersden, Kent. I found my own feelings about these recordings coincided exactly with those of a friend, the well-known musicologist and author of *Nineteenth-Century Piano Music*, Mrs. Kathleen Dale, who writes as follows:

> The average musician, if contemplating Beethoven's works being played on a piano of his time, would most likely imagine them as sounding tinkling, jangling, lacking in resonant tone or in sustaining power.
>
> The reality is simply astounding: warmth, clarity, poetry and the wonderful feeling that the lovely sounds are simply emanating from the instrument and are not being hacked out of it by an over-emotional performer. The music speaks for itself, with no uncertain voice, with quiet authority. It is *there* of its own accord.
>
> One has always dreaded the first *fortissimo* chords of the 'Appassionata' Sonata, Op. 57 (at bar 17), almost having to seal one's ears against their blatancy. On the correct piano they lose all their stridency and sound purposeful and convincing—not

hard and antagonizing. Especially, one notices all through the 'Appassionata' and the 'Waldstein' that whenever a single line of the texture had to be made conspicuous the surrounding texture did not retreat into the background (i.e. melody and accompaniment were equal partners). *All* parts of the texture remained within the musical context; no finesse of part-writing was lost. It was like looking at the west front of a great cathedral and seeing every detail clearly as well as the contour as a whole. Pedal-effects, which would sound smudgy on a modern piano, sounded magically ethereal, lifting the music into the sphere of impressionism.

At the end of these performances one was left with a feeling of having breathed mountain air—exhilarated, not exhausted, as one so often is after a concert pianist today has butchered one's ears with his heavy attacks on the instrument.

What is so refreshing to me about these remarks is that they were made by someone whose musical training began at the turn of the century. Kathleen Dale became a pupil of Fanny Davies in the 1920s and is thus an inheritor of the Clara Schumann tradition. These impressions of hers go to strengthen my opinion that if pianists in general could hear these recordings and accustom their ears to the exciting possibilities of tone-colour and textural clarity that they offer to the player, a new era in the interpretation of Beethoven might well be within sight. Nevertheless, it cannot be too strongly emphasized that it needs a really sensitive musician and pianist to achieve the right results.

★ ★ ★ ★

In the collected letters of Beethoven translated by Emily Anderson (*LA*) there are only a few direct references either to the piano in general or to his own instruments, but these are very interesting and worth assembling here with a commentary. Miss Anderson's numbering of the letters is used; the reader is referred to her edition for her annotations.

There are more references when he was young than during his middle and last years. The first two are:

17   To Johann Andreas Streicher   *19 November 1796*
Dear Streicher!

I received the day before yesterday your fortepiano, which is
really an excellent instrument. Anyone else would try to keep it for
himself; but I—now you must have a good laugh—I should be
deceiving you if I didn't tell you that in my opinion it is far too good
for me, and why?—Well, because it robs me of the freedom to
produce my own tone [this is akin to Chopin's preference for the
Pleyel piano, rather than the Erard, which he said had a ready-
made tone]. But, of course, this must not deter you from making
all your fortepianos in the same way. For no doubt there are few
people who cherish such whims as mine.

. . . But I trust that, without my having to remind you of this in
my letter, you are wholly convinced of my heartfelt desire that the
merits of your instrument should be recognized in this country and
everywhere . . .

18   To the same   *1796*

. . . I assure you in all sincerity, dear St[reicher], that this was
the first time it gave me pleasure to hear my trio performed; and
truly this experience will make me decide to compose more for the
pianoforte than I have done hitherto. Even if only a few people
understand me, I shall be satisfied. There is no doubt that so far as
the manner of playing it is concerned, the *pianoforte* is still the least
studied and developed of all instruments; often one thinks that one
is merely listening to a harp. And I am delighted, my dear fellow,
that you are one of the few who realize and perceive that, provided
one can feel the music, one can also make the pianoforte sing. I
hope the time will come when the harp and the pianoforte will be
treated as two entirely different instruments . . .

These are Beethoven's only references to the piano before his
deafness began. Five years later he can write:

53   To Karl Amenda   *1 July 1801*

. . . Let me tell you that my most prized possession, *my hearing*,
has greatly deteriorated. When you were still with me, I already
felt the symptoms; but I said nothing about them. Now they have

become very much worse . . . I hear that you have ordered
pianos from S[treicher] . . . (When I am playing and composing,
my affliction still hampers me least; it affects me most when I am
in company) . . . My pianoforte playing too has considerably
improved . . .

The question of Beethoven's deafness is of great importance
when considering his pianos, his remarks about them and his
attitudes towards them; the degree of his deafness is, however,
extremely difficult to assess accurately.

Beethoven's first-mentioned preference for a particular maker is
for Anton Walter. He obviously thought very highly of this maker's
work, as he was prepared to pay him for a piano when he could
obtain one from several other makers for nothing. It does not
surprise me that he thought so well of Walter's pianos. One in
particular, in the Kunsthistorisches Museum in Vienna, as I have
mentioned before, has the most remarkably beautiful tone. Mozart
certainly liked them; Haydn preferred Johann Schanz and said of
Walter's that they were expensive and that only one instrument in
ten was a good one. In the next letter it is particularly interesting to
note that Beethoven was anxious to have a piano with a true *una
corda*, a device which the Viennese makers had never fitted.

66[1]   To Nikolaus Zmeskall von Domanovecz   *November 1802*

Well, my dear Z[meskall], you may give Walter, if you like, a
strong dose of my affair. For, in the first place, he deserves it in any
case; and, what is more, since the time when people began to think
that my relations with Walter were strained, the whole tribe of
pianoforte manufacturers have been swarming around me in their
anxiety to serve me—and all for nothing. Each of them wants to
make me a pianoforte exactly as I should like it. For instance,
Reicha has been earnestly requested by the maker of his pianoforte
to persuade me to let him make me one; and he is one of the more
reliable ones, at whose firm I have already seen some good instruments—so you may give Walter to understand that, although I can
have pianofortes for nothing from all the others, I will pay him 30

---

[1] This letter has been partially retranslated by the author; see plate 6.

ducats, but not more than 30 ducats, and on condition that the wood is mahogany. Furthermore, I want a stop built into it to give one string only [i.e. *una corda*]—If he won't agree to these conditions, then make it quite plain to him that I shall choose one of the others to whom I will give my order and whom I shall take later on to *Haydn* to let the latter see his instrument—About noon today a foreigner, a Frenchman, is coming to see me. Herr R[eicha] and I shall then have the pleasure of *seeing myself compelled to display my art on Jakesch's piano* . . .

Beethoven had to wait another year before his wish for a true *una corda* was fulfilled. For technical reasons relating to the Viennese action, Walter was unable to comply with his wishes. In 1803 Sébastien Erard presented Beethoven with one of his pianos. This, as we have seen, has four pedals: lute-stop, sustaining pedal, *sourdine* and *una corda*, which is a true *una corda*, i.e. the hammer can be made to strike one only of the three strings. A particularly noteworthy example of its use occurs towards the end of the slow movement of the Fourth Piano Concerto, where Beethoven writes first '*a 3 corde*' and four bars later '*due, poi una corda*'. This is an effect which cannot be produced on a modern piano.

A year later he wished to hire or borrow a piano from Matthäus Andreas Stein (son of the famous pianoforte manufacturer at Augsburg, Andreas Stein), who came to Vienna with his elder sister Nanette, who had married Johann Andreas Streicher, another pianoforte manufacturer. It was the Streichers who opened a salon for musicians, which became the centre of Vienna's musical life. They also established a piano factory. Stein started his own business as a pianoforte-maker in Vienna in 1802.

80   To Ferdinand Ries   *Summer 1803*

You probably know that I am here—Go to Stein and find out whether he can't send out an instrument to me here—against payment—I am afraid of having mine brought out here . . .

In the next letter he is merely recommending pianoforte-makers; but it is interesting to note that they are two fresh ones. It is possible that this restlessness is due to the onset of his deafness, and not to dissatisfaction with the piano, which is borne out in the subsequent letter, written six years later.

86   To Breitkopf & Härtel   *23 November 1803*

Since you wish to have instruments from other manufacturers as well, I am suggesting to you also Herr Pohack, whose work is sound and whose prices and types of instrument are enclosed in this letter. I should like to add Herr Moser, a list of whose prices and instruments will be sent to you shortly. His work is also reliable and leads one to hope that in time he will make instruments equal, or even superior, to those of the leading manufacturers.

220   To the same   *26 July 1809*

. . . I have only a few samples of Emanuel Bach's compositions for the clavier; and yet some of them should certainly be in the possession of every true artist, not only for the sake of real enjoyment but also for the purpose of study. And my greatest pleasure is to play at the homes of some true friends of music works which I have *never* or seldom seen . . .

Possibly Beethoven's confidence was being undermined by his deafness, which may account for the opening of the next letter, since after the Sonata in F minor, Op. 57 (1804–5), he composed no piano sonatas until 1809:

226   To the same   *19 September 1809*

. . . I don't like to spend much time composing sonatas for pianoforte solo, but I promise to let you have a few . . .

Less than five months later he sent Breitkopf & Härtel not only three sonatas but a number of other works involving the piano, including the Fifth Concerto.

The next mention of a particular make of piano, in the spring of 1810,[1] is his choice of an actual instrument, and the maker, Schanz, may well have been the choice of the buyer, Frau von Malfatti, as his pianos were considered to have a sweeter, softer tone and an even lighter action than Walter's. Certainly it is unlikely that Beethoven himself would have been interested in a piano by Schanz at

[1] Cf. *LA*, letter 255.

this date, if it was softer. But time proves one wrong, in fact. The following letter shows the first expression of real criticism, not of Schanz, but of Streicher:

257   To Johann Andreas Streicher   *6 May 1810*
   . . . But I do ask you to ensure that the instruments do not wear out so quickly—you have seen your instrument which I have here and you must admit that it is very worn out; and I frequently hear the same opinion expressed by other people—You know that my sole object is to promote the production of good instruments. That is all. Otherwise I am absolutely impartial. Hence you must not be annoyed at hearing the truth . . .

It is possible that by this time, because of his increasing deafness, Beethoven was 'punishing' his piano in an effort to hear it properly. He obviously used the instrument a very great deal, which would in itself account for its wearing out. There seems no doubt at all about his enthusiasm for Streicher's pianos in the next letter.

267   To the same   *Shortly before 27 July 1810*
Dear S[treicher],
   I can't help it, the pianoforte beside the door near your entrance is constantly ringing in my ears—I feel sure that I shall be thanked for having chosen this one—So do send it. If you think that it may be even heavier than you suppose, why, we can easily get over that difficulty—

269   To the same   *July 1810*
   . . . I am already looking forward to the new instruments and I hope too that the Archduke [Rudolph] will soon take one.

He was obviously very pleased with Streicher's pianos when they were new and was not looking forward to returning to his now old 1803 Erard in Vienna, having hired or borrowed one of Streicher's while he was at Baden.

275   To the same   *18 September 1810*
Dear Streicher!
   As I shall be back in Vienna by the beginning of October, let me know whether I may again have a piano from you—

My French piano is no longer of much use; in fact it is quite useless. Perhaps you can advise me where we can find a home for it . . .

N.B. The Archduke R[udolph] would like to have some good strings. So I am asking you whether you could provide him with some; and, if so, I shall then let you have the numbers. But, of course, they must be *Kürnbergers.*

The following letter speaks for itself:

283   To the same   *Middle of November 1810*
Dear Streicher!

You promised to let me have a piano by the end of October; and now we are already half through November and as yet I haven't received one—My motto is either to play on a good instrument or not at all—As for my French piano, which is certainly quite useless now, I still have misgivings about selling it, for it is really a souvenir such as no one here has so far honoured me with—

On account of my foot I cannot yet walk so far. But if you keep me waiting any longer I will invade your premises with a horrible modulation; and then a murrain upon you—Forgive my *filthy ink-blots.*

In regard to the remover, if any further damage was done to the instrument perhaps while in my possession, which is quite possible in view of the state of my household at that time, then let me know this frankly, for I am perfectly willing, of course, to compensate you for the loss.

All good wishes, if you send me a p[ianoforte];
     if not, then all bad wishes,
                         Your friend
                         Beethoven

By the way, since my home is now in better order your i[nstrument] will certainly suffer no damage.

In 1813 we find Beethoven wanting his piano repaired or put in order before taking it to Baden. It is fairly obvious that Stein has suggested that he has the piano in the workshop in Vienna and that Beethoven should hire one in Baden, but . . .

420   To Matthäus Andreas Stein   *Early May 1813*
Dear Stein!

At Baden people charge 34 gulden a month for a wretched piano.
I consider that to pay that sum amounts to throwing money out of
the window—If you could only spare one of the people whom you
have at your place, that would soon be remedied. I would certainly
pay him well!

Be sure to bring the mattresses with you! I think that on these
and some straw my instrument could, after all, be brought safely
to Baden. Kindly let me have your opinion . . .

Beethoven took a great interest in the pianos of his day and went
to a great deal of trouble to advise his friends and acquaintances
what make to buy and what they would cost. Notice that in his
next letter he talks of a 'sound and *durable* piano' (my italics).

536   To Joseph von Varena   *21 March 1815*
My dear V[arena]!

Being unwell and very busy I found it impossible until yesterday to make the necessary enquiries—Here are my results. You can
have from *Schanz* as good a piano as he is able to supply for the
price of 400 gulden V.C., including packing. This piano has six
octaves—*Seiffert* asks 460 gulden, but would probably let you have
one for 400—There are, however, other excellent makers, I hear,
from whom you could purchase a sound and durable instrument
for a good deal less than 400 gulden—But one cannot *look for* and
find one of this type very quickly—I mean, *a good one*—such as you
must have by right—Hence I should require more time—Well,
let me have an early reply informing me whether you agree to these
prices and then in a few weeks you will have a sound and durable
piano—As for payment, well, the Viennese instrument makers
insist on being paid here at once in loco before despatching their
instruments; for they declare that delay in obtaining payment has
frequently caused them inconvenience—That is all I can tell you
for the moment, my dear V—As soon as you let me have your
views on this subject, I will take steps to serve you as best I can . . .

Having recommended Schanz's pianos to Frau von Malfatti in

1810 and again to Joseph Varena in March 1815, Beethoven him-self decided to have one, but with disastrous results. Whether Schanz's pianos really were softer- or sweeter-toned I have not been able to ascertain, and it is impossible to guess why Beethoven decided to try one. He certainly keeps quiet about his own Schanz piano in the second of the next two letters!

539 To Johann Xaver Brauchle   *Spring 1815*
. . . in spite of all the kindnesses of the Countess I shall have [to ask] . . . to have one of her pianofortes in my room just for a few days. For *Schanz* has sent me such a bad one that he will soon have to take it back again. And I don't like to send out to you his instrument which I cannot keep . . .

557 To Joseph von Varena   *23 July 1815*
You will certainly receive it [the piano], my dear V, in twelve days at latest. It was impossible to get it off to you before . . . If you want to add 50 gulden more for embellishments, write to me at once.—The instrument has been made by *Schanz*—I too possess one of his . . .

It is possible only to make wild guesses about the next letter, which concerns an organ. Mine, for what it is worth, is that Beet-hoven thought he might be able to hear the sustained tone of an organ better than a piano and wanted it purely for composing purposes.

594 To Herr Riedel   *1815*
Herr Riedel, organ-builder
Be so kind as to come to me so that I may have a talk with you. For I cannot use the instrument you have installed . . .

In 1816 he asks Baron Joseph von Schweiger and Joseph Czerny to help an unknown pianoforte-maker at Baden sell 'his very small but elegant and well-made pianos'.[1] It was in a letter to Sigmund Anton Steiner on 23 January 1817 that he decided to use the word '*Hammerklavier*' on all his piano music with German titles. 'This is to be clearly understood once and for all.'[2]

[1] *LA*, letter 730, to Schweiger; that to Czerny is 731.
[2] *LA*, letter 737.

At this time in many of his letters to Nanette Streicher, wife of the pianoforte-maker (and indeed one herself), it is difficult to decide sometimes which is the most important, his pianos, his meals, or his laundry! Nanette Streicher must have had the patience of a saint, doubtless because she could see his frightful household troubles and because she realized the colossal hindrance that his deafness was to him and also how very bad his general health was becoming. She realized what a dreadful liability it was for him to disrupt his way of life in order to bring up his nephew Karl. Some of these letters or parts of letters may seem to have nothing directly to do with his pianos, but they give a picture which illuminates the period when some of his most remarkable piano music was written; and they *were* written to a pianoforte-maker!

785   To Frau Nanette Streicher   *7 July 1817*
My beloved friend!

. . . I have a great favour to ask of Streicher. Request him on my behalf to be so kind as to adjust one of your pianos for me to suit my impaired hearing. It should be as loud as possible. That is absolutely necessary. I have long been intending to buy one of your pianos, but at the moment that would be very difficult for me. Perhaps, however, it will be possible for me to do so later on. But until then I should like *to borrow* one of yours. Of course I don't want to do so without paying for it . . . Perhaps you are not aware that, although I have not always used one of your pianos, since 1809 I have always had a special preference for them—Only Streicher would be able to send me the kind of piano I require . . . Whatever proposals you make to me in this connection I will accept, and I will gladly comply with your conditions . . .

789   To the same   *20 July 1817*

. . . I have spoken to your husband. His sympathy for me has helped me and has also pained me; for Streicher very nearly shattered my resignation. God knows what is going to happen. But as I have always helped other people whenever I could, I am trusting to His being merciful to me . . .

Beethoven was nothing if not importunate in his demands for an instrument to alleviate the desperate condition of not being able to hear the piano properly:

792   To the same   *Between 22 and 27 July 1817*

As to my health . . . the chief trouble is still there; and I fear that it can never be removed . . . I am spending next Wednesday and Thursday in town, where I shall again have a word with *Streicher*.

These next two letters probably refer to a new model of piano that Streicher had made with six and a half octaves:

807   To the same   *26 August 1817*

. . . Your patent piano certainly does not need my approval, but for my own sake I have long desired to make its acquaintance . . .

808   To the same   *After 26 August 1817*
Dear friend,

I am willing to look at this instrument with you tomorrow. At what time tomorrow? . . . But I must ask you to be patient with me. In my present circumstances I can no longer *behave* as I *used to behave*, although my name is still *Beethoven*—

There are some extraordinary letters to Nanette Streicher which follow on in quick succession from these last two. They show how closely pianos, laundry and household problems were linked together in Beethoven's mind at this time. The latter take pride of place. His stockings, laundry-lists and many other long sentences relating to them are all underlined. (They correspond to *sfz* and *ff* markings in his music!) In the following letter he is still concerned that Streicher should not give up trying to help him hear the piano:

810   To the same   *August 1817*

. . . My warmest thanks to Streicher for his trouble. Please ask him to continue his efforts. Surely God will again enable me sometime to repay good with good, since the opposite is what grieves me most of all . . .

One more letter to Nanette Streicher is important, as it shows

Ludwig van Beethoven *c.* 1819

Piano made by Anton Walter, 1785

Beethoven's Erard piano, 1803

Beethoven's Broadwood piano, 1817

The Broadwood action, 1819

Beethoven's Graf piano, 1825

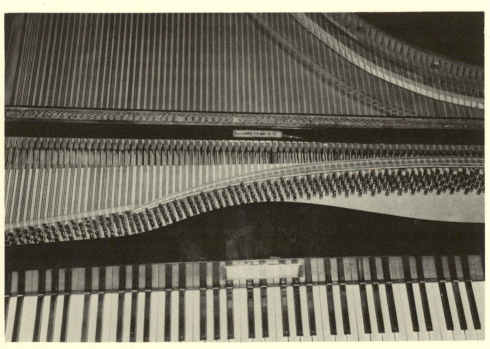

The interior of the Graf piano

Beethoven's letter to Nikolaus Zmeskall von
Domanovecz, dated 1802

Some of Beethoven's hearing-aids

Part of the first edition of the slow movement
of the Third Piano Concerto, published in
Vienna in 1804

The opening bars of the song *Der Liebende*
(*a*) as first written down in score by Beethoven
(*b*) as written out by a copyist

how hard she and her husband tried to help Beethoven to hear better:

844   To the same   *December 1817*
I thank you. Things now seem to be greatly improving. I am sending the *ear-trumpet* as well. Please let me have it back to-morrow, for with its help I have gained a considerable amount of information.

Your grateful
Beethoven

Apparently Streicher suggested to Beethoven that he should have an upright piano, as it would be easier to fit a hearing-aid to a sound-board that was upright. He mentions fitting two horns to it and says that as it will cost a lot he will make it in wood first.

It was fortunate that Thomas Broadwood, head of the firm of John Broadwood and Sons, in London, visited Vienna some time in 1817, made Beethoven's acquaintance and offered to present him with a six-octave grand piano (No. 7632; see plate 4*a*, and also plate 4*b* for the action of a Broadwood of 1819). Although it is doubtful if Beethoven heard the piano as someone with normal hearing would have done, there is no doubt that it was a great stimulus at a very difficult time for him. To send the piano to Vienna was no light undertaking in those days. It was packed in a tin and deal case, shipped to Trieste and then carted over the Alps by horses or mules along 360 miles of cart-tracks.

Beethoven was extremely pleased with this piano and would not let anyone else touch it at first—not even to tune it!—except Stumpff, of London, who came with a letter of introduction from Broadwood. Cipriani Potter, who tried the instrument after Streicher had unpacked it, told Beethoven that it was out of tune (not surprisingly), whereupon Beethoven apparently replied: 'That's what they all say; they would like to tune it and spoil it, but they shall not touch it.'[1] There is no record or letter from him after he had received it—only his letter of thanks to Thomas Broadwood when he heard from the latter that the piano had been dispatched to him:

[1] Cf. *TF*, p. 695.

891[1] To Thomas Broadwood   *3 February 1818*

My very dear friend Broadwood!

I have never experienced a greater pleasure than that caused by your informing me of the promised arrival of this piano which you do me the honour of presenting to me; I shall look upon it as an altar on which I shall place the most beautiful offerings of my spirit to the divine Apollo. As soon as I receive your excellent instrument, I will send you the fruits of the inspiration of my first moments that I spend at it as something for you to remember me by, my dear Broadwood, and I only hope that they will be worthy of your instrument. My dear sir and friend, believe me your friend and very humble servant

Ludwig van Beethoven

He enlisted the help of Count Moritz Lichnowsky, who knew Count Stadion, the then Austrian Minister of Finance, and also Nanette Streicher's cousin from Cracow, to see that he received the piano free of customs charges, as they had arranged. Broadwood paid the freightage.

At the time of writing I have not seen this piano, but in the Colt Clavier Collection there is one exactly similar, which is a very fine piano and far superior in tone to the four-stringed Graf. There is a similar model in the Germanisches Museum, Nuremberg, but it is not the equal of the one in the Colt Collection. There seems little doubt that Beethoven preferred the Broadwood to all his other pianos. Thayer describes Beethoven's Broadwood piano thus:[2] 'The case of the instrument, simple, plain but tasteful in design, is of mahogany and the structure generally of a solidity and strength paired with grace which caused no little surprise at the time. The compass is six octaves from C, five leger-lines below the bass staff. Above the keys is the inscription: *Hoc Instrumentum est Thomae Broadwood (Londini) donum, propter Ingenium illustrissimi Beethoven.* On the board, back of the keys, is the name "Beethoven", inlaid in ebony, and below this the makers' mark: "John Broadwood and Sons, Maker of Instruments to His Majesty and the Princesses, Great Pulteney Street, Golden Square, London". To

[1] Author's translation from the French printed in *LA*.
[2] *TF*, loc. cit.

the right of the keyboard are the autograph names Frid. Kalkbrenner, Ferd. Ries, G. G. Ferrari, J. B. Cramer and C. Knyvett.'
That Beethoven was delighted with the piano there is no doubt:
the last three Sonatas, Opp. 109, 110 and 111, are proof of this.

In February 1822 Beethoven wrote to the cellist Bernhard
Romberg and told him: 'Last night I again *succumbed to the earache*
which I usually suffer from during *this season. Even your playing*
would only *cause me pain* today.'[1] Obviously he *could* hear the cello.
Strings can sustain tone, and this may well account for Beethoven's
turning to the string quartet again in his last years, while largely
abandoning writing for the piano.

There are a few more references to the piano in his letters. He
tells the Archduke Rudolph in 1823 about exercises in composition: 'when sitting at the pianoforte you should jot down your ideas
in the form of sketches. For this purpose you should have a small
table beside the pianoforte. In this way not only is one's imagination stimulated but one learns also to pin down immediately the
most remote ideas. You should also compose without a pianoforte . . .'[2]

On 15 December 1823 Beethoven lent Moscheles his Broadwood
piano for a concert at the Court Theatre, so it must still have been
in quite good condition. In October 1824 he asks Johann Andreas
Stumpff to call on Stein and 'kindly tell him exactly what ought to
be done to my Broadwood instrument'.[3]

It is fitting that Beethoven should have the last word, and it is
interesting and encouraging to note that he was concerned about
his pianos to the end of his life. It gives the lie to those who have
made out that by the mid-1820s he had lost interest in the piano
and did not care about it any more:

1440   To Karl van Beethoven   *12 October 1825*
Dear Son!

. . . The chief thing is the pianoforte, for just now the weather
is very fine and dry—The Stein pianoforte can be attended to later.
As soon as I am in Vienna I will have it seen to and will gladly pay
him for it, since otherwise it will be completely ruined . . .

[1] *LA*, letter 1072.   [2] *LA*, letter 1203.
[3] *LA*, letter 1314; this Stumpff is not the tuner referred to above, p. 65.

THREE

The Piano Music—I

HAROLD TRUSCOTT

THE PIANOFORTE was the result of a desire to improve the harpsichord by adding to it certain features: for example, the ability to produce legato tone and to grade volume with the fingers. What arrived was not a harpsichord, improved or otherwise, but a totally new instrument; although it made its appearance early in the eighteenth century, the history of piano music begins disproportionately late. By piano music I mean music conceived specifically for the new instrument, not treating it merely as an improved version of any older instrument. Although there were spasmodic attempts to realize its newness in concrete terms, it is true to say that, quality of music aside—and this includes Haydn and Mozart —it is difficult to discover, in music written up to the early 1770s a passage which asserts its piano origin so positively that one cannot imagine it on any other instrument. On the other hand, examine such a passage as this:

Ex. 1

and, even allowing for the state of the instrument at the time, the absolutely pianistic nature of this music is manifest at a glance. Ex. 1 is the beginning of the first movement of Clementi's Sonata in C, Op. 2, No. 2;[1] it is one of a group of six sonatas, of which three, Nos. 1, 3 and 5, are for flute or violin and piano and the other three for piano alone. They were published in 1779, but may have been composed by 1770, when he was eighteen, and only a few months before Beethoven was born; the three solo sonatas possibly constitute not only the first genuine piano sonatas ever composed but the first genuine piano music of any kind, in the sense that the piano and the piano alone is their inspiration.

If we are to understand the origins of Beethoven's mature piano style it is necessary to know a fair amount of Clementi's music, as

[1] The numbering of Clementi sonatas in this chapter accords with that given in Alan Tyson, *Thematic Catalogue of the works of Muzio Clementi* Tutzing, 1967).

well as that of another composer, Dussek.[1] By mature style I mean that shown by the music Beethoven considered fit for publication, from Op. 1 onwards. It is true that the early works with opus numbers do not represent full maturity, but they do show the style which gradually grew to maturity. It is also true that Beethoven was writing music, a good deal of it piano music, from his early teens; in fact, his first preserved composition, some variations on a march by Dressler, was composed in his twelfth year. A good deal of this early music is for wind instruments, with a more or less classical outlook without many individual features, and there is some vocal music of varying quality, but the piano music is a different matter. For one thing, it shows a steadily cohering style, from the three sonatas written in 1783 (his father wanted them published as by an eleven-year-old, but this the boy strenuously opposed, which accounts for some editions giving their date of composition as 1781) up to the early sets of variations of his late teens and early twenties. It is evident from some of the early piano music, which includes the Piano Concerto in E flat, WoO 4, of 1784, that he started by founding his style on a rather clumsy attempt to imitate Mozart; this much is clear, in fact, as early as the variations on Dressler's theme, although this is almost the only work of Beethoven in which an overt attempt can be found. Many of the older composer's characteristic features are there, slightly gone wrong, but the resulting sound, as usually happens when composers, however young, try to imitate other composers, is nothing like Mozart. The interesting thing is that out of this muddle a genuine personal style begins to emerge, so that it is disconcerting to find that by the time he writes his Opp. 1 and 2 in the early 1790s the influence is less firmly established than might have been supposed.

Here, for instance, is the beginning of the rondo of the E flat Sonata, WoO 47, No. 1:

[1] There are several editions of sonatas by Clementi. The best edition of Dussek's is in four volumes of *Musica Antiqua Bohemica*, XLVI, LII, LIX and LXIII, ed. Jan Racek and Václav Jan Sýkora (Prague, 1960–3). Also cf. Tyson, op. cit., and Howard A. Craw, *A Bibliography and thematic catalog of the works of J. L. Dussek (1760–1812)* (Diss., University of Southern California, 1964, unpub.; also Ann Arbor, University Microfilms).

Ex. 2

This is a Mozart-type rondo theme, characteristic of many of the older composer's concerto rondos, but as one listens it sounds less and less like Mozart without being any more like the Beethoven we know. The ultimate of this style is the beautiful little Rondo in A, WoO 49:

Ex. 3

where the one thing that can remind us of the later well-known Beethoven is the presence of passages with a strong, sturdy tonic-and-dominant bass:

Ex. 4

To some extent the Op. 33 Bagatelles stem from this style. Most of these pieces were certainly written, or at least sketched, some years before they were published in 1803.

One of the strongest impressions left by the style of this music is a curious angularity, a result of Beethoven's misfired Mozart imitation, but in the end this angular quality is the most potent ingredient of its individuality. Just once in this early piano music does Beethoven show the influence of Haydn, and this is in the variations of the D major Sonata, WoO 47, No. 3, with a theme characteristic of early Haydn:

Ex. 5   Sostenuto

Some of the early sets of variations well repay examination, such as those on Salieri's 'La stessa, la stessissima' (1799) or Grétry's 'Une fièvre brûlante' (1796). All these sets—there are over a dozen—show a good deal of Beethoven's awakening natural sense of how to develop thematic material. Perhaps the most remarkable of them all was written in 1790. This is the set of twenty-four on a theme of Righini, 'Venni, Amore', which has a strong claim to be considered Beethoven's earliest masterpiece. Here, already, we have a work of size built up in a manner intelligently anticipating such a later set as the 32 Variations in C minor (not in material, however). In fact, the variety of approach and certainty of touch, in the knowledge of how to suggest a framework through the use of the simplest keyboard materials, make it not inappropriate to mention this work with the Diabelli Variations. In it Beethoven makes use of the different levels of the keyboard to unify simple statements; legato theme is put against rising shakes, imitation is used to yield new depth, development figures arise from the simple chords of the theme, the same chords are turned into rising and descending chromatic thirds, and there are even anticipations of Brahms's variation technique. In the coda one tiny figure is made to yield a harmonic tour and a fade-out of imaginative power which would not be out of place in mature Beethoven and which also anticipates one of Schumann's favourite coda devices. All these things are presented in a complete unity. Not only is there tremendous variety in the variations as such in this set, but they are grouped to form a single unit of constantly growing power. One could not displace a single variation without disturbing the balance of the whole.

This great work is, in my view, without a rival in the piano music until we get to the Op. 10 Sonatas, some six to eight years later, and, with certain others, two of which I have mentioned, stands on a borderline in Beethoven's development. Within a fairly circumscribed but slowly expanding style, founded partly on new elements absorbed from Clementi and Dussek, there is an astonishingly wide range of piano writing. Beethoven obviously used these sets of variations in part as experimental try-outs on a small scale of textures and techniques he later applied and further transformed in larger and maturer works.[1]

The prototype of these early sets of piano variations is the final movement of a Sonata in E flat by Clementi, Op. 23, No. 3, composed no later than 1789. This is a set of variations on a theme of his own:

Ex. 6   Allegretto

and it may or may not be coincidence that this turns up, faster, as the beginning of the finale of Beethoven's Septet, Op. 20:

[1] Cf. below, pp. 197–8, where Beethoven's variations are linked to his powers as an improviser. (Eds.)

Ex. 7

although the connection here goes deep into Clementi's variations also. I think it is true that Beethoven absorbed so much of this music of Clementi and Dussek that many times themes crop up in his work which go right back to themes in their work and that it seems probable that he was unconscious of any origin; they had become part of him. We should be careful to distinguish between such unconscious connections and real influence, although the mere fact that these themes penetrated so deeply into his musical make-up seems to show that they had had a great impact upon him. Here are two such themes:

Quintet for wind and piano, Op. 16, finale:

Ex. 8

and its possible model:

Clementi, Sonata, Op. 8, No. 2 (published 1782), first movement:

Ex. 9

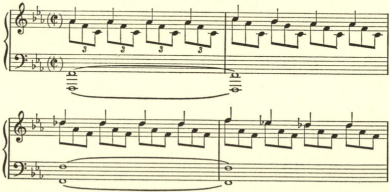

Sonata for violin and piano, Op. 24, opening:

Ex. 10

and *its* possible model:

Clementi, Sonata, Op. 25, No. 4 (published 1790), opening:

Ex. 11   Maestoso e cantabile

which itself could have grown from the first movement of Clementi's A major Sonata, Op. 2, No. 4:

Ex. 12

I have given only two of these strong premonitions or pre-echoes; they can be found in dozens all over the work of Clementi and Dussek. What I have quoted shows one facet of Clementi's influence on Beethoven, although not the deepest. What is much more potent is that both Clementi and Dussek had an atmosphere in which Beethoven found himself in his right element, and he proceeded to make full use of it. Atmosphere and structure: these are the fundamentals with which these two composers were able to supply Beethoven. We have arrived at Beethoven's first works published with opus numbers, the three Piano Trios, Op. 1, composed in 1792–4, and the three Piano Sonatas, Op. 2, composed during 1794 and 1795; and immediately Clementi is concerned, and a little later Dussek also. I shall not deal with the trios here,[1] beyond saying that there is a good deal of Dussek in the piano writing of all three, and especially in the first movement of the second, in G.

The three Sonatas, Op. 2, form a trio of contrasts. Two show a good deal of influence, the other a little. The F minor, in spite of attempts to link it with the early F minor Sonata, WoO 47, No. 2, really bears no relationship to it. The passion displayed in the early sonata is short-lived in each passage in which it occurs and is the result of the early angular style I have discussed; also it is simply liberated for a moment and then left. Nothing is done with it. There is nothing angular about Op. 2, No. 1, and the style is continuous in each movement. It is simply *not* Beethoven's style of 1783; it *is* the result of Clementi's style of about 1784. Much has been made of the resemblance between the opening theme:

Ex. 13

of the Beethoven and the beginning of the finale of Mozart's Symphony No. 40 in G minor. Again I can hear no resemblance. They look a little alike, but that is all. The sound generated in each case is completely different, and the world of the Beethoven at no point touches that of Mozart; and, within that world, the writing is assured, the movement of the music continuous within each stage of the piece. I have said that the most potent connection with Clementi is one of atmosphere and structure. One of the most notable features of Clementi's style is the complete through-running of first group, transition and second group as one continuous growth; this happens in movement after movement, at a time when it was not the norm for either Haydn or Mozart. It has

[1] They are discussed below, pp. 201–5.

not been a marked feature of Beethoven's writing up to now, but it is very noticeable in his F minor first movement: the swift, gradual approach to the dominant, the beginning of the second group without a break and still on the dominant, and the opening-out to make a climax to the exposition, built on a figure released from the second subject theme and all non-stop. All this, indeed the whole movement, is redolent of a new approach executed with confidence because he has behind him the support of many Clementi movements in which this non-stop through-running in the exposition is a marked feature: notably, the first movement of a remarkable Sonata in E flat, Op. 5, No. 3, of *c.* 1780–1, and a Sonata in F minor, Op. 13, No. 6, of about 1784. Also, there is the fact that Beethoven's second-subject theme:

Ex. 14

is a sort of inversion of Ex. 13, again a firm Clementi characteristic. The separation of the turn from Ex. 13 in the development is the beginning of a typical Beethoven habit, also taken over from Clementi, as in this theme from the latter's Sonata in B flat, Op. 8, No. 3, published in 1782:

Ex. 15   Presto

with its purposeful development in a passage which, its composer apart, one can associate only with Beethoven:

Ex. 16

Anything less characteristic of either Haydn or Mozart or the eighteenth century in general, or more typical of Beethoven, than the following passage, it would be hard to find:

Ex. 17   **Allegro agitato**

poised quietly on the indeterminate dominant, fairly high, and
gradually falling and opening out with a crescendo to reach the
tonic with a crash at the end of the sentence. By comparison with
most music of the time, this is not of 1784, about when it was
actually composed: it is the beginning of a new world—Beethoven's
world, of his first and quite an amount of his second period; but it is,
in fact, the opening of Clementi's F minor Sonata, Op. 13, No. 6.
One passage in particular contains in a nutshell the atmosphere not
only of Beethoven's F minor first movement and finale, but of a
good deal of his first period as a whole:

This is from the development of the first movement. But the effect of this Clementi sonata, the world, atmosphere and language it presents so graphically, spreads out over the whole of Beethoven's first period, in work after work, with very few exceptions. There is one such exception in Op. 2, No. 1: the *Menuetto*, which is the first of a series of completely individual movements in these early sonatas, owing nothing to any influence, and therefore perhaps the quintessential Beethoven in all this early mature piano music. There are five in all, the others occurring in Op. 7, Op. 10, No. 2, Op. 10, No. 3, and Op. 14, No. 1: one should also perhaps include the scherzos of Op. 2, Nos. 2 and 3. The present movement and that of Op. 10, No. 3, are called '*Menuetto*', but neither is really a minuet. Indeed, none of these five movements is either a minuet or a scherzo; without exception they are quiet, gentle, reflective movements, such tension as there is being obtained by the intense quiet of the trio in Op. 7, or the extremely subtle anticipation of Schubert in the trio of Op. 10, No. 2. These movements therefore have the curious effect of showing the most individual early Beethoven to be quiet and reflective; while the sharp, forceful dramatic sounds of the approach most often associated with him actually received their impetus from other sources: Clementi and Dussek. The writing in all these movements is extremely grateful— their technical difficulties are not arduous, but only a very fine musician can display the depth of this music.

For the *Adagio* of the F minor Sonata Beethoven made the first of two borrowings in Op. 2 from his own earlier music, both from the same work, the Piano Quartet No. 1 in C, WoO 36, of 1785. The sonata slow movement begins with precisely the same idea as that of the quartet, the later version being filled out to some extent. The middle portion in D minor is new; most of the figuration otherwise is of the same kind, though extended a little, so that this far the very early piano style fits well enough with the new one. It is a simple little movement, with more below the surface than its lightly decorated melody shows at first.

The second of these three sonatas, in A, is a much more independent conception in its first movement than the corresponding movements of the other two works; as a result, it displays the jerky, nervous, dig-in-the-ribs style he often shows in this first period when he knows he is branching out on his own, a manner entirely absent from the first movements of the other two sonatas. Even so, it owes something to movements like the first of Clementi's B flat Sonata, Op. 10, No. 3 (published in 1783), mainly for its vivid progress through an inexorable rapid tempo. The most potent individual effect in this first movement is the treatment of tonality. There is nothing in any earlier work by anybody like Beethoven's opening-out on the dominant of E minor at the start of the second group, with an epitomized tour round the key before arriving at a climax, asserting a reference to his main theme, and finally descending to E major. There is no coda; apart from developing this feature, one of Beethoven's greatest early assets was knowing when to leave it out.

The *Largo appassionato* is a very fine movement, not without its precedents in Clementi. Its fine treatment of the bass can be matched in the magnificent opening slow movement of Clementi's E flat Sonata, Op. 6, No. 2, of *c*. 1780–1:

Ex. 19

Again, Beethoven's episode is beautifully balanced:

Ex. 20

and

So, too, is Clementi's second subject, and its emergence from the previous harmony:

Ex. 21

None the less, Beethoven's *Largo* is individual; especially is his use of the staccato bass his own. The deeper Clementi's music went the more creative was Beethoven's reaction.

The scherzo is largely swift and quiet; its spareness is Clementian, but the sound is Beethoven's, especially the wonderful crescendo to a climax on G sharp minor, and the even more wonderful reaction, the gradual fade-out to a suspended home dominant and ensuing silence. The use of a simple broken-chord idea, too, is here personal rather than an echo. The trio is also mainly swift and quiet, but with a slightly tenser atmosphere.

The final rondo has the relaxed ease such a movement should have, in spite of the fact that it wastes no time and its progress is as straight as an arrow, both to the first episode and throughout the movement. The opening tune results in one of Beethoven's characteristic qualities, in the gradual development throughout the movement of the arpeggio that begins it, until it reaches its apex with the long rising scale of A major which is the outcome of the middle episode's staccato triplets. He also begins, in the first episode, to develop the Alberti bass to something as yet not thought of, even in the developments Clementi and Dussek had already given it. The sound of the movement is, almost at every point, quite new.

The origin of Beethoven's piano world is fascinating enough to dwell on for a moment, since all writers I have read on the subject avoid it. I have tried to show a little of one important origin of what we call typically Beethovenian. The C major Sonata of Op. 2 is concerned with another, which rocked Beethoven as much as Clementi had done. The whole of Beethoven's first movement is founded on a mixed virtuoso and musical basis first propounded in an electrifying sonata by Dussek—Op. 9, No. 2, in C, composed in 1782. Beethoven begins quietly, Dussek *fortissimo*:

Ex. 22

They reverse things at the end, Beethoven ending loudly, Dussek quietly. Dussek follows Ex. 22 with a quiet continuation which leads with an explosion to a passage taking the music to the home dominant:

Ex. 23

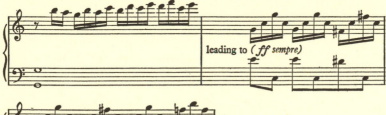

Beethoven follows his opening with *his* explosion, taking him to *his* home dominant. As with the Clementi influence, Beethoven's work here is a creative imitation.

For his transition theme Beethoven has the second borrowing from the early piano quartet:

Ex. 24

Here his idea is larger; Ex. 24 is the start of a passage which drops in harmony step by step until it reaches the G major dominant with a figure taken from the same piano quartet; this very soon leads to the second subject.

One must be full of admiration for the way in which Beethoven has managed this, beginning with the two unpromising borrowed bits of material. But Dussek's idea is subtler. He follows Ex. 23 with a transition passage, vast for the size of the movement, of which Ex. 25 is only part:

Ex. 25

leading to

Its energy is phenomenal, and its goal, twenty-eight bars later, is the second group in a fully established G major, beginning with the tune which begins Ex. 25; Dussek's subtlety, to which at this time Beethoven does not rise, is the presentation of the same theme at the same pitch in two totally different functions, with a complete difference of tonal level, between home dominant and new key, fully audible in the music.

Beethoven's exposition is neatly contained within its own length; the energy of Dussek's music is so great that, while the music comes to a perfectly natural point for the exposition to end, it refuses to stop there, but goes boiling on quite a way into the development before it runs itself out:

Ex. 26

(continuing for another 10 bars before there is a change of mood)

Beethoven's development deals with two exposition themes in two passages separated by some bars of themeless cadenza (a suggestion which is realized more fully before the movement is over). Dussek's development grows, as naturally as art can make it, from what has already been presented, without using any particular feature, and comes to a preparation for C major in truly Beethovenian fashion, so that everything comes together in this return:

86

Ex. 27

This is sonata; *this* is what we recognize in Beethoven as evidence of his supreme mastery, but it did not come first from him. This is mastery of one's material, of the shape and living form of the classical sonata, and it was Dussek's superbly, as it was Clementi's, before it was Beethoven's. It is important here to stress that all examination of the music of Beethoven's two great influences must be treated fairly, *with all movements felt strictly at the indicated tempos and with indicated dynamics;* in other words, the music must be treated with the scrupulous courtesy we should show to Beethoven.

The *Adagio* of the C major Sonata is a rondo in E, which has a short main tune, punctuated by rests; this dominates the movement, in spite of the single, much larger episode in E minor. The scale of the movement is considerably enlarged by a startling wrench to C major harmony to bring back the episode. The most characteristic feature of the movement is that the main tune is built on a turn-like figure which is specifically Beethoven's. Turns were very much eighteenth-century thematic material, and they early became staple diet for Beethoven; they provide a definite line of growth in his string chamber music, while their use in other media is more spasmodic. None the less, when he uses them the results are his, not an echo of anyone else. This feature also sets off the main theme of the C major scherzo:

Ex. 28

The swift expansion of this theme through magnificently spontaneous yet completely logical harmonies could not be more subtly set off than by the contrast, of theme and texture, made by the simple rapid arpeggios of the trio; the subtle relationship between cadence chords and a twist of the turn theme:

Ex. 29

shows Beethoven's thinking to be expanding.

It expands still more in the rondo finale, in which a mass of material is contained and controlled in a very short space, with equally varied keyboard textures. The middle episode is remarkably prophetic of the corresponding episode in the finale of Brahms's F minor Piano Sonata, Op. 5. There is again a tendency towards cadenza writing near the end of the movement; as with many other features originally borrowed from other music, he retained this device and allowed it to grow into integrated musical thinking. The whole of this movement has a sense of growing freedom, which breaks out even more potently in the next sonata, in E flat, Op. 7.

Throughout his career the essentials of Beethovens' piano writing changed little from what is displayed in these three sonatas. It was the writing of a virtuoso, using the basic techniques of Clementi and Dussek, but gradually developing their potential in his own way to meet new expressive demands as they arose. Always Beethoven's development of essential technique, like that of his predecessors, went along with his development of material and form, and it is rare indeed to find a technical device in his work which lacks a musical explanation.

Regarded as sonatinas, which is what they in fact are, the two works published in 1805 as Op. 49, but composed about 1796, have a certain merit—the G minor, a beautifully shaped little work, much more than the G major, which, even among sonatinas, is much inferior to a number by Clementi and Dussek, especially the latter's F major and E flat from his Op. 20. The G major's main claim to fame is its anticipation, in a more inhibited style, of the minuet theme later brought to its full stature in the Septet, Op. 20.

The writing in the next four sonatas expands swiftly on the technical premises outlined above through a wide variety of ideas, involving constant revision of structural processes in a new light, seesawing back and forth between the influenced (in part or almost entire) and the completely individual. The first movement of Op. 7, composed only a few months after Op. 2, seems to carry on directly the mood and style of the previous finale, partly in the $\frac{6}{8}$ rhythm but also in that many themes seem to have spilled over from the C major rondo to produce similar successors in the E flat movement; but the treatment is not similar. The movement institutes a growth virtually from three ideas:

this growth expands without a break in the thought for fifty-seven bars, to the beginning of the second group. One suggestion grows into the next, which grows into the next; Beethoven is growing up as a composer. This process involves the second subject—a contrast, but also another stage in the gradual evolution of thought. There is growth, too, in the rhythmic changes which characterize the various appearances of *a* in Ex. 30. The movement is Beethoven's first complete masterpiece of sonata style for piano.

The *Largo* is the first of the deep, broad slow movements which Beethoven made so much his own, but the originals of which are in Clementi and Dussek; I shall have more to say about this in connection with later examples. Rests are again an important part of the theme, while the texture is full and rich, but restrained, with a test for the player in maintaining the very slow tempo with full musical interest; particularly must there be no hurrying of the quavers in the coda.

The third movement is the second of the five reflective pieces I mentioned above. The rondo is one of a type he used again later, notably in Op. 22, gentle but swift, with strength lurking behind the gentleness; the archetypal Clementi movement for this kind of expression in Beethoven is the finale of his B flat Sonata, Op. 8, No. 3:

Ex. 31   **Allegretto grazioso**

Compare this for style with the opening of Beethoven's E flat rondo:

Ex. 32   **Poco allegretto e grazioso**

and the derivation is obvious; but the dissimilarities between the two movements as a whole are greater and equally obvious. The Beethoven is a larger and looser movement. In the middle episode, however, we are confronted with an astounding paraphrase of Clementi:

Ex. 33

That is the beginning of Beethoven's episode; here is the beginning
of the middle episode from the finale of Clementi's Op. 2, No. 2:

Ex. 34

The right-hand part in bars 5 and 6 of Ex. 34 shows the origin of
Beethoven's left-hand part in Ex. 33; the Clementi is, among other
things, considerably further developed.

The rondo in Clementi's Op. 8, No. 3, is a superb example of his
allowing music to relax and yet go to the point with no waste anywhere. It has seventy-nine bars, Beethoven's rondo 183; as a rule
nothing is to be gained by such arithmetic, but in this case the
weightier movement, in impression and result, happens to be
Clementi's, and this does prove something. Beethoven cannot yet

rely on being able to drive his music to the main point with minimum effort and maximum effect, although such mastery as a constant quality was only round the corner.

The next sonatas are the three of Op. 10, composed in 1796–8. They are a mixture of the borrowed and the individual, but the mixture is handled with a much more assured hand than before. The swiftness and, to some extent, the mood of the first, in C minor, is certainly a legacy from Clementi, the originator and original master of such swiftness, with its inevitable concomitants of right proportion and texture. And the swiftness lies on different levels. Beethoven's transition passage brings with it a contrasting relaxation and yet manages to do so without relaxing the tempo one bit. The middle movement of this first three-movement work in the sonatas is another wonderful *Adagio*, intensifying his broad, deep style a notch or two more. Again, it is in a very slow tempo. The real beat unit is a semiquaver; only on this basis does *every* part of this movement make sense. It is a sonata movement without development; the end of the exposition sounds a quiet dominant chord, then a loud dominant seventh, followed by the beginning of the recapitulation. It is ruinous to cut short the rests between these chords. In place of a development there is a large coda, in which the full inwardness of the extremely slow tempo comes fully to the surface.

This is the most finely proportioned and balanced movement in Beethoven's piano sonatas so far, but yet again it had a part-model: the *Mesto*,[1] also in A flat, from Clementi's Sonata in E flat, Op. 7, No. 1, composed probably in 1781. Here is its main theme, with the follow-up:

Ex. 35

---

[1] Thus in the earliest editions; *Maestoso* in some later ones, including the 1820 one supervised by Clementi himself.

This brings the music to E flat major, and the second group starts with the beginning of Ex. 35:

Ex. 36

Ex. 36 is the complete phrase; it is repeated and comes to a cadence theme; at its end we have arrived at the same point in

Clementi's movement as that at which Beethoven wrote his detached chords. And here is a way in which Clementi's imagination goes beyond Beethoven's at a roughly similar age: Ex. 37 shows Clementi's cadence phrase, *his* dominant chord, and what follows:

Ex. 37

The third bar from the end of Ex. 37 contains the imaginative development of those silences in Ex. 36. Also, until the music is resumed after that silence, the breathless second chord in this third bar from the end of Ex. 37 gives no indication of where it is going. The last-inversion dominant seventh and the resolution to a first-inversion A flat chord make one of the most thrillingly unexpected sounds in all music, and it is capped by the wonderful moving bass that now accompanies Ex. 35.

In the finale, Beethoven wrote a movement which is short, pungent and absolutely individual, and this in spite of the fact that it is based on any number of thematic devices from earlier music—a main theme derived from a turn, for instance. Again the obvious influence is Clementi, but a Clementi so pushed out of sight that almost all that remains on the surface is the intense rapidity of the music. Here, also, we get the repeated-note rhythm that Beethoven later used so much, and this, too, had been used by earlier composers. But for an earlier version of Beethoven's manner of using it one must go back to Clementi's G minor Sonata, Op. 34, No. 2, published no later than 1795 (and said to have been rewritten from a symphonic original), in which the first and last movements are impregnated with this figure in Beethoven's style.

There is humour in plenty in Beethoven's music (in fact, there is far more music with it than without it), but a complete comedy is unusual. The second sonata in this set is exactly that. The subject-matter of the first movement; the proportion of the two groups of themes, the first short, the second large; the impudent use of the exposition cadence octaves as the *only* exposition material in the development, starting the recapitulation in the wrong key (the result of the development being mainly pitched round D minor), only for it to be overcome with blushes and stammer its way into the right key (the stammering accentuated by the fact that the triplets which originally descended with the harmonies of the theme now stay on the same note): all this speaks of comedy almost of a Mack Sennett type. The middle movement is one of the five reflective ones I have mentioned, and a wonderfully gentle contrast before the mock fugal-cum-sonata heroics of the finale break-out. The work is a completely individual masterpiece.

The third Sonata, in D, has, as its third movement, the fourth of the five meditative and highly individual movements referred to above. The work as a whole is heroic in the first movement, tragic in the second, and rapidly and explosively triumphant in its finale, which is another very individual rondo, consummately written, and releasing the opening theme with great impetus. There are three episodes, the first a mere gesture on the dominant, the second without a definite key, but searching for one—the home key of D major; but the whole movement is simply in D major, even the final episode only exploring harmonies of that key. The other two movements, superbly written, owe a good deal to Clementi. Here is the opening of the first movement, omitting the introduction, of the latter's B minor Sonata, Op. 40, No. 2.[1]

Ex. 38

This must be played at its indicated speed. The material here is similar in manner to that of Beethoven's first movement, the energy and piano writing even more so. But with the development the likeness is astounding:

Ex. 39

[1] Clementi's Op. 40 Sonatas were not published until 1802 (cf. Tyson, op. cit., p. 80), and although they may have been composed before Beethoven composed Op. 10, No. 3, there is no evidence that they were. (Eds.)

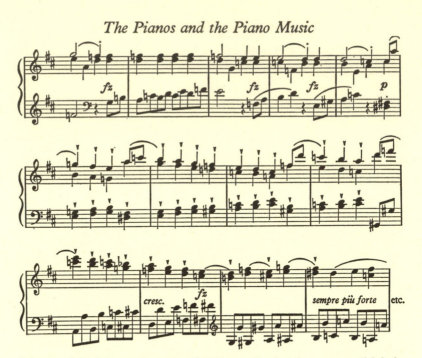

I have picked just one part of Clementi's development, which is actually continuous for 135 bars.

With Beethoven's *Largo e mesto* there is again, apart from its masterly handling of the sonata style in this very slow tempo, a strong similarity in material and mood with Clementi—from the slow movement of the D major Sonata, Op. 40, No. 3:

Ex. 40

a　**Adagio con molto espressione**

The *Sonate Pathétique* (Beethoven's own title), Op. 13 (1798–9), is a famous work, even where people are not generally knowledge-able about these things—partly because it has a title, partly because tragic or sombre music always has more adherents than cheerful or humorous music. The work itself is a mixture of the new and the borrowed, also of the weak and the strong. The introduction is splendidly new, perhaps the finest individual passage in the first movement, and its partial use on two later occasions may or may not be an echo of a similar procedure in the early F minor Sonata, WoO 47, No. 2. I do not think so: the imagination displayed in each of the later uses in Op. 13 is well beyond the scope of the thirteen-year-old composer of the early sonata; in fact I believe that much has been read into that work which is simply not there, merely in the light of later events. The weakness of the 'Pathétique', for me, is in the main *Allegro*, where the arrangement of the material has what is the rarest thing in Beethoven: an air of having been manufactured. Certainly the movement cannot compare with its slightly earlier neighbour in the same key, from Op. 10. Added to this is the fact that what Beethoven is manufacturing is a repetition of the mood and style of the C minor Sonata by Dussek, Op. 35, No. 3, first published in 1797 and probably composed two or three years earlier. Apart from its superbly inevitable structure and the freshness of the material, the Dussek also supplied Beethoven with the rhythmic shape of his main theme, as Ex. 41

shows. I give two versions of the second theme of Dussek's first movement, which, incidentally, has no introduction:[1]

Ex. 41

Beethoven's *Adagio cantabile*[2] is a beautiful movement, rather like that of Haydn's Symphony No. 88 in G in that it consists of a melody with two ineffectual attempts to get away from it. The reaction each time is to repeat it. As in earlier cases, Beethoven's real grip and mastery come to the fore in the magnificent rondo.

I have often wondered why, among the mass of writing on Beethoven that has been pouring out in an unceasing flood ever since his death, there has never been, to my knowledge, a real attempt to get to grips with the piano writing as a medium for his music. Like his orchestration, it is either taken for granted or, on rare occasions, adversely criticized. Even Sir Donald Tovey, who

[1] Cf. Ex. 10 in Chap. 5, p. 220, for another quotation from Dussek's Sonata in C minor and its possible influence on another C minor work of Beethoven's.
[2] Opening quoted as Ex. 15a in Chap. 7, p. 309.

examined practically every aspect of Beethoven's music with a fine toothcomb, is content in this matter with hero-worship. The only sentence I can discover in Tovey's writings on this subject is that 'Beethoven's knowledge of the piano was unfathomable', which does not help much. And yet I think Tovey has said all that can be said, for I believe that the reason why there has been no study of Beethoven's piano writing as such is that he added nothing new to the technique of the instrument, at least before his third period, and even there it is much more a case of new adaptations of the old. The one partial exception in his piano work as a whole is the gradual development of the Alberti bass, and even this had been to a large extent anticipated by Clementi and, especially, Dussek. What is it, then, that makes Beethoven's handling of the piano so unique, particularly once he has completely absorbed his influences? Clementi and Dussek were also two great composers in their own right, but there were any number of very worthy composers of the time who had all Beethoven's knowledge of, and experience of, the piano, and yet do not produce anything like *his* results. Cramer, for instance: there are any number of fine sonatas by this pianist-composer, some I would call outstanding and some with no mean individuality. Many of these use precisely the same technical means as Beethoven used in many of his sonatas, but Cramer nowhere arouses the excitement in his excellent sonata movements that Beethoven can arouse in a few bars—bars which, on the surface, look no different in essentials from many of Cramer's. Clementi and Dussek were creators; they were also discoverers. Most of what Beethoven is using he has no more discovered—except through their means—than Cramer had, and yet Beethoven's use of these means is as individual as is that of his two influences. Here is the reason, I think, for the lack of any study of this subject; it is well-nigh impossible to put one's finger on the activating cause of the individuality.

The two sonatas of Op. 14 and the B flat, Op. 22, illustrate ideally Beethoven's use of quite ordinary technical means. In the two earlier works (1798–9) there is nothing discoverable on the printed page that had not already turned up many times before, and yet the impact of these two sonatas is of two quite unique little specimens. Beethoven has at last absorbed his influences, and these two works are quite individual. The E major is seriously happy, like a child completely absorbed in what it is doing, and contains in its middle movement (both are three-movement works) the last of the five completely individual reflective movements referred to above. Beethoven did tentatively introduce here one other addition to piano technique, which grew very much in later music: a tendency to write for the piano in the manner of an adaptation of string-quartet texture. This is suggestive in this instance, since two or three years later he wrote a quartet version in F of this sonata. The G major is a glorious little comedy, different from but matching the F major of Op. 10, and it is characteristic that the highlight of the comedy is the middle *Andante*, with its variations, and that the balancing intrusion of the serious occurs with the C major section of the scherzo-finale. Schindler reports Beethoven as saying of these two works: 'everyone had recognized in both opus 14 sonatas the dispute in dialogue form between two principles, without the aid of words written above the score';[1] however, his detailed interpretation of these sonatas is unusually fanciful for Beethoven, and it is possible that in thus allegedly speaking of them he was impatiently fobbing off Schindler.

The extraordinary ordinariness of Op. 14 is even more to the fore in the B flat Sonata, Op. 22, completed in 1800, especially in its first movement, where the themes are turns, chords, scales or broken chords, with equally simple support; it is almost as though Beethoven were determined to show just how extraordinary ordinary things can be. The work is the grandest 'Grand' sonata he had written, which is not to say that it is necessarily the finest to date; however, it is a magnificent close to his first-period piano sonatas. The slow movement has a leisurely approach, and a long main tune, which belies the speed with which it gets through a large-scale sonata form—shades of Dussek's wonderful slow movement from his C minor Sonata, Op. 35, No. 3, which is not like this one in any other way—and is allied in style to some of the early chamber-music slow movements. One new and, in the manner of its execution, unique feature is the manner in which the development

[1] Cf. *SB*, p. 406.

drifts into and out of beautiful three-part counterpoint, perhaps the earliest application of such a technique for a new sound in Beethoven's piano works.

The minuet is again new-style—no eighteenth-century composer ever wrote a minuet like this; the newness is even more in the manner of accompaniment, with a wide-ranging bass, than in the theme, which is itself not of the normal minuet type. Every part of the texture is made to tell, although nothing is in itself particularly new; the newness is in the conjunction of items. New, too, is the second part, which sets two tremolandos each against a cadence, and a trio which is not melodic but simply rumbles a rapid bass against changing syncopated chords. Here is the really original Beethoven, bringing forward the most basic things in conjunctions no one had thought of before. In the face of such thought, new technique is not necessary; the oldest will inevitably sound new.

The finale picks up the style of the corresponding movement of Op. 7, to make a quite different rondo; apart from the similarity of tempo and of the mood of the two main themes, the later movement also uses as a transition theme and middle episode material a theme very close to one from the Op. 7 rondo. Variation plays a much bigger part here than in earlier rondos, with the various returns of the theme, and one return is cunningly extracted from the final note of a shake (bars 110–12), an idea he liked so much that he re-applied it in the following year to a return in the final rondo of the F major Sonata for violin and piano, Op. 24.

The first piano sonata of the so-called second period is Op. 26 in A flat (1800–1). There is nothing notably indicative of a new period in either first or last movement, both of which could quite easily have been written a few months earlier. (There are no hard and fast lines of demarcation for such a change of outlook, which happens gradually, and of which the composer is usually unaware until it has happened.) The variations are a beautiful melodic set, with a hint in the final variation of the persistent shakes above or below a melody of which he was fond in later life, and a short coda which strikingly anticipates for a few bars a passage in the *Arietta* variations of Op. 111. The finale is a rondo conveyed entirely in an unbroken rapid texture, of a type which by some composers of that time would have been miscalled a toccata. Its newest feature is the suspension of the first episode on a dominant seventh to the last possible moment, and a final resolution, with hurtling scales, on to the tonic. In between are the scherzo and a remarkable funeral march, in that order, reversing the customary position of such middle movements, as Haydn had done years earlier. The first-period sonatas had produced nothing like the scherzo, for rapidity of actual speed and of harmonic movement, nor had the chamber music, where the nearest thing is the scherzo of Op. 18, No. 6; the only comparable movement so far is the wrongly-named *Menuetto* of the First Symphony, of the previous year. The funeral march (*Marcia funebre sulla morte d'un eroe*) is as unique on its smaller scale as that of the later 'Eroica' symphony and achieves this quality without the colour of the orchestra and with the severest restraint in harmony, plus a theme which is for the most part only a rhythm; the muffled grief which spreads its pall by this means is as moving as the most impassioned oratory and as austere as the Cenotaph. Even simpler in its means and just as moving is the trio—drum rolls answered by funereal trumpets in a jerky march rhythm. Again Beethoven's originality shines by reducing the music and its technique to basic elements.

Romanticism, too, is mixing with the other elements, and this shows plainly in the two sonatas of Op. 27 (1800–1) and the D major, Op. 28 (1801); Beethoven unnecessarily apologized for interfering with movement order by qualifying each of the two of Op. 27 as 'quasi una fantasia'. Later he rightly did not think this necessary; nor did Mozart in 1774, when he wrote his E flat Sonata, K. 282, or Haydn in certain of his keyboard sonatas. The romantic element in Beethoven's Op. 27 does not lie in movement order but rather in the passion and use of sudden mood changes behind the movement shapes. Nor does it seem to matter what kind of themes he uses, or if he uses any at all. No movement in these two sonatas shows this romantic mixture more than the first in the E flat Sonata, with its almost excessively simple square-cut classical first theme. The answer to this, which is also a development of it, sounds a more obviously romantic note but still exhibits a classically lyrical shape. The later episode, in C major, is rapid but equally square. The middle appearance of the opening theme applies the simplest, almost Mozartian, rhythmic variation to the upper part, the last restores the original rhythm, but also switches parts, while a little coda on the repeated-crotchet idea leads to a beautifully poised final chord. On the surface Beethoven seems to have reverted almost to childhood, but the movement develops an extraordinarily mature and romantic sound as it progresses, and finally reveals itself as probably the first romantic use of the form so dear to Schumann in his earlier music—the classical sectional rondo, romantically adapted.

The one-in-a-bar scherzo shoots to the other end of the romantic universe, again with an almost Schumannesque epigrammatic touch, and in the trio builds up tonic and dominant harmonies on A flat to make them sound as though they had just been discovered. The shape of the other two movements, an *Adagio* in A flat framing a full-scale rapid rondo (which echoes one theme from the finale of Op. 26 and the general type and mood of the finale of the E flat Violin Sonata, Op. 12, No. 3), is the most obviously romantic thing in the sonata, and yet, content aside, this general idea goes right back to the Clementi E flat Sonata, Op. 5, No. 3, in which a *Prestissimo* finale-type movement is enclosed in a grave *Andante* which ends the work. The mood there, too, as well as the shape, is romantic, but admittedly Beethoven here goes beyond the Clementi in content, as well as returning to an abbreviated version of his *Adagio* in E flat, and including a short *Presto* coda, which Clementi does not. Undoubtedly this is one of the most neglected of Beethoven's sonatas and also one of his most subtle masterpieces.

It is, indeed, far more so than its well-known companion in C sharp minor, fine as that work is. The comparatively weak part of this work, for me, is the finale, in which the passionate drama seems, in no matter how fine a performance, somewhat leaden-footed and never gets off the ground. This, I think, is partly due to the nature of the two main themes, which seem to be clogged and hampered in their attempt at flight; partly because of a rare occurrence in Beethoven's work—very static harmony, with low-pitched clogging Alberti chords, in the wrong place: in music which is meant to be fast. It succeeds only in sounding as though it is *trying* to be fast. I can think of no other examples in Beethoven's music. Perhaps this is why, when people ask for the 'Moonlight' sonata, they really mean the opening *Adagio sostenuto*; how right they are, even though they are at the same time slighting the very fine scherzo middle movement. But the *Adagio* is the really original, individual, classical, romantic thing in this work; and it is a tribute to the deep melodic power of harmony that people who will tell one that they only like music with a tune or a melody will ask over and over again for this movement, which has no melody as such and only a rhythm and a cadence for themes.

The D major Sonata, Op. 28, is the other cheerful, happy, much less known neighbour of the C sharp minor. The main theme of its first movement is strikingly original and individual, with the veiled subdominant harmony at its very beginning. And yet this phrase is a projection (quite accidental, I am sure, in this case) of the suggestion from two widely separated Clementi themes; none the less, it is astonishing how much of Beethoven's theme is suggested by this short opening phrase of Clementi's Sonata in D, Op. 10, No. 2, published in 1783:

Ex. 42

with its anachronistic reference to the figure in bars 9–10 of Beethoven's subject. And the beginning of the first *Allegro* from Clementi's D major Sonata, Op. 40, No. 3, even has the C natural, the subdominant flavour and the D pedal:[1]

Ex. 43

[1] But cf. p. 97, n. 1, above. (Eds.)

Beethoven's theme, including the initial bars of repeated D's, is ten bars long; it is repeated an octave higher, there is an eight-bar answer, still featuring the C natural, and this is repeated and extended to eleven bars. Throughout the D is repeated, mostly an octave higher than at the start, with a slight deviation at cadences. Another leisurely theme begins a transition passage—two identical phrases, the second a fifth higher. Both are repeated with quaver decoration and the second phrase extended to emphasize a chord of E major. This, being the dominant of A, should bring the second group, but, tonally at any rate, it does not. There has been much debate and controversy over this matter; there is no need for any. Beethoven has made it quite clear where A major is established, and it is not at this point. What has caused confusion is that it *is* established in the middle of a long passage in which the writing is similar throughout. Following assertion of E, Beethoven makes a detour through F sharp minor and B minor harmonies, to close momentarily on A. But the same detour, repeated and foreshortened, leads to the beginning of the long passage I have mentioned, starting on C sharp major harmony; from this point introductory material in a new, simple but beautifully effective keyboard texture leads to the actual point of establishment, and the theme proper blossoms out:

Ex. 44

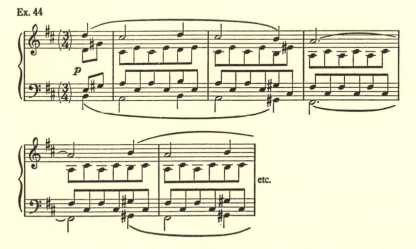

In description Beethoven's procedure may seem roundabout; in sound it is absolutely right. This theme provides a climax which, like most things in this movement, comes twice, the second time with more emphasis, and subsides into a cadence theme with a rhythm which is a trap for the unwary pianist.

It was no new thing for Beethoven to found development on a small figure, and it had been done before him. But no one had ever before done what he does here. The whole first subject is, apart from containing a number of themes, a self-contained melody. Beethoven begins his development by sliding on to G major and sounding it on that harmony. As before, he begins a repeat, for the first time filling out the first bar with quaver decoration (similar to that in the transition of the exposition) and a minor inflection; but this time the last four bars, still minor, initiate a development of their own, with a sweeping bass counterpoint:

Ex. 45

This, as always, is repeated, on the dominant of G minor. Both phrases come again with parts switched, after which the decapitation process is taken further, and the figure in Ex. 45, bars 3–4, continues alone, still with quaver counterpoint, switching from part to part and harmony to harmony, until it begins a rising sequence which lands us at the climax of the development, on F sharp major. F sharp remains the basic harmony for thirty-eight bars, although with B minor and major connections, with the same figure heaving and surging, descending into the bass, rising into the treble, accompanied all the time by booming F sharps, until the chord of F sharp major gradually subsides into the depths and at last comes to rest. The reaction is B major with the cadence theme from the exposition, now four bars and a pause. This is repeated on B minor, and the cadence is echoed, *Adagio,* unfolding the dominant seventh of D.

I have given a good deal of space to this movement because it is perhaps the most individual thing Beethoven had yet written, and the farthest flight he had taken away from the eighteenth century. The gradual decapitation of his theme is a new process; no other composer had even remotely thought of such a thing; while Schubert, Brahms and Bruckner are the only other composers I can think of in the nineteenth century who were capable of maintaining one harmony for so many bars without a break. And yet the umbilical cord is not broken, as it is with Schubert and Bruckner. This music is not like them at all and never ceases to own its eighteenth-century roots. It is a huge and hitherto unforeseen extension of eighteenth-century principles; and this, too, is a secret of Beethoven's originality.

The disturbing of the norm is balanced by an almost exact recapitulation, the only changes being those necessary to bring the second group in D, which makes a great deal of harmonic effect, but does not alter the actual order of the music. There is a short coda on the first subject, separating the tag in Ex. 45 again, leaping up the tonic chord to the tonic itself. Perhaps the most Beethovenian thing of all, and the least eighteenth-century, is the prim perfect cadence which ends this cataclysmic movement.

Czerny tells us that for years the slow movement was a favourite with Beethoven;[1] I can well understand this. It is not one of the deep, broad slow movements he had already experimented with but a sectional *Andante*—almost a sectional rondo. But there are few more fascinating or more haunting sounds than the lovely main melody, with its persistent staccato bass. The D major episode is even simpler: another of Beethoven's miracles, fashioned from a bit of rhythm and a broken chord. The lack of either a second episode or a restatement of the first one is compensated for by the rich double statement, with complex variation figuration, of the opening group. There is a coda which begins thoughtfully by drawing out the third bar of the first theme to a pause, with differing harmonies, and a reminiscence of the episode brings a wonderfully glowing final cadence, crowning a phrase which has gently climbed from the depths.

[1] Quoted in *TF*, p. 296.

The scherzo presents a rhythmically subtle (because ambiguous) scheme attached to an equally simple thematic outline—Beethoven's one-in-a-bar idea reduced to its barest bones. With a slight but real contrast of tone in the middle, the whole thing is really a gradual crescendo. The tempo needs careful working out, since the trio, which obviously cannot go as fast, must present the smallest possible relaxing of tempo. Here simple subtlety rules again—one simple melodic four-bar phrase played, with repeats, eight times, with changing bass harmony.

It was presumably the final rondo, with its rustic drone-bass rhythm, which tempted someone to attach the inadequate label 'Pastoral' to this sonata. Thematically the movement is simple, but it is complex in its layout and still more so in its reactions. The opening bass figure:

exists at three levels. If played entirely alone, it makes a quite complete four-bar thematic idea, as Ex. 46 shows; it also provides a sort of ground bass to the whole opening group. On top of this the rising notes of the first two bars are answered by the treble entry, so that those rising notes have two different thematic meanings. Complexity in simplicity could go very little further. The treble figure in Ex. 46 produces a little refrain figure and also gives rise to rhythmic variation. An arpeggio-figure transition leads to a short first episode, similar in rhythm to Ex. 46, stated in imitation, and again with rhythmic variation. A sweeping octave figure leads to the first return, which itself leads straight on to a transition, on the same galumphing rhythm, to the middle episode, starting on G. This is fugal, on a figure with not a little suggestion of the G major Bagatelle, Op. 126, No. 5, of 1823 or 1824. This leads in a powerful crescendo to an inversion of the octave figure in a return to Ex. 46, which is stated entire, with the original transition passage taken in a slightly different direction and the first episode now in D; a coda starting on G gives a subtle version of Ex. 46 and opens out gradually to a *Presto* wind-up, with a rapid counterpoint over the original bass in octaves. It can scarcely be accident that the quiet perfect cadence which closes the first movement is answered at the end of the rondo with a *fortissimo* one, reversing the movement of the upper notes.

With the three Sonatas, Op. 31, written in 1801–2, Beethoven's second period was well under way. About the D minor Sonata especially he was to exhibit wisdom after the event by remarking that henceforth he would write in a new way; he had gradually been doing so for some time. But it is probably true that the full force of this new manner is felt only with these three sonatas—and in one of these there is still a backsliding to his earlier manner. This is the G major, whose beautifully rich and luxurious slow movement steps straight from the period of the Septet and F major String Quartet of Op. 18, and, indeed, from even earlier chamber works such as the Octet, Op. 103. This quality is the more emphasized by the radically forthright new-type first movement, in which the main theme is again a rhythm and a combined turn and scale:

Ex. 47   **Allegro vivace**

The dotted rhythm is immediately developed into a further idea, as this example shows, and leads through the dominant to a restatement of Ex. 47 on completely unexpected flat-seventh harmony, swinging round to a swooping development of the turn-and-scale motive, which is brought up eventually on the home dominant. Ex. 47 begins again, short-circuited this time to the dominant of B.

One writer has said that she can find nothing new in this work, which prompts me to wonder with what sort of ears she listened; the whole of the procedure I have first outlined is so graphically foreshortened, taking so much normally stated for granted, as to be not so much second-period as a foretaste of the third. The rest of the movement follows this same pattern. To find another piece with commensurate language and movement one must go to the middle movement of the E major Sonata, Op. 109. I do *not* claim that the content has the depth of the later work. The whole sonata is a mixture of styles, for the final rondo is pure second-period music, and it is a remarkable feat on Beethoven's part that he managed to make the work sound like a unified whole.

As often, it is the minor-key work, the middle one of this group, which has captured the limelight. It has no mixture of style, and it has many new ideas, the two that have perhaps brought it the most fame being the use of recitative in the first movement and the galloping rhythm of the finale, kept up unbroken throughout the movement. However, just as individual and original is the fact that, in spite of appearances, the first movement does not have a slow introduction. What it has is one opening idea, formed of a *Largo*, with *Allegro* answer. When this is raised a third, the *Allegro* expands to come to the original slow arpeggio used now with a turn continuation to form a new theme (bars 21 ff.). There *is* a case for regarding the whole of the beginning, up to bar 20, as an introduction, since that is what it sounds like, although the passage beginning at bar 21 initiates a transition. This movement also gives, in the second subject, possibly the first structural use of the Neapolitan sixth in Beethoven's work:

Ex. 48

Note that the theme itself, in its upper notes, is the inversion of the turn of bars 22–4, although with a different rhythm and different harmony, but with the actual upper notes at the same pitch as the original turn. But perhaps the strongest evidence of the new look of this music, and of Beethoven's power of transforming the ordinary into the extraordinary, is the alternation of simple tonic and dominant harmony (most potent in its context) as the exposition closes.

The development expands the use of the opening *Largo*, with rippling arpeggio approach, to F sharp major, alters this to minor and concentrates on bars 21 ff., which explains why this theme plays no part in the recapitulation. Beethoven is now responsive to whatever situation arises. The development comes eventually to dominant preparation for D minor and the recapitulation, which begins with the opening *Largo* arpeggio, expanded to the first of the pathetic recitative passages, and the original *Allegro* answer; the lift to C major harmony brings the second recitative but not the original expanded answer. Instead there is a passage of chords and arpeggios, remarkably apt in these surroundings, which brings the music to the original transition passage, the dominant of D minor and the second subject. A rumbling bass arpeggio on the tonic chord provides all that is needed for coda, plus two tonic chords.[1] This is the kind of movement that led eventually to sonata movements in the late string quartets which have stimulated writers to describe them as capricious or as fantasias, etc., implying (and sometimes saying) that Beethoven had broken with sonata style. In fact his attitude became gradually stricter, following every nuance and suggestion offered by the music. This is one of the most important features of his middle-period music.

The somewhat austere expressiveness of the *Adagio* is another facet of his second-period attitude to the classical-romantic combination. Its opening rhythm can be misleading, as the phrasing imparted to it by many concert pianists shows; none the less, the opening whole-bar chord *is* the beginning of the eight-bar melodic phrase. Beethoven's counter-statement adds proof of this, if proof is necessary. There are few movements in the whole of Beethoven's piano music in which he employs so great a range of nuance, or where every note counts to such an extent. It is not a long movement, although every facet of sonata-movement shape is used, even to a return to the restatement which serves adequately as a real

[1] These chords have curious echoes in Sibelius's first two symphonies.

development; the coda, long for the proportions of the movement, is based on the same little development phrase and makes melodic use of every note up to the final low B flat.

The first thing most people notice about the finale is that it has an all but unbroken flow of semiquavers throughout its length, the bulk of it expressed in the brief, highly pungent rhythm of its beginning. This is a remarkable feat; but if it were just that it would not deserve either the reputation it has or the place it has as finale to this expressive tragedy. What gives it its most potent flavour is that it sums up the work in a sonata movement expressed in an almost unbroken texture, yet there is all the contrast one requires. Already it comes close to the frozen dramatic tableau that is the finale of the 'Appassionata', with the equally frozen texture of the slow movement of the third 'Razumovsky' Quartet, but without the pathetic and impotent appeal of the latter's little second subject. In other words, Beethoven is hitching his finale to the main drama in a way he has not done before and will rarely do again. But the main drama is already over. The finale is an echo frozen in its grief; such grief is either incapable of thought at all or it revolves round one thing—as this movement does.

The E flat member of this group, especially in its first and third movements, can be a misleading work, and has, accordingly, misled many commentators into believing it to be a reversion to Beethoven's earlier manner, and, even beyond that, to a Mozartian type of writing. On the contrary, while it is not in style the most obviously mature work of the three, it is probably in the long run the most potently so; practically everything in the first movement which superficially suggests an earlier period turns out to be among the strongest proofs of its 'second-period' quality. Let us take the most obvious thing: the Alberti bass, used in this movement more than in any music for some years, and more than it will be again, without adaptation. It occurs in the second subject; that is its first statement, and even here the manner in which the harmony is adapted to the implications of the upper part are far from eighteenth-century. But in the counter-statement at bar 57 it releases a figure that quite definitely grows out of this bass, and this is quite new. On the other hand, the most obviously individual thing about the movement as a whole, its ambiguous opening, realized afresh at different parts of the movement in a manner we can only associate with Beethoven, is a definite 'second-period' characteristic, although developed from certain signs appearing in an unrealized state in earlier works. The use of the opening chord, with a minor inflection and transition material growing from it, has a new romantic depth that would not have come from Beethoven a few years earlier. The tune of the second subject, on its own, could perhaps suggest an earlier period, but the cadenza-like extension of it before its resumption could not. Finally, perhaps the deepest and most wonderful single stroke in the movement, which proves its modern quality: the last few bars approaching the second subject descend through five F's, followed by a crotchet rest; the tune begins on the second half of this rest; in the recapitulation the descent concerns four B flats, and what was a crotchet rest is occupied by a descending bass note, A flat, connecting it to the bass of the tune:

Ex. 49   Exposition

a

b   Recapitulation

There are few single notes in Beethoven's entire work more wonderful than this A flat.

The $\frac{2}{4}$ scherzo, in A flat, is one of the most individual conceptions in all Beethoven's piano music: light, staccato, will-o'-the-wispish, with sudden outbursts which sink back again almost immediately; and with the simplest of main themes, which nevertheless went through five or six main versions in his 1802–3 sketchbook before assuming its final form.[1] The piece is a sonata movement with a strong rondo suggestion which never quite materializes (it is this teetering between one style and another which gives an essentially simple movement an effect of great complexity); as a test of pianistic control it has few superiors.

There is no slow movement, as such; instead, Beethoven follows the scherzo with a minuet, full of deep-throated grace and charm, and with a trio so original and individual, as well as satisfying in itself, that it inspired Saint-Saëns to one of his real strokes of genius, in selecting it as the basis of his fine Variations for two pianos, Op. 35. There is no relapse in style in Beethoven's minuet— no composer of eighteenth-century classical outlook would have written such a piece in such a way; the absence of a slow movement helps to emphasize the light but deeply happy mood of the whole sonata. In mood and style the minuet is closely akin to the isolated Minuet in E flat for piano, WoO 82, which possibly originated about 1785. It was published in 1805, by which time Beethoven must have revised it to such an extent that it became a new piece. In particular this wonderful exploration of the dominant, and the depth of the syncopated repetition:

Ex. 50

etc.

[1] See Ludwig Nohl, *Beethoven, Liszt, Wagner* (Vienna, 1874), p. 100.

are mature second-period features without parallels in Beethoven's juvenilia.

Beethoven whips up the substance of this sonata to a concentrated finish in his finale, a sonata-form tarantella, and one of the two greatest pieces of this type ever written for the piano, the other being the finale of Schubert's C minor Sonata, D.958. One reason for the comparative obscurity of this wonderful sonata (it is seldom picked for performance unless a cycle of the sonatas is to be performed) is probably that, in contrast to the lively demonism of the G major, in its first movement, at least, and the tragic quality of the D minor, the E flat is a happy work.

The year 1802 saw also the composition of two of Beethoven's finest mature sets of variations, the Six Variations on an Original Theme, Op. 34, and the so-called 'Eroica' Variations, Op. 35. The *Adagio* theme of Op. 34 has the luxurious sprawl of so many of his first-period slow movements—on the surface; in fact, it is as tight as a drum, and there is not a note that does not contribute to the basic theme and harmonic texture essential for the variations. The whole outlook is utterly different from that of any first-period work. The first variation conveys the theme in lavish but controlled decoration, a quality which is almost completely relaxed in the next five variations, which are respectively a virile $\frac{6}{8}$, a gentle *Allegretto*, a minuet, a funeral march and a sort of $\frac{6}{8}$ *Ländler*; with the return of the theme in its original form in the coda, the decoration also returns in force and leaps ahead to preview the type found in the *largo* $\frac{6}{8}$ variation of Op. 35, and much further still to the $\frac{9}{8}$ *largo* of the 'Diabelli' set. The key scheme is interesting: F major for the theme, D, B flat, G, E flat, C minor and F for the variations. It was an experiment that fitted this work, but one that Beethoven did not repeat.

E flat is obviously the right key for the theme which forms the foundation of Op. 35: it is in this key in each of its appearances in four different works; but it is this key which causes the piano writing in the 'Eroica' variations to hover at times on the borderline between difficulty and awkwardness. This is a quality frequently found in Beethoven's keyboard writing, although no one ever mentions it (it would appear that there is a tacit agreement on the part of musicologists not to mention it); there is, in fact, far more of such awkward writing in Beethoven's piano music than in Schubert's, although it is always mentioned in the latter case (I imagine as a result of another tacit agreement). In every case in Beethoven's music that I can recall this awkwardness in writing results from the key used; the key is right and Beethoven is right in not sacrificing that key—but it still results in awkwardness, though not in real difficulty.

The 'Eroica' set is a masterpiece for the most part unique in his work. In most ways it stands alone, not least in the manner in which the variations, mainly harmonic, at times blend theme and bass to such an extent that they become one entity—or one a projection or extension of the other. Also, even when the accent is on the bass (that is, the original bass, although it may be placed on the top of the music) the theme is brought to mind, though not a note of it may appear in the music. The piano writing often has more affinity with aspects of twentieth-century keyboard writing (see Variation 9, for instance) than with anything of Beethoven's own time or even later in the nineteenth century—to a much greater extent than in the majority of the sonatas. One final point: on the strength of this work and the 'Diabelli' set Beethoven has often been credited with starting the habit of ending sets of variations with a fugue; in fact, he did not. To the best of my knowledge, this habit still starts with Brahms. In neither Beethoven case is the fugue the last thing to be heard; in Op. 35 it is true that it is headed 'Finale', coming after the *largo* fifteenth variation, but it is cut short for the music to plunge into yet two more slower variations and a final wind-up. In Op. 120 it is the thirty-second variation out of thirty-three and is followed by the minuet and a coda, which begins yet another variation before stretching its last energy to the final chord.

The virtuoso trend found in the 'Kreutzer' Sonata spilled over into the next piano sonata, Op. 53, known as the 'Waldstein', but produced a much nobler work. Here the virtuosity is, in fact, unleashed to an even greater extent, especially in the coda to each of the quick movements, but does not obtrude on the attention as the lesser application tends to do in the 'Kreutzer'; rather, it deepens the ideas and reveals their greatest depth. Here, Beethoven is master of the virtuosity; in the violin sonata we may feel that it rather mastered him.

Scarcely, if ever, did Beethoven conceive a finer rondo theme than that of the final *Allegretto*; calm and simple, its three-tier presentation is absolutely right, culminating in the famous passage with left-hand scales and the theme presented amid a persistent shake. Nothing more calculated for technical display could be imagined, and yet this technique comes as an absolute *musical* necessity at this point; and this is a mark of the whole movement, to the end of the *Prestissimo* coda. From this point of view, the work has affinities with two Clementi sonatas, both also in C: his Op. 34, No. 1 (published no later than 1795), and Op. 36, No. 3 (published in 1797), the first of which at least is said to have been rewritten from a piano-concerto original. Poetry also emerges from this accent on technique, as in the wonderful passage towards the end of the middle episode, where the right hand floats above the three-note figure derived from the opening of the movement.

Beethoven made many new discoveries in his music about the basic perfect cadence, but few more remarkable than those which form the basis of the main idea of the first movement. His manner of investing them with mystery at the beginning of a movement which plays out its drama mainly in daylight is twofold: delaying the cadence by quiet chord repetition, to make the move the more rewarding when it comes, and the gradual semitonal descent of the bass during the first eight bars. There is yet a third feature: the harmonic rise, after the pause in bar 13, which not only leads to the dominant preparation for E major but also to the first real outburst in the movement, practically all of which has so far been conducted in intense quiet. I will add that the habit that some pianists have of playing the main theme of the second group as a sort of slow hymn effectively destroys any sense of poetry or motion which may already have been set up. The whole of the second group from the start of its second, broken-chord theme is worth study for a perfect use, for a musical reason, of pure concerto-type virtuosity to reveal the latent poetry of this music, which is the closing theme of the exposition, following the shake which would normally end the exposition.

Beethoven uses two simple methods to produce the complex effect of his development: one is the 'cutting-down' method, by which the third and fourth bars of the movement are first crammed into one bar, and then the third bar is allowed to develop alone in its new rhythm, building a quite new theme in the most natural way. This passage leads to the second method, built on the arpeggio theme from the second group; this propels a use of large-scale sequence rare in the work of Beethoven, who was not as a rule given to much sequential writing. This eventually sinks down to *pianissimo* on the home dominant, and a short scale stutters its way up to a climax and the recapitulation in a manner peculiar to Beethoven and somewhat prophetic of the corresponding passage in the first movement of the Fourth Symphony, although harmonically different. No one will miss the miraculously simple expansion of the original twelfth and thirteenth bars of the first group; it is a justly famous stroke.

In these two movements Beethoven finally mastered the use of extreme virtuosity on a keyboard for purely musical and poetic ends, without the ameliorating influence of an orchestra—an important step forward. He was not so successful in the balance of the work as a whole. His first attempt at a slow movement slipped back to the rather luxuriant type found at times in his first period and certainly out of joint with his present outlook as a whole. It is a beautiful movement and, when he proved amenable to a suggestion that it should be removed, immediately revealed its full beauty when he had released it from its intimidating position between its two athletic neighbours; it was published as the *Andante favori*, WoO 57. So far, so good. But the *Adagio* with which he replaced it, which proved to be an introduction to the finale (the original *Andante* was self-contained), also proves to have missed the mark as widely as the earlier movement, but in the opposite direction. One of the profoundest passages Beethoven ever wrote, it leaps ahead by many years to the world of his third period; its fit companions are works such as the Opp. 101 and 109 Sonatas, or the Cello Sonatas of Op. 102. To this extent the 'Waldstein' Sonata remained unbalanced, with one problem Beethoven never solved.

The 'Waldstein' and 'Appassionata' Sonatas (1803–5) are two

towering peaks. In between comes, as far as the piano sonatas are concerned, one of his subtlest and smallest works, Op. 54 in F (1804). A gem in every way, only its lack of size prevents it from figuring in recital programmes, which it does very infrequently indeed. Its two movements are as simple in construction as anything in the classical period, but it is this very simplicity of outline that makes possible the rich burgeoning of detail that clusters round the structure in the first movement, a simple sectional rondo–minuet, and the immense control displayed in the action of the *perpetuum mobile* sonata movement which is the finale. This is related in the use of certain figures to the finale of Op. 26, but the result is very different. Quiet humour informs both movements in quite different ways. It is somewhat of a shock to realize that in the beautifully urbane main minuet theme of the first movement Beethoven has, in fact, consciously or unconsciously, returned, though utterly transforming it, to the rapid and purposeful main theme of the first movement of his First Symphony.

Beethoven capped his sonata writing at this momentous period with the F minor Sonata, Op. 57, the 'Appassionata', not Beethoven's title, but an apt one. Ferdinand Ries related[1] that while on a walk with Beethoven the composer began humming in a most devilish manner (his humming being a sort of raucous croak to other ears) and ran on, leaving Ries behind. When Ries reached Beethoven's lodgings the composer was already at the piano, and, said Ries, he sat quietly in a corner and heard Beethoven improvise practically the whole of the finale of this sonata 'in the beautiful form we know'. How much credence one can give this is difficult to assess; certainly it could not have been 'in the beautiful form we know', for Beethoven's sketches contradict this. But that Ries heard a version very nearly as impressive as the final one may very well be true.

Technically, apart from one or two passages, the work is not difficult to play. It contains some of the most playable keyboard writing in his whole output and yet can still sound very brilliant. Its real difficulty, however, is control of its varied elements and of the

---

[1] Cf. O. G. Sonneck (ed.), *Beethoven: impressions by his contemporaries* (repr. New York, 1967), pp. 52–3.

great expressive power which is their sum. Emotionally it is expressive of tragedy, and a tragic drama is enacted and completed in the first movement. The slow movement is in suspension throughout, and the finale is an emotional echo of the first—in fact, the emotional residue of the first movement is here frozen into a great tragic tableau, which comes to no solution except that 'this burden shalt thou carry'. Its triumph is in the strength wrested to enable the load to be carried. There are, as noted above, only two other movements in Beethoven's work comparable in atmosphere, and they are the finale of Op. 31, No. 2, and the $\frac{6}{8}$ *Andante* from the C major 'Razumovsky' Quartet; but the latter does have the relief of its pathetically appealing little second subject, a relief denied to either Op. 31, No. 2, or to the finale of Op. 57.

But, even more than on its themes, which for character reasons alone are important, this sonata depends upon its highly individual structure for the expression of the music it contains. Its opening is sometimes quoted as an example of the Neapolitan sixth on something more than a small, local scale, and so it is. What I have not yet seen noticed, except in so oblique a fashion as to make one wonder if the writer has felt the full import of what he has noted, is that the entire sonata, all three movements, is built on an extended use of the two Neapolitan harmonies, on tonic and dominant, unprecedented in Beethoven's work, and never explored in this way in any earlier music. We have in this work a large preview of what Schubert expanded throughout his instrumental music on a scale which makes even this sonata *seem* small in comparison. I write 'seem', and this is all it is. There is nothing small anywhere in this work, least of all in its structure.

Not only is the tonic chord of the opening phrase answered by the Neapolitan G flat chord, but the dominant to which the phrase leads is emphasized by a rise to the submediant—the Neapolitan effect, in a minor key, leaning on the dominant. (In a major key it would be the *flat* submediant.) This alternation and answering process goes on all through the movement. Dominant preparation for A flat major and the second group have it. It is this leaning of a Neapolitan chord on its fundamental, essentially a two-note, two-chord, figure, which is so fundamental to the harmonic structure of the whole and which Rudolph Réti[1] distorts by obliterating intervening rests to try to prove a point for which the Beethoven movement, *as Beethoven wrote it*, is no proof. The second subject first theme, derived from the opening, is free from this harmonic effect until the close, where it suddenly intrudes, leading to a new theme in A flat minor, again impregnated with Neapolitan harmony. This theme fades out in echoes of this effect, and, except for one bass alternation, Beethoven keeps his development free from it, until the tail-end of the climax, when the three-quaver figure shouts it just as the recapitulation is approached. Again, having been insisted upon for some bars before the outburst of the coda, the coda itself is free from it, as far as the actual chords are concerned, although the use of a D flat upper note in a chord of the added sixth twice carries its impression.

The slow movement is as nearly motionless as is possible in music; not even the slow movement of the Violin Concerto has more of this quality, but the effect here is very different. Here it is as though one held one's breath until the outbreak of the finale. Everything contributes to this stillness, even the fact that the theme is not much more than an alternation of tonic, dominant and submediant. There is slightly more thematic substance in the bass. The chords are the simplest possible, and the most potent effect of all is that each phrase of the theme ends on the tonic. Taken right out of context one might say that here is support for those who have maintained that Beethoven could not write a tune. He could, when he wanted to, and there are hundreds to prove it. But the apparent crudeness of this theme is its most distinctive feature. *This* is what achieves the wonderful breath-held suspense— and the key contributes also. Not that it is a key *per se*; it is simply the submediant of F minor, held in suspense throughout the movement; hence the harmonic immovability, with nothing in the slightest to disturb it. The first three of the four variations maintain the simplicity by gradually activating the texture through figurations which outline the harmonies. The final variation adds poignancy to simplicity and breathlessness by its placing of parts

---

[1] Cf. Rudolph Réti, *Thematic patterns in sonatas of Beethoven* (London, 1967), pp. 97 ff.

of the harmonic structure at different levels of the keyboard, until it is dispersed by a soft, spread diminished seventh, immediately followed by a very loud one, only the lower part of which should be spread, although many editions show an arpeggio sign for the whole chord. The same diminished seventh sets off the finale and leads, via a semiquaver figure which vaguely suggests something fugal, to the beginning of the movement proper.

This starts with a theme obviously designed primarily to display the Neapolitan sixth. This comes twice, the second time with a jerky addition (first heard at bar 28), and is followed by two statements of a derivative of the opening, extending the jerky-rhythm figure. The second statement leads to a swoop through a rapid transition passage, based on the opening, to come without a break at bar 76 to a short second-subject theme which combines the Neapolitan sixth of C minor with a simple turn shape. A cadence theme based on the first subject leads to the development (the exposition is not repeated, although everything from the beginning of the development to the end of the recapitulation is, or should be). The first subject on a dominant minor ninth of B flat minor begins the development, and a derivative leads to the alternation of tonic and flat supertonic in simple arpeggio form, as at the beginning of the movement, and repetition with a new crotchet detail (first heard at bar 134); this leads to a new rhythmic theme (bar 142), which features the submediant thematically, but— subtle point—not harmonically. The music swings to F minor, and overlapping entries of the first subject swoop to the home dominant and build a big crescendo to the famous arpeggio passage of return, which begins by switching to the home flat supertonic, or tonic Neapolitan sixth, and culminates in a long ascending and descending quaver diminished seventh. This whole passage is redolent of Beethoven's rhythmic subtlety with very simple means. The harmony comes to rest on the home dominant *half-way* through a four-bar phrase; the remaining four bars are an inevitable result, the final bass dotted rhythm clinching the whole effect of exact proportion.

The opening subject gains a new little counterpoint in the recapitulation, which produces an effect of intense poignancy, but which is in fact simply augmenting bits of it:

Ex. 51

Otherwise, except for a change of harmonic outlook to bring the second subject in F minor, the recapitulation is exact up to the point of repetition from the beginning of the development and then the plunge into the coda. In the latter, with a new *Presto* theme, all tonic and dominant, with a counter-statement on the mediant, and a last apotheosis of the opening, complete with Neapolitan sixth, the music rushes to the final arpeggio descent and the last chords, heaving and surging in an attempt to break its bonds—and failing.

With this great work Beethoven closed an era in his piano-sonata writing. When he restarted, after an interval of some five years, the works he wrote are still within his so-called second period, but, especially in Opp. 81a and 90, a new manner is emerging.

FOUR

The Piano Music–II

PHILIP BARFORD

INTRODUCTION

THE WORKS THAT BEETHOVEN composed for the pianoforte in the last eighteen years of his life are monumental structures and enduring sources of inspiration. Despite his view that the piano 'is and always will be an unsatisfactory instrument',[1] the later sonatas and the Diabelli Variations are so tremendous in their impact, so challenging to pianists and audiences all over the world, that they can only be classed in the realm of timeless masterpieces. The composer's use of his material arouses renewed admiration in our own day, and it is upon this that a modern assessment must be made. It has been the special distinction of the twentieth century, reacting against the romantic excesses of the nineteenth, to draw attention to Beethoven's structural methods. At the same time, the seeds of a deeper insight into the structures and forms of music had, in fact, been sown in the nineteenth century. In traversing ground previously reviewed by earlier critics[2] we shall try to relate our own analytical observations both to recent developments in music theory and to those deeper currents of cultural insight in an earlier generation of criticism which have still to make their way outside Germany.

[1] Reported by his friend Karl Holz, who was an important figure in Vienna's musical life. Cf. Friedrich Kerst, *Beethoven: the man and the artist as revealed in his own words*, trans. and ed. Henry Edward Krehbiel (London, 1906), p. 45.

[2] See, for instance, Eric Blom, *Beethoven's piano sonatas discussed* (London, 1938), and Donald Francis Tovey, *A Companion to Beethoven's pianoforte sonatas* (London, 1943).

In our own time there have been two complementary developments which, when fully understood in their reciprocal relationship, must inevitably deepen our musical awareness. On the one hand, functional analysis has done much to illuminate as a musical, not as a merely abstract philosophical principle, the unifying force of basic thematic shapes from which contrasting themes and motives are derived.[1] Josef Rufer, for example, in his book *Composition with twelve notes*,[2] demonstrates in detail the unifying figure which appears in each of the three movements of Beethoven's Sonata in C minor, Op. 10, No. 1. Such analysis places a strong emphasis upon the *Grundgestalt* or 'basic wholeness' of a work in terms of some figure from which its varied and contrasting structures are derived. Further questions are now being raised about the deeper significance of this compositional procedure.[3] Is it, for instance, conscious or unconscious? If it is conscious, as Réti suggests,[4] then the thematic and formal structure of a sonata is largely a matter of 'tonal engineering'. If it is unconscious, the creative act is an outflow from a positive core or nucleus experienced under a creative compulsion which seems to have origins beyond itself. The musical *process* would be all one with the psychological *state*—taking account of subconscious mind-energies and images. The development of a basic shape in composition would be the actual exploration, in musical thought, of an area of the composer's experience which would be of the greatest interest to all who study the workings of his mind through the symbols of musical notation. Thus the notion of a symbology of music invites elaboration, and may well become a major department of musicology, especially when serious study of nineteenth-century music and music theory gets under way.[5]

[1] Broader cultural implications of functional analysis are discussed in Philip Barford, 'Urphänomen, Ursatz and Grundgestalt', *Music Review*, XXVIII (1967), p. 218.

[2] Trans. Humphrey Searle (London, 1954, rev. repr, 1969), pp. 38–44.

[3] See Alan Walker, *A Study in musical analysis* (London, 1962), and idem, *An Anatomy of musical criticism* (London, 1966).

[4] Rudolph Réti, *The thematic process in music* (London, 1961).

[5] See Gordon Epperson, *The Musical symbol: a study of the philosophic theory of music* (Ames, Iowa, 1967). A recent meeting (1967) of the American Musicological Society discussed the problems of 'opening up

On the other hand, Deryck Cooke has already attempted to establish themes and motives as *tonal images*.[1] It now appears to his critics that Cooke has somewhat overstated his case that specific shapes are consistently associated with specific psychological contents. The case is far from proven. Nevertheless, some over-emphasis was indeed necessary to avoid the danger of insensitivity to all creative functions other than those demonstrable in purely *notational* analysis—a danger which is very real in some areas of contemporary music theory. To the present writer it seems very possible that in the climate of modernism we may lose that element in musical sounds which corresponds to the image-content in speech. It is interesting that even Beethoven once said to Neate in Baden that he always had a picture in mind when composing.[2] This should not, perhaps, be taken too literally, especially when we remember that on this occasion conversation turned on the subject of the 'Pastoral' Symphony. But what would happen to our appreciation of Beethoven's late music if we brought to it only those categories of analysis applicable to a limited number of contemporary works, and totally discounted the notion that every theme and figure is an image—not necessarily in the literal sense of something seen, but as a quantum of spiritual force subjectively formed in a unit of thematic energy?[3]

---

the nineteenth century' to musicological investigation. From the special standpoint of musical symbology this would bring many interesting ideas into renewed consideration.

[1] Deryck Cooke, *The Language of music* (London, 1959; repr. 1962).

[2] Cf. Kerst, op. cit., p. 24.

[3] Aware of a parallel danger in literature, Owen Barfield, in his collection of essays entitled *Romanticism comes of age* (London, 1966), has wondered if the increasing phenomenon of word-blindness in children is the effect of a cultural environment in which the logical, i.e. structural, relations of words are increasingly valued at the expense of their image-content. As he points out, linguistic analysts have professed no interest in etymology. And he is 'not surprised to hear it. I do not suppose a Crystal Palace is much interested in dynamite.' The sterility of purely relational analysis of poetry has its equivalent in a merely numerical analysis of music; and both reflect an uncritical acceptance of habits of thought and standards of judgement which bear no immediate relation to aesthetic experience. In music it is important not to apply retrospectively methods of analysis and (by implication) standards of judgement which only apply

In the following discussion, the assumption is that Beethoven's themes, motives and harmonic relations are such quanta, and it is maintained in order to safeguard the vital contribution which the listener's imagination can make towards the understanding and enjoyment of Beethoven's late works. The constructional interest of Beethoven's music cannot be a merely scientific matter of 'tonal engineering'.[1]

His thematic material, as the sketchbooks reveal, arose painfully into its final form through the stress of subconscious pressures, often over a considerable period of time. Figures from the *Allegro* of Op. 111 were first written down twenty years before the sonata was composed. The composer had to struggle to bring out what he knew to exist within himself. There is a sense, too, in which their final emergence into consciousness coincided with the right psychological moment for their creative use. Beethoven's themes frequently convey, especially in development, the feeling of the stress of their slow birth. Sometimes, in listening to a speaker struggling to articulate a difficult concept, the *feeling* of the struggle is empathetically experienced by the listener. It is like this with some of Beethoven's late music—the creative journey and the achieved destination seem to be one. The stress of the tonal pattern becomes a function of our inwardness.

Yet there is another side to this. As Goethe tried to demonstrate

---

to a few modern experiments. If there is something of a justifiable analogy between the human brain and the electronic computer, there is none between the computer and the unconscious mind of the artist, which works by deeper principles of organic co-inherence. Coleridge knew this 'deeper' level of creative activity as the imagination, i.e. the mental force which fuses images inspirationally. It is quite arguable that as the eye conditions itself negatively by television, which reduces images to black and white in two dimensions, so can the ear condition itself negatively by reducing tonal relations to a mere construction of aural sensations.

[1] This phrase was used by a concert pianist whose warm and brilliant playing seemed to deny the coldness of his theories; but he was discussing the 'Hammerklavier' Sonata, and it must be confessed that there are passages in that work to which the phrase is not entirely inappropriate. There Beethoven was working out a problem; but he solved it by a brilliant imaginative stroke in the preparation of the recapitulation in the first movement. See Ex. 25 below.

to sceptical scientific contemporaries, the imagination can be used in the process of fantasy to gain creative insight into the world of nature. He called such use of the imagination 'exact sensorial fantasy' and illustrated its function in the observation of transformation processes in plants. Unwittingly, perhaps, he provided an exact analogy of functional musical analysis. When we actually *hear* the different parts of a sonata as a wholeness of musical function, as distinct from merely arriving at an abstract understanding of formal arrangements, we are exercising 'exact *tonal* fantasy'—that is, sensorial fantasy concentrated into tonal images.

As an example of this, consider the thematic material of Beethoven's Sonata in A flat, Op. 110 (Ex. 1). Listen carefully to the opening bars, and then transform the melody into the fugue subject which is contained in it. Soon you will hear and *feel* both figures in a relation of mutual transformation. Now in the performance of a great piece of music such an experience can be supremely inspiring, far transcending in its impact a merely formal knowledge of the common thematic stock of the themes involved. The melodies come alive with a wonderful inwardness and seem to be formed of the very substance of mind and spirit:

Ex. 1

a   Fuga: allegro ma non troppo

b   Opening bars of sonata: **Moderato cantabile molto espressivo**

The condition of this kind of musical experience is a positive use of the imagination, not passive absorption of programme-notes.[1]

---

[1] Relations between the fugue subject and the sonata's first few bars have been pointed out by Réti, op. cit., pp. 89–90, and also by Donald Mitchell, prefatory note to Réti, op. cit., p. vii.

Musical experience is a consciously-directed waking dream, built up from the substance of inspired intuitions. The creative genius makes music within himself, as a spiritual force using mind and imagination to create tonal forms out of its own dynamic energies.

If the thematic movement of Beethoven's thought comes through with compelling force, with or without explicit recognition of an underlying basic shape, we must not lose sight of the harmonic impetus which is so closely related to it, the factor which in Schenker's view is of primary importance. In the later sonatas, the formal structure is knitted together by dynamic harmonic rhythm. The time-space of Op. 81a, for example, is really determined by an extended I–VI–II–V–I progression. Again, a large volume could be written on the subject of Beethoven's rhythmic organization; and it is quite true, as has been pointed out, that theory has hitherto concentrated upon thematic and harmonic at the expense of rhythmic analysis.[1]

It is necessary, then, to observe thematic structures against harmonic and rhythmic movement and to recognize that the entire thematic-harmonic flow is generated from a subjective 'in-stress' guiding the listener's creative fantasy. A Beethoven sonata is a tonal drama played out in the listener's own being. In this psychotonal fact lies the real origin of the 'transcendental' element in Beethoven's late works which has moved so many writers to rapturous enthusiasm.

Increasingly in these masterpieces Beethoven conceives the sonata as a tonal world unifying different spheres of experience, and this is reflected in the expanding and varied organization of separate sections and movements. Op. 110, for example, consists of a slow movement in sonata form, scherzo, recitative, slow movement, fugue, varied restatement of the slow movement, inversion and diminution of the fugue, and triumphant finale on the fugue theme, the whole structure being conditioned by the close relation between its opening bars and the fugue subject, and subsidiary relationships affecting both melodic and harmonic elements.

[1] Cf. Leonard B. Meyer and Grosvenor Cooper, *The Rhythmic structure of music* (Chicago, 1960).

The unifying force of musical thought is necessarily expressed in motion; and if it is true that the tonal *process* and psychological *state* are two sides of the same coin, it is nevertheless true that *motion* and *flow* are the two main categories in which we first apprehend music. For Ernst Kurth[1] motion is paramount, and to some extent he shares the same world as Hugo Munsterberg, who also wrote idealistically on music under the influence of Schopenhauer. He was much concerned with the inner psychological energies informing harmony and counterpoint, experienced as movement, and he attempted a systematic theory based upon them. He is therefore heir to the tradition of German music theory which owes so much to C. P. E. Bach, and his views seem particularly applicable to Beethoven's later music. 'Sound', says Kurth, 'is dead; what lives in it is the will to sound.' Music's 'true and original, supporting and formative contents are psychic tensions unfolding, and these it merely transmits in the perceptible form . . . The musical phenomenon merely manifests in sound but is not based upon them . . . It is mistaken to emphasize only the acoustical phenomena—the sounding and the sounds themselves with all their latent harmonic relationships—as the most essential and truly significant moments of melody, without paying attention to the connection with perceptions of a proceeding of forces between the tones . . . The original form of the volitional impulse in music . . . are physical tensions that press toward resolution in motion; all musical phenomena are based upon the occurrence of motion and its inner dynamic . . . Music is therefore no reflection of nature, but rather the experience of [the latter's] mysterious energies within ourselves.'

Anyone who looks below the surface of both functional analysis and Cooke's theory of musical language to make contact with the 'psychic'—or 'spiritual'—or 'subconscious' will to achieve unity through contrast must reach the same general conclusions. In view of the tremendous psychological oppositions which found expres-

[1] The writer is indebted to the article by Dolores Menstell Hsu, 'Ernst Kurth and his concept of music as motion', *Journal of Music Theory*, X (1966), p. 2, for the references and quotations. This article includes a comprehensive bibliography of Kurth's theoretical writings.

sion in Beethoven's character, and musical projection in his earlier and middle-period sonatas, the application of such conclusions to the later piano music is profound, and to embark upon discussion of the last sonatas without in any way making contact with the psychological world underlying the sounds, the 'mysterious energies' which are also 'within ourselves', would seem a fruitless undertaking, a mere codification of musicological data already worked over by others. But to avoid any one-sidedness lurking in Kurth's theoretical approach, let us remember the presence of fixed elements of construction, the unifying figures (when they are present) which initiate the musical flow, and their significance not merely as moving elements but as psycho-tonal shapes symbolizing originating centres of musical experience. In Beethoven's late music, it often seems particularly important, as we shall see, to realize that the growth of complex forms occurs between these two polarities of motion and fixity which express the logical development of musical thought and the psycho-thematic constants inspiring it. In one great instance, namely the last sonata, it even seems that this polarity is itself symbolized in the two complementary movements, the inner relation of which is revealed in the introduction. The true recognition of these principles leads the mind away from sterile concepts of calculated pitch-relation and timbre, which debilitate so much contemporary music theory, to dignify the creative process as an inspirational force in the human mind.

THE NEXT FOUR SONATAS

In 1809, four years after the stress and passion of Op. 57, Beethoven composed the wonderfully serene little Sonata, Op. 78. 'They are incessantly talking about the C sharp minor sonata (Op. 27, No. 2),' said Beethoven to Czerny: 'on my word I have written better ones. The F sharp major sonata (Op. 78) is a different thing!'[1] It is indeed a most beautiful composition, in two movements, opening with the following meditative statement:

[1] Cf. Kerst, op. cit., p. 42.

Of this opening, analogous in position and function to the opening of Op. 110, one editorial board opined that, 'though without thematic connection with the first movement, [it] stands in an intimate aesthetic relation to it'. This is misleading, because there are associations in the first movement with these introductory bars. Some pointers to the continuation, *Allegro ma non troppo*, are shown by square brackets in Exx. 2 and 3; they assume progressively greater meaning as seminal fragments inspiring the continuation, even if the derivation of ideas is not always literal:

The ascending fourth C sharp–F sharp is inverted in the *Allegro*. The anacrusis in the *Allegro* (*b*) is hidden in the prelude (*e*), whereas the initial fourth (*a*) appears transposed in bar 3 of the *Allegro* and is followed by a descending figure (*c*) foreshadowed in the prelude. A few bars further on, (*b*) and the entire group (*e*) of the prelude are taken up in the chord sequence at the end of the example. The descending scale of triplets also echoes (*c*); and so on. In fact, the influence of the figures referred to permeates the entire movement. Especially beautiful are the three chords (*f*) at the end of Ex. 3, as they reverse the order of the three notes, A sharp, C sharp and B, which form the anacrusis and the first beats of bars 1 and 2 of the *Allegro*, respectively. A modified form of (*f*) appears in the second subject of the first movement (Ex. 4*a*) and also generates impetus for the finale (*b*):

Ex. 4

The thematic material of the finale is also related to the prelude. Especially interesting is the shape in the prelude's fourth bar at (*g*) and (*d*) of Ex. 2, the third bar of the *Allegro* (*d*), and bars 9–10 of the finale, Ex. 4 at (*g*). Subsequently the finale runs away with the B sharp–C sharp figure of Ex. 4*b*. Throughout this sonata the composer works with the utmost economy not only in the derivation of themes and subsidiary figures but in their development. For example, running semiquavers of the development section of the first movement pick up again and again the falling figure (*c*), and there is a suggestion of (*f*) in the left-hand part:

Ex. 5

It can be no accident, either, that the four octave F sharps in the bass of the prelude are balanced at the end of the first movement by four tonic chords in the treble. In the finale (*c*) is important in the main theme and in the coda.

Op. 78 is deservedly a favourite of amateur pianists, not only for its formal perfection, which unfolds a beautiful structure from the wonderfully expressive microcosm of the opening statement, but also because it offers an enriching experience which can be gained without too much technical stress. However, if the notes are easy, their interpretation requires maturity, sensitivity and that insight which can convey in performance the intimate and subtle cross-references between often minute details of structure in which this sonata abounds.

The Sonata in G, Op. 79,[1] also composed in 1809, is a light-hearted romp in its two outer movements; but these enclose a romantic and warm-hearted *Andante*. The first movement shares the designation '*alla tedesca*' with the fourth movement of the Quartet in B flat, Op. 130, and their common thematic motivation is

---

[1] It is really a sonatina. Beethoven called it '*Sonate facile ou sonatina*'.

amusing to note; Ex. 6 shows the theme from the sonata, Ex. 19 in Chapter 6 shows that from the quartet:

Ex. 6

The falling third B–G in the sonata theme is made the basis of development, and on account of it the work was once ridiculously styled 'The Cuckoo'. In its rhythmic flow the movement unmistakably suggests the Austrian peasant-type dances that were forerunners of the Viennese waltz: that is to say, it is ebullient and bouncy, rather than sentimental like the *Ländler* of Josef Lanner, which were soon to become popular in the taverns of Vienna. The sforzando markings in the development seem designed to cancel out the waltz effect, because they emphasize the second beat instead of the first. However, in the recapitulation of the main theme the emphasis is suddenly returned with characteristic zest to the first beat. This is a familiar and exhilarating device in all Beethoven's music; it is, for instance, used with tremendous verve in the first movement of the Eighth Symphony. The movement has a delightful dancing coda, heightened with appoggiaturas, when the main theme is answered by a consequent which it has implied all along, with much merry interplay between treble and bass.

A melodious barcarolle serves as a middle movement which in its short span manages to become quite expansive in its lyrical expression. The finale synthesizes substance from the first two movements and yet seems to make much sound and fury about very little. Is the derivation of the rondo theme from the *alla tedesca* figures of the first movement and the melody of the barcarolle a matter of deliberate contrivance (see Ex. 7, p. 138), or happy subconscious theme-transformation? There can be few creative procedures more interesting than those that arise when a master turns his mature attention to lightweight composition.

With the Sonata in E flat, Op. 81a (1809–10), programmatically styled *Sonate caractéristique: Les adieux, l'absence et le retour*,[1] we

[1] *LA*, letter 325, shows that Beethoven disapproved of this French title given it by the publisher. The sonata was dedicated to the Archduke Rudolph on his departure from Vienna for nine months.

enter a tonal world characterized by powerful emotional expression and formally by the utmost structural economy. As the title indicates, there are three main movements, and the first one has an *Adagio* introduction. It is a big sonata; but not, compared with later works, a long one. Its wide emotional range is indicated by German directions, which Beethoven uses for the first time in this work. He required the sad slow movement to be played 'in a flowing movement, though with much expression' and the finale to be taken 'in the fastest possible tempo'—a direction that places some strain upon unpractised fingers. Thematic structure apart, the entire scheme is unified by an extended cadential movement embracing E flat, C minor, B flat (dominant seventh of E flat) and a return to tonic. These keys are arranged in relation to the different sections as follows:

E flat major   Introduction and first movement
C minor   Slow movement
F minor   Concluding section of slow movement,
          leading to:

Dominant seventh Beginning of finale
    of
E flat major   Finale

The harmonic flow in terms of overall tonality can therefore be symbolized:

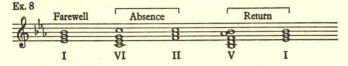

Thematically the 'Farewell' is based upon the unifying figure presented at the outset:

This 'dying fall' in the warmest 'horn' register of the piano is a tonal symbol of tremendous thematic importance throughout the first movement, and many changes are rung upon its descending tones. Notice first of all that its primary harmonic direction is from I to VI, thus anticipating in microcosm the relationship between the first and second movements (see Ex. 8) and justifying the emotional link between parting and absence. Notice also the three *upward* steps, G–A natural–B natural, which invert the motto in the tenor

139

register in bar 4. Chromatic progressions lead to a restatement beginning with a diminished seventh, an increasingly important chord in Beethoven's later music, where it is always used with power and originality; the harmony here is most affectingly transmuted. The climbing progression anticipates rhythmic and melodic shapes from the slow movement (cf. Ex. 13) and in its inner parts echoes the fall of the motto theme at different pitches. Preparatory chords then invert the sequence—three steps up instead of three down, prefiguring what is to come. The main theme of the *Allegro* then presents these basic steps in disguised form, after an assertive subdominant chord:

This is immediately continued by a leaping theme (Ex. 11) of which a ghostly echo is heard in the *Andante espressivo* (Ex. 12):

Ex. 12 is in fact the second appearance of the ghost and comes at the
end of the long passage centred in F minor.

Secondary material inverts the motto and then leads to an
augmented statement of its original form; and this is rounded off
by a closing group once again grounded in the falling series.
Development is terse, pungent and sinewy, and the recapitulation
orthodox; but this is followed by a long and brilliant coda in which
Beethoven breaks free from formal convention to launch out into
poetic rhapsody upon the 'Lebewohl' theme which holds the entire
movement together. In this wonderful passage the original 'horn'
tones reappear, with overlapping I–V chords, to cast a romantic
glow over the closing bars. Throughout the movement taut, powerful construction and masterly use of the omnipresent figure
contribute to the drama and subjective intensity of the musical
experience.

The slow movement is an essay in expressive nuance recalling
passages in C. P. E. Bach's sonatas which explore the inner world of
fluctuating feelings, the ebb and flow of the emotions. Compare this
passage in Beethoven's movement:

Ex. 13

with these examples from Emanuel Bach. The first is from the
'Prussian' Sonata in A major, the other from the finale of a Sonata
in A flat from the Württemberg set:

Ex. 14   Adagio

Ex. 15

Beethoven's teacher, Neefe, himself an admirer of C. P. E. Bach's sonatas, had made his pupil study them, and there are many indications that the earlier master's freedom of modulation and appoggiatura had provided Beethoven with useful models. He once told Breitkopf & Härtel in a letter of 26 July 1809, 'I have only a few samples of Emanuel Bach's compositions for the clavier; and yet some of them should be in the possession of every true artist, not only for the sake of real enjoyment but also for the purpose of study'.[1] In fact, Beethoven copied out the fourth and fifth Württemberg Sonatas.

However, most untypical of Emanuel Bach is the ebullient finale, 'Le retour', with which Beethoven concludes this highly integrated work. This finale, which emerges ecstatically from the slow movement in an uprush of arpeggiation on the dominant seventh, is rapid in movement and joyous in effect, only slowing down for a few bars of tranquil contemplation before the final explosion of tonic harmony.

With the beautiful Sonata in E minor, Op. 90 (1814), the composer explored a world of nervous, mercurial, scintillating delicacy and flowing lyricism. The most obvious and delightful characteristic of the first movement is a tendency to 'sideslip' in semitones, which weakens the sense of harmonic stability and sometimes implies a Neapolitan effect. Related to this, there are some interesting enharmonic modulations. Semitonal step modulations and enharmonic effects become pronounced in Beethoven's third period, and this sonata clearly belongs to the final phase of his musical development. The following example, quite apart from its kittenish musical effect, which is wholly delightful, is worthy of close scrutiny. It comes from the bridge passage leading to the second subject:

[1] *LA*, letter 220.

Ex. 16 **Mit Lebhaftigkeit und durchaus mit Empfindung und Ausdruck**

After defining the chord of E minor, the harmony slips suddenly to a dominant seventh, and the ensuing downward scale, in C major, leads to a conventional cadence in that key. An unprepared dominant seventh in A minor is likewise confirmed by a cadence. The bare octave B flat is then a masterstroke. It has a Neapolitan relation to the preceding A minor chord, but characteristically is without harmonic filling, and this enables Beethoven to exploit its ambiguity. Another downward scale misleadingly suggests the key of B flat; but as the bare note is sustained it mysteriously turns into A sharp and burgeons into a diminished seventh resolving on the orthodox key of the dominant, B minor. In the penultimate bar of Ex. 16 there is a sharp semitonal clash—another feature of the movement, pleasingly astringent in effect, and used, too, in the material that closes the exposition. Beethoven was well aware of the facile opportunities offered by the diminished seventh chord for enharmonic modulation; but his own use of it is never cheap. In fact, as the Diabelli Variations reveal, Beethoven was one of the few composers who really knew its magic and used it with masterly effect.

The semitone slip G–F sharp is a feature of the second subject:

Ex. 17

When the writer practised this sonata, with that special zest which seems to belong to the later years of adolescence, he inscribed the word 'transcendentally' over this passage. It was not intended to have mystical implications. The point was that the wide spacing of the left-hand part, together with its rapid movement, made proper execution difficult. It seemed only possible to play it if the hand danced lightly over the keys with an exceptionally loose wrist. The next discovery was that if the eye read only the right-hand part, the left would look after itself; and as the melody had a light, ethereal quality, this somehow spontaneously transferred the requisite freedom and energy to the music of the lower stave. It was necessary, then, in order to master the technical difficulties, to pay attention only to the innermost nature of the music—an implication which the writer has since generalized into a principle with very fruitful results. With the music of Beethoven, in particular, it is always better to work outwards from the musical essence to the means of its realization rather than to become preoccupied with technical problems at the expense of the music.

The development of the first movement is alternately capricious and sweetly lyrical; it is based on skipping chromatic relationships and delicate exploration of the Neapolitan key (F major) and the subdominant (A minor). An amusing sequence vacillates between augmentation and diminution immediately prior to the recapitulation.

The concluding rondo is music of gentleness, peace and great beauty. In its lyrical flow it recalls some of C. P. E. Bach's wandering rondos, although the satisfying pianistic texture is developed through a richer harmonic scheme.

BEETHOVEN'S LATE MUSIC: INTRODUCTION

Let us pause here and gather breath, so to speak, before entering upon a brief survey of the tremendous sonatas which lie before us. There are five of them—overwhelming in effect, tremendous in musical substance, and profound in a psycho-spiritual depth that has provoked many writers to metaphysical speculation. Wilhelm von Lenz, a century ago, characterized the two movements of Op.

111 as 'Sansara' and 'Nirvana' and thus may have put mystically and poetically what responsive listeners feel intuitively. At any rate, he stands with a company of others who reacted to the impact of Beethoven's music with the language of mysticism and romantic enthusiasm, encouraged by the idealistic ethos of a Germany already conditioned by the writings of Goethe, Hegel and Schelling. This company includes Romain Rolland, who testified in more than one book to the enduring inspiration of Beethoven in his life, and J. W. N. Sullivan, a mathematician, whose *Beethoven: his spiritual development*,[1] remains popular.

The present writer, in the abiding memory of a fine performance of Op. 111 by Denis Matthews in 1947, and brooding over Thomas Mann's *Dr. Faustus*, retired, Faust-like, to a garret in an old Georgian house in Liverpool, vowed to master the technical problems of performance and also, through critical study and meditation, to fathom the music once and for all. The immediate outcome was a youthful article,[2] affectionately remembered by its author as the outward and verbal sign of a profound turning-point and of a deepened interest in the processes of musical thinking, which survives the impact of more recent trends in analysis. If only more music-lovers would feel excited about music, the way Mann's imaginary lecturer Wendell Kretschmar felt when talking about Beethoven's last sonata . . .[3] Today we overcondition and gravely limit our responses by critical webs of our own making. Beethoven broke through all critical webs, and so his late music is not only profoundly inspiring; it can lift consciousness into the free air, away from that kind of intellectual flatness which characterizes the mind imprisoned by its own machinery, the mind which turns aside from *experience* to take refuge only in the outward form as a mechanic would describe it, not as the poet would apprehend it. As Mahler once put it in a letter to his wife: 'At the stage where men of higher development are found, production . . . is accomplished by an act of self-realization; and hence its creativeness is

[1] London, 1927, repr. 1964; for a passage from Rolland, see pp. 514ff. below.

[2] Barford, 'Beethoven's last sonata', *Music and Letters*, XXXV (1954), p. 319.

[3] Cf. below, p. 524.

heightened on the one hand, and on the other is manifested as a challenge to the moral being.'[1]

It is surely unquestionable that in Beethoven's late sonatas 'production' was 'accomplished by an act of self-realization'. To be deaf is to reinforce the ideal experience of sound, so that tonal imagination, musical thought and contemplation come into a deeper fusion than might otherwise be achieved. In the light of his known attitudes, Beethoven would surely have agreed with Rudolf Steiner[2] that perception, imagination, conceptualization and intuition are all modes of spiritual activity and that our freedom (valued by Beethoven in both a political and spiritual sense) lies in acts of self-realization wherein we condition our individual life-expression through the concept we have of our own nature and the world around us. We have only to look around to see that this is true; it applies equally to music. If we believe, with the avant-gardist, that music is only an arrangement of sensations, then our musical experience unfolds within the limitations of that thought. But Beethoven's last sonatas open wonderful doors to those who will go through them. As acts of self-realization—Beethoven's self-realization—they are symbols of our own. The mind cannot realize wholeness in its comprehension and enjoyment of great music without living in the experience of wholeness and thus coming to a new knowledge of itself. As a tonal structure, each sonata is a musical experiment into the very structure of consciousness.

What distinguishing features, then, may we expect to find in the late piano works ? In the first place, we should note the re-evaluation of the simplest ingredients of classical music—commonplaces of harmonic structure and progression which reappear in a transmuted form. The *Arietta* of Op. 111 is simplicity itself, possibly even an offshoot of the theme of the Diabelli Variations. But its widely-spaced harmonization creates a mood of almost mystical intensity. In this exquisite harmonization the notes do not make

[1] Alma Mahler, *Gustav Mahler: memories and letters*, trans. Basil Creighton, ed. Donald Mitchell (rev. ed., London, 1968), p. 322.
[2] Rudolf Steiner, *Philosophy of freedom* (*Die Philosophie der Freiheit*), trans. Michael Wilson (London, 1964).

their own track—the way we play them depends upon the way we catch the inner vibration of the thought between the notes, and this will condition every nuance of shading. The pressure of the hands on the keys is absolutely determined by this inwardness. This is also true of the variations of Op. 109, the opening movement of Op. 101, the entire length of Op. 110. The secret is to play the music as if listening to an ideal performance in the mind and heart; by such a route should these works be approached.

Another prominent feature of the third period is the use of prolonged trills. By means of a trill, the primary tone is kept in sustained vibration analogous to liturgical cantillation on a reciting tone. In Opp. 109 and 111, under the hands of a pianist who can respond to the inner challenge of the music (Mahler's 'challenge to the moral being'?), they rise to a trance-like condition of contemplation. However, although long and often difficult trills occur in all the last five sonatas, they are not all of this nature. Some, like those of the 'Hammerklavier', act like irritants within the texture and rivet concentration on the convolutions of a restless counterpoint. One of the most difficult trills of all occurs at bars 106 ff. in the *Arietta* of the last sonata, the difficulty lying not in the movement of the fingers but in their control. The mental control required here is a good indication of the overall concentration required in the performance of this music. After this triple trill a high level of intensity is established which is not relaxed until the final bars. Technical problems apart, it often seems that Beethoven deliberately aims to heighten the musical effect by tightening up the mental control required to play it. And yet the secret of such control lies in an extreme inner relaxation. This relationship between relaxation, control and the innermost nature of the music itself is worthy of study. In the closing stages of Opp. 109 and 111 the trills are terminal save for restatement of the theme in the former and a few bars of coda in the latter. The melodic notes, picked out slowly against the trill, seem to be heard in a timeless context.

Related to the magnetic pull of the trill upon consciousness is the use of variation form, which is a prominent feature of the third period generally. It occurs, for instance, in the Quartets, Opp. 131

and 132, the Ninth Symphony and in combination with fugue in the *Grosse Fuge*; and there are the Diabelli Variations. This heavy emphasis upon variation technique suggests a contemplative as opposed to a dialectical development of thematic ideas, and it hints at a change of inner orientation in Beethoven's mind. In considering this point it is important to remember the tremendous dialectical stress of the sonata principle, which is worked out again and again in the sonata-form movements of earlier sonatas and which indeed persists right through to the struggle of the first movement of Op. 111 (to say nothing for the moment of Op. 106). The last period, however, precisely because Beethoven can be observed veering towards variation and fugue, could be regarded as the period of transcended antitheses—or at least as the period marked by the emergence of a new emphasis upon what can be experienced above and beyond antithesis. In variation form (perhaps best regarded, like fugue, as a method, not a form), key conflict, harmonic stress, emotional drama, all developed from the dialectical enhancement of the interplay of feeling known as *Empfindsamkeit* and cultivated in the eighteenth century, are far less important than meditative reassessment of an idea, of such a kind that the simple melodic and harmonic elements of which it is composed undergo a deepening, a constant intellectual exploration which finally seems to release an imprisoned, super-sensible vibration in the inner ear. In the Diabelli Variations, thematic and harmonic exploration is extreme. Strange harmonic transmutations occur through masterly use of the diminished seventh, and remote echoes are evoked from the *Ursatz*[1] of Diabelli's commonplace little waltz. It often seems to

---

[1] This word is much used by Schenker, who initiated a system of harmonic analysis based upon the assumption of an essentially simple and fundamental basis of formal movement through harmonic progression. For example, in a complex chromatic progression of chords, analysis could well reveal an underlying diatonic structure. The chromatic chords, suspensions, elisions and so on would then be interpreted as 'enhancements' of this. It is possible for quite different pieces of music to grow from a common *Ursatz*. The *Ursatz* is thus a principle of universal harmonic relationship, whereas the actual music that springs from it is its particular expression or modification. Literally the term means 'primary movement' or 'initiating principle'. The word is very interesting in its latent implications because it has dynamic reference. If the musical

amount to a revelation of the spirit of music locked up in root figures of the classical idiom. There are passages in the Diabelli Variations which will always sound new—a salutary reminder that new music does not emerge from new ways of manipulating sound but from new developments in the mind and spirit. In the absence of such new developments, mere tonal manipulation void of inner content will make no headway.

To some extent, fugue[1] appears in the late works as a contemplative idiom; but the emphasis is different. Dialectical stress remains as a powerful, even violent linear tension, as in Opp. 101 and 106. The fact that this stress is expressed in counterpoint makes it an intellectual matter, a process of thought to be distinguished from the emotional antithesis arising from the conflict of different elements in successive rhythmic impulsions, which is the essence of the sonata principle. Thematic interest in Beethoven's fugues is explored for its energy-content, and this establishes constructional unity through dynamic momentum. If we allow an ideal oversimplification of the development of Beethoven's musical mind, a threefold evolution presents itself. In the first place Beethoven grapples with the sonata principle, achieving the

---

enhancement of an *Ursatz* has its own unique expressive force, which will be subjective to the composer, the *Ursatz* itself must have a hidden, universal expressive potential, and, because universal, *objective*. It can have as many particular applications as the composer can draw out of it; but *what* he draws out of it will depend upon the depth of his imaginative-conceptual penetration of the universal form. The condition of such creative penetration seems to depend upon the extent to which the composer can invest the *Ursatz* with his own emotional energy. The process is the artistic equivalent of religious meditation upon a symbol no more complex than a circle, cross or triangle. Beethoven's belief, reported to Goethe by Bettina von Arnim (cf. *TF*, p. 495), that music mediates between the spiritual and the sensuous, reveals a clear insight into the principle involved. In this case 'the spiritual' is the universal principle, 'the sensuous' its particular modification in tone. The art of musical variation, in particular, can thus be understood as a form of creative meditation upon a universal form. It is especially in variation that Beethoven ultimately revealed his musical mastery. See the entry 'Urlinie, Ursatz' in Willi Apel, *Harvard Dictionary of Music* (London, 1946).

[1] On Beethoven's piano fugues cf. John V. Cockshoot, *The Fugue in Beethoven's piano music* (London, 1959).

unification of conflicting subjective contents through the musical procedure of thematic and tonal antithesis and synthesis. Towards the end of his life he begins to introduce fugal development as an integral feature of sonata-form movements, as in the first movements of Opp. 106 and 111. This overcomes the emotional antithesis of thematic contrast, to build up a driving intellectual momentum. For ebb and flow, conflict, contrast and opposition, Beethoven substitutes a linear dialectic. Symbolically this suggests the victory of thought above subjective involvement with warring emotional elements. Finally there are those wonderful variation movements where all dialectical conflicts are left behind. If this notion of a threefold evolution is valid, it offers a clue to the psychological unfolding of third-period Beethoven. His mind moved in creative self-realization from subjective conflict (sonata principle), through the structure of thought (fugue) to contemplation (variation). Beethoven's mighty struggle with fugue thus represents a necessary link between emotional life and the spiritual intuition which vastly transcends it, as the universal spirit which so occupied Goethe and Hegel transcends the finite ego. What Beethoven discovered, through music, was what we may all discover—that the internal stresses of the psyche have to be mastered by the mind, which thus wrestles with its own substance before consciousness can achieve balance, integration and fulfilment in that which is greater than itself.

A clear image of the driving forces of all Beethoven's later music is gained by relating the contemplative to the dynamic element. They have their musical symbols in the two movements of Op. 111, the first of which is hard, driving energy, laced with contrapuntal development, the second mostly contemplative stillness. How can use of the word 'stillness' be justified? Does not all music depend upon divisions of time for its very existence? Careful scrutiny of the second movement of the last sonata—and also of the variations of Op. 109—reveals an exploration of the keyboard in depth and height. The extreme contrast of register in Op. 111 particularly has the apparent effect of almost eliminating forward movement through emphasis on the wide harmonic spaces involved. Are these spaces, vast in terms of the keyboard, tonal symbols of the ex-

perienced inner spaces opened up in contemplation? At one point
momentum is almost completely lost:

Ex. 18

Also characteristic in Beethoven's late-period works is his
exploration of wide-ranging schemes of harmonic relationship, not
only between but within movements. Reference to his use of the
diminished seventh has already been made in connection with Op.
90, and it will come up again in connection with the last sonata. For
the moment let us look more closely at the structure of the sonatas
leading up to it.

THE LAST FIVE SONATAS

Op. 101 in A major (1816) begins with a beautiful meditation on a
flowing theme in $\frac{6}{8}$ time. It contains subsidiary phrases; but the
melodic elements represent a continuous thematic and textural
evolution. Especially characteristic of the sustained poetry of this
music, the beguiling simplicity of which masks a rigorous concentration of tonal procedures, is the following passage (from bar
34 onwards) in which the added C sharp in the right hand seems to
elicit the subtle modulation of the left:

Ex. 19   **Etwas lebhaft und mit der innigsten Empfindung**

The movement comes to a wistful conclusion with wide spacing, a few bars after interesting cadences involving diminished sevenths. It is well worth noting that although this fascinating movement is in the key of A major, the exposition hangs around the dominant chord, and modulation to the dominant is early established with no more than passing utterance of the root-position tonic. The intention of the wealth of subtle harmonic enhancement which pervades the movement seems to be to avoid unequivocal tonic affirmation until near the end, when firm cadences appear, and then the tonic key is confirmed by the pedal note underlying the diminished sevenths referred to above. The entire structure is framed within a prolonged and enhanced perfect cadence. The following harmonic abstract of bars 34–52 will give some idea of the beauty of the modulations, which are enriched with expressive appoggiaturas:

Ex. 20   see Ex. 19

A vigorous march follows, the mood of which conflicts almost brutally with the soliloquy which precedes it. Its driving dotted rhythms somewhat anticipate the insistent repetitions of the scherzo in the E flat Quartet, Op. 127. The harmonic connection between the movements—A to F major—is experienced with something of a shock; but this same relationship (one of many such submediant ones in mature Beethoven) occurs at a significant moment (bars 327–31) in the finale of the Ninth Symphony, immediately before the introduction of the march theme in B flat, when the A major triad (here the dominant of D major) is divested of its third and fifth, and just as violently thrust forward as a chord of F major in a dominant relation to the key of B flat. The progression is interesting in so far as it partly follows what happens in the sonata. The middle section of the march movement is largely a canon in B flat. Towards the end it has some wonderful 'third-period' magic before re-introducing the march figure. The slow movement, *Langsam und sehnsuchtsvoll*, is a prelude in A minor to the ensuing fugue and is based mainly on an exquisitely moulded turn developed in the manner of a baroque improvization through a falling chromatic sequence. Its final cadence, enhanced with a chain of diminished sevenths, leads pointedly back to the opening theme of the first movement and then, after meditative pauses, explodes into the final fugue. The material is developed with tremendous élan and homophonic episodic sections, the running passages being dotted with wide leaps, dramatic changes in the rhythmic pattern, hesitations and galloping sixth-chords. There is an interesting moment near the end, when the fugue subject threatens to break out in D minor; but the introductory notes of the fugue subject are immediately used to redirect the flow into the tonic key through F major and A minor.

Busoni did not always discuss music with the same searching intelligence with which he performed it; but he spoke good sense when in 1920 he noted '*the subservience of virtuosity to the Idea*'[1] in Beethoven's music. Beethoven's concern is indeed always with the idea, and we should remember that to the German mind the word 'idea' has greater richness of content than it has in casual English usage. It really denotes the indwelling, all-permeating force of which the outer form is a vehicle, and it therefore relates to the wholeness of the formal conception. As Schenker revealed, this wholeness is detectable in an overall harmonic framework through which movement is canalized. It is more apparent when common thematic elements are also observable. Op. 101 unfolds through the following harmonic scheme, with, of course, an inexhaustible wealth of harmonic enhancement:

Ex. 21

[1] Ferruccio Busoni, *The Essence of music and other papers*, trans. Rosamund Ley (London, 1957), p. 132.

but we should not ignore the significant thematic movement in the opening theme. The falling third D–B (sixth and seventh notes) suggests the falling third of the fugue subject, whereas the first five notes (Ex. 22*a*) *are* the essential notes of the fugue subject (Ex. 22*b*) in retrograde:

Ex. 22

The structure of the fugue is complex, being worked out in an extended sonata form with an episodic secondary figure (Ex. 23*c*) related to the turn (Ex. 23*a–b*) that is such a feature of the slow movement:

Ex. 23

The figure which follows the turn in this example also appears in the fugue (see the bracketed notes in Ex. 24, p. 156), and the melodic line of the homophonic passage introducing the development again picks up the opening theme of the sonata—not exactly, but near enough to signpost integral connections.

The 'Hammerklavier' Sonata in B flat, Op. 106 (1817–18), may well, as Alan Walker suggests,[1] 'lie somewhere in the future of the

---

[1] Cf. Walker, *An Anatomy of musical criticism*, p. 24.

Ex. 24   **Geschwinde, doch nicht zu sehr, und mit Entschlossenheit**

piano'. We are confronted here with a work which seems to be ultimately incapable of definitive realization. It exists for us as a colossal tonal conception just beyond the limit of perfect pianistic expression; but, as Walker points out, the work was composed against the nature of the instrument. 'The chronic sense of friction that you get throughout the *Hammerklavier*, but especially in the Fugue, is . . . an essential part of the music.'[1] The *'idea'* is always present as the force of the thought developed from it, as the innermost essence of the tonal movement; but if it can be intuited, or analytically defined, it is hard to express it in performance. The experience of the 'Hammerklavier' generates the feeling of an ultimately unresolved intellectual activity, because that is what the music is—intellectual activity projected into a vast tonal structure offering endless scope for analytical study. At the same time, the fugue, which is vastly more than the rattling of academic bones, and the *Adagio sostenuto*, one of the loveliest romantic movements Beethoven ever conceived, require the utmost in interpretative power.

The sonata consists of four extended movements, thematically linked by the relationship of descending thirds (see Ex. 27). However, the harmonic relationships, about which an extended treatise could be written, are perhaps of greater interest and significance, not forgetting that one of the work's most characteristic features,

[1] Ibid., p. 25n.

the pitch of the *Adagio* a major third below the tonic key, in F sharp minor, is a formal projection of the falling third D–B flat in the grandiloquent opening theme. Related to this is the fact that Beethoven pulls away from the traditional procedures of dominant modulation. The resulting scheme, in terms of harmonic-formal relationships, goes a long way to explain that 'chronic sense of friction'. The harmonies are so arranged as to generate movement within an orbit which, while seeming to allow infinite room for manoeuvre, nevertheless creates a feeling of intensity and unremitting attention to structural function. Expansive though the opening gesture is, emotional outflows are held in check, so that the ear can battle with a latent antithesis between B flat major and B natural, G flat and G natural. The antithesis is in the nature of a technical proposition, and the first movement of the 'Hammerklavier' is Beethoven's solution in terms of sonata form.

The following example reveals the major pivotal points, with intermediate progressions:

Ex. 25

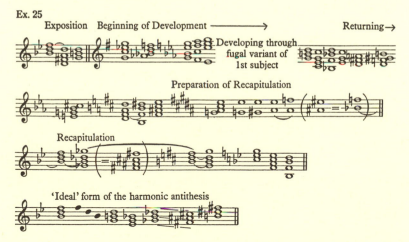

The first great thrust in this tremendous architectural scheme is the abrupt transition in bars 37–8, where Beethoven exploits his favourite third-period device of emptying a chord of its harmonic content and filling it up with different harmony, often, as here, that of a chord a third away from the previous one. The significant pause which follows is highly disruptive. Eventually the chord unfolds dominant seventh harmony to the submediant key, G major, in which a second subject is presented. The modulation is confirmed at length; but for a repeat of the exposition the music simply steps up assertively G–A–B flat. At the beginning of the development there are four more steps, G–A–B–C–D, and then the battle really begins. This D is once again the dominant note of G major; but now the harmony moves away to E flat for fugal development of the main theme. In order to understand succeeding events it is necessary to realize that the original transition to G major through the pivotal tone D established the note B natural (mediant of the new key) in opposition to B flat, tonic key of the sonata. In terms of classical harmony, almost the greatest distance between two keys is one semitone, and here we have it. Later in the movement B major emerges as an important key when it is actually used, with enharmonic audacity, to prepare the return to B flat major for the recapitulation and is justified in retrospect by the presentation of G flat major, which as enharmonic F sharp is dominant to B major. In this case the pivotal link is the tonic note, B flat.

Following the fugal development, the movement of the harmony is extremely interesting. The diminished sevenths lead to the D major chord, the approach to it being strengthened by the persistence of D as a note in the first seventh and a pedal in the second (bars 192 ff.). Once again the chord is stripped, and the hollow octave D then slips up a semitone to D sharp, the supporting harmony establishing the key of B major. The recapitulation is then deviously prepared by a progression which leads to a clear implication of the key of A sharp (A sharp–F natural, which is, of course, E sharp enharmonically). What this really means is that the tonic, B flat, emerges enharmonically from A sharp, the leading-note of B major. As soon as the F natural is heard, the main theme crashes in (at bar 227) without any further preparation. But in a very short space its secondary phrases are heard in G flat major, and from here there is a modulation to B minor. Ex. 25 explains the rest without further comment; the brackets indicate enharmonic pivotal notes, which are such a feature of this amazing structure. To play the progression through on the piano is to savour something of the tense atmosphere which pervades the entire movement.

It is worth noting that in the finale of the Eighth Symphony Beethoven magnificently exploits a somewhat similar situation. The main theme contains an obstinate C sharp (at bars 17–18) which subsequently emerges (at bars 376 ff.) as the dominant of F sharp minor, a semitone away from the tonic key of F major. When the main theme is being heard in the new key, trumpets batter away at E sharp until it transforms itself enharmonically into the tonic, F natural.[1]

The scherzo of the 'Hammerklavier' Sonata is a fairly straightforward movement, with a main theme based on the two principal thirds introduced at the very beginning of the sonata. Falling and ascending thirds also characterize the trio, which is in the tonic minor. A special feature here is the canonic imitation masked by the running triplets, which keep up a sense of dynamic energy. Return to the main figure is by way of a subsidiary *presto* in $\frac{2}{4}$ time, ultimately evaporating in a *prestissimo* upward rush. The coda once again returns to the B flat–B natural antithesis, with an enharmonic B flat–A sharp to create temporary mystification in B minor. *Presto* B natural octaves in $\frac{4}{4}$ gallop recklessly away to an unknown goal; but their flight is brusquely cut short by a sideslip to B flat. A four-bar statement of the opening phrase (*Tempo I*) concludes the movement with a gesture of deceptive innocence.

The F sharp minor *Adagio sostenuto—appassionato e con molto sentimento* is a wonderful movement in sonata form, traversing harmonic vastnesses, intensely subjective in its overall mood and marked throughout by the depth-spacing which is such a feature of the third period. This feeling of depth and immensity is expressed immediately in the potent double-octave A–C sharp that Beethoven added as an introductory bar after completing the rest of the sonata. It has an effect somewhat analogous to the vibrating fifth which opens the Ninth Symphony, in symbolizing the pregnant void from which an enormous structure is going to evolve. In one significant step it opens up an interior space in the mind and heart. The main theme it introduces at once reverses the relation as C sharp–A and proceeds to unfold a richly harmonized cantilena, the effect of which is both deeply moving and mysterious after

[1] Cf. below, p. 306.

the heavy emphasis on B flat in the scherzo. Before introducing a secondary theme in the first subject group, Beethoven explores the Neapolitan relation of G major—significantly, of course, one semitone up from the tonic—and this is later justified by a return to the same region in the coda. The second theme of the first subject group is also in the tonic key, and the accompaniment has expressive syncopated beats. These gradually dissolve by a chromatic transition to D major for the second main theme, which is introduced low down in the bass and then answered in octaves in the treble. The sonority of this beautiful passage must have been, in Beethoven's day, a wonderful revelation of the rich possibilities of the pianoforte. Dussek explored rich sonorities in his later sonatas (as we have seen in the previous chapter), and both Clementi and Hummel understood the new range of power which Beethoven's work opened up. None, however, penetrated the innermost abyss of human experience as Beethoven did here.

At the end of this great statement the texture passes through chromatic veils into development. Here again the working-out is on shifting sands, harmonically speaking, and E flat appears briefly in the key-signature. The momentous return is wreathed in a tapestry of demisemiquavers. By a bold stroke the second figure of the first subject group is brought back in an unprepared D major. It is worth noting here, and also with reference to the solemn second main subject in the exposition, that D major stands in the same relation to F sharp (enharmonic G flat) as F sharp does to the overall centre of the sonata, B flat. In this sense we see the idea of the whole sonata working itself out. Let us not forget, either, that the D major triad, on the mediant of the tonic B flat, is the lever used in the first movement to wrench the texture away from the tonic.

In due course a transition is made to the tonic major for restatement of the second subject. The coda is introduced in the Neapolitan region by brief references to the main theme, and then we have another, though modified, statement of the second subject. The main theme returns starkly in F sharp minor; but the hollow minor-key effect is finally overpowered by a persistent *tierce de Picardie*. This deliberate archaism has an almost painful effect of melancholy sweetness, enhanced in the very wide spacing of the final chords. In this sonata A sharp must always seem to be hovering suspiciously on the brink of enharmonic transformation. Here its effect is powerfully emotional; but we should note that the chord of G flat major appears early in the *Largo* introduction to the fugue which now follows.

The *Largo* proceeds to build up a powerful expectation of the three-part fugue soon to be unleashed. Essentially it is a free fantasia distantly recalling the keyboard fantasias of C. P. E. Bach, and it is based on a plunging series of thirds. The harmonic scheme is set out as Ex. 26, but it is, of course, only the background principle of a dynamic variety. Note that the *Largo* begins with the note F natural. Coming immediately after the F sharp major chord of the *Adagio sostenuto*, it is bound to be heard as E sharp, the leading-note of the key of that movement. The formal problem, then, is to arrive at a conclusive preparation of the dominant chord of B flat on the basis of this F natural. To do this Beethoven explores a scheme of harmonies implied in the relation of descending thirds, thus allowing himself once again a rhapsodic survey of the prevailing germinal idea. The required dominant chord is finally reached by using the A of the A major triad in bar 10 as a leading-note and (after removing its harmonic filling) bolstering it up with the 'proper' harmony.

Ex. 26

5 bars of canonic counterpoint

entry of fugue

The end of all this preparatory material is interlaced with the fugue subject, which now enters *Allegro risoluto*, with the proviso '*con alcune licenze*' ('with some liberties').

The art of fugue probably implies a greater intellectual detachment in the business of putting notes together than any other form of composition, with the possible exception of strict canon. The intelligent way of tackling fugal composition on a grand scale, as Bach supremely demonstrated in *Die Kunst der Fuge*, is, of course, to compose passages in multiple invertible counterpoint which combine the different subjects to be used. Each subject can then be fugued separately, with or without a regular counter-subject, before the final invertible combination is demonstrated in a climactic *tour de force*. Fugues built up in this way are tremendously exciting, the thrill arising from a supreme activity of the intellect and imagination working together. In the special case of keyboard fugues there is the further satisfaction of grasping the texture quite literally with both hands, a satisfaction in the sheer physical feel of the music. In playing a fugue the complex thought-process is brought right down into the hands; one is truly thinking with one's hands. For the lonely pianist condemned to rely exclusively upon his own musical resources there are few experiences more rewarding than regular sessions with Bach.

From the theoretical angle, the method of fugue is analytic. Fugal composition draws out the structural implications of the subject into a two-, three- or four-part texture (sometimes more), and the counter-subject provides an element of linear dialectical tension which strengthens and enhances the dynamic forward momentum of the analysis. Sonata composition relies more upon the dialectic of contrasts, when material contrasted in rhythmic shape and key is presented successively: its method is synthetic.

In view of the analytical nature of fugue, the overall affective tone of the texture is 'pre-set' by the subject. If the primary subject is exciting, then the emotional impact of the fugue will be progressively heightened in development, especially when the subject combines with new material.

The main subject of the 'Hammerklavier' fugue (Ex. 27) is powerful and arresting. Beethoven expands the omnipresent third into a tenth. The first note is cut off as the hand leaps to a challenging leading-note trill. Trills have a galvanic effect in fugal textures and can lead all too soon into passages where the pianist wishes he had fingers to spare. In general they seem to act like a goad, injecting new power and force into the music every time they appear. (This is particularly true of the fine three-part Fugue in A minor in Book II of Bach's '48'.) Beethoven's trill resolves on the tonic, and there are then downward steps of a third (cf. the upper stave in Ex. 27) linked by running semiquavers which fix the underlying momentum of the composition. Here we see the deeper meaning of the introduction:

Ex. 27

The fugue as a whole evolves with two counter-subjects and two further subjects, and this material is variously combined, use being made of retrograde and inverted presentations of the main theme. Throughout, except in a short fugue on the third subject and some episodic matter, the trill vibrates forcefully like an electric current and is pursued to the end with determined ferocity. However, this fugue is the finale of Beethoven's longest sonata, and it is far more than a supreme intellectual achievement based on a stirring subject. The entire contrapuntal texture is built on a dramatic tonal scheme. Now, dramatic modulations are the essence of the sonata style, and they are present here in abundance. As with the first movement, the range is vast; but the overall effect is extremely intense, and it arises

163

from avoidance of the more obvious classical procedures. Dominant progressions are only the subsidiary or clinching moments in a forceful wrenching of the tonal scheme, which creates an emotional effect like the bending of iron bars. To a considerable extent the harmonic contrasts are introduced *against* the natural gravitational force of the contrapuntal texture. The result is a collision between the analytic procedures of fugue and the synthetic dialectic of harmonic contrasts that is the essence of the sonata principle. Out of this galactic event new and strange musical forces emerge like the brilliant lights which glow around ingots of white-hot metal. The following harmonic abstract sets out the main compass-bearings of the whole enormous structure, the progressions in square brackets giving only a brief indication of interesting and important transitions:

Ex. 28

The forces of harmonic drama and intellectual virility are further heightened by the gritty, uncompromising counterpoint, which arises in great part from the significant B flat–B natural and E flat–E natural juxtapositions in the main subject. This quality is immediately apparent in the counterpoint at the entry in bar 35 of the third voice in the exposition.

Generations of music students studying this and many similar passages must have wondered about the relevance of traditional textbooks on harmony and counterpoint to the technique of *musical* composition. The gap between examination exercises and real music—a gap which academically trained minds all too often fail to bridge—arises because of a divorce between the notational symbols of sound and the subjective energies which they were originally invented to express. To many music students academic training becomes a kind of death. Beethoven, throughout this fugue, is dealing at first hand with the energies of life. His counterpoint cannot remotely be approached from the critical standpoint of the conservatoire, any more than Hegel's thought can legitimately be dismissed by the passionless dissections of linguistic analysis. Beethoven's notes, like Hegel's words and concepts, are embodied energies. The expression and forming of these energies resulted in both cases in conflicts, tensions and oppositions structured by the power of thought.

On the assumption that examples are more helpful than pages of noteless description, a sketch of the overall layout of the fugue is now offered; this will at least clarify the main outlines:

Ex. 29

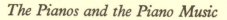

Ab Recurrence of 'regular' episode
bar 130
etc.

New subject against retrograde of original subject.

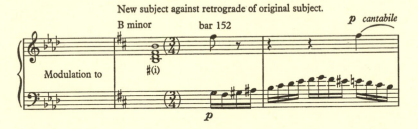

B minor   bar 152   *p cantabile*

Modulation to

D bar 196
Subject in original form leading to:

III

G Inversion bar 208

etc.

167

The fugue is tonal. After the exposition, which has presented two counter-subjects, there is a brief relaxation into episodic matter. Following this the subject appears in D flat with new accentuation; and then there is modulation to the flat submediant at bar 85, where Beethoven proceeds to build up a regular episodic passage—regular because it is used again in A flat. In E flat minor the main subject appears augmented, with augmentation of the counter-subject. This then moves to a terrific, shattering outburst where stretto of the first bar of the main subject is brought in by augmentation and inversion. This passage is literally an explosion of trills over grinding accented discords and elisions. Nothing behaves quite as it should; but somehow everything is bent in the direction of a dominant seventh which ushers in the regular episode, this time in A flat, at bar 130. From here Beethoven strikes out remorselessly into the significant key of B minor, where a new subject appears above the retrograde first subject. This retrogression is quite obvious in performance, as it gives rise to a curious jerky rhythm, ending, of course, with the trill and the falling tenth. There is some episodic extension before the original subject reappears in D major. It is then promptly inverted as the texture modulates at bar 205 to G and again unfolds episodically. Now follow some violent harmonic wrenches: G major yields to E flat for a third entry of the inverted subject, and then everything is broken up in a series of skips of a tenth through a few brusque bars which crash to a pause on the dominant of D major.

What follows is the quiet expression of a new subject. However, after twenty-eight bars the texture reverts to the tonic key, in which Beethoven displays the new subject in combination with the first. After this there is a gradual build-up of intensity, with a further developmental episode, stretto using both original and inverted forms of the first subject, dominant pedal, trills low down in the bass, and final brutal trills to bring the movement to an overwhelming conclusion. In this last, long final phase of the fugue, Beethoven stays close to the tonic centre. The rigours of this incredible sonata require it. The long harmonic journey is over; but the excitement of this most dramatic of all fugues never ceases until the sonorities of the last B flat chord fade away.

The fugue has terrified pianists for a long time, and performance of this movement alone used to be taken as conclusive proof of keyboard virtuosity. In fact, the awkward texture will yield to slow practice, bearing in mind the important fact that the fibrous, knotty, finger-twisting sensations to which it gives rise are essential to the nature of the music. Its real difficulties are difficulties of insight, acceptance, assimilation and endurance, in that order. Many amateur pianists fight shy because they do not like the frightening appearance of the printed page—indeed, the entire 'Hammerklavier' can induce a failure of nerve. It is certainly not music for babes; but it amply repays attempts to know it at first hand.

The last three sonatas must ever provoke reflection on the creative process. Bearing in mind his dealings with publishers, and his personal troubles, it seems that Beethoven must have had fantastic powers of mental abstraction, that his creative life went on ceaselessly at subconscious levels, even as his everyday consciousness enmeshed itself in machinations with the outer world. There is, indeed, a type of mind which deals, well or badly as the case may be, with mundane involvements while yet inwardly engaged in ceaseless creative meditation, the inner consciousness being in a permanent 'listening' attitude. Beethoven was surely an extreme case of this type, with a natural tendency to introspection heightened by deafness. Friedrich Kerst observed that 'his personality, on the whole, presented itself in such a manner as to invite the intellectual and social Philistine to call him a fool'.[1] This strongly suggests a mind living in its own inwardness, and no doubt vastly impatient of the myriad concerns in which little minds seek to project their own image. 'I much prefer the empire of the mind', he wrote in 1814, 'and I regard it as the highest of all spiritual and worldly monarchies.'[2] Practice of the last three sonatas tends to induce introspection, because there is much in the very nature of the music which requires an inner listening, as if the sensation of sound is being internalized. This statement represents a feeling, an intuition born of personal experience, and it may not be valid for all. Certainly the sonatas do not yield up their secrets merely to a competent technique, and it sometimes seems to the writer that the last place they should be played in is a huge concert-hall before a large gathering of people. Technical virtuosity is largely an irrelevance. It is true that strength, power and endurance are required, although not in as great a measure as in many later piano works of the nineteenth century. What is really wanted is the ability to place the energies of one's entire musical being in the service of the spiritual form, the *idea*, the principle of inner movement which, as Kurth said, is the real energy of the music, perhaps not even to worry about finer points of interpretation until the mind becomes incandescent with the inspiration of the musical thought.

[1] Kerst, op. cit., p. 69.
[2] *LA*, letter 502, to Johann Nepomuk Kanka.

The principle of unity manifest in each sonata is not easy to define. In Op. 109 it is most ethereal, least susceptible of reduction to basic shapes, far more a matter of subconscious reciprocal echoes and overall atmosphere. In Opp. 110 and 111 there are very clear thematic links in the internal structure; but again the nature of the material is so intrinsically beautiful, so formed of purely musical energies that the principle of unity lies rather in the nature of mind itself. In other words, unity is not solely a matter of structure; the structure is unified because mind itself is a unity, and because the music directly synthesizes the multiplicity of its tonal elements as mystical intuition spontaneously reveals the unity of *becoming* in *being*.

Op. 109 was composed in 1820, Op. 110 in 1821 and Op. 111 in 1821–2. Each is a uniquely individual creation in which the sonata concept is completely transformed. The E major opens with an alternating *Vivace, ma non troppo* and *Adagio espressivo* movement, the fast part consisting of graciously curving arabesques requiring the utmost sensitivity in performance. This yields after five more bars to the improvisatory *Adagio*. Having presented this basic material, Beethoven subjects it to a broad expansion. Links between these two intensely poetic utterances are more a matter of feeling than formal contrivance; but a fusion of elements occurs near the end, in this procession of chords:

Ex. 30

The discerning ear will feel the force of the descending scale interwoven with the thematic outline of the opening *Vivace* theme and perhaps detect its pre-echo in the *Adagio*. Altogether this is one of the subtlest movements Beethoven wrote.

The very first bar of the fierce *Prestissimo* which follows is reminiscent of the opening of the sonata. Canon features in the middle of this wild gallop, and its austere figures, played softly, sound mysteriously prior to recapitulation of the main material. The descending line first presented in the bass against the main theme suggests, though in E minor, the line of the opening of the first movement.

The deeply moving theme now to be varied is a wonderful example of how the unity of a complex work can be sensed even when there are no obvious thematic interconnections. The greater one's familiarity with this sonata, the more conviction grows that the opening phrases are highly significant; something is expressed there which is resolved in the last movement. What is it? Well, as the following example shows, fragments of this *Andante* are hidden in the material of the first movement, and it is because of this that the variations seem to define explicitly what is only hinted at earlier:

Ex. 31

Each four-note phrase in the abstract (*b*) lacks a B natural to complete a statement of the first four bars of the variation theme (*a*). Bar 9 of the opening movement aims at it (see Ex. 31*c*); but the expected resolution does not occur. Instead, the *Adagio* cancels the A sharp in a diminished seventh chord. In the variation theme, the two B naturals are heard, and a sensitive ear will recognize, at least subconsciously, the link this implies with the first movement. Moreover, the supertonic chord towards the end (bar 13) of the variation theme, moving to a dominant seventh which marks its climax, proceeds by a falling series to the final cadence, and this has an outline similarity to what happens at the beginning of the *Adagio* section. The last two bars of the variation theme should also be compared with the procession of chords in Ex. 30.

The variations themselves are the purest poetry, although one is an awkward-to-play polyphonic structure, characteristically placed immediately before the glorious soliloquy of Variation VI, which dies away into a restatement of the theme. In this last variation the theme is picked out in ethereal tones above and below a sustained trill which gradually gathers momentum until it reaches gyroscopic stability in a cantillation of exquisite purity. There are moments of ecstatic soaring when the right hand explores arpeggios high upon the keyboard above the vibration of a low dominant trill (Ex. 32*a*) before relaxing into the ethereal space of the syncopated melody notes (*b*):

The approach to this passage recalls the preludial arpeggios of the first movement; but now the hands are liberated as the heart sings.[1] Always, in listening to great pianists, one waits for these moments with bated breath; but sometimes they are past before the 'final bound' has been dared. Technique imprisons the soul, and memory reminds the disappointed listener that this is the age of behaviouristic psychology and tonal engineering.

Sensuous richness flowers again in the sustained intellectual development of Op. 110 in A flat. As previously indicated (see Ex. 1), the beautiful opening phrase contains the fugue subject in embryo. Of great importance is the descending phrase of four notes F–E flat–D flat–C which determines the affective tone of the entire sonata: for example, they appear in bars 4–5 (see Ex. 1*b*) and in bar 11 (the bracketed notes in Ex. 33). The continuation of the lyrical first subject (Ex. 33), somewhat disguised by the repeated chords (of which only the essential bass is given in the example), seems to foreshadow important shapes in the *Adagio ma non troppo*:

Ex. 33   **Moderato cantabile molto espressivo**

---

[1] Perhaps, after all this analysis, we can permit a poetic reference. Emily Brontë's lines from her poem *The Prisoner* seem not inappropriate to these wonderful sounds:

> Mute music soothes my breast—unuttered harmony,
> That I could never dream, till Earth was lost to me.

> Then dawns the Invisible; the Unseen its truth reveals.
> My outward sense is gone, my inward essence feels:
> Its wings are almost free—its home, its harbour found,
> Measuring the gulf, it stoops and dares the final bound.

Another disguised figure is the ascending scale which links a chain of arpeggios (bars 12–18). Both ascending and descending scale figures, sometimes with chromatic elements, appear throughout the sonata, and the descending patterns especially heighten the affective tone of the four-note figure referred to above. This last reappears with significant emphasis in the recitative introducing the *Adagio*. The following skeleton excerpts should be considered in relation to the 'parent' scale hidden in the arpeggios (*a*) and the four-note fragment (*b*):

Ex. 34
a Chain of arpeggios

Retrograde

b 'Affective tonal determinant'

c 1st movt., bars 20—1

d 1st movt., bars 25—7

So different in culture, in talent, in environment, there is yet a common element in the Yorkshire novelist and Beethoven. They both knew the elemental life of nature and exulted in lonely walks in the country. Both derived creative inspiration from the contact of the earth, and neither cared a rap for wind or weather. According to Charlotte Brontë, Emily used to practise Beethoven's earlier sonatas with fire and spirit.

e 1st movt., bars 29—33

f 1st movt., transition to development, bars 38—40

g 1st movt., transition to coda, bars 100—5

h Theme of Scherzo

j Theme of Adagio ma non troppo

Now that we have observed these subtle similarities and links, the tonal layout of this huge conception merits some attention, and once again the phenomenon of falling step relations springs to notice, this time in connection with pivotal points of the harmony:

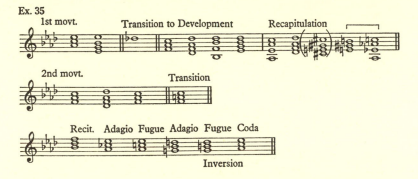

Ex. 35

The first movement modulates in an orthodox way to the dominant key, E flat. The transition to the development is achieved through a profoundly thoughtful and characteristic 'sideslip' through a bare octave D flat (Ex. 34 *f*, bar 39) to the key of F minor. This development is a purely lyrical extension of the opening figure, and it moves through D flat and B flat minor to the recapitulation in the tonic. Further modulation in the recapitulation leads through the chain D flat, enharmonic C sharp minor, E major and back to A flat at bar 78 by one of Beethoven's magical reorientations of tonality. The opening of the fugue subject is twice mooted in the last six bars of the movement.

The scherzo evolves between F minor and a tenuous D flat major. It sounds like quite different music, and indeed it is; but it is surprising what attentive scrutiny reveals. For instance, there is the falling shape of the opening theme, already quoted as Ex. 34*h*, and the continuation takes up once again the four-note phrase of the opening bars of the sonata at different pitches:

Ex. 36

The wraith-like trio is a disguised descending scale which yet again gives prominence to the prevailing affective tone of the sonata (see Ex. 34*b*). The approximate shape of the bass of Ex. 33 is used to prepare the recitative. With sustained pedalling, the F major chord at the end of the scherzo, dominant in function to the incipient B flat minor of the recitative, awakens the whole keyboard to ghostly sonorities, and the harmonic scene dissolves into astral mists which dimly recall the heartfelt chromaticism of C. P. E. Bach's fantasias, especially as Beethoven dwells on a repeated A in imitation of the *Bebung* effect of the clavichord. It is obvious that deeply subjective utterances are to follow this passionate declamation. The mood is that of the *Cavatina* of the B flat String Quartet, Op. 130, and for this *Klagender Gesang* in A flat minor (whose opening melody is quoted as Ex. 34*j*) Beethoven employs an accompaniment of throbbing chords as he does in the most emotional 'sobbing' passages of the *Cavatina*. From this doleful outpouring emerges the fugue (see Ex. 1*a*), with a serene flow which quite transcends the extreme subjectivity of the *Adagio*. After reaching a climax, it slides amazingly from a dominant seventh in the tonic key to a $^6_4$ chord in G minor for a varied restatement of the *Adagio*. The expressive effect of a falling chromatic progression is well known: here it is applied to linked sections with far-reaching formal effects. A glance back to the fourth bar of the sonata (see Ex. 1*b*) reminds us that a descending chromatic movement E flat–D natural–D flat is closely related to the falling phrase F–E flat–D flat–C, and this further illuminates the overall affective tone which binds everything together. Subsequently the fugue reappears, inverted, in G major, finally modulating with augmentations and diminutions to A flat. Immediately before the re-emergence of the fugue, massive G major chords and a rising arpeggio similar to that at the end of the scherzo create an awesome, even frightening effect. 'Fate knocking at the door' in the Fifth Symphony is not nearly so impressive as the shattering sounds which give birth to the inversion of the fugue subject a semitone below the tonic key. Once the key of A flat has been reached the contrapuntal texture dissolves and the fugue theme, part at least of which has overshadowed the entire sonata, rises to a triumphant peroration over a running accompaniment of broken chords.

It is interesting that the harmonic architecture of the sonata gives prominence to minor keys on either side of the tonic, and that this is emphasized in the last great section (beginning with the recitative) as a fall from B flat minor through A flat minor and major to G minor and major. If we look at the roots only—B flat, A flat, G natural and (omitting subsidiary modulation through the inversion, augmentation and diminution of the fugue) A flat—we have a cadential series which Beethoven uses melodically just before the final outburst of A flat arpeggiation which concludes the sonata:

Beethoven's last sonata defines with absolute assurance the two polarities within which his creative consciousness evolved. That is the real answer to Schindler's query as to why he did not write a third movement to wind up the sonata in the grand heroic manner. (Beethoven simply said he had no time).[1] The two movements completely symbolize the two primary functions of the mind—dialectic and theory; or, to put it another way, analysis and synthesis of conflicting elements on the one hand and the transcendence of all oppositions on the other. From this point of view the sonata projects, in the abstract structure of musical thought, at once the inner conflict and tension of consciousness and the unmoving ground of that conflict and tension. In human experience this unmoving

[1] Cf. *SB*, p. 232.

background is really there all the time; but to know it intellectually is one thing and to experience it is another. The breakthrough to realization—if only in brief moments throughout a lifetime—is the victory of consciousness over its own dialectical functions. These functions have to be recognized and objectified precisely so that consciousness can be free of them. Once they are recognized, the dialectical movement continues as before; but consciousness no longer identifies itself with the push and pull of attraction and negation. The way now lies through the consciousness which contains all antitheses as they occur, as being contains becoming, space form, time rhythm, silence harmony, stillness movement and, as Beethoven might well have speculated to himself, God everything.

Performances of the last sonata often fail because the mind of the pianist does not contain his technique. The technical mastery of difficulties does not necessarily yield insight into their musical substance, although an exception might be made in the case of the triple trill which occurs in the variations. It cannot be played if there is tension in the hands and the mind. The conditions of its performance relax all tensions. In such a psychological condition, new insights into the relation between mind and body, and, by implication, between mind and matter, life and form, can sometimes arise. The real problem is psychological. How does one pass, *with deep and communicable conviction*, from the *Allegro*, which demands dynamic energy, powerful control and intellectual mastery, to the *Adagio*, which elevates and transmutes all these qualities into a seemingly effortless and transcendent meditation upon a melody expressed in the simplest elements of the classical style? Mastery of the first movement sets its own tremendous problems. Apart from technical difficulty, which is not beyond the solution of anyone who can attack the keyboard with reasonable skill and unwavering conviction, the fiercely contrasted dynamic rhythms, hesitations and resumptions demand a finely-developed perception of the relation between rhythm and form. How does the pianist avoid conveying to the listener in the second movement a residual impression of unassimilated nervous energy and momentum left over from the first? In solving this problem a kind of insight and inner poise are required which few of us possess. We have not had the kind of experience which would give it. And, let the truth be faced, few of us have sought it. Music, for the majority, is not what it was for Beethoven at Heiligenstadt, a way of committal. It is a way of escape; a way out of life, not a way leading further into it. In concerning ourselves with the pleasures of sound we seldom rise above a refined hedonism to examine the significance of our musical interests. For Beethoven, we may be sure, the dialectic of the sonata led to new musical and spiritual insights, and these may well have been gained reciprocally, in terms of one another. In Op. 111 the dialectic of the first movement has to be lived in every dimension of our musical experience before we can fully appreciate the strength of the forces poured into it. The fusion of imagination, conception and will then paradoxically brings us to the standpoint of the second.

The first movement is in C minor, the second in C major, and the sonata begins with a *Maestoso* exposing left-hand plunges of the diminished seventh in a dramatic and tightly-spaced rhythmic relationship. The second movement varies a theme which, in its opening intervals, closely resembles those of Diabelli's waltz. It touches wonderfully in its second phase upon the submediant region, and this is a transcendent reflection of the I–flat VI relation between first and second subjects in the first movement. The harmonic relations implicit in diminished harmony determine the overall tension and structure of the *Allegro con brio ed appassionato,* whereas the C major chord establishes the stability, orientation and atmosphere of the *Adagio molto semplice e cantabile.* The harmonic flow of the whole sonata could be *ideally* symbolized like this:

Ex. 38

the first chord indicating the affective tone of the first movement, the second that of the *Arietta*; but a deeper exploration of this is very rewarding. It is obvious from study of the opening theme of the *Allegro* that the diminished seventh implied by the sforzando leading-note and the following A flat functionally and symbolically enclose the C minor chord which is the tonic centre of the movement. However, the heavy emphasis upon the diminished seventh in the introduction (only three diminished sevenths are possible, and Beethoven uses them all) puts the formal stress of the movement upon the discord rather than the chord of resolution it requires. The destined resolution is not reached until momentum collapses upon the *tierce de Picardie* in the coda.

It is now time to consult the following harmonic abstract of the introduction, which lays out the main areas of conflict in which battle is to be joined in the *Allegro* and which also gives at least thematic hints of the protagonists and a few clues about the *Arietta*:

Ex. 39

These thematic hints are given in black notes either above or below
the chords. Notice first of all the first five black notes, the series E
flat–C–B natural–C–D, and then listen more closely to the opening
figure of the *Allegro* and the melody of the *Arietta* with respect to
the pivotal tones of each (*a–b*):

Ex. 40

Retrograde form of the phrase marked *x* also yields the opening of
the second subject of the first movement (Ex. 40*c*). It should be
noted that the characteristic figure E–C–B features prominently in
Variation II of the *Adagio*, and the rising pattern B–C–D occurs in
the C minor interlude after the long trills (cf. Ex. 42). But the most
interesting point is perhaps that the all-important E flat–C–B natural in the *Allegro* grows initially from the powerful diminished
seventh chord opening the sonata, as the opening of Ex. 39 indicates.

In general theoretical principle the diminished seventh arose
from chromatic enhancement of the diatonic triads of the classical
system. Psychologically, and paradoxically, the premiss of chromatic
inflections and relations in Western classical music is the ideal
construct of the triad. Symbolically, the consciousness projected in
triadic concord *underlies* all that is relatively discordant that flows
from it by suspension and chromatic inflection and returns to it by
resolution. Put another way, tonicity, which by analogy is the
hidden 'I' centre of the musical consciousness, 'recognizes' itself
and 'defines' itself through its regional and chromatic excursions, all

of which it implicitly contains, orders and assimilates. The un-
moved stillness of the contemplative mind likewise defines its own
centre through the experience of transcended antithesis. This
principle of Hegelian analysis and Buddhist psychology applies to all
assimilated musical experience.[1] In this connection it is relevant that
the harmonization of the *Arietta* is almost entirely free of discordant elements, the emphasis being upon those root elements of pure
triadic relationship that underlie everything in the classical tradition.

In some ways the challenging introduction to the sonata is like
second thoughts about the *idea* (the *idea*, not the literal harmonic
procedure) of the opening bars of the First Symphony, which
settles down to C major after laying out three regional points of
harmonic orientation.[2] The first diminished chord in the sonata
encloses the dominant chord of C minor. The second moves to the
subdominant. The third crashes on to a $^6_4$ on the B flat minor triad
(IV of IV) and then resolves deviously on the major chord of A flat
—the key in which the second subject is to be presented. There
follows a wonderfully sustained *pianissimo* progression featuring
diminished harmony and landing upon the dominant. The next six
bars consist of massive dominant preparation for the eruption of the
main *Allegro* theme. This passage is worth scrutiny because it anticipates not only the upward-rushing triplet from V to I with which
the *Allegro* theme begins but also, in the bass, the downward curve
on which so much contrapuntal extension is later based (see Ex. 39).

Following the forceful exposition of the first subject, an extended transitional counterpoint, invertible in spirit if not in
point of detail, introduces at bar 35 another powerful figure, first in
in the lower and then in the upper part:

Ex. 41　(Allegro con brio ed appassionato)

etc.

[1] See Barford, 'Tonality', *Music Review*, XXIV (1963), p. 195.
[2] Cf. below, p. 282.

It has affinities with the retrograde form of the bass in the first two bars of the introduction (see the bracketed notes here, and also Ex. 39), of which it is probably a subconscious, if not literal, reminiscence. Equally interesting is the original form of this bass, which relates to the episode in the variations, like the rising figure B natural–C–D already mentioned; this passage is from bars 121–3:

Ex. 42   See Ex. 40*b*

The invertible counterpoint in the first movement leads to the key of A flat, and there are two dramatic bars (48–9) immediately before the emergence of the second subject:

Ex. 43

Ignoring the octave displacement, the figure is:

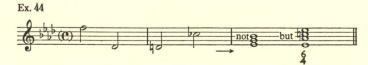

Ex. 44

The diminished seventh D natural–C flat could be expected to imply the dominant chord of A flat, the E flat triad. However, it clearly resolves directly upon the $^6_4$ of A flat. Beethoven writes only a bare E flat octave in the bass before leaping into the second subject with a high E flat. The implied $^6_4$ carrying through the whole bar is literally anticipated in the introduction, where the same diminished seventh resolves upon the same $^6_4$. This passage offers another striking instance of what was said earlier about the emphasis in this movement being placed upon the chord of the diminished seventh rather than on its chord(s) of resolution. Psychologically the force of the diminished chords tends to persist and to override the point of rest. The melodiousness of the second subject is not dwelt upon; after a brief pause, plunging diminished arpeggios race on towards the closing group, where at bar 64 the inverted second subject, now a bristling, uncompromising figure, points the way to a high A flat (Ex. 45), finally confirmed by a fierce chromatic upward rush. The inverted form in this closing group is joined on to three preliminary affirmations of the first three notes of the first *Allegro* theme:

Ex. 45

The second subject gives prominence to the falling second of the opening phrase of the sonata, C–B natural becoming A flat–G (see Ex. 40*c*).

From the final *fortissimo* A flat there is a dramatic sideslip to the dominant, G, and this is confirmed by an anticipatory sforzando on the secondary dominant. Development begins with an echo of the threefold repetition of the opening figure as in Ex. 45, and then moves to six bars of imitative writing involving what sounds like an augmentation of the important first three notes of the main theme of the *Allegro*. However, these are closer to the first three bass notes of the introduction (see Ex. 39). The climax of the development is reached with high-powered diminished-seventh clusters, which are used to harmonize once again the opening of the *Allegro*. As there are three diminished sevenths, there are three statements of the ubiquitous figure in three different positions. A fourth in the original position at bar 87 dramatically brings back the full restatement of the main theme. As these clusters pile up, the left hand is busy with broken arpeggios, and it needs a lot of faith to strike the low G from which they erupt with volcanic force. It *has* to be struck, because that G is a dominant pedal bringing back the recapitulation in double octaves. From here onwards the texture drives on relentlessly to a return of the second subject in the tonic major. It is repeated shortly afterwards in a poetic F minor version before diminished-seventh arpeggios plunge down once more to the closing group, where the inverted second subject appears in C minor. The coda, beautifully ushered in with the three diminished sevenths, which resolve upon a $\frac{6}{4}$ F major triad, is really an extended plagal progression (IV–I), with the diminished chord asserting itself for the last time between the subdominant triad and the tonic major. The spacing of the broken chords in the penultimate bar emphasizes E natural, and thus the shift to major tonality for what is to come:

Ex. 46

With the *Arietta* we enter a new world. Perhaps no more should be said than has been suggested already. In this case it seems offensive to reduce to conceptual analysis a musical experience which so transcends conceptual activity. The movement establishes a sense of immediacy which fuses the perception of sound in a stream of contemplation. Where consciousness and tonal essence are so completely one the way is open for intuition to contribute its own wordless insights. But there is one special moment for which the listener should prepare himself. Towards the end of the episode which follows the long trill trembling on the edge of an abyss five octaves deep, there is a magical progression through the diminished chords heard in the first movement. It steals upon the ear like the voice of memory whispering on the heights of the soul. It even leads, at bar 129, as in the introduction, to a B flat minor chord and thence to A flat; but this is gloriously swept away in the ecstatic C major of the fifth variation. At the end of this extended and trans-figured version of the *Arietta* the music, under the hands of a pianist who has long since submerged himself in the indwelling spirit of the sounds, rises to a pitch of lyrical ecstasy unscaled, in the writer's view, by any other composer before or since. Isolde's 'highest bliss' can in no way compare with it. But there are levels beyond the heart's emotion. The last two pages of this wonderful sonata lay bare the simplest atoms of classical C major, and the last word is with the commonest sound in piano music.

THE DIABELLI VARIATIONS AND OTHER WORKS

C major, once again, is the key of the Diabelli Variations (1819–23). Diabelli, indeed, wrote a good deal of music in C major, including sonatinas in the contemporary Viennese idiom, and much charming music for the classical guitar, which was enjoying a considerable vogue at that time. Prominent amongst the guitar music are sets of *Ländler* popularizing a style which Lanner and the elder Johann Strauss were exploiting, to the delight of Schubert, with the aid of a small band in a tavern in Vienna. The idea of a waltz with varia-tions contributed by composers of the day was a good one, especially from the standpoint of Diabelli's interests. His delight at receiving thirty-three variations from the greatest composer of the day ex-pressed itself, as Tovey points out,[1] in an uncommonly perceptive announcement which extolled the excellence of the fugal variations and ranked the work with Bach's Goldberg Variations.

Tovey sees in Diabelli's 'cobbler's patch' (Beethoven's own description) 'a theme . . . rich in solid musical facts'.[2] Eric Blom, in an excellent historical and analytical essay to which the reader is also referred,[3] tends to note its faults, in particular the 'rosalias'

---

[1] Cf. Tovey, *Essays in musical analysis: chamber music* (London, 1944), pp. 124–5.

[2] Ibid., p. 126.

[3] Blom, 'Beethoven's Diabelli Variations', in *Classics major and minor* (London, 1958), p. 48.

(literal sequential phrases involving modulation) to which Beethoven made scathing reference. The main point about Beethoven's treatment of such material is that every variation is a masterly transmutation of the original; moreover, all the characteristics of the third period are in evidence—trills, tensely developed rhythmic figures, forceful counterpoint, slow contemplative sections, and moments of mysterious, searching depth which seem to anticipate the music of a later day. No useful purpose would be served here by adding yet another descriptive analysis to the work of Blom and Tovey; but a few indications may illustrate some remarkable features of Op. 120 which show the composer voyaging still further out into strange seas of musical thought.

The early variations of a set usually keep recognizably close to their main theme; but in these variations Beethoven moves rapidly away at the outset from anything resembling 'literal' treatment of Diabelli's harmonic simplicities. The combination of subtle phrasing and adventurous harmony suffices to free Beethoven's music within its own idiom. The relation of a variation to its originating centre thus becomes intuitive and inspirational rather than derivative in any conventional sense. The opening of the third variation is an example of the way Beethoven frees himself from the outlines of Diabelli's theme:

Ex. 47

The trills at the end of Variation VI show another kind of forceful emancipation recalling the world of the 'Hammerklavier' Sonata. The solemnity of Variation XIV is immeasurably deepened in the fascinating progression of Variation XX and the meditative abstractions of Variations XXIX–XXXI. These sections contain some of the loveliest lyrical excursions Beethoven ever conceived:

The suave fughetta (Variation XXIV) is offset by the unrelenting attack of the big fugue that constitutes Variation XXXII. Its collapse after a brilliant cadenza is one of the most amazing transitions in the entire work:

What follows, modestly headed '*Tempo di minuetto moderato*', re-enters the heavenly atmosphere of the *Arietta* of Op. 111, as this passage from towards the end shows:

Ex. 50   Variation XXXIII

Once again, and for the last time in a major piano work, Beethoven initiates the ear into the wonderful world which lies hidden in such obvious matter as tonic-dominant progressions. It is difficult to study such music, to be enraptured by fine performances, or to play it to oneself without feeling convinced of the more-than-tonal but essentially musical principle expressed in it. Op. 120 is an amazing variety, a quite fantastic assembly of reflections rayed off from a vibrating centre. It is easy to believe that what really inspired Beethoven here was not Diabelli's trivial waltz, however 'rich in solid musical facts', but the spiritual force of the *Ursatz*[1] embedded in it. If any reader objects to the word 'spiritual' in this essay, let him substitute a term of his own. The main point here, as Kurth might say, is that the primary force of a musical idea exists before it is realized in sounds which die away as soon as they are uttered. What Beethoven grasped in the Diabelli waltz is eternally of the same order as what he heard inwardly in each of its variations. Any one of the variations could serve as the ideal centre of the work.

The late Bagatelles, Opp. 119 and 126, a total of seventeen pieces, contain many splinters and chips of third-period quality, and

[1] Cf. above, p. 149, n. 1.

some of them at least are great music. A few of the Op. 119 set
originated much earlier in Beethoven's career, but the Op. 126 set,
which Beethoven composed in 1823–4 when completing work on the
Ninth Symphony, is surely a unity; they certainly sound well
played in series, which is becoming standard practice. Of the sundry
other piano compositions which belong to the second half of
Beethoven's career there is nothing which really approaches the
standard of the sonatas, the best of the Bagatelles or the Diabelli
Variations; although the Fantasia in G minor, Op. 77, composed in
1809, is an unusual and interesting composition which deserves to
be better known. Czerny thought it conveyed an accurate impression
of Beethoven's style in improvisation.[1] In construction it really
manifests what has come to be called 'progressive tonality'.

CONCLUSION

The great works we have considered belong to one of the most
significant cultural epochs in the history of Europe. Timeless
masterpieces though they are, they grew out of an era of profound
reflection, which discovered new insights into the nature of mind
itself. Perhaps it is true to say that at no other period of history has
a prime intuition of unity so inspired composers, poets and
philosophers as it did in the world that nourished Goethe, Hegel,
Schelling, Coleridge and Beethoven. Each in his own way experienced the world in terms of an *ideal centre*. Goethe grasped the
principle of unity through an aesthetic vision of nature, and he
believed—and he may well be right—that a science which ignores
this vision is an impoverished science. Beethoven knew Goethe's
Theory of colour; it is quite possible that he also knew the *Essay on
the transformation of plants,* the significance of which in relation to
the aesthetic transformation of the different stages of a phenomenon
into one another could not have escaped him. It had nothing to do
with his own growth as an artist; but it could have been part of his
own cultural background. And the subconscious force of ideas is
often far greater than we realize. Hegel, Schelling and Coleridge in
their philosophical work discovered the unity of the mind in itself—

[1] Cf. *TF*, p. 368.

Hegel through thought, Schelling through mystical intuition, Coleridge through imagination; but the creative insight radiated from the consciousness of each of these men intermingles and overlaps. The essential inspiration is always unity—unity as experience, unity as idea, unity as a system of interrelated parts, unity as contrast, unity as an invisible world-spirit manifesting itself in the transformation of organic forms and the transmutation of life-energies through perception, imagination, thought and intuition. Beethoven knew unity through discovery of the formative forces locked up in musical shapes. These shapes are 'moments' of the dialectical movement of an inwardness intuited as a universal continuum.[1]

That is a personal view. All Beethoven said about his later music was that it was better than what he wrote before.

[1] Cf. Agnes Arber, *The Manifold and the One* (London, 1957).

III
The Chamber Music

FIVE

The Chamber Music with Piano

NIGEL FORTUNE

THIS CHAPTER is not a series of analyses but a survey, roughly chronological, charting developments in Beethoven's treatment of the media of piano chamber music and more generally in his career as a composer in so far as his works in these media illuminate it.

In his youth Beethoven was one of the finest pianists of his day; in the Vienna of the 1790s he was the finest of all. 'All the contemporary authorities, and all the traditions of those years agree in the fact of [his] success, and that his playing of Bach's preludes and fugues especially, his reading of the most difficult scores at sight and his extemporaneous performances excited ever new wonder and delight.'[1] His skill as a pianist and in particular as an improviser appears to have determined for him his early development as a composer. It might even be said that he relied on the piano to 'get going' as a composer. Not only is a high proportion of his early music for solo piano, but when he turned to certain other media he still used the piano: his first big orchestral works are piano concertos and not symphonies, and nearly all his early chamber music in the more serious forms involves the piano. The frequency of variations in his early output is also linked with his improvising, as is made clear by the following extract from a letter of early June 1794 in which he is referring to his variations for violin and piano on 'Se vuol ballare' from *The Marriage of Figaro*, WoO 40: 'I should never have written down this kind of piece, had I not already noticed fairly often how some people in Vienna after hearing me

[1] *TF*, p. 161.

extemporize of an evening would note down on the following day several peculiarities of my style and palm them off with pride as their own. Well, as I foresaw that their pieces would soon be published, I resolved to forestall these people.'[1]

It need cause no surprise, then, to find Beethoven writing for the piano in probably his first chamber works, but it *is* surprising to find that they should be in the virtually unknown medium of the piano quartet. They are a set of three (WoO 36) dating from 1785, when he was fifteen, and now, in the new Henle complete edition (Section IV, Vol. 1), correctly published for the first time in the intended order: No. 1 in C, No. 2 in E flat, No. 3 in D. They antedate by a few months the only two late eighteenth-century piano quartets in the repertory, Mozart's K.478 and K.493. Beethoven thought well enough of two ideas in his C major Quartet to incorporate them in his Op. 2 Piano Sonatas;[2] the second subject of the E flat minor sonata-form *Allegro con spirito* that forms the second movement of the E flat Quartet is even like a pre-echo of the main theme of a later piece still, the last movement of the C minor Sonata, Op. 13 (the 'Pathétique'); and its first theme presently reappears, also in C minor, in the so-called Kafka sketchbook in the British Museum as the opening theme of a projected symphony. This E flat Quartet is, in fact, the maturest of the set. E flat minor is an extraordinary choice of key for the *Allegro con spirito*, though there is a precedent in, for example, the fifth of C. P. E. Bach's Württemberg Sonatas (1744): indeed, the stylistic basis of the quartet and its fellows is—not surprisingly, since Beethoven grew up in Bonn and was still there—the North German music of C. P. E. Bach and his contemporaries, and they are quite un-Mozartian. The works give a general impression of being piano sonatas with strings. There is virtually no three-part string writing without piano as at bars 91–101 of the finale of Mozart's G minor Quartet, K.478, but even the cello has a certain independence, as it does not in, for example, Haydn's piano trios; the variations of the last movement include elaborate solos for viola and cello. The following extract from the first movement, *Adagio assai*, illustrates a characteristic balance of forces:

[1] *LA*, letter 9, P.S.　　[2] See pp. 80 and 84, including Ex. 24, in Chap. 3.

The sequence of movements in the E flat Quartet—slow movement leading into a tonic-minor sonata-form movement, with a concluding theme and variations in the major—is as far from an 'orthodox' fast-slow-fast sequence as many a work by Haydn. Overall formal variety is a continuing feature of Beethoven's subsequent piano chamber works, several of which are trios, a medium that, like other composers, he clearly found more congenial than the piano quartet. It must be remembered (cf. Chap. 2) that the tone of the piano then was much less powerful than it is today and that in terms of balance and cohesion the combination of two stringed instruments and piano was less unequal than it may seem today. In fact, what may have been Beethoven's next chamber work is a G major Trio (WoO 37) for two more penetrating instruments— flute and bassoon—with piano, composed between 1786 and 1790 and again rather C. P. E. Bach-like, but with a more orthodox sequence of movements; there also appears to be some influence from Mannheim, for example in the 'skyrocket' opening subject of the first movement. The use of wind instruments, whose parts are not very idiomatic, links it with other early works, such as the Octet, Op. 103, written in the tradition of entertainment music. There is also a *Romance cantabile*[1] in the Kafka sketchbook for the same instruments.

For the normal piano trio of violin, cello and piano there are a dull *Allegretto* in E flat in the same book (*HV* 48), written about 1790, and an incomplete and immature Trio in D (*KH*, Anhang 3), now published in the Henle complete edition (though it is by no means certain that it *is* by Beethoven). There are two further works in E flat, which was one of Beethoven's favourite keys in his early years: he employed it in some of his finer works, such as the Piano Trio, Op. 1, No. 1, and the Piano Sonata, Op. 7, and also seems to have fallen back on it when inspiration was burning more fitfully. This seems to be true of these two E flat works. One is a three-movement Trio, WoO 38, of 1791. The outer movements are respectively in sonata and rondo form; the middle one is a scherzo, so, since such movements were at this period in the tonic key and there is no slow movement, all three movements are in E flat major,

[1] Ed. Willy Hess (Wiesbaden, 1952).

a rather unsatisfactory feature paralleled in one or two other classical works such as Haydn's Piano Trio in F, H.XV.2, of 1769. A theme in the development of the first movement reappears in the Piano Sonata in F minor, Op. 2, No. 1 (at bar 20 in the first movement),[1] and elements of two other themes in this movement are reworked in the main theme of the last movement of the First Piano Concerto. A notably mature passage is the concealed return to the recapitulation, suggesting that Beethoven profited by Haydn's many such moments (within a few years he manages a specially subtle return in the last movement of the G major Trio, Op. 1, No. 2). The rondo is the most ambitious movement here: the part-writing includes a good deal of thematic independence for the cello. The other E flat work is a conventional set of fourteen variations (including two slow ones in E flat minor), which are, however, no more conventional than the rather unpromising theme would lead one to expect; the work was published as Op. 44 in 1804, but written about 1792.

The last six works mentioned contain fewer hints of the great creative personality to come than do the piano quartets of 1785; it seems as if, in chamber music at least, the subsequent five or six years of study somewhat cramped Beethoven's incipient individuality. However, an individual personality reappears in the first works he allowed to be published with an opus number, which, not surprisingly in view of his assiduous practice in the medium, are piano trios. In 1792, in his twenty-third year, he moved from Bonn to Vienna, where he remained for the rest of his life: the three Piano Trios, Op. 1, are among the first music that he wrote for Viennese audiences. These were private audiences in the houses of the nobility, for we must remember that public concerts were scarcely known in Vienna in the 1790s: there was no parallel there to London's many public concerts such as those for which Haydn composed his last symphonies.[2] The three trios must have been composed, at least in their first versions, by the end of 1793, for they were first performed in Haydn's presence, and he left for England in January 1794; Beethoven certainly revised them before

[1] See Ex. 14 in Chap. 3 above.
[2] Cf. *TF*, pp. 152 ff.

publishing them in 1795. According to fairly reliable evidence,[1] Haydn advised against publication of the third Trio, in C minor, not, it appears, because he disliked it or was offended by it (as has sometimes been said), but because he thought the public might not be ready for it; this was surely well meant, for he had given Beethoven lessons since December 1792, and, while the pupil seems to have been rather dissatisfied with the tuition, there is no conclusive evidence that Haydn was ever other than proud of his pupil.

Haydn, then, was worried about the possible reception of at least one of the trios, and the set as a whole aroused 'extraordinary attention'.[2] It is difficult, but important, for us to try to hear this music with the ears of its first attentive listeners and to try to forget the greater masterpieces to come, and thus to determine which elements must have sounded new and arresting and even disconcerting. First, and most superficially, these are the first piano chamber works—possibly the first works involving a piano—to have four movements: three had always been the normal maximum for such works, though of course four movements were quite usual in what were doubtless thought of as the more venerable forms of string quartet and symphony. The 'extra' movement is a scherzo in the first two trios, a minuet in the third. Continuing the tendencies of Beethoven's earlier works, these trios include some genuine independent writing for the cello. This need be mentioned here only because his master Haydn, even in his mature piano trios of the 1790s, still treated the medium almost as a piano sonata, with obbligato violin and a cello part slavishly tied to the bass of the piano part; Beethoven must have thought such a texture incomprehensibly old-fashioned, but in Mozart he had an example of a composer who had already treated the three instruments as equals, as can be seen in, for instance, the canonic four-part writing at bar 63 of the first movement of his Trio in B flat, K.502. In freedom of key relationships between movements the roles of the two senior composers are reversed, and Beethoven again follows the more adventurous one: the slow movement of the second, G major Trio is not in the more usual C major but in the submediant key, E, an extremely common tonal relationship in his later music; it is

---

[1] Marshalled in ibid., p. 164.   [2] Loc. cit.

found a good deal in Haydn, together with more disruptive relationships of a kind that Beethoven also occasionally adopted, as when
he put into E the slow movement of his C minor Piano Concerto.

More arresting and 'disturbing' than any of the features so far
mentioned is the new dynamism in Beethoven's music, especially in
alliance with abrupt, a-melodic lines and offbeat sforzandos. The
C minor Trio in particular abounds in such writing as bars 18–30
of the first movement:

Ex. 2

Beethoven's sketches show that some of his most dynamically personal ideas were forged from blander, more conventional beginnings; the theme of the trio of the scherzo in the second Trio is a case in point, and that of the minuet in the third is another.[1] Sometimes we find him fashioning a longer theme in order to generate, through order and consistency, a greater intensity and sense of momentum than in any earlier music: the definitive form of such a theme, the first of the *Allegro vivace* of No. 2, is much more suitable for his purposes than the capricious diversity, reminiscent of C. P. E. Bach and Clementi, of an earlier version:[2]

Ex. 3 *a:* Sketch

b: Published version

Like so many composers' youthful productions, these Op. 1 Trios are laid out on a leisurely scale. This is specially true of the first movement of the E flat Trio. If any of the trios contains material from Beethoven's Bonn days, as has been suggested, this must be the one, but even here there are original ideas to which Beethoven was to adhere in later works. One is a chordal theme, usually appearing in a second subject group and sometimes tonally unstable, which introduces a contrast of tempo and texture and allows for the possibility of more chromatic harmony; the example here is at bar 33 of the first movement. If one feels in this movement a certain disparity between scale and content, which one

[1] Cf. *NZB*, pp. 23 and 25.
[2] Cf. *NZB*, p. 21.

never feels in work after work of Beethoven's maturity, this is certainly not true of the first movement of the C minor Trio. This movement, in fact, illustrates the most epoch-making of his creative conquests: the expansion of long-range tonal drama intensified by the nature of the material, dynamic contrasts and the generation of momentum. However much we may respect Clementi and Dussek for their suggestive master-strokes of invention and their development of keyboard technique, no younger composer but Beethoven had at this time so commanding a grasp of scale in relation to all the constituent elements of music or the genius and determination to expand it—and eventually to compress it—in more and more dramatic ways. Consider in this C minor *Allegro con brio* the number of keys established or touched upon in the exposition; the insistence upon the foreign note of C flat (new light on the leading-note) and the consequently satisfying emergence of the enharmonic key of B major at the start of the development. We are thus prepared for, even if we do not expect, what is possibly Beethoven's most original inspiration so far in his career—the tonal variety at the start of the recapitulation, where the unstable passages of C major and D flat do not just flout tradition but continue the tonal unrest of the development and still explore the tonal implications of the exposition; the passage is enhanced by the scoring as a cello solo of bars 224–9, which must have seemed specially novel to those for whom Haydn's trios were models of piano-trio writing.

I have dwelt on this movement at some length because it has so many purely 'Beethovenian' features. The remaining movements are scarcely less fine. Beethoven seems to have been struck by the further possibilities of the coda to the variations that form the slow movement, since the piano Bagatelle in C, Op. 119, No. 2, is in effect a reworking of it; despite the high opus number, it quite possibly dates, like other pieces in the set, from not long after 1795. In his next trio, the B flat Trio, Op. 11, for clarinet (or violin), cello and piano, of 1798, he relaxes and writes more 'entertaining' music. This trio has usually been patronized, but it is a delightful piece worth taking seriously; its craftsmanship surely shows that Beethoven did, and the work was found 'difficult' enough by a critic in the *Allgemeine Musikalische Zeitung* for him to chastise him with composing 'unnaturally'.[1] In the first movement there is another chordal theme of the type mentioned above, highlighted by mediant or submediant relationships when it is introduced in the exposition (bar 39) and, especially, at the start of the development (D flat after F): such relationships become a prominent feature of Beethoven's tonal thinking right from so early an example as the startling second phrase (D after F) in the piano Bagatelle, Op. 33, No. 3. The little cello phrase delightfully enhances the first cadence and propels the music on as minims and semibreves change back to crotchets:

Ex. 4

The next new theme, the 'true' second subject in the 'expected' key of F, is subtly related to it. The sketches of the *Adagio* show that the main theme was originally almost the same as that of the minuet from the G major Piano Sonata, Op. 49, No. 2 (*c.* 1796),[2] and in the key, E flat, in which Beethoven did re-use it in his Septet (1799–1800); only in the final, published version of Op. 11 is the theme given at the start to the cello. The variations that form the last

[1] Cf. *AMZ*, I (1798–9), col. 541.
[2] Cf. *NZB*, p. 516.

movement are among the most resourceful of all Beethoven's sets at this period. The theme is that of the jaunty trio 'Pria ch'io l'impegno' from the opera *L'Amor marinaro* (1797) by the then popular composer Joseph Weigl. Operas were among the most sought after of all musical fare in Vienna, and variations on recent popular tunes from them were sure of an enthusiastic welcome; this one was later used by Hummel, Joseph Wölfl and Paganini. According to Czerny, Beethoven 'frequently contemplated writing another concluding movement for this Trio, and letting the variations stand as a separate work'.[1] This suggests that he may have thought the finale too lightweight, though it can boast serious elements such as the second variation entirely for clarinet and cello and the strenuous imitative writing at the start of the ninth variation.

Another set of variations for piano trio, on Wenzel Müller's song 'Ich bin der Schneider Kakadu', Op. 121a (published in 1824), seems to date basically from this period. The song came out in 1794 in the musical play *Die Schwestern von Prag*; Beethoven is likely to have made use of it when it was still popular, and he says, moreover, in a letter of 9 July 1816 that the variations 'belong to my early works, but they are not poor stuff'.[2] He also writes, in further letters of 1816 and 1818, about an otherwise unidentifiable 'new' trio. Now it has been plausibly argued[3] that this could be the same work, which Beethoven could pass off as 'new' because he had revised the variations and because the introduction, certainly, on grounds of style, and the coda, too, could date from 1816: it is possibly significant that they are mentioned separately in the full title of the printed score. In layout these variations are not unlike those in Op. 11: for instance, the first in each set is for piano alone, and there is a duet here, too, for violin and cello. Again a comic tune produces relatively serious variations: it is deliciously offset by the portentous G minor introduction with its florid piano writing, offering the sort of piquant contrast one finds between the slow

[1] Quoted in *TF*, p. 214, along with another, less probable anecdote about this movement.
[2] *LA*, Letter 642.
[3] Cf. Alan Tyson, 'Beethoven's "Kakadu" Variations and their English history', *Musical Times*, CIV (1963), p. 108.

introduction and first subject at the start of Haydn's Symphony No. 100. There was clearly a demand for piano trios at the beginning of the new century, and although it was 1808 before Beethoven produced any more original works for the medium (the two Trios, Op. 70), in 1805 he arranged his Septet, as Op. 38, for the same forces as Op. 11, and his Second Symphony for normal piano trio; in 1808 he could write to his publishers, when sending them Op. 70, that 'such trios are now rather scarce'.[1]

There are two sonata-length works by Beethoven for wind instruments and piano, as well as, much later on in 1817–18, sixteen variations on national airs for piano with *ad lib* flute (or violin), published as Opp. 105 and 107.[2] The Horn Sonata in F, Op. 17 (1800), need perhaps detain us long enough only to admire the way in which the C major second group in the opening *Allegro moderato* turns to its mediant, E minor, a very surprising key in an F major movement. The other work is finer: the Quintet in E flat for wind and piano, Op. 16 (1796–7; published 1801), which has suffered from otiose though perhaps understandable comparisons with Mozart's great work for the same forces in the same key, K.452. While Beethoven must have known Mozart's quintet, composers as great as he do not just copy works by their seniors, and a detailed comparison sheds no light on his work. Nevertheless, it is, like the Second Piano Concerto, one of very few of his works that can be called 'Mozartian', and the only one provoking stylistic reminiscences of Mozart's mature E flat mood as found, for example, in the quintet and in parts of the Piano Concertos, K.449 and K.482. The first theme of Beethoven's final rondo superficially recalls that of the rondo of K.482, but the association cannot be pushed further, and indeed Mr. Truscott finds Clementi behind the E flat minor passage starting at bar 92.[3] As in so much of Beethoven's early ensemble music, the piano plays the leading role. Nor do we feel, as Hans Keller has pointed out, that the scoring for wind instruments is 'inevitable': 'thought and sound do not come across as indivis-

[1] *LA*, letter 169.
[2] Cf. C. B. Oldman, 'Beethoven's variations on national themes: their composition and first publication', *Music Review*, XII (1951), p. 45.
[3] Cf. p. 74.

ible'.[1] Beethoven possibly felt this when he returned about 1810 to the rare medium of the piano quartet by arranging the quintet for it. There are no wholesale changes, but in the rearranging of parts, the adding of counterpoints and so on, one senses his desire to bind together the two sound elements, the piano and the other instruments: for instance, in the wind version the piano has the opening eight-bar melody of the *Andante cantabile* to itself, but in the re-working the strings join in at bar 5.

We are still concerned with Beethoven's early music, but except for the three great piano trios of Opp. 70 and 97 we have now covered all of the music for more than one instrument and piano and all of his piano chamber music involving wind instruments. Everything else that remains to be discussed, except for two trivial pieces (WoO 43–4) of about 1796 for mandolin and piano, is for either violin or cello and piano, and a good deal of this is early, too. Early or no, the two Cello Sonatas, Op. 5, are historic works, for they seem to be the first classical cello sonatas with a written-out piano part; even the sonatas that the cello virtuoso Anton Kraft published in the 1790s are accompanied by continuo. Beethoven wrote his sonatas for another virtuoso, Jean-Pierre Duport, who served at the Berlin court of Friedrich Wilhelm II, to whom they are dedicated. The cello writing is emancipated and mature, with no padding, and must have done a lot to raise the status of the instrument as a solo performer; as Beethoven was so fine a pianist, and indeed played these works with Duport for the king, the piano writing is also sonorous and spectacular. Formally both works are unusual in starting with what is in effect a slow movement, rather than an introduction, leading into an *allegro*, and in that the only other movement is a rondo. Just as in seventeenth-century Gothic one cannot always distinguish between Gothic Survival and Revival, so here it is not immediately clear if this formal outline survives from less stereotyped practices of the early classical period or whether it is an early anticipation of the free ordering of movements found in some of Beethoven's late works; historical considerations cause one to take the former view. Possibly the only

[1] 'Communication and experience', *The Listener*, 16 January 1969, p. 89.

slow music in the sonatas comes first in order to establish the cello at once as a sonorous, singing instrument, a suggestion possibly supported by, among other features, the long cantabile first subject of the ensuing *Allegro* in the F major Sonata. Since the cello sonata was still a continuo form at this date, Beethoven may also have been more aware of the tradition whereby baroque sonatas often started with a slow movement, leading into the first fast movement; and with his dynamic inclinations he may have thought that one such movement, even a short one, was enough in each work.

These two sonatas are among the finest of Beethoven's early works—the G minor especially—and still too little recognized as such. The first movement of the G minor Sonata is arguably his most notable achievement to date, as a study of even a small part of it will suggest. I am thinking here of both slow and fast parts, though, in fact, the 'introduction', a powerful fantasia comparable to the one in the piano trio Variations, Op. 121a, in the same key, gives a specially strong impression of being a separate movement. The energetic dotted-rhythm scales look back to things like Mozart's piano fantasias and, in conjunction with the filigree writing for piano from bar 22 onwards, forward to Beethoven's later music. The opening page of the *Allegro molto più tosto presto* offers early support for Joseph Kerman's thesis that Beethoven was 'deeply interested in the principle of contrast at every stage of his career'.[1] The quiet scalic opening idea subtly runs at bar 25, through a figure which establishes a cadence four bars earlier, into a totally different idea—loud, dynamic, and dominated by arpeggio figures:

Ex. 5

[1] Cf. Joseph Kerman, *The Beethoven quartets* (London, 1967), p. 227.

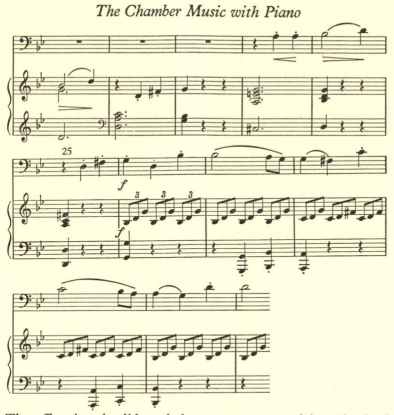

The effect is splendid, and the energy generated is maintained through three further stages: the strong B flat second subject, which is subtly related to the first theme through its rising scales and falling cadential figures; and the characteristically explosive piano writing at bars 100 ff., and the disruptive rhythm at bar 114, both of which transform and extend an element in the B flat theme. Ex. 6 shows this element at its three stages: (*a*) original version, bar 86; (*b*) bar 108; (*c*) bar 114:

Ex. 6 *a:* Vc.

[*p*] *dolce*

b: Piano r.h. (triplets in l.h.)

[*p*] [*cresc.*]

c: Piano r.h. (triplets in l.h.)

The variation technique which stimulates such momentum is a hallmark of Beethoven's maturing style as of no other composer at this time. Like Mozart in two G minor works, the Piano Quartet, K.478, and the String Quintet, K.516, Beethoven puts his finale, a rondo, in the tonic major, but with no loss of dynamism: the ubiquitous demisemiquavers, in the piano part especially, whether to intensify sforzando main beats or in both hands together to produce richly articulated harmony, certainly ensure this; and harmonic piquancy derives from the fact that the main theme begins with the subdominant chord.

Three sets of variations further illustrate Beethoven's enthusiastic response to the medium of cello and piano at this period. Two vary popular operatic tunes, both from *Die Zauberflöte*: 'Ein Mädchen oder Weibchen', in F (Op. 66; 1798), and 'Bei Männern', in E flat (WoO 46; probably 1801). The third and finest of the sets of cello variations, though the first to be written (*c.* 1796), is the set of twelve, WoO 45, on the theme of 'See, the conquering hero' from Handel's *Judas Maccabaeus*, an extraordinary choice of theme at this period, possibly prompted by Baron von Swieten, the noted admirer of Bach and Handel, whom Beethoven knew. One can already hear in this work an affinity between the more forthright or 'public' manners of Beethoven and Handel, who later in life was the composer he most loved: the vocal parts at 'und der Cherub steht vor Gott' (bars 85 ff.) in the finale of the Ninth Symphony and parts of the Overture *The Consecration of the House* are notable later instances. The variations are a resourceful set, following the general plan of many a late eighteenth-century set such as the finale of Mozart's D major Piano Sonata, K. 284: two are in the tonic minor, No. 11 is a florid *adagio* and No. 12 a skittish *allegro*.

Through these five works, especially the two sonatas, Beethoven established the combination of cello and piano as a true duo. We have seen that in doing so he raised the status of the piano from that of a continuo instrument to genuine partner. The classical violin sonata, on the other hand, grew out of the solo piano sonata, and violin sonatas were for long published and advertised as 'sonatas for piano with accompaniment for violin' (or some similar wording). This is true of the first publications of some of Beethoven's violin sonatas, and the piano is always mentioned first. This, however, was surely a selling-point: certainly it did not reflect his own view of the medium as a true partnership, a view that had clearly been Mozart's, too, as his own sonatas demonstrate (if less consistently than Beethoven's).

Beethoven's first violin-and-piano music is to be found in three slight works (WoO 40-2) from the period 1793-6. The set of twelve variations on 'Se vuol ballare' from *The Marriage of Figaro* is the most important and characteristic of these works. An interesting point in the letter about this piece, already quoted on pp. 197-8, shows Beethoven giving primacy to the violin. 'The v[ariations] will be rather difficult to play, and particularly the trills in the coda. But this must not intimidate and discourage you. For the composition is so arranged that you need only play the trill and can leave out the other notes, since these appear in the violin part as well.' He seems to have included such difficulties in his works in order to embarrass other pianists, 'some of whom are my sworn enemies', when they tried to play his music.

Beethoven turned to the more serious business of sonata composition in 1797-8 with the three sonatas published shortly afterwards as Op. 12. Even if, as Kerman says, the violin sonata was for Beethoven 'never a very solemn form'[1] (which is questionable), it was still a vehicle for his increasing individuality. The first movement of the second, A major sonata may distantly hark back to movements in Mozart's Violin Sonatas, K.305 and K.526, in the same key, but it is individual enough to have served as a possible model for Beethoven himself in another A major piece, the first movement of the String Quartet, Op. 18, No. 5, to which it is superior. The first movements are in general the most original ones in Op. 12 and the ones that through their tumbling succession of fresh material must have done most to attract the puzzled scorn of

[1] Op. cit., p. 57.

the reviewer of 1799 who cried: 'Gelehrt, gelehrt und immerfort gelehrt und keine Natur, kein Gesang!'[1] The opening of the first sonata (Ex. 7b) shows this new manner as well as anything in the set; as such concentrated profusion of material is scarcely paralleled elsewhere in his output Beethoven himself may have considered it self-defeating: there are five different figures in little more than a dozen bars, and always three simultaneously from bar 5. Moreover, to compare the very opening with the not dissimilar outline at the start of Mozart's Violin Sonata in E flat, K.302, with its more urbane continuation, too (Ex. 7a), sets in relief Beethoven's generation of a typically gruff dynamism from a discontinuous line, staccato final notes, and a disruptive rest in the middle longer than the others:

[1] *AMZ*, I, col. 571. 'Learned, learned, always learned, no naturalness, no melody!'.

214

However distinctive the first movements, nothing in these works is more individual than the C major *Adagio con molt'espressione* in No. 3, in mood not unlike the corresponding movement in the same key in the E flat Piano Sonata, Op. 7. With its violin melody against a wide variety of figuration low in the piano part, this rapt piece displays some of Beethoven's most original invention from this period in his career, its piano writing hardly surpassed even in the piano sonatas. The slow movement of No. 1 in D is a theme and variations, a rare form for such a movement (for all its popularity elsewhere) in Mozart as in Beethoven's early music; the C minor Piano Trio from Op. 1 affords another example. The first F major episode of the A minor rondo forming the slow movement of No. 2 again has a 'new' piano texture not unlike that of Ex. 7*b*, bars 5 ff., with slow sonorous left-hand chords supporting more active writing in the right hand, this time in approximate canon with the violin. Beethoven still respects the three-movement convention in these works, as he had not done in Op. 1, so there are no minuets or scherzos; the finales are genial rondos, an unambitious form that Beethoven was gradually to outgrow.

The next two violin sonatas (1800–1) are very different works from these and from each other. Op. 23 is in A minor, a key that Beethoven used only rarely, as had Haydn and Mozart, and then for something special like Mozart's Piano Sonata, K.310. This Beethoven sonata is unique, too, in being dominated by so much tense and bare linear writing. The extraordinary energy of the opening ⁶₈ *Presto*—a very exceptional marking for a first movement, repeated in the 'Kreutzer' Sonata—is so relentless that diversity of figuration such as we see in Ex. 7*b* could not possibly coexist with it, and so it gives way to a much starker uniformity. The closing rondo is also spare and relentless except for one or two contrasting chordal episodes and, as has been pointed out, offers another foretaste of the first movement of the 'Kreutzer' Sonata. Even the 'slow' movement is an *Andante scherzoso, più allegretto* and includes —exceptionally for a slow movement—a fugato at bar 33 on a theme that contrasts vividly with the slurred and halting motion of the opening idea.

The well-defined contrast between the two main subjects in the first movement of the F major Sonata, Op. 24, is more traditional in terms of, say, Mozartian sonata form than are such movements in earlier violin sonatas by Beethoven, but the traditional roles are reversed, which is possibly an even more original stroke than anything in the earlier sonatas. The first subject is the famous lyrical melody—conceivably, as Mr. Truscott shows, on p. 75 above, owing something to Clementi—that has given the sonata its nickname of the 'Spring' and is one of the earliest harbingers of a new relaxation, even in traditionally energetic forms, that informs a number of Beethoven's middle-period works, such as the 'Pastoral' Symphony and the Fourth Piano Concerto. The second group is much more powerful and significantly veers to C minor from C major, the expected key for it. The relaxed lyricism of the main theme of the final rondo complements this movement; it is reminiscent of certain themes by Mozart—in the same medium there is the first subject of the first movement of the Sonata, K.378, and one might also mention the *Allegro* of the aria 'Non più fiori' in *La Clemenza di Tito*. The B flat slow movement, on the other hand, far from recalling an earlier composer, anticipates a later one. It is one of Beethoven's earliest evocations of intense feeling whose characteristic expression was later to find a response in Schubert: the singing violin line and the rich piano part combining with the change to G flat at bar 40 are especially significant. The 'Spring' Sonata is Beethoven's first violin sonata in four movements. The added scherzo is extremely short (nor is the first part repeated) and also highly personal in the quick flicks of its incisive rhythm: a sketch shows that it was less incisive at an earlier stage than in the final version.[1]

Except for possible changes in the Op. 121a Variations we now move for the first time in this chapter towards what is commonly regarded as Beethoven's second-period music. The borderline works here are the three Violin Sonatas, Op. 30 (1802), roughly contemporary with, and counterparts in this medium to, the three Piano Sonatas, Op. 31. In each set the central minor-key sonata is the crucial work, but the flanking sonatas should not be overlooked. If of the two in Op. 30 I concentrate briefly here on No. 3 in G, it is because it is so short and unpretentious that it can easily be under-valued. Yet there is no Beethoven sonata remotely like it, and it is one of his wittiest and most delightful works. Again he seems at once to revitalize the past and to point to the future. The perpetuum mobile finale is an entirely personal recreation of a Haydn rondo, with slight Lydian, folklike overtones in the subject, plenty of tonic pedal and at bar 177 an outrageous switch to E flat, complete with 'till-ready' accompaniment. The middle movement is an exceed-ingly beautiful slow minuet which, far from being old-fashioned, as it has been described, adumbrates the nineteenth-century inter-mezzo and generates the sort of expressive warmth we have already found in the slow movement of Op. 24 and which is later developed in the third movement of the Piano Trio, Op. 70, No. 2, and in the slow movement of the Op. 96 Violin Sonata; the theme first appear-ing at bar 59 is so sonorously harmonized with $^6_4$ and $^4_2$ chords as to look even beyond Schubert to Schumann. The first movement has several Beethoven fingerprints: an impudently simple opening subject; contrastingly complex sinuous counterpoint at bar 42 lead-ring to a typically assertive minor-key subject, with off-beat sfor-zandos against double-stopping; and another delightful tonal side-step, at bar 35.

The originality of the C minor Sonata lies especially in its outer

[1] Cf. *NZB*, p. 235.

movements. The *Allegro con brio* is one of Beethoven's grandest first movements to date in any medium. As later on in the first 'Razumovsky' Quartet, there is no repeat of the exposition. Instead the opening theme, originally announced in short abrupt phrases (Ex. 8*a*), steals in, after a tremendous build-up, in E flat (*c*) in a more expansive treatment of the form it takes at bar 9 (*b*); the tonal disturbance intensifies and 'fulfils' that introduced at that point (a suggestion of F minor):

Ex. 8 *a*

The closing *Allegro* is also grander than most of Beethoven's earlier finales; he now discards simple rondo form and writes a tempestuous sonata rondo. The main subject, stated after explosive dynamic contrasts, introduces another type of melody that is unmistakably Beethovenian: a rough, rather square type, emphasizing only tonic and dominant chords at its first, incomplete appearance. The simplicity is qualified by the originality of the dynamics:

Ex. 9

The melody appears in 'complete' form in C major from bar 106, including jaunty imitations and an equally jaunty cadence: it is of a daring, almost banal simplicity that reappears in later works by Beethoven, in such places as the very end of *Fidelio* and the finale of the Ninth Symphony. The texture of a forthright tune with chordal accompaniment possibly owes something to a passage such as the following from the first movement, *Allegro agitato assai,* of Dussek's Piano Sonata in C minor, Op. 35, No. 3, published in 1797:

Ex. 10

A similarly forthright subject appears at bar 144 in the second group of the first movement of the Sonata in A, Op. 47, completed in 1803 and known as the 'Kreutzer' after its second, indifferent dedicatee, the French composer and violinist Rodolphe Kreutzer. It is one of Beethoven's characteristic modulating subjects that introduce such striking tonal fluidity into so many of his sonata movements; it is preceded a little earlier by another of his quieter chordal melodies such as we have found in early trios such as Op. 1, No. 1, and Op. 11. The virtuosity and scale of this famous sonata proclaim it even more decidedly a middle-period work. In composing it in, as the original title-page says, 'a very concertante style, almost like a concerto', Beethoven transferred the violin sonata from the private salon to the concert hall (at a time when public concerts were becoming established in Vienna) and did for the medium what the 'Razumovsky' Quartets did for the string quartet and the 'Waldstein' and 'Appassionata' Sonatas for the piano sonata. The fact that the two outer, sonata-form movements are marked '*Presto*' emphasizes the brilliance. The first, the finest of the three movements, is a dramatic, tonally wide-ranging structure in A minor introduced by an *Adagio* that starts most originally in A major with four bars for violin alone in double- and triple-stopping. The last movement is a hectic tarantella in the major whose headlong rush is interrupted only by a charming insouciant $\frac{2}{4}$ tune near the end of the exposition and recapitulation. That it was originally the finale of the A major Sonata, Op. 30, No. 1, supplements the evidence of Op. 30, No. 2, that Beethoven was consistently 'thinking big' in his violin sonatas by 1802—indeed, the A minor Sonata,

Op. 23, of a year or two earlier contains, as we have seen, hints of the 'Kreutzer'. The middle movement of Op. 47 is a set of variations in the flat submediant, F, more elaborately perky on the whole than slow-movement variations usually are—not inappropriately in the context, like the *Andante scherzoso* of Op. 23. It is not one of Beethoven's most interesting sets (though the delayed tonic in the bass at bars 207 and 211 in the coda is as fine a moment as any in the work). Indeed, the work as a whole, possibly through its attractions for virtuoso players, has unfairly overshadowed violin sonatas with possibly greater claims to attention—Op. 30, No. 2, and Op. 96, certainly, the lovable little Op. 30, No. 3, too.

Only now, late in this chapter, do we come to the really mature works from the exceptionally creative years of Beethoven's so-called second period. Yet only seven major works remain to be discussed; of these the two Cello Sonatas, Op. 102, dating from 1815, are the last, so in the last dozen years of his life Beethoven turned away completely from chamber music with piano. Five piano sonatas and the Diabelli Variations date from those years, but his neglect of piano chamber music, and piano concertos too, may well reflect the sad decline in his powers as a pianist and his abandoning of social music-making, as consequences of his ever-worsening deafness. In his autobiography Spohr draws a terrible picture of Beethoven rehearsing one of his piano trios: 'It was no pleasure, firstly, because the piano was out of tune, which bothered Beethoven not at all, since he could not hear it, and, secondly, because little was left of his once celebrated virtuosity. In *forte* passages he hit the keys so hard that the strings rattled, and in *piano*, so softly that whole groups of notes never sounded at all, with the result that it was impossible to follow without the piano score as a guide. I was deeply moved by so tragic a fate.'[1]

The two Trios, Op. 70, in D and E flat respectively, and the A major Cello Sonata, Op. 69, form a magnificent group dating from 1808, one of Beethoven's most fertile years; they are contemporary

---

[1] Cf. *The Musical Journeys of Louis Spohr*, trans. and ed. Henry Pleasants (Norman, Oklahoma, 1961), pp. 106–7. Spohr seems to date this episode about 1812, referring to Op. 70, No. 1, but *TF*, pp. 577–8, attaches it to a performance of the 'Archduke' Trio, Op. 97, in 1814.

with the Fifth and Sixth Symphonies. The first two of the three movements of Op. 70, No. 1, are astonishing, the first for its drama of contrasts, the second for its atmosphere, unique in Beethoven, of almost gothick mystery, which caused the work to be called the 'Ghost' Trio. There is surely no more abrupt or pregnant contrast in Beethoven, certainly not within a few bars of a first-subject group, than that between the first two elements in the first movement—an explosive theme in octaves, and an aching tender melody such as we find later on in the D major trio of the second movement of the F minor String Quartet, Op. 95, or as the second subject of the first movement of the A minor Quartet, Op. 132, in each case, as here, as relief after darker or tenser music. The highly charged contrast is accentuated by an exposition remarkable for its terseness and worked out in a more extended development and recapitulation. Even so, the movement reminds us that not every-thing from Beethoven's middle years is big and expansive, just as the 'Pastoral' Symphony reminds us that all is not highly-charged drama. We do find a foretaste here of the more elliptical music of Beethoven's last years: the hectic wide-ranging imitative writing starting at bar 124 and derived from the first bar of the movement is a new, typically 'late' element in Beethoven that we shall meet again in the last cello sonata and which intensifies the element of strife in the drama; this, however, is very soon counteracted by the fast, consolatory piano scales added to the recapitulation from bar 183, recalling the similar effect of the scales beginning at bar 631 in the coda of the first movement of the 'Eroica' Symphony.

Just as the D minor slow movement of the Quartet in F, Op. 18, No. 1, is said to have been inspired by a scene in Shakespeare (the tomb scene in *Romeo and Juliet*), so may the one in this trio have been prompted by *Macbeth*, since the main thematic idea appears in a sketchbook among sketches for a projected *Macbeth* opera.[1] If one compares this movement in its slowness, small amount of basic material, and elaborate figuration with other middle-period slow movements such as the one in the Triple Concerto, this still leaves out of account its extraordinarily dramatic implications. It is far from static and includes a most impressive modulation to the flat-

[1] Cf. *NZB*, p. 226.

seventh key, C major (later paralleled in the scherzo of the Ninth Symphony), and an equally powerful return to the tonic twenty bars later: this is a concentrated tonal drama no less remarkable than, and complementary to, the concentrated exposition of the preceding movement.

If the last movement is less arresting, in the E flat Trio the finale crowns a work which is in any case one of Beethoven's chamber-music masterpieces—and a strangely neglected one. It is his first sonata-form work to have movements in three different keys. The second movement is in C and follows the Haydnesque plan of alternating variations on two themes, one major, one minor. The third is in A flat. According to a sketchbook Beethoven conceived it as a minuet, but he finally marked it simply '*Allegretto ma non troppo*', and the impression it gives, like the middle movement of the G major Violin Sonata, Op. 30, No. 3, is of a languorous intermezzo, a typically nineteenth-century 'character piece' with, in the 'trio', a distinct pre-echo of Schubert's famous Impromptu in the same key, D. 899, No. 4; violin double-stopping enhances the romantic atmosphere.

The outer movements are both based on an exceptionally large amount of material. A striking and significant formal point in the first movement is that an idea introduced while the dominant is being established (Ex. 11*b*) is derived, in speeded-up form, from the slow introduction (*a*) (which returns at the original tempo in the coda to the movement):

Ex. 11 *a*

It has, moreover, two features increasingly common in Beethoven: since it begins in G flat it has a mediant relationship with the preceding tonic, and the next key, the dominant, is itself a mediant away from it; and it is a modulating subject, itself moving to the dominant as Ex. 11*b* ends. Textures and material in the closing bars of the development seem to foreshadow the already mentioned 'trio' of the third movement. They are followed at once by what Tovey calls 'perhaps the most unexpected return in all music':[1] the cello starts off the first theme of the exposition in D flat, only to be brusquely corrected by the piano in the tonic. There are at least five distinct themes in the exposition of the finale, the first two of which, apparently disparate, are brought into relation with each other, to the illumination of both, at the start of the recapitulation. At the moment of union all stress is transformed into restrained

[1] Cf. Donald Francis Tovey, *Beethoven* (London, 1944), p. 101.

224

jubilation comparable to that of the passage from bar 183 of the first movement of the D major Trio. Beethoven continues in F minor, which prepares for the second-group key of C—for a recapitulation an unusually long absence from the tonic, which is then stressed in a long extension of the material of the exposition. G (minor and major) is the tonal area of the three second-group ideas in the exposition—another instance of Beethoven's growing fondness for mediant relationships not just between but within movements. The second of these ideas, like the second in the first group, is based on a tonic pedal which contrasts tellingly with more mobile basses elsewhere in the movement. The last is one of Beethoven's most infectiously perky inspirations: at its second statement bar 5 magically transforms the line of bar 3 and is repeated sequentially in the next bar to form the cadence:

Ex. 12

The whole work is full of such splendid inventions on both a small and a large scale.

As in Op. 70, No. 1, contrast is established on the first page of the Cello Sonata, Op. 69, but this time quite differently. The movement (*Allegro non tanto* only) begins with a long, quietly unfolding melody first heard on unaccompanied cello. When the second main idea appears it is loud, dislocated by offbeat sforzandos and in the minor, but it is clearly derived from the first theme:

Ex. 13 *a:* Vlc. (Piano silent)

b: Piano

Contrast also informs the E major second group—this time between bland counterpoint and a much more dynamic melody whose restless drive is enhanced by transitory modulations; the contrastingly relaxed cadence figure that follows can also be heard, certainly through its initial rising interval, to relate to the very first theme (Ex. 13*a*). The asymmetrical rhythms of the final version of the main theme of the scherzo are already present in the earliest surviving sketch, which is, however, more symmetrical in parts;[1] in an intermediate version the symmetry disappears, but the last phrase is still a third higher than it finally became.[2] The scherzo is heard three times, interspersed by an A major trio whose sonorous piano writing in thirds and sixths, sometimes with the two hands playing the same chords an octave apart, is the sort of piano writing that Schubert developed in his late music; as in the corresponding place in Op. 70, No. 2, double-stopping on the violin makes the

[1] See the valuable article by Lewis Lockwood, 'The Autograph of the First Movement of Beethoven's Sonata for Violoncello and Pianoforte, Op. 69', *The Music Forum*, II (New York, 1970), pp. 1–109.

[2] Cf. *NZB*, p. 534.

texture even richer. Like that of the 'Waldstein' Sonata the slow 'movement' in this work consists of only a few bars leading into the finale (the last one, Op. 102, No. 2, is the only one of Beethoven's five cello sonatas with a fully-fledged slow movement). It is almost as if the lyricism one might have heard unfolding here is absorbed into the first subject of the *Allegro vivace*, which is notably suave and rounded. The change of the fifth note from tonic to dominant when the theme is played loudly in the coda is a magnificent moment which announces that the end is near and crowns the work; it would be as impossible at the start of the movement as it is absolutely 'right' here. The lyricism of the second subject:

Ex. 14

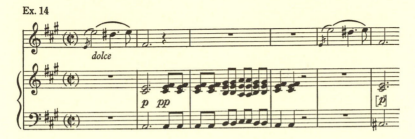

is suffused with 'romantic' feeling, especially because of the falling minor seventh; it is echoed at bars 16 and 17 of the first movement of the Piano Sonata, Op. 101, in the same key, a 'key' phrase in one of Beethoven's most concentrated expressions of romantic feeling; and it stands at the beginning of increasingly romantic trends in nineteenth-century music that led within fifty years to the yearning sevenths of *Tristan* (see, for example, the opening phrase of—significantly—the cello melody beginning at bar 18 in the prelude to that work).

The incredible variety of Beethoven's output, the uniqueness of each masterpiece, are abundantly clear: consider, for instance, the Fifth and Sixth Symphonies, which he composed simultaneously. Even so, certain dominant moods recur. One is a relaxed expansiveness in sonata-form movements, markedly different from the stormy dramas that perhaps first spring to mind in such a connection. We have already seen that the first movement of the A major Cello Sonata is only an *Allegro non tanto*; those of the Sixth Symphony,

the Violin Concerto and the Op. 78 Piano Sonata are all marked
'*Allegro ma non troppo*'; it is no surprise a few years later to find the
lyrical opening of Op. 101, just referred to, moving only at *Allegretto, ma non troppo*. The most spacious of all such movements in
Beethoven's lyrical transformation of dramatic sonata form is the
Allegro moderato that opens the Piano Trio in B flat, Op. 97, the
'Archduke' (dedicated to the Archduke Rudolph); the work dates
from 1811 at a time when Beethoven was slackening his feverish
pace of composition of the preceding years, though, in fact, he
wrote it inside three weeks in March (using sketches made in 1810).
All the hallmarks of his relaxed style are here: the moderate tempo;
the measured lyrical melody at the start, which could well have
subconsciously inspired Schubert to the first theme of his B flat
Piano Sonata, D.960, but which despite its lyrical nature still has
enough separate elements to launch Beethoven on one of his most
exhaustive developments; the sonorous textures, heard at their
richest at the double-stopping on both stringed instruments and
the full chords for the piano's left hand from bar 43; the characteristic side-stepping at the same point into the submediant key,
G (involving a change of key-signature), a type of modulation which,
as we have seen, Beethoven increasingly prefers now to sharper,
more 'black-and-white' dominant and subdominant relationships.
The subject that follows this passage recalls the opening of another
middle-period *Allegro moderato*—the first movement of the Fourth
Piano Concerto. Here is the whole of this section:

Ex. 15

The transformation of the last idea into a 'new' subject shows Beethoven's art at its subtlest. This theme is a late example of the type of chordal melody we have seen as early as Op. 1, No. 1. The repeated notes of the opening, with constantly changing harmony underneath, later become one of Schubert's fingerprints: the opening of the A major Piano Sonata, D.959, is only one of many examples.

The densely sonorous textures are perhaps the most remarkable feature of Ex. 15. Beethoven at the same time uses the developing resources of the most up-to-date pianos of his day—indeed, causes the makers to keep up with him—and increases the sound of the stringed instruments in order to match the piano; one feels the developments in instrument manufacture, instrumental technique and Beethoven's own art to be indivisible. Increasingly elaborate textures are also a notable feature of the slow movement (which is placed third), and the *Andante cantabile* tempo allows them to be more sumptuous than ever; the piano textures of the third and fourth variations in particular are of a complexity and originality such as Beethoven developed in his later piano works such as the Diabelli Variations and the last Sonata, Op. 111. There is less scope for such writing in the other two movements. The principal theme of the extended scherzo is a marvellous example of Beethoven making something utterly memorable out of elementary materials—a rising octave scale and a straightforward cadential figure. It is soon transformed by totally different articulation, and the new version is fulfilled by the extension marked *x* in the following passage, which has a strong feeling of inevitability about it:

Ex. 16 (Vln. silent)

In the 'trio' Beethoven's passion for contrast juxtaposes a mysterious chromatic fugato in B flat minor and a brilliant piece of salon music—really a waltz—in D flat. The finale, which leads out of the slow movement, is a rondo, not for Beethoven the most serious of forms and not one he would have used to complete so grand a work had he not wanted to show how serious he could make it. The movement is not the flippant piece it has sometimes been taken for —though it is true that the strings play a subsidiary role compared with the preceding movements—and tonality is one of the main agents of its seriousness. A strong subdominant feeling[1] is induced at the very outset by the several A flats in the principal subject, which is, in fact, one of Beethoven's many modulating themes, moving from E flat to B flat, and this tempers the jaunty rhythms of melody and accompaniment, which are further offset by the markings '*dolce*' and '*espressivo*'. Moreover, there are few themes of Beethoven more subtle and original, melodically or rhythmically, than that of the episodes, again starting *dolce*, but further enhanced by a wider dynamic range in subsequent statements:

Ex. 17 (Vln. silent after first beat; in Vlc. F and C for two bars each)

A surprising enlargement of the tonal scope of the movement is provided by the A major in which the *presto* coda begins. There is a much inferior separate *Allegretto* in B flat for piano trio, WoO 39, which, it has been suggested, was a rejected finale for the 'Archduke' Trio. However, this is certainly not so, even though the Trio was not published until 1816, though Beethoven may have kept the *Allegretto* in reserve as a substitute finale, easier in every respect: he composed this piece only some eighteen months after completing the 'Archduke' Trio, and it bears a separate dedication, suggesting that he always meant it as an isolated movement, however unusual that may be in this medium.

[1] See Tovey's detailed tonal analysis of this movement, op. cit., p. 102.

In piano chamber music the sole true companion to the 'Arch-duke' Trio at this period in Beethoven's career is his last Violin Sonata, Op. 96 in G; it dates from 1812, but, as with the Trio, publication was delayed until 1816, and it, too, is dedicated to the Archduke Rudolph. Here again the first movement is marked '*Allegro moderato*'; there is once again, at bar 20, an echo of the opening rhythm of the Fourth Piano Concerto in the same key, to set beside bars 51 ff. of the first movement of Op. 97:

Ex. 18

When Beethoven modulates to D he introduces an idea reminiscent, notably in rhythm, of the one at bar 29 in the concerto, and the next idea to appear in the second group does so after a relaxed sub-mediant modulation to B flat, the key in which a new theme is introduced at bar 105 in the concerto; in each case the change of key is intensified by more languid figuration. Given that the individual qualities of Beethoven's greatest works are among the most arrest-ing manifestations of his genius and also that too much has been made of an allegedly single mood in his C minor works (cf. p. 247), the admittedly superficial resemblances between the G major music just discussed do seem to hint that one or two keys at least may have suggested to Beethoven at different times ideas linked by common characteristics. Or did the ideas prompt the keys ?[1]

None of his great first movements flowers from such unpretentious seeds as does the first movement of Op. 96 from its 'throwaway' opening phrase: the material so far mentioned does not exhaust what is presented in the exposition, which is rounded off by a 'romantic', drooping cadential melody. There is a prolonged passage in E flat starting only a few bars after the beginning of the recapitulation, an instance of Beethoven's increasing tonal freedom that balances the submediant modulation in the second group in the exposition and would indeed be unconvincing without it. The slow movement is in the same flat submediant key. It is a deeply expressive piece which illustrates an intensifying of a mood we have seen developing since the slow movement of the 'Spring' Sonata. The harmony and texture of the opening, especially the frequent chromatic alterations (notably in bar 7), the use of $^6_3$ chords, the progression at the beginning of bar 3, and the dense textures, would not be out of place in a Schumann song of 1840, such as 'Du Ring an meinem Finger' in *Frauenliebe und Leben*; and this movement may well have influenced Brahms in the slow movement of his own G major Violin Sonata, Op. 78. The ultimate debt to Beethoven even of some of the most personal inspirations of Schubert and Schumann, to mention just two composers, is remarkable and has never been fully explored. The specific gravity of the last two movements of Op. 96 is lower, but not at all at odds with what has gone before. The scherzo is even in the minor—a rare occurrence in a major-key work—and the E flat trio again emphasizes the submediant inclinations of the sonata. It is no surprise to find intrusions of E flat and G minor near the end of the final variations, a particularly discontinuous section, including at the very end a repetitive, mock-serious *poco adagio* between *allegro* and *presto* passages, reminiscent of Haydn's 'joke' endings. The theme of the variations is of popular cast; Nottebohm draws attention[2] to a similar tune in a then very popular *Singspiel* by J. A. Hiller, *Der Teufel ist los* (1766). The variations are not specially showy and are

[1] Also cf. below, p. 307.　　　　[2] Cf. *NB*, p. 30.

somewhat akin in temper to the variations also on *Allegretto* tunes that form the finales of the A major Violin Sonata, Op. 30, No. 1, and the Quartet in E flat, Op. 74. The following extract from a letter that Beethoven wrote to the Archduke Rudolph in December 1812 explains the nature of the finale of Op. 96 and also throws light on more rumbustious finales: '. . . I have not hurried unduly to compose the last movement merely for the sake of being punctual, the more so as in view of Rode's playing I have had to give more thought to the composition of this movement. In our Finales we like to have fairly noisy passages, but R[ode] does not care for them —and so I have been rather hampered.'[1]

In Op. 96, the finest of his violin sonatas, Beethoven invests simplicity with serious elegance, a conspicuous 'second-period' quality that greatly diminished in the music of his last years, together with his obsession with the symphonic ideal. We have noticed one or two intimations of Beethoven's later music, for example in the terseness of the exposition and in the imitative writing of the development of the first movement of the 'Ghost' Trio, but the only two works that remain to be discussed in this chapter are in general very different from any earlier works. Composed in 1815, the two Cello Sonatas, Op. 102, stand on the threshold of Beethoven's last period, following his comparative silence in 1813 and 1814; the elliptical quality of the first one in particular, their textures—especially the fugal finale of No. 2—and the nature of their profoundities, such as the final section of the slow movement of No. 2, place them firmly with his late works.

The first sonata, in C, is in two balanced halves, each slow-fast. The opening *Andante* of twenty-seven bars leads into a *Vivace* sonata-form movement not in the key of the work but in A minor. The E minor second group is no less urgent than the dotted-rhythm scales of the first group, to which it is rhythmically linked near its close. Since the first idea (Ex. 19*b*) can be heard as an inversion of the main theme of the *Andante* (*a*) and as the recapitulation, following a very short development, is comparatively regular, the whole of the first half of the work is very tightly organized.

[1] *LA*, letter 392. Pierre Rode was the great French violinist who gave the first performance of the sonata with the Archduke.

The sonata continues to be so as the nine bars of rhapsodic *Adagio* after the break lead into seven bars in which Beethoven intensifies the material of Ex. 19a before leading straight into a sonata-form movement whose unassuming first subject reinforces the feeling of terseness generated earlier. It starts with one of those cheerful phrases—introduced in a typically hesitant way and surely stemming from popular music—that occasionally burst in in late

235

Beethoven, somewhat disconcertingly, it may seem at first, into weightier surroundings, which indeed enhance them:[1]

Ex. 20

This chirpiness, however, is immediately modified by dragging triplets in the cello. Again the whole movement is terse—simply 233 $\frac{2}{4}$ bars of *Allegro vivace* without a repeat. The energy it soon works up still sounds like 'second-period' energy, especially in the coda, where the dactylic figure from Ex. 20 is thrillingly worked up in conjunction with sforzandos, and when a little phrase burgeons so finely at bars 59–60 with rather like the effect of Ex. 12 in the finale of the E flat Trio from Op. 70. What is really new here, however, is what follows at the start of the development—Ex. 21, at first both static and explosive and then leading into smooth and spare imitative writing, foreshadowing Beethoven's first fugue in a sonata-form work.

That appears as the finale of the second Op. 102 Sonata, in D. Of the two preceding movements the first is another terse sonata-form structure starting with the subject shown in Ex. 22*a*, which

[1] Dr. Simpson makes a similar point below (p. 267) when discussing the finale of the Op. 127 Quartet.

Ex. 21

may not have been lost on Schubert when he wrote the opening
Allegro of his D minor String Quartet ('Death and the maiden',
D.810), bars 114–15 of which are shown in Ex. 22*b*:

Ex. 22a: Piano r.h. (Vc. silent)

It is symptomatic of the two composers' different methods that Beethoven should take the opening rather a-melodic but strongly rhythmic five-note figure as the starting-point of a movement, whereas Schubert uses it to intensify a climax (which he does much more insistently at bars 134–7 just before he completes his exposition). The second movement is a D minor *Adagio con molto sentimento d'affetto* in ternary form, and we can for once confidently echo Schindler when he puts it 'among the richest and most deeply sensitive inspirations of Beethoven's muse.'[1] Its textures, especially in the reprise, are of a distinctive elaboration peculiar to Beethoven in his late works and even more complex than those found in the variations of the 'Archduke' Trio. The middle section is in D major, which, as Philip Radcliffe has pointed out, is often for Beethoven a key of warmth and richness, especially when he uses it as a key of modulation (and sometimes to contrast with D minor).[2] He was a long time settling on the final version of the main theme (Ex. 23), as the sketches show;[3] for example, in all the versions that

---

[1] Cf. *SB*, p. 213.

[2] Cf. Philip Radcliffe, *Beethoven's string quartets* (London, 1965), p. 117. Also cf. below, p. 307.

[3] Cf. *NZB*, p. 325.

preceded it he moved up to D in the first bar, which, he no doubt felt, detracted from the leap up to G in the next bar, which was present from the start.

Ex. 23: Piano r.h.

When the D major *Allegro fugato* leads out of this sublime *Adagio* we realize that, like the E major works that Dr. Simpson refers to below,[1] the whole work is going to centre on a single tonic: we are far now from the three tonal centres and wealth of material of Op. 70, No. 2. The vehement hostility that greeted the two Op. 102 Sonatas was no doubt generated principally by this fugue, with its 'want of clearness' and 'confusion'.[2] Despite some more rounded contours, it is one of Beethoven's 'rough' fugues, first cousin to the fugal writing in the finale of the A major Piano Sonata, Op. 101, and unlike the softer fugues typified by the finale of the A flat Piano Sonata, Op. 110. This is not the most appropriate chapter in which to discuss Beethoven's fugues, but it is worth pointing out here that all the movements just mentioned are finales and that Beethoven may well have turned to fugue as a new way of crowning a work now that simpler forms such as rondo and sonata rondo possibly appealed to him less and as he was outgrowing the dynamic sonata ideal. As far as Op. 102, No. 2, is concerned, it might be added that a cello would be harder to balance against a typical new piano of 1815 than against the lighter piano for which he had composed Op. 5 nearly twenty years earlier, and that a linear, fugal piano texture in three or four parts would allow it to 'speak' more convincingly than the denser, more harmonic textures of earlier works. The subject of the fugue cost Beethoven an immense amount of trouble before he was satisfied with it: many pages of sketches unfold before the more concise, less chromatic definitive version emerges.[3] The climax of the fugue is brilliantly achieved through

---

[1] Cf. p. 256.
[2] Cf. *SB*, loc. cit.
[3] Cf. *NZB*, pp. 318 and 326.

smooth scales, sometimes in sixths on the piano, and dominant and, particularly, tonic trills lasting for bar after bar; at the end of the last work to be considered in this chapter we for the first time hear Beethoven in the aspiring transcendental vein that he worked out so magnificently in his last piano sonatas.

SIX

The Chamber Music for Strings

ROBERT SIMPSON

TO UNDERESTIMATE BEETHOVEN'S earlier works in the light of his later achievements is one of the commonest blunders of critic- ism, and one of the most natural, in view of the magnitude of the last and greatest works. It is all too easy to take for granted that the Op. 18 Quartets are works of genius and then to treat them as advanced student essays; more than one writer has been guilty of this, and with the best of intentions. Listening recently to an exceptionally fine performance of the C minor String Trio, Op. 9, No. 3, I suddenly and for the first time heard it as perhaps it seemed to its first hearers; the furious perfection of its first movement must have struck them with great force, and the more perceptive of them must have been overwhelmed by its unprecedented concentration and structural tension, to say nothing of the unheard-of richness and power of Beethoven's writing for three instruments. It is less common to look askance at these string trios than at the Op. 18 Quartets, simply because of the element of virtuosity with which Beethoven solves the notoriously difficult problems of string-trio writing. But the view that they are 'superior' to the quartets is one that tends to regard composition as some kind of athletic feat, that is less likely to grasp the real merits of both sets than one that eschews dangerous and invidious comparisons. It is not unreason- able to see that the E flat Trio, Op. 3, does not reach the level of the Op. 9 group—it does not aim at it—but it would be unreasonable, in my view, to criticize it with hindsight, as if it were a sketch for later attainments. Much may be learnt from viewing a composer's life work as a continuous process (if his development is powerful

241

enough, as Beethoven's decidedly is); the danger in this rather popular approach, however, is that it may lead to the blurring of individual works. Ultimately, individual works of art are all that exist, and that is how they are meant to be experienced. We cannot get out of Op. 18, No. 1, what Beethoven put into it if we listen to it with the ears we use for the *Grosse Fuge*, or even for the 'Razumovsky' Quartets. And it is what the composer put into each work that is what we should try to find, rather than damaging the concentration of our perception by telling ourselves what it was that he was not yet able to say.

It is perhaps not surprising that Beethoven, before embarking on the adventure of his quartets, and with the achievements of Haydn and Mozart in mind, should tackle the more rigorous medium of the string trio—more rigorous, that is to say, in the sense that it is more difficult to create a sonority productive of momentum with three than with four parts. His three Op. 9 Trios are rightly quoted as the *locus classicus* for astonishing weight and richness of sound in this medium; the real difficulty, however, is not to find the means of producing a full texture (the liberal use of multiple stopping and luscious harmony can easily take care of that), but to make the movement of the parts themselves develop an organic energy without attenuating themselves. It is surprising how often the second violin in a quartet will be found to save the situation; the string trio must live without it. The miracle of Beethoven's trios is that nowhere do they suggest its absence, and where double-stops are used, the purpose is more often to provide contrasts of colour than to fill out harmony that could be expressed in no other way. Beethoven could easily have found a pleasing way to harmonize the second theme of the G major Trio in three parts, without recourse to double-stopping; but he wants the consistent, fascinating sound of the violin chords mingled with the other two instruments playing single notes (see Ex. 1). The four-part texture is emphatically not quartet music *manqué*—it is a sound possible only with a string trio, and the succeeding counter-statement, in three parts, confirms the composer's freedom and security in handling the medium, emphasized by the way in which the violin crosses the other two parts.

Ex. 1

Beethoven resorts to the obvious trick of giving see-saw arpeggios to the viola (so leaving the other instruments free to play tunes on either side of it) only when the demands of contrast make it desirable—and this happens surprisingly rarely. He knew only too well all the devices his contemporaries and forebears used automatically. The E flat Trio, Op. 3, clearly suggested to him by Mozart's masterly Divertimento in the same key (K. 563), makes remarkably sparing use of this device (of which Mozart is not shy), and although this early *jeu d'esprit* cannot match Mozart's masterpiece, it is evidence of Beethoven's taking absolutely nothing for granted.

Trio-writing, then, is proved by Beethoven early in his career to be something notably different from quartet-writing—more different, in fact, than the string quintet, which medium may not unreasonably be regarded as an enriched quartet, while the quartet itself cannot by any stretch of the imagination be thought of as an enriched trio, or a proper trio as an impoverished quartet. It is possible (when confronted with some performances, at least) to sympathize with Sorabji's unfriendly description of Bach's solo violin works as 'ghastly grinning skeletons', but one wonders if even Verdi (who dismissed Mozart as a '*quartettista*') would have found Beethoven's string trios in any way inadequate. By virtue of their very sufficiency they compel us to regard quartet-composition as another matter altogether.

The essence of classical music is momentum, generated by vigorous reactions between tonal, harmonic, rhythmic and thematic elements in equally functioning proportions—equally, that is, when the totality of the work is considered, though they may at different times during its course leap individually into the foreground. The

basis of classical harmony is the manipulation of four parts; this is
not the place to examine the reasons for this, and it must suffice to
observe that in classical music the triad and the seventh (which
modifies the extra-note octave and turns the dominant triad into a
genuine four-note chord) are fundamental, that functional harmonies of more than four different notes are extremely rare and
that when they occur may almost always be construed as distor-
tions or intensifications of simpler forms. This somewhat brusque
description may serve to hint at why the string quartet became one
of the central interests of classical composers. Stringed instruments,
too, are capable of the finest intonation, the most flexible expressiveness, and the greatest range and agility. Beethoven was not the man
to spend too long performing balancing feats with a string trio;
as soon as he had learned to enjoy handling a three-wheeler his
interest in making more purposeful journeys took over, and for this
four wheels were more comfortable than three, enabling the driver
to concentrate on the road rather than sometimes wondering if he
is going to overturn on sharp corners. The medium of the quartet is
less obtrusively acrobatic than the trio; so it recedes into the background, allowing full concentration on the character and structure
of the music itself. This is one of the reasons why Op. 18 seems at
first impression less adventurous (in general) than Op. 9; the first
of the quartets to be written (D major, No. 3) rejoices for the most
part in smooth euphony, while his revision of the second (F major,
No. 1) is an absorbing study in clarification and in the closer
articulation of counterpoint and form.

Too many writers have treated Op. 18 apropos Haydn and
Mozart, and particularly Mozart, to whom Beethoven's backward
glances are sometimes so obvious as to distract attention from his
own individuality. Yet the most ostensibly Mozartian movement in
the group (the first of the A major, No. 5), for all that it is almost the
slightest piece in the whole set, could have been written only by
the young Beethoven. It shares with the more aggressive C minor
Quartet (No. 4) a guilelessness that is positively sardonic in the
other work and which perhaps needs some pugnacity if it is to be
effective. The sardonic side of Beethoven in his earlier years is
prominent in his music and if we appreciate it to the full we shall not

be in such a hurry to find crudities in the C minor; but it is almost reduced to casualness in the first movement of the A major and turns into his own brand of elegance in the other three movements. Comparisons with Mozart do not help here—Beethoven's elegance has different aims, and the grace of Mozart's A major Quartet, K.464, is intellectually self-conscious compared with Beethoven's (in this case) much more naïve pleasures. Why should we want it otherwise? It was not until his last period that Beethoven was able to achieve an elegance that might just be called Mozartian, and there it serves a range of expression beyond Mozart's ken. If we merely try to see how the young Beethoven falls short of the Mozart on whom sometimes he appears to be modelling himself, we miss the fact that this music is so deeply different that comparisons are not really possible. Harmonic range and a vaster sense of movement (even in apparently entertaining music) have something to do with it—very much, in fact. The last movement of the D major Quartet has sometimes been unfavourably compared with the finale of Mozart's D major Quintet, K.593, also in a lively $\frac{6}{8}$ time; but from the very start Beethoven is setting out bigger lines and already shows a more comprehensive sense of movement than his senior. It would be possible wickedly to point out the 'superiority' of Beethoven by quoting both main themes and noting that Mozart's (Ex. 2a) persists lumpishly in squatting every two bars or so, while Beethoven's (b) soars with the freedom of a bird in full flight:

Ex. 2

Beethoven's tune is actually shorter than Mozart's, but it contains in itself the momentum of the whole movement—from the start we have the sense of a large stride—whereas Mozart's energy develops only after the theme, with its circling repetitions, is over. But such comparisons are basically as unfair as the more common reverse kind, which are made all the easier by the confrontation of Beethoven's youth with Mozart's experience. Where we may perhaps permit ourselves to speak of Beethoven's superiority, however, is in this very matter of scale-potential, or power of suggestion where momentum is concerned. In this even the young Beethoven can be superior to any other musician who ever lived. And it is this power that is fundamental to the immensity of his later achievement, that is behind his unequalled range of human expression. So we must be careful not to fall into any traps when thinking about his early music against what we fondly imagine to be its 'background' in Mozart, Haydn or Clementi. And in the limited space of this essay it is only the surpassing power of the quartets of Op. 59 and later that makes discussion of Op. 18 perforce constricted.

Nevertheless, we must not leave Op. 18 without making at least one point about each of the quartets. Despite some inequalities (and we need not blind ourselves to the fact that Beethoven had never written quartets in his life before) these six works, sometimes to the point of recklessness, express a wider range of colour and feeling than any group of six by Haydn or Mozart. Opposite the bluntness of the C minor lies the almost genteel elegance of the A major, informed by an amused restraint with a trace of irony in it—'So you think me crude?' The C minor goes in for crunching homophony, the A major for suave polyphony; the young composer whose rude manners could shock was also at this time very careful about his dress. But neither work courts superfluity, and the disconcertingly slender first movement of the A major is in its way as ironically elliptic as that of the C minor, which bluffly shoulders its way past. Where polyphony enters the C minor (as in the second movement) the effect is directly flippant, much more so in this context than in the First Symphony, whose *Andante* is less spiky and more relaxed. Neither the C minor nor the A major aims at profundity—only the F major does that— and, so far as the C minor

Quartet is concerned, much harm has been done by the expectations aroused by Beethoven's famous 'C minor mood', as if there were such a thing in a generalized sense. C minor often incites Beethoven to blunt energy, but never to the same mood twice. Contemplate his C minor works individually, for once—Op. 1, No. 3 (piano trio), Op. 9, No. 3 (string trio), Op. 10, No. 1 (piano sonata), Op. 13 ('Pathétique' Sonata), Op. 18, No. 4 (quartet), Op. 30, No. 2 (violin sonata), Op. 37 (Third Piano Concerto), Op. 62 (*Coriolan* Overture), Op. 67 (Fifth Symphony), Op. 80 (Choral Fantasia), Op. 111 (piano sonata): are they really all in the same 'mood'? Parts of them share a certain trenchancy, but the difference between the trenchancies of, say, Op. 10, No. 1, and the first movement of Op. 111 is as wide as between Op. 10, No. 3, and the 'Eroica', which are in different keys. We seem to digress, but the point is that most criticisms of Op. 18, No. 4, miss its sardonic humour by expecting a C minor Titan.

One might pair in contrast, both with these two and with each other, the D major and G major Quartets, one for the most part consciously serious and smoothly architectural, the other overtly witty and dry (the dryness decidedly petrifies the *Adagio* of the G major—in my view the only really perfunctory movement in Op. 18). The G major is essentially epigrammatic, which perhaps explains why its slow movement, in the manner of the finale of Haydn's Op. 54, No. 2, has to resort to a quick middle section. Haydn's movement, however, is a finale, and that is its point—the quick section sounds deceptively like the beginning of the 'proper' finale, and when it is dismissed by the original slow music the entire work is given a new dimension. Without sensing the full genius of Haydn's idea (and without an *adagio* theme as beautiful as Haydn's) Beethoven could do no more than give the impression of interrupting tedium, and with something that lacked the teasing deceptiveness of Haydn's *Presto*: we are not expecting any kind of finale. But the rest of the G major is as witty as all but the most brilliant Haydn and, in the last movement, fiercer. One of the wittiest strokes is at the recapitulation in the first movement, where the cello comically anticipates the event, causing the theme, when it does enter at the right time (on first violin), to fall over itself in canon. The stiff crotchets and minims paradoxically suggest the kind of weightily spacious preparation for the recapitulation we might have expected in the D major's first movement. But there Beethoven magnificently allows the moment to happen as a harmonic surprise—straight to D major from the dominant of F sharp minor (as at the same point in the later Second Symphony):

Ex. 3

In the G major Quartet the harmonic (or tonal) surprise is reserved for a little later, with a delightful turn to E major.

The two quartets Beethoven placed first and last in the published set are also markedly contrasted, but they both have a penchant for extremes of expression. The F major, however, is perhaps the strongest and most concentrated of all six works, and it may be significant that it was the only one to have undergone rigorous revision. The B flat quartet, on the other hand, is ostentatiously disparate in its content; some suggest that it may instinctively be foreshadowing the enormous variety of Op. 130, which oddly enough is in the same key. But whereas Op. 130 (*pace* Joseph Kerman[1]) is a magnificent unity (with the *Grosse Fuge* as finale), this work does not digest its disruptive elements. Its incredible syncopated scherzo (the most original in Op. 18, and one that could have occurred in a late quartet) and the groping, explora-

[1] The work by Kerman referred to here and later in the chapter is *The Beethoven quartets* (London, 1967).

tory *La malinconia* are opposite extremes, but neither is remotely like anything that had ever been heard before. The last movement, deeply split between *La malinconia* and a bland *Allegretto*, leaves a strange atmosphere behind it, through which one can still hear the cold brisk wit of the first movement. From all this the statuesque, occasionally ornate *Adagio, ma non troppo*, with its indolent expansiveness, seems curiously detached. All the same, the B flat Quartet is a work of genius, unconvincing, not because Beethoven has failed to say what he managed to say later, but because he has not quite succeeded in giving unity to the elements he has brought together. He failed, perhaps, to say what he wanted to say at the time. It is too fanciful to drag in Op. 130, either as the goal at which Beethoven was unconsciously aiming or as a later and vaster dissociative essay.

The F major shows the most perfect mastery of all the early quartets, both in equality of part-writing and succinctness (as well as breadth) of form. From its first page great tension is developed, and the nervous energy and concentration of its first movement give rise naturally to the dark and dramatic, yet finely disciplined *Adagio affettuoso ed appassionato*. Most unusually, the scherzo—rather than rekindling energy, as is normal—is quietly soothing after the slow movement, and its humorously modulating, dynamically varied trio does not really disturb this impression. Relaxed and brilliant, the finale completes the sense of a maturely dispersed knot of feeling; the last two movements are curiously complementary to the first two. It is important that the finale should not be taken too fast—in fact, Beethoven's original version marks it *Allegretto*, and his subsequent change to *Allegro* means that he felt *Allegretto* to be too slow, *too* easy-going. But there is no excuse for rushing it (as is often done) and trivializing it. Beethoven's revision of this work two years after its original composition caused him to remark: 'I have now learned to write quartets properly'. We cannot do justice here to the wealth of detail in his revising, nor to the lessons to be learnt from it by all students of composition, and it must suffice to note a couple of characteristic points. It was not merely a question of quartet-writing *per se*, but of composition; for Beethoven the two things were inevitably inseparable. Notice

how as an afterthought he tightens the thematic tissue—in the
first version the cello at bar 30 in the first movement is answered by
a new violin figure:

Ex. 4

A little later he extends the main figure of the first movement thus
(bar 42, first violin):

Ex. 5

In the revision (and surely he must have thought of it before but
for some obscure reason restrained himself?) he decisively brings
the two figures into close relationship (bar 42):

Ex. 6

Phrase-proportions, harmonic and tonal relations, chordal
balance, rhythmic and thematic interrelationships, all are made
more powerful in the revision. Again in the first movement, a great
stretch of the development is not only bodily transposed first by a
minor sixth and then by a fifth but is also made rhythmically more
concentrated, and the approach to the recapitulation is more
strongly energized by a fresh use of the Neapolitan D flat that was
not, and could not have been, possible in the original scheme. The
two versions are published in Section VI, Vol. 3, of the new Beethoven edition published by Henle, and readers are advised to
compare bars 137–84 in the original with bars 129–78 in the revision.
In revising the slow movement Beethoven severely controlled its
originally rather gusty dynamics and greatly refined its earlier
operatic flavour, so that the explosive moments are all the more
potent. Many hours of pleasurable enlightenment may be had from

studying the differences, large and small, in the two versions of all four movements.

Between the Op. 18 Quartets and those of Op. 59 lie about six or seven years and the 'Eroica'. A whole world, in Beethoven's terms —but we cannot properly appreciate it if we persist in regarding Op. 18 with complacent indulgence, as do many writers; the more we find in Op. 18, the more we are capable of getting from Beethoven's greater works. The bridge between the two worlds is built of works other than quartets, and the only piece of chamber music for strings belonging to this interim stage is the splendid Quintet in C, Op. 29 (with two violas), which lies nearer to the first than to the second period. This work, which may be in some ways regarded as a crown to Op. 18, is still shamefully neglected. As a whole it has greater breadth and economy of line than even the F major Quartet, Op. 18, No. 1; fine works for this medium are not so plentiful that chamber players can afford to ignore it as often as they do. Although there is a sufficiency of accomplished five-part writing and one gets the strong impression for much of the time that the quintet is (as suggested earlier) an enriched quartet, Beethoven contrives also to create from time to time an almost orchestral richness and weight, especially in the vividly resourceful 'storm' finale (which, however, twice defies all precedent by disgorging a curious jocular few bars of *Andante con moto e scherzoso*). The first movement is magnificently broad and sustained, and anticipates the Triple Concerto by placing its second group in A major and minor, an uncommon direction from C major (at least at this stage in Beethoven's career). The slow movement, richly elaborated yet of deep simplicity of expression, is one of Beethoven's most spacious from this period, while the large-boned, expansively genial scherzo must surely often have been in Schubert's mind, and the trio even more so (it can be ruined as much as many of Schubert's trios by playing it slower than the scherzo). Unlike some of Beethoven's earlier works, this quintet shows few traces of a desire to absorb influences from or to rival superficially similar works by Mozart or Haydn. It is possible to fabricate an elaborate pseudo-critical scaffolding on supposed relationships between Beethoven's and Mozart's wind-and-piano quintets, or between

Op. 18, No. 5, and Mozart's K.464 (many writers have led themselves gaily and plausibly into exaggeration along these lines). But none of Mozart's string quintets is a possible model for Beethoven's; there may be a dim forerunner somewhere else, perhaps among Aloys Förster's by no means negligible works (which Beethoven knew and spoke well of), but Op. 29 is likely to escape this kind of critical treatment.

With the deceptively plain opening of Op. 59, No. 1, we enter a world fantastically remote from that we have been considering. The years 1803–6 (this last the year of the 'Razumovsky' Quartets) were the most amazingly prolific period of Beethoven's life. From the 'Waldstein' Sonata onwards there is a close succession of masterpieces of terrifyingly consistent quality; the 'Waldstein' is Op. 53 and was followed by the small but subtle F major Sonata, Op. 54, the 'Eroica', Op. 55, the Triple Concerto, Op. 56 (which solved Beethoven's concerto problems once and for all), the 'Appassionata', Op. 57, the G major Piano Concerto, Op. 58, the three 'Razumovsky' Quartets, Op. 59, the Fourth Symphony, Op. 60, the Violin Concerto, Op. 61, and the *Coriolan* Overture, Op. 62. At the same time he composed the first version of *Fidelio* and its staggering retinue of overtures, and was sketching the Fifth Symphony (indeed more than sketching—half of it was fully composed before the 'Razumovsky' Quartets, of which more later). If there are still any romantic illusions about Beethoven the laborious Titan wrestling with recalcitrant muses, this list of works alone, and the speed with which it was accomplished, should do something to disperse them. Not one of these works is remotely similar to any other; think of the beginnings of all of them, and the far-reaching uniqueness of each is at once manifest. That of the F major 'Razumovsky' Quartet is both plain-sailing and astounding. Who else, before or since, began a classical *allegro* with two stretches of what is basically $^6_4$ harmony? The opening cello theme is from the beginning what must be felt as a decorated root of a $^6_4$ F major triad, and when F appears on a strong beat (bar 6) the immobility of the harmony above it (which has not changed since the start) makes sure that the hollow $^6_4$ feeling is still prevalent. When the harmony itself changes in the second half of bar 7, the cello G is at the bottom of a second inversion dominant seventh, which feels like yet another $^6_4$. No wonder there is such tension behind this unemphatic beginning, and the tension is enhanced by the obstinacy of the harmony and (until the harmony becomes explosively orthodox in bars 17–18) by the steady regularity of the phrase-lengths. And no wonder the first strong F major emphasis in bar 19 gives rise to serious harmonic question-marks within the new theme that immediately follows it, a theme that one would expect to be comfortably consolidating the tonic. That function is held off until as late as bar 30, by which time the sense of scale is gigantic. A huge book could be devoted to the means by which Beethoven creates a sense of size at the beginning of a work.

The sublime instability of the opening progression of $^6_4$ chords has, of course, even larger consequences—at the beginning of the development (this is Beethoven's first repeatless *allegro* in a quartet, and the theme returns *on* rather than *in* F before the development, as if a repeat has begun) and in the recapitulation. In both places the G becomes a disruptive G flat; in the development it is at first explained away as a flat sixth in B flat, and in the recapitulation, by acting as an insistent subdominant, it forces the tonality to D flat. And just before the recapitulation the 'harmonic question-marks', intensified, after a long and breathtakingly orthodox dominant preparation, anxiously jumping the gun, as if to forestall the terribly disturbing $^6_4$ progression, make the sudden *piano* of the actual reprise seem sphinx-like, almost like a serene but minatory judgement. It is not until the coda that the main theme is heard with strongly rooted F major harmony—and what tremendously tense harmony it is! This strange and stupendous movement, with its vast calm fugato in the middle and its extraordinary blend of serenity and inner force, is, like all Beethoven's great conceptions, unique. In it fate does not knock at the door—it stares through the window.

After this the remarkable *Allegretto vivace e sempre scherzando*, covered with subtly conveyed confusion, permeated by human pathos, is the only possible immediate reaction—disturbed humour and a frequent stammer. Despite ingenious theories to the contrary, it is a sonata movement—of great irregularity, certainly, but organic. The width of its tonal range is very different from that of the first movement, yet like that it is founded (if that is the right word) upon productive tonal instability. But where the first movement grows from a direct harmonic phenomenon, this scherzo relies on abrupt juxtapositions of tonalities, such as the switch from B flat to A flat in bar 9, and the incursion of D minor (the remotest key from A flat) at bar 39. It is characteristic that the whole first group, enormous and seemingly unstable, occupying the first hundred-odd bars, should make its final transitional modulation with sudden dispatch, so that the second group (in the dominant minor) can start at bar 115. The unstable first group is suddenly given stability in the recapitulation by the turn to the dominant at bar 304, and everything hangs on our perception that this passage is *on* not *in* the dominant of B flat. Such subtleties (and here the effect is truly subtle) are the very life-blood of sonata.

The stare of fate is discomfiting, but it cannot be met for long with nervous humour, nor with tears: if the F minor *Adagio* is rightly played, and not distorted with lushly applied emotionalism, it is heard as the withdrawn music it really is, a private kind of funeral march, comparable with that in the 'Eroica' just as Op. 95 may be compared with the *Egmont* Overture. Such ceremonial accents as it has are faint echoes of the larger human issues raised in the personal experience of any single individual. The use of appoggiaturas is curiously formal and unsentimental (of course, the bad artistry we so often hear in performance can easily falsify it), and the movement of the parts confirms Beethoven's intentions. It is a sonata design of the utmost spaciousness (all four movements of this work are sonata structures); like the scherzo it puts its second group in the dominant minor—but this is a minor-key movement, so the effect is strongly oppressive, and the rare gleams of major serve to intensify the darkness when it returns. A sense of strength is created by the many instances where Beethoven harmonizes otherwise what any other composer would have made an appoggiatura. At the end the gloom lightens almost imperceptibly; suddenly the atmosphere is Arcadian. After the first movement the whole of the rest of this quartet must seem dreamlike, and although the *thème russe* with which the finale opens suggests some kind of awakening, its tonal ambiguity, suspended between Beethoven's F major and the original folk-song's Dorian D minor, has a magical air. The magic is both confirmed and enhanced by the F sharp Beethoven substitutes for D at the beginning of the development; no note could have been more marvellously chosen, and to omit the repeat of the exposition literally halves its effect. The whole movement is full of gliding and floating harmony, and there is a sense in which the $^6_4$ progression that began the first movement is never far away; like the main subject of the first movement, the *thème russe* starts by decorating a $^6_4$ root, but here the Dorian tendency makes for a greater air of insubstantiality. At length Beethoven allows the tune to slip into its native melancholy and the slow tempo in which Razumovsky must have known it, but with a wonderful harmonization; B natural slips to B flat and C sharp to C natural, recognizing, but instantly and touchingly repudiating the Russian D minor, before the whole vision is dismissed by the clapping of hands.

Two sharp handclaps, and a new vision—that might be one way of describing the beginning of the E minor Quartet:

Ex. 7 Allegro

But Beethoven would, I suspect, resent the description. The profound nervous sensitivity of this first movement does not lend itself to picturesque fancies. But it would not, perhaps, be too fanciful to see the E minor Quartet as a reaction to the whole F major work in the way that the scherzo of the F major is a reaction to its first movement; the E minor's anxious questionings are purely human, as is the wry restiveness of the scherzo of the other work. In contrast to the F major, the E minor states its tonalities solidly; the frequent Neapolitan inflexions confirm rather than undermine them, emphasizing the anxiety and its basis. E minor is clearly defined, the adrenal glands located. Yet a romantic subjectivity is no more behind this quartet than the F major or any other great Beethoven work; everything is too sharp and clear for that. There is also an objective element of contrast in the whole—the serenity of the slow movement is the reality against which the rest functions. In the first movement Beethoven exceptionally directs both exposition and the whole development and recapitulation to be repeated, with powerful confining, circling effect, against which the calm expanses of the *Molto adagio* are all the more impressive and to which its moments of intensity refer. All four movements of the quartet are in E, minor or major, and it is curious that this phenomenon occurs in all four of Beethoven's works in E, the others being the Piano Sonatas, Op. 14, No. 1, Op. 90, and Op. 109. So far I have been able to think of no easy explanation of this, and the matter is perhaps aesthetically complicated by Beethoven's transposition of Op. 14, No. 1, into F major when he arranged it for string quartet— the value of the cello's low C outweighed in this case any attachment he may have had to the original tonality.

The immense contrast between the first two movements is mitigated by a subtle melodic link. The first movement concentrates on the interval of a semitone, often Neapolitan, but equally often E, D sharp and back again. The last point of comparative relaxation in its coda occurs at bar 240, now significantly over a tonic as opposed to the original dominant pedal at its first appearance in bar 13:

Ex. 8

The interval is reversed at the end of the movement:

Ex. 9

The slow movement at once makes it a new point of departure:

Ex. 10   Molto adagio

The climax of the *Adagio* achieves an extremely intense harmonization of the transformed main theme by accentuating semitonal movement in the bass. This has sometimes been compared with an even more intense passage in the slow movement of Op. 132, but the point of the later passage lies in its incandescent diatonicism. In the present work the harmonic structure is powerfully and organically chromatic.

The quietly obsessive *Allegretto* anticipates the characteristic Brahmsian third movement. Again semitonal and Neapolitan inflections are prominent, melodically, harmonically, tonally; we begin to see the sense of the monotonality of the quartet as a whole. In this and the Piano Sonatas, Op. 90 and Op. 109, wide contrasts are knit by common tonality and by melodic connections: in the trio Beethoven gives Razumovsky the promised Russian theme; as in the F major Quartet, the concession is not without whimsicality, and here it occasions some canons as rough as some of Beethoven's puns. He was to write more such trios. In this movement the return to something like the nervous sensitiveness of the first movement brings about a double repeat of scherzo and trio—confining, circling movement again, to be finally emphasized in the last movement, a kind of sonata-rondo with a powerful irregularity in its development-cum-recapitulation. It begins by hitting the flat sixth very hard, as if it were a key (C major), so at a blow consolidating the Neapolitan tendencies of the quartet as a whole and relieving the ubiquitous E tonality. The approach to the recapitulation (and the coda) is one of three variants in the use of a texture by Beethoven at similar points in different works, the other two being the 'Waldstein' Sonata and the Fourth Symphony (both, however, in their first movements). They represent three stages in the idea, the quartet in the middle. In the sonata the preparation is straightforwardly on the home dominant. In the quartet it is on the dominant of the apparent foreign key in which the movement and its main theme began. In the symphony comes the highest subtlety; the development gets into a very remote key (dominant of B major), and then the drum treats its A sharp as B flat (it can do nothing else because its associations with the tonic are irresistible) and a crescendo brings about the recapitulation without intervention of the home dominant.

The third 'Razumovsky' Quartet, with its very mysterious

introduction, has a (more clandestine) rapport with two of the symphonies. Beethoven had suspended work on the C minor Symphony at the end of its second movement, knowing that he needed to have a special magnetic kind of scherzo. But apparently it would not come, and in the meantime he wrote the Fourth Symphony, with is dark groping introduction. He also produced the C major 'Razumovsky' Quartet, with another even more secretive opening. Then came the scherzo of the Fifth Symphony (which was originally to have been the Fourth); at first it ended formally, *forte*—then, surely as a result of the introductions to the B flat symphony and the C major Quartet, he got the tremendous idea of reducing the final reprise of the C minor scherzo to *pianissimo* and linking it mysteriously to the finale of the symphony. A further development of this train of thought was the storm in the 'Pastoral' Symphony—only the known course of events enables us to trace this extraordinary chain of ideas.

At once the most 'classical', the strangest and the least describable work in Op. 59, the C major Quartet fits no category, either in Beethoven's world or outside it. Its incredible themeless introduction, with its cryptically exhaustive treatment of the diminished seventh, is yet far from static, as we might expect it to be. Joseph Kerman makes a penetrating observation when he points out that the sense of harmonic direction 'seems to hinge on the fact that while embellishments to the diminished-7th chords may sound very excruciating, in actual fact they limit the ambiguity of these chords'.[1] Beethoven's appoggiaturas both increase the mystery and point the way. The sphinx finally indicates a country more Arcadian even than the finale of the F major Quartet, and the first *Allegro* is as sunny as that of the Fourth Symphony. It is also capricious yet balanced, expansive yet in the end abruptly truncated—full of strangely complementary contradictions, with a marvellous development which slowly turns the first two notes of the movement into a mighty song of mountain air, as mysterious in its way as the introduction.

How to describe the A minor second movement, as uniquely hypnotic as the *Allegretto* of the Seventh Symphony? Like the

[1] Ibid., p. 136.

introduction to the quartet, it is a kind of fixation, now on thematic as well as harmonic elements; the contrasts between plain diatonicism and sharply accented chromaticism are themselves obsessive, and the almost ceaseless rhythm produces a fateful fascination. Apart from the innocent second subject everything is in minor keys, and the movement exploits the strain between the polar regions of A and E flat; the unusual sonata design, with reversed recapitulation, adds to the sense of strangeness. So far, what is real in this work, the painful mystification or the light of common day, or both? Both, says the amazingly bland minuet—*minuet*! A powerful but mysterious C major scherzo would not have been impossible here, an uprushing of energy such as Beethoven was always capable of wresting from the dark. But the power is to come; in the meantime normal light is switched on. Its very 'normality' is mysterious, for it is still the normality of Arcadia, not the everyday world—it is the memory of the world that Beethoven has seen vanish, though he was born into it. After this—reality, the fight to exist and be something: 'Make no secret of your deafness, not even in art', wrote Beethoven over the sketches for the finale. Would it be far-fetched to deduce a connection between the extraordinary plan of this work and the composer's now severe affliction? Could the introduction be deafness itself, and the ensuing *Allegro vivace* relief that the inner ear is unimpaired? Is the obsessive pain of the *Allegretto* perhaps what Beethoven felt about the outward effects of his deafness? Might the minuet be a memory of the kind of music he once heard most clearly? The words 'not even in art' must be particularizing, meaningful. In my view it would be neither romantic nor sentimental to suppose what I have tentatively suggested; the inner life of the music seems to support the idea, which does not suggest that Beethoven was subjectively dwelling on the mood of the moment, any more than he was in the 'Eroica'. The introduction is like a man struggling to *hear* something, and the *Allegro* his inward success. As for the finale, its tumult comes from within, blotting out the despair and nostalgia of the two previous movements, drowning the sense of failure where ordinary means of communication were concerned. Fugato and sonata, fused together with a heat that Mozart could never have conceived, generating defiant realistic energy—with these means Beethoven hammers out his greatest quartet finale so far, fiercely stretching the medium, yet never breaking it.

By 1809 Beethoven's enormous burst of creative power was, for a time, waning; but in this year his works show a calm sense of consolidation, the Fifth Piano Concerto, the Piano Sonatas, Opp. 78, 79 and 81a (the first of these the beautiful work in F sharp) and the next quartet, in E flat, Op. 74. His circumstances and personal problems were more than troublesome, yet his work, though less momentous than in previous years, shows an impressive quiet confidence. Op. 74 is an underrated masterpiece of deep, consummate beauty of thought and execution. Much of the subtlety is grounded in the introduction, with its marked subdominant tendency, influencing the first movement proper, and in particular its majestically lyrical main theme. The introduction has some labyrinthine harmonies and mysterious touches but is lit from within by a deep, quiet, human warmth—so different from the frozen rigour of its counterpart in Op. 59, No. 3. Characteristic of this work (and already prophetic of the last period) is the anticipation of the tonic major on the very last quaver of the introducton, which cunningly makes the authoritative start of the *Allegro* more surprising than it would have been had Beethoven held up the resolution a half-beat longer. The first movement has two superb flights. The development generates magnificent energy in a sustained C major passage, perhaps more simply powerful than anything in the earlier quartets, except for some parts of the finale of Op. 59, No. 3, and here the relaxation produces a wonderful exhilaration, enhancing the easy but strong tension with which it subsides into a long and equally simple stretch of dominant preparation, pervaded by the pizzicatos that give this work its rather silly nickname of 'The Harp'. The other outstanding passage is the main body of the coda, where the crescendo is gloriously dominated by the brilliant bravura of the first violin while the texture forms and solidifies beneath it, a new and daring way of creating a quartet climax, impossible to repeat or imitate. This movement is bolder and more adventurous than it looks on paper; I never fail to find it thrilling.

The beautifully composed *Adagio ma non troppo*, in A flat, lives upon fine melody. As with the slow movement of Op. 59, No. 1, it has suffered from too heavily upholstered performance; Beethoven marks the main theme '*cantabile*', not '*molto vibrato*'! It is a kind of slow rondo with a fine-drawn coda, upon which the fiery C minor scherzo bursts. Any scherzo in C minor must recall the Fifth Symphony, but this demonstrates yet again the falsity of the hoary old notion about Beethoven's 'C minor mood'; there is no minatory quality here—simply masterly control of energy, and even the rhythm of the symphony's first movement (eased by the triple time) elates rather than threatens, while the rough counterpoint of the blustering trio has more in common with that of the E minor Quartet than with its more superficially comparable counterpart in the symphony. But there is an ironic connection with the symphony all the same—the scherzo almost vanishes in a muttering *pianissimo*, and action nearly ceases in what is obviously a link (this after double repetition). Instead of fierce triumph, however, there follows an impudently amiable theme that is not nearly so naïve as it sounds; we do not realize that it begins with an upbeat until we get the gentle jolt of its cadence, and the repeat; and its first half ends on a bright G major chord (the dominant of C minor, the key that has just evaporated). A set of simple variations ensues, simple but far from naïve, always with a more than interesting treatment of the half-close, culminating in the perennially fascinating sixth variation in which an obstinate pedal E flat defeats the original half-close. In Brahmsian vein, the second part finds the pedal throbbing on D flat—a cunning hint of the subdominant overshot, in reference to the tendency of the first movement, and touched lightly but formidably again in the coda. This finale could not be more right, or more unexpected.

About a year later came the fantastically concentrated F minor Quartet, Op. 95. 1810 was lean, but the two major works completed were the *Egmont* music and this quartet. The overture and the quartet have something in common: both are in F minor, and both end with a deliberately dissociated coda in the major and a new tempo. In the overture the intention is plainly programmatic—the blatant fanfare ordered by Alva to drown Egmont's speech on the scaffold proves, despite the tyrant's intention, inspiring. Is it possible that in composing the quartet Beethoven expressed the inner thoughts of Egmont, as opposed to the public effect displayed in the overture? If it were so, the astoundingly lithe and delicate F major coda to the quartet finale could aptly represent the hero's fleeting sense of justification and release at the moment of death, and the dissociative nature of the music itself, oddly convincing as such, might have an additional extra-musical motivation. The same key, the same dissociation, and the quartet, moreover, written without a commission, from inner compulsion alone—Beethoven must have been absorbed in Goethe at the time, and I do not see how an inner connection between the two works can be disproved.

One of the most important consequences of the F minor Quartet's extreme concentration is the amount of space Beethoven is able to create. The action in the first movement is packed into short periods, so that there is a surprising degree of what might almost be called leisure in the piece. The structure itself is unique. Like the E minor Quartet, Op. 59, No. 2, it exploits Neapolitan and semitonal elements, but in a different way. The abrupt start is answered on the dominant by a leaping octave figuration that already produces trenchant rhythmic irregularity (a bar more than expected, not a bar less, as would be devised by anyone else bent on achieving startling bluntness!):

Ex. 11

The answer on the flat supertonic being held up a fraction, the steam goes out of it and it melts back into the home dominant:

Ex. 12

262

This already makes a sense of space that one would not have fore-
seen from the opening; imagine Ex. 11 reduced to absolute
regularity, followed instantly by an equally regular flat supertonic
answer, thus:

Ex. 13

We may have shortened the second phrase so that the answer can
come in 'on time', but in making room for it we allow it to occupy
too much space, to say nothing of the platitudinous effect compared
with Beethoven's. His extra bar seems to warn the platitude off—it
approaches, but turns away. The harmonic point of the Neapolitan
relationship, however, is made, time and space are won, the urgency
heightened where Ex. 13 would have reduced it. The apparent
relaxation on to the home dominant gives a sense of giant muscles
being flexed, and the main subject returns with added power and
authority in F minor. Now it stretches, and there is a very quick
modulation to D flat, where the second group begins at once.
This change is so sudden that we cannot quite believe in D flat
(especially after the repudiation of its *alter ego* G flat), but Beethoven nevertheless keeps the music floating in this harmonic region
for some considerable time. This is not the place for an extended
analysis, but the point of the foregoing is that F minor is never
undermined by anything that happens in this movement; the
development breaks in sharply and turns out to be even more of a
dominant preparation than the passage following Ex. 12, and it
leads, not to the opening, but to the counter-statement that came at
bar 18. This turns exactly as before to D flat for the second group!
But, says Beethoven, we were right to be suspicious about the
reality of D flat, and it slips quietly to F, where the second group
continues as if nothing had happened. The coda savagely (and in
the end mysteriously) consolidates the tonic. The unreality of D

flat in the exposition is emphasized by the flat supertonic D major scales that break in on it at bars 38 and 49; the normality and solidity of F in the recapitulation is confirmed when Beethoven changes this relationship to the ordinary supertonic G minor at bars 107 and 118.

The D major of the extraordinary *Allegretto ma non troppo* is, despite the remote harmonic clouds in the centre of the piece and the tortuous chromaticism of the fugato that gives rise to them, as strongly in possession as was F minor in the first movement. Yet its remoteness from F minor and the manner in which it is introduced make it and the terrain it colours seem so unreal as to be almost hallucinatory; the effect would be impossible without the extreme solidity of F minor in the previous movement. The whole quartet is concerned (perhaps like *Egmont*) with two worlds, the real and the ideal, the first embodied in the harsh F minor (Beethoven's 'barbarous' key), the other imagined in remote keys, or keys deliberately made to seem unreal, such as the D flat in the first movement, the D major in the second, or the marvellous translations into distant keys in the two trios of the scherzo. When the D flat of the first movement eventually slips back to F it is like a vision held in spite of circumstances (hence also the blunting of the D major interruptions into G minor, instead of the analogous G flat major). By the time the finale comes the vision is lost, and the only hope lies in total dissociation—hence the astonishing F major coda. Beethoven was neither romanticist nor pessimist; human realism in a terminal situation is perhaps the burden of this, his most genuinely revolutionary work. It may be that *Egmont* did not give him the outlet he needed to explore the nature of the revolutionary mentality; the F minor Quartet certainly did.

The revolutionary element in Beethoven's nature was never iconoclastic or destructive; he was always consolidating—not only his own discoveries, but also the past, whose achievements he never ceased to study with the deepest respect. We can understand the late quartets only in the light of this. The F minor is often regarded as a kind of anticipation of the 'third period'; decidedly its elisions and compressions, and its dissociations, freed him for new courses of action, but that work remains a special case nevertheless.

The later works take advantage of ground broken by the F minor, but they go further in the direction of consolidation of a vaster past than he had hitherto been able to reach. None of his works is more 'classical' than Op. 127. By the time he started it (1824) he had entered another phase of prodigious creative energy. There is a fearful sense of effort in Op. 95; effort is certainly conveyed by the *Missa solemnis*, the Ninth Symphony, and the 'Hammerklavier', yet there is already a mighty expansiveness in these works that puts them in another category altogether. Between 1816 and 1825 came the last five piano sonatas, the Diabelli Variations, the *Missa solemnis*, the Ninth Symphony, the overture *The Consecration of the House*, the E flat Quartet, Op. 127 (as well as much of the A minor and B flat Quartets), and other things, including some of the wonderful Bagatelles of Opp. 119 and 126. The remaining last quartets were done by the end of 1826. When one considers the magnitude and the exploratory nature of most of these works, this period, though longer, becomes comparable with the burst of 1803–6; and Beethoven's circumstances were much more difficult.

As in most such periods of fruitfulness, consolidation and exploration go hand in hand. The late E flat Quartet, for instance, is even greater in scale than that eminently exploratory work, the first 'Razumovsky', yet the work is self-contained, compact, economical —in a word 'classical'—while at the same time the sound world is utterly new. Its very opening is a new blend of formality and rhythmic ambiguity, while the ensuing *Allegro* is thematically one of the most close-fisted he ever wrote, yet still giving a sense of superb ease and expansiveness out of all proportion to its length. Its disturbing elements (and it does contain these, despite its reputation for serenity) are encountered and dispatched with concentrated abruptness, finally when the introduction majestically dismisses them in C major at the height of the development. They attempt to invade the music again (see bars 147 ff.), but are beautifully absorbed by one of the most exquisite moments of recapitulation that Beethoven ever devised (bar 167). The introduction never comes back, but its appearance in the development in C major rather than at the recapitulation in the tonic is a stroke of genius

that enables the composer to discover magic in the last movement—
we remember it in that foreign key, but would not if we heard it
once more in E flat. Its C major also deepens the effect of the subdominant in which the variations of the second movement are cast,
and of that sublime third variation in E (really F flat), to which in
retrospect it seems like a bright foil. Four variations and a coda—a
simple enough plan, but the theme is vast and the variations of the
utmost subtle elaboration, contrasted in character with surprising
sharpness, every note inspired. The last full variation, with its
great striding arpeggios marching skywards past the slow soaring
of the theme, the air alive with the singing of birds, surpasses even
the 'Scene by the brook' in the 'Pastoral' Symphony as a response
to nature. The only possible reaction to it is mysterious, and the
coda (in true classical vein) opens *sotto voce* in the subdominant,
turns to a shadowy minor (D flat minor spelt as C sharp minor),
brightens, and drifts into another (repeatless) variation before
settling quietly, not without a brief reference to the E major of
Variation III.

There follows one of the largest and strangest of Beethoven's
scherzos, contrasting fragmentary counterpoint with vivid jagged
unisons—the suppressed disturbances of the first movement are
rising to the surface. Curious thematic transformations manifest
themselves:

Ex. 14

The last-quoted of these is marked '*Allegro*'; the time is changed for
those few bars to $\frac{2}{4}$. With Beethoven *allegro* is always slower than
vivace (the main indication for the scherzo); what he requires here

is two crotchets in the time of the previous three, or so is my belief. If he wanted no change of tempo, why add '*Allegro*'? It is astonishing how rarely this marking is at all interpreted; the crotchets are usually allowed to go marching on at the same pace, with a complete loss of the mystery the composer clearly intends. Perhaps many quartets fear that two in the time of three would be too slow—but most of them play the scherzo too slowly anyway. This absorbingly capricious movement gives way to a wild trio in the minor that disappears as suddenly as it came. Like the trio of the Ninth Symphony, it is cut off before it can come round a second time, but more kindly and wittily.

The finale exploits a popular vein that was no less dear to Beethoven than to all other classical composers; indeed, the late quartets, besides being complex beyond anything in his earlier chamber music, show a determination that this side of his art should be more than ever clarified and lightened. The use of simple folklike couplets is more evident in these works than in any earlier music, by Haydn, Mozart or Beethoven, and the depth of their context makes certain that triviality is impossible. The regular irregularity of the main theme of this finale (it is twice eight bars, but does not feel like it) displays what Tovey used to call the cloven hoof and is made all the more unpredictable by the weaving tonal ambiguity (at first on the dominant of C) that introduces it. Both these elements give rise to glorious developments, but there is an added subtlety in the use of C major—inevitably brought about by the introductory phrase at bar 106 and later on emerging to initiate a magical coda in a new tempo (*Allegro con moto*). This refers to analogous events in the first movement and adds a dimension to what would otherwise be a charming but plain-sailing finale.

The last quartets were not written in the order of their opus numbers. No greater contrast could be imagined than between the E flat work and the one Beethoven composed next, the A minor, Op. 132. Even the keys are poles apart; the A minor is predominantly dark, though it rises in the *Adagio* to a luminosity that makes the E flat seem like a warm coal fire compared with the sun. A great deal has been written about the ramifications of the phrase with which the A minor begins, not only in that work itself, but in the two following quartets, the B flat and the C sharp minor. I do not propose to amplify it here, but may perhaps be permitted to express some scepticism about attempts to attach too great a significance to the phenomenon. It is not unnatural that Beethoven should have found various meanings and possibilities in this series of notes, both melodically and harmonically, and even tonally. I do not see, however, that our understanding of any one of these master-pieces as a work of art is substantially increased by an awareness of any elements it may have in common with the others. Each is self-contained, an organism; we must grasp each individually as such before generalizing further. I have no objection to such generaliz-ing, provided it recognizes the integrity of individual works of art. As soon as it ceases to do so, my interest evaporates. Unfortunately much writing on this subject, however ingenious, is as valuable as a survey of the surface of Mars from a submerged submarine in the Atlantic.

The truly imaginative ingenuity of Beethoven may be seen in a comparison of two utterly different movements that on the face of it might be thought to have nothing in common—the first movement of the A minor Quartet and the finale of the Eighth Symphony. The latter creates an exhilarating 'circular' motion by means of two developments and two recapitulations, thus producing a gigantic-ally magnified rondo effect. Rondo is a potentially endless form that could go on as long as one cared to add segments to it; sonata, on the other hand, is a closed structure that dictates its own end, yet is packed with strictly canalized energy. To break it open is like exploding a hydrogen bomb in space above the earth—the debris would spread round the planet in a great ring. If there were enough debris, the ring (like those of Saturn) would be visible and, though it would be revolving, would appear static. Beethoven's purpose in releasing such a 'ring' at the end of his Eighth Sym-phony is a sublime one—to make the dynamic so immense that it seems in a magnificent sense static, an illusion based literally on revolutionary principles. The effect in the symphony is thrilling; in the A minor Quartet it is indescribably tragic: the 'ring' in the symphony seems as if it has been released; in the quartet it seems trapped. The quartet movement has not the energy for a second development (the second recapitulation follows almost at once), and it seems to fall into a low orbit around a dark and gloomy planet, seemingly in danger of being sucked down at any moment. One dares not try to imagine what Beethoven would have thought of such an analogy, though perhaps his would not have been much worse than the opinion of some of my readers; but it seems to me a possible, though inadequate, means of describing two amazing imaginative feats.

Circling motion of a different kind is present in the second movement, *Allegro ma non tanto*, another example of remarkable thematic economy. The tightness of its principal section is offset by the expansive freedom of the ethereally folklike trio (all his late trios are in the same keys as their parent scherzos), a freedom that allows him to break rhythmically and thematically into it with grotesque, barely related material:

Ex. 15

Modal elements had already entered late Beethoven—in the *Missa solemnis* and the Ninth Symphony notably—but never quite with the frankness of the Lydian mode in the *Molto adagio* of the A minor Quartet. He consolidates his link with a remote past in a hymn of thanksgiving on recovery from an illness, an intense serenity soon to be shattered again, and in this very work. The classical ear (and our own) can never be sure that it hears the old modes as their original creators did—classical tonality breeds almost ineradicable habits, instincts if you prefer. Schoenberg might blot them out, but an ancient mode has too many things in common with a classical key for that. Otherwise Beethoven would not have been able to move at all from the Lydian F to the classical D major for the contrasting material (*Neue Kraft fühlend*); and the strange convalescent lightness of the Lydian mode as Beethoven uses it is probably not a sensation that would have been felt by Palestrina— on our ears (and, I think, on Beethoven's) its effect is due to the fascinating gentle pull of classical C major, from which we cannot and should not try to escape by a conscious effort to archaize our habits. Sibelius relies on similar productive confusions in his Sixth and Seventh Symphonies. The A major chord that eventually brings about D major is not only an ancient textbook way of cadencing the Lydian mode—A lies midway between the quietly tugging F and C, and it is a disruptive A major that finally shatters the mood altogether, in the *Alla marcia* that follows the *Adagio*. I cannot attempt to describe the wonderful static power of this slow movement; too many have tried already. Before leaving it, we may as well note that there is a serious misprint in many editions; in the penultimate bar, the first violin should sustain A throughout the bar, not fall to an F halfway through—it is vital to the cadence, and I have heard very few performances that observe the correct reading.

There is nothing more startling in music than the little *Alla marcia* that follows all this with such cruelly bland abruptness; it provokes protest, in recitatives closely related to those in the Ninth Symphony, for whose finale the theme of the quartet's seems to have originally been intended. How stupidly and coarsely these recitatives are often played! Beethoven does not mark them '*fortissimo, molto vibrato, violente e brutto*'! The dynamics, until the last tearing phrase, are restrained, as indeed they are in the finale itself, for all that it is marked '*Allegro appassionato*'. The first *ff* occurs in bar 71. This heartrendingly beautiful rondo is perhaps a kind of translation of Mozart into a different sphere; the pathos of the A major in the coda is very near to that of some of Mozart's last-minute transformations to the major, now informed with a new kind of wild intensity, conveyed with high originality by switching the registers of viola and cello.

Op. 130 seems to be Beethoven's most controversial quartet. For some reason the key of B flat became for him the vehicle of immense power-struggles—witness the 'Hammerklavier' sonata, the 'Credo' from the *Missa solemnis*, the *Grosse Fuge*. Joseph Kerman has some hard (and I think strange) things to say about the 'dissociative' nature of Op. 130; rather than attack his viewpoint, I would put forward some positive observations of my own. First, dissociation is a positive factor for unity in this utterly original work; it functions most successfully with the *Grosse Fuge* as finale. To take the largest aspect first, tonality is certainly the strongest large-scale dissociative factor. The opening movement puts its second group in G flat—but how ?—by a modulation so abrupt, after a powerful preparation on the *home dominant*, that the 'key' of G flat is no more than a hugely extended chord, not a believable established tonality at all. One is reminded of Op. 95, though now the large calmness of the whole second group is curiously mesmeric. The return to B flat at the repeat (which includes the introduction) sounds as if B flat has never been seriously challenged. We can hardly fail to re-member this when the same phenomenon occurs (though there we can expect no repeat to rub in the point) in the *Grosse Fuge*, whose second stage comes in a G flat approached with equal lack of cere-mony and equally unreal as a key. With a vengeance the sound of G flat is now associated with a sense of unreality, and in this case with a particular subject, rather than a string of ideas such as emerged in the first movement:

Ex. 16

pp

As soon as B flat is restored (the ⁶/₈ *Allegro molto e con brio*, bar 233) it is taken for granted as never having been really disturbed, just as B flat is, in fact, never seriously shaken in the whole of the first movement (which is why Beethoven is able to slip so casually into his recapitulation). Much later in the *Grosse Fuge* he reaches a tremendous climax in the astonishing key of A flat, the one key most likely to undermine B flat by making it behave as an 'enhanced dominant' (the dominant of the dominant). But this climax is crowned by Ex. 16, which we decisively associate with an unreal key—so A flat is placed in real doubt, it collapses, and dark rumblings lead to B flat and a resumption of the *Allegro molto e con brio*. This music, associated with stability, settles the matter, and B flat sounds again as if it had never been attacked. So the dissociative use of G flat has an associative long-term meaning, making it possible for Beethoven to erect a great climax in the 'impossible' key of A flat without destroying or even damaging the real tonic. Even without the first movement this scheme is effective enough in the *Grosse Fuge* alone, which is why Beethoven felt able to issue it separately, but if the fugue is played as finale to Op. 130, we have gigantic 'dissociative' uses of G flat at each end of the vast quartet. At the very centre of the work lies the *Alla danza tedesca* in G, magically dissociated tonally from the preceding movement in D flat (a polar opposition); and the D flat has been reached through the B flat minor of the second movement. So there is a violent break, or dissociation, in the middle of the quartet, from which the tonality is eased back again to B flat through the E flat major of the *Cavatina*. The central dissociation produces a jolt where it is most needed as a reminder that such things are in the air—midway, and symmetrically, in the work.

Thematically Op. 130 is perhaps the most closely integrated of all the late quartets, a tissue of a density to offset the large-scale associative dissociations. Thematic derivations cannot of themselves ensure organic unity. But everywhere one listens in Op. 130 (with either finale) one hears pairs of notes clearly derived from the opening phrases of the introduction:

Ex. 17

It is not possible here to list the instances that strike me as deliberate and genuine—almost every important theme makes prominent use of these pairs or is accompanied by them. The prevalent semiquaver motion of the first movement is plainly evolved from them, and the piece makes play with them up to its last bar. The *Presto* constructs its theme from them. The *Andante con moto, ma non troppo* begins with them, and makes them an integral part of the accompaniment to its first theme and the backbone of its second:

Ex. 18   Cantabile

The *Alla danza tedesca* points them markedly:

Ex. 19

The *Cavatina* is positively permeated by them. The opening 'note-row' of the *Grosse Fuge* is like a devilish contraction of Ex. 17 and its G flat section concentrates entirely on the pairs of notes. So does the $\frac{6}{8}$ movement that follows it. There is scarcely a moment's escape from them. In the other finale they characterize the main subject and swarm all over the place, actually elongating themselves into an ending for the exposition (see bar 89, second violin and viola); they not only infiltrate the flowing A flat theme that starts at bar 109, but accompany it, too.

This brings up the question of the change of finale that Beethoven made under persuasion. The *Grosse Fuge* is clearly part of a grand design, if my observations are sound; it was with the greatest reluctance that he agreed to supplant it with something slighter. He knew it would stand alone, for the reasons already shown above, and it is possible that the thought of providing another ending to the quartet, totally different, was something of a challenge to his imagination. Obviously he did not subscribe to the absurd notion that music and logic are connected, that there can be but one consequent to a musical statement; from the same beginning he could have written a million satisfying 'Eroicas' if he had had the time, energy or inclination. But one thing he could not do. The scale of the new finale, if he were to provide anything like what was expected (and what he himself was certainly intrigued to try), could not encompass the dissociative-associative tonal dénouement so tremendously achieved by the *Grosse Fuge*. He must be largely content with the kind of thematic integration I have already outlined, though there is a sly element of dissociation in the use of A flat for the 'middle' theme, approached with amusing circumspection, left by an ostentatiously careful modulation to the dominant of B flat, and finally recapitulated in the tonic to disperse any suspicions of disruptiveness it might have aroused. A humorous ending to this compendious quartet is, as he proved, not impossible or inapt, but there can be no doubt that such a conclusion cannot integrate the whole as comprehensively as the fugue; vast issues may be hinted at, or dismissed, by a joke, but they cannot be exhausted. Nevertheless, we must not decry this marvellous and by no means small movement; it was the last thing Beethoven wrote and is in its way just as much a triumph over adversity as the *Grosse Fuge* itself. Alas, there is no space to speak of the prodigal variety and profundity of Op. 130, with whichever finale we choose; with the *Grosse Fuge* it is one of the greatest and most overwhelmingly impressive of Beethoven's compositions.

The C sharp minor Quartet has a perfection that is perhaps beyond controversy. Beethoven himself thought it his finest, and no one of any consequence has disagreed with him. Sometimes in the late quartets we feel that his attitude towards tonality is changing; the muscular athleticism so characteristic of the sonata principle dominant in his work seems at times to be giving way to a calmer, older method. He is now apt, Bach-like, to step on and off a tonality as one might get on and off a table (to recall Tovey's analogy). This is another aspect of his consolidation of history, his absorbing of influences from further back than ever he did in his earlier music. The C sharp minor Quartet thus opens with a fugue and reserves its first full treatment of sonata for its finale. Tovey has accurately analyzed the work, and others have noted the subdominant answer in the fugue, accentuating the note D natural, so that the wraith-like second movement floats upon the senses in that key. The miraculous variations come naturally in A major (which was also carefully illuminated in the fugue), where they stay for a very long time without deviating, their wonderful variety unified by the key as much as by the theme. The amazing thing about the scherzo is that it is not (as is usually assumed) in E major; it is *on the dominant of A*. This is where the cello interrupts the variations, and E major is never rid of that association, never substantial as a tonality—if it were, the very scale of the scherzo would make the emergence of a finale very difficult. Notice how Beethoven always avoids a strong dominant of E by blunting it into G sharp minor; as soon as the dominant of E tries to assert itself the music positively wilts:

The trio inevitably drops (half way through) into A, and the return each time to the scherzo (with detached pizzicatos) does not assert the dominant with enough weight to redress the matter fully; the last time these pizzicatos occur, in fact, the note D sharp is pointedly eschewed, and they are on the dominant of A. The tendency towards G sharp minor in the scherzo produces the elegiac introduction to the great C sharp minor finale. The dominating anapaest rhythm of this last movement recalls that of the E minor 'Razumovsky' Quartet, but now there is a vast sweep and scope completely beyond the terms of the earlier work. The flat second, D, performs miracles of unification, especially at the recapitulation of the second group. (Is there a more marvellous piece of quartet-writing than this passage?) The unity of this mighty conception, from the profound contemplation of the fugue to the magnificently conclusive statement of the finale, is so clear, so utterly convincing, so completely original, that it defeats all attempts at criticism, rendering them impertinent. The work has the clarity of the simplest classical quartet, and a power beyond that of any other composer's mightiest symphonies.

Before considering Op. 135, there is one more intriguing point about a passage in Op. 131, made here simply because I have not seen it explained anywhere else. It concerns the third of the variations, *Andante moderato e lusinghiero. Lusinghiero*—coaxingly: 'curious coaxing', says Kerman (and he is not alone in being thus mystified), 'with those carping trills and *sfp's* and hair-raising dissonant clashes in the repeated second strain'.[1] But surely it is the *first* strain that is doing the coaxing, with its sweetly persuasive canon—the second strain is being coaxed, like some recalcitrant animal sticking its nose out of a hole. At first the nose only is visible (bar 105); later the brute creeps out with slow reluctance (bars 113 ff.) to emerge into the glorious light of the next variation. Programme music! God knows why, wonderful though it is.

Beethoven's final quartet, the F major, Op. 135, is his last completed composition, except for the second finale to Op. 130. It has the light touch of infinite wisdom and charity; smaller than the others, in scope as well as dimensions, it is nevertheless something only the vastly experienced Beethoven could have written. Its exquisitely reticulated first movement draws on what he had learnt in such passages as Variation II in the second movement of Op. 127, the *Andante* of Op. 130, or the *Neue Kraft fühlend* section of the *Heiliger Dankgesang*. Even as far back as the coda to the *Andante cantabile* of Op. 18, No. 5, we can find the beginnings of this particular genius, a delicately ambling style, light, airy, never mincing, the parts very free and strong and fine, with a great variety of detail, and deep subtlety of harmony. It is the most sensitively coloured quartet-writing in existence. He has not done it in a first movement before, though the piece in Op. 130 is a full-sized sonata design, without development, but with an extensive coda. Now it sets the tone of a work. There is much quiet humour in it, as well as the mystery of all perfect things. It leaves us unprepared, perhaps, for the extraordinary scherzo that follows it, a movement of astoundingly dislocated rhythms and syncopations and fire-breathing, suppressed energy—suppressed, that is, until the trio, which lets fly the force of an exploding atom. The staggering A major climax of the trio, which eventually subsides, muttering, into the scherzo with the most weird transition Beethoven ever wrote, makes a violent polar opposition to the fierce unexplained E flats that with rhythmical disruption invade the scherzo.

After this the utter quiet of the *Lento assai, cantante e tranquillo* is so extreme as to breed another kind of tension, equally great. It is a set of three very slow variations on a theme of the utmost simplicity,

[1] Ibid., p. 335.

the middle variation in the minor, full of breathless oppressed pauses, more frozen then the *beklemmt* section of the *Cavatina* of Op. 130, and the last moving quietly into a trance-like coda. There is nothing relaxed here, nothing decorative—only an iron self-control; the contrast with the scherzo is too enormous for anything else to be possible. The key of D flat is heavily subdued, and rarely do the instruments explore beyond moderate registers. The reaction to this is F minor, and *Der schwer gefasste Entschluss*—the difficult resolution. Solemn Germans have breathed much philosophical hot air into this situation, which arose from a joke of Beethoven's about someone who owed him some money, who, when asked to pay up, moaned, 'Muss es sein?', to which Beethoven, with some lack of originality, replied, '*Es muss sein!*', thereupon setting the words to an atrocious canon. Kerman treats the introduction to the last movement of Op. 135 (above which Beethoven quotes these words against the relevant themes) as a not very good joke. While deploring too much dismal theorizing, I feel that his attitude takes too little account of what has been happening in the quartet. Some kind of difficult resolution *is* necessary after that fantastic scherzo and the sublime paralysis of the slow movement. The hard step-wise progression of this introduction, painfully edging its way upwards towards light and freedom of movement, is inescapable, and it breaks out with delighted relief into what *must* be—life again. The F minor and the slow grind return once more (twice more if the second repeat is observed, as it should be), now intensified and more theatrical in an inextricable blend of humour and seriousness, and more subdued questions precede the delicate laughter of the end. Beethoven, as always, is in favour of life and at this late stage is not prepared to argue any more. There is, I think, some significance in the fact that the second group of this movement, the gayest and simplest material, is cast in A major, the key of the trio's overwhelmingly vital climax, while the only traces of D flat are elliptically hinted at in the struggling introduction.

Beethoven's quartets may not be summed up. They represent most of the main stages in his development, though not all; the piano sonatas show a more continuous process, but the quartets reach further into his last period. Falling conveniently into three groups (or four if you regard Op. 74 and Op. 95 as a separate pair), they reveal Beethoven at crucial stages in his incomparable career. There is nothing else like them in the whole of music, except in Beethoven's own work, and they reveal, like the sonatas and the symphonies, that of all composers he possessed the widest, deepest, most active and most realistically hopeful genius. It is a platitude to say that his range of expression is Shakespearean; so it is, but he has a commitment to humanity that Shakespeare does not reveal. There has been no greater artist, and it is to be doubted whether any can match him.

IV
The Orchestral Music

SEVEN

The Symphonies and Overtures

BASIL DEANE

THE SYMPHONIES

THE UNIQUENESS of Beethoven's historical position, standing as he does between two ages and two philosophies, is nowhere more apparent than in his attitude towards the symphony. The symphony in the eighteenth century was essentially an aristocratic entertainment; to the Romantics it was a vehicle for self-confession on a grandiose scale. For Beethoven it was neither. It was a public work, not a private one. It did not reflect his immediate personal situation, not did he use it to symbolize an intimate human relationship: the Second Symphony was written at the time of the Heiligenstadt testament; and no woman was paid the compliment of receiving the dedication of a symphony or of an overture. But Beethoven's public was mankind, and he was mankind's spokesman. In his symphonies and overtures he proclaimed his concepts about life, concepts which, he believed, are of universal application: love of nature, desire for peace, freedom and brotherhood, the reality of conflict, of defeat, of triumph. To achieve his aim it was necessary for him to forge a new symphonic language, one direct in its impact, yet capable of a hitherto unexplored range of expression. The story of his symphonies is the story of his creation and extension of this language.

Beethoven's First Symphony (C major, Op. 21, 1800) has been dismissed as derivative or timid: Edwin Evans, for example, referred to 'the composer's hesitation to trust himself too far ahead of his compeers'.[1] But Beethoven never hesitated to advance beyond his contemporaries on his own path, as some of the earliest works show, and the First Symphony, in fact, declares its individuality from the opening bars of the *Adagio molto* introduction. Its originality does not reside in the opening chord itself—a dominant seventh on C—which is reputed, wrongly, to have offended contemporary critics; but rather in the nature and function of the introduction as a whole and in its motivic structure and its instrumentation. Just as the first chord is a dominant resolving into a tonic, so the harmonic function of the introduction is to create a dominant tension which will lead into, and be resolved by, the beginning of the *Allegro con brio*. To this end Beethoven avoids stating the tonic chord at the opening, and he moves in the first three bars on to a dominant chord, through three cadences, none of them a perfect cadence in the home key. These cadences develop the motive that is one of the generating forces of the movement, the diatonic semitone from leading-note to tonic. Further melodic tension is added by the fact that the interval connecting these pairs of cadential notes is the tritone:

Ex. 1

Beethoven's relationship to two different traditions is epitomized by the first theme of the *Allegro con brio*. The connection with the opening theme of Mozart's 'Jupiter' Symphony has often been remarked upon. But, despite the superficial similarity of the first bars, Beethoven's theme is worlds removed from the stately contrasts of Mozart's. Arnold Schmitz drew attention to another, more relevant antecedent, the opening of the *Ouverture de la journée de Marathon* by the French composer Rodolphe Kreutzer, to whom Beethoven later dedicated his Violin Sonata, Op. 47:[2]

[1] Cf. Edwin Evans, *Beethoven's nine symphonies fully described and annotated* (London, 1924), I, p. 19.

[2] Cf. Arnold Schmitz, *Beethoven* (Bonn, 1927), pp. 99–100.

Ex. 2

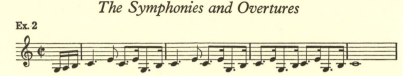

Kreutzer went to Vienna in 1798 with Count Bernadotte, who was often in Beethoven's company. Whether or not Beethoven knew the French work, his theme is closer in spirit to Kreutzer than to Mozart. At the same time it far surpasses that of the Frenchman in its intensity and vitality. The theme is generated melodically by the semitone, and the first four bars are linked to their repetition a tone higher by the woodwind semitone motive. Thus, although the melodic line of the opening paragraph is continuous, its structure and provenance are made explicit by the orchestration. This technique, which might be described as 'motivic orchestration', is not, of course, without precedent: the second subject of the first movement of Mozart's Symphony No. 40 in G minor offers a striking example. But it plays an increasingly important role in Beethoven's symphonic thinking. The second subject in this movement is another example of its use:

Ex. 3

The other features of the exposition may be summarized: a 'primitive' preparation for the second key—a half-close on to the dominant of the home key; an extension of the second subject by a modulating bass melody; and a re-introduction of the opening motive in the codetta. The development demonstrates the seriousness of Beethoven's conception of this section, and also his instinctive tendency to start from simplification and symmetry. It is based on three passages, each consisting of a triple sequence on a four-bar phrase, and each dealing with one aspect of the thematic material. The first two are descending sequences, the third ascends by step. The result is a curious blend of energy and colour provided by the material and its instrumentation, and scholasticism arising from the excessive use of sequence. The return to the tonic key is by way of the dominant of the relative minor, a Haydnesque device. If this method of approach is unoriginal, Beethoven's triumphant restatement of the opening theme on the full orchestra is a stroke of individual genius and underlines his sense of the importance of this point in the movement. The brilliant coda confirms that he conceives of the recapitulation, not as a repetition, but as the culmination of the movement.

The slow movement is less successful. The opening theme and its manner of exposition suggest that it was originally conceived as a fugue subject. Its weakness lies in the fact that the paragraph loses its contrapuntal impetus and comes to stagnate on a four-times repeated half-close. (A comparison with the beginning of the slow movement of Mozart's Symphony No. 40 is illuminating.) The main interest of the movement is in the detail of the instrumentation: the woodwind in development and coda, and the *pp* trumpets and drums, whose dotted rhythms add a new emotional dimension to the music. The *Menuetto*, on the other hand, is a splendid achievement and marks the transformation of the form into a fully-developed orchestral scherzo, breaking free from traditional binary proportions. The opening eight bars are followed by a second section of seventy-one bars, which include a remarkable development, a *f–ff* restatement and a codetta. The same instinct for full restatement leads to the surprise entry of the whole orchestra at the end of the otherwise lightly scored trio.

The *Adagio* introduction to the last movement, *Allegro molto e vivace*, with its gradually expanding scale figure, has often been regarded as a Beethovenian joke, and not always as a good one. But it has two useful, and serious, functions. It cancels the effect of the *ff* conclusion of the minuet; and it draws attention to the rising scale which forms the anacrusis to the main theme and which plays an important part in the subsequent thematic argument. The movement has been described as Haydnesque. It is not one of Beethoven's most inspired conclusions; but, in the character of its themes, its formal directness and above all its orchestration and its rhythms, it is distinctly characteristic of its composer.

In some respects the Second Symphony (D major, Op. 36, 1802) represents an important advance in Beethoven's conception. The sketches of the work that have survived, and in particular those of the first movement, throw a revealing light on the composer's methods and attitudes.[1] In this case Beethoven does not follow his general practice of hammering out his themes before sketching the entire movement. Instead he conceives the exposition as a whole from the start, and refines his ideas in successive versions. The first sketch shows the principal theme of the *Allegro* used also as the introductory material:

Ex. 4

In the next version the *Allegro* theme is recast, and an independent short introduction is added:

Ex. 5

In subsequent sketches the composer expands, then rejects, his introduction completely, substituting a new idea, which was to lead eventually to the final version. The *Allegro* theme, however, remains, its rhythm sharpened by the dotting of the minims and the consequent compression of the turn. This change is illuminating for its relevance to Beethoven's attitude to thematic unity.

---

[1] For a valuable presentation and discussion of these sketches, see Kurt Westphal, *Von Einfall zur Symphonie* (Berlin, 1965).

Two important passages in the exposition, the transition to the second group (Ex. 6a) and the continuation of the second subject (b), are derived *rhythmically* from the original version of the opening theme:

Ex. 6
a

b

By changing his opening theme Beethoven obscures this particular thematic derivation, especially as the note sequence is different in each case. This suggests that he was not concerned with establishing a motivic relationship between different themes in the same movement, although he was very concerned with their subsequent working-out.

In its final version the *Adagio molto* introduction is at once traditional and original: traditional in that, unlike that of the First Symphony, it establishes the tonic harmony at the outset; and original in its subsequent harmonic and thematic range. Haydn was accustomed in his late symphonies to beginning a major work with an introduction in the tonic minor. In this symphony Beethoven takes up this relationship and applies it within the movements themselves. Thus the introduction is in D major; but its climax is a *ff* arpeggio of D minor. In the *Allegro con brio* another *ff* arpeggio of D minor occurs in the second group. The development sections of the first, second and fourth movements all lead off from a tonic minor version of their respective opening themes.

The second theme of the *Allegro con brio* (bar 73) has in its shape and orchestration a military flavour, and its non-lyrical character enables Beethoven to introduce it into the development. In his earlier works his struggles with the second subject are often apparent. He clearly feels it desirable that it should be used in the development, along with other material from the exposition; yet the lyrical nature of so many of his second subjects militates against the

dramatic continuity of the section. So in the first movements of the
E flat String Trio, Op. 3, and the Piano Sonata in G, Op. 14, No. 2,
for example, the second subject sits uneasily in the developmental
sequence. In the Second Symphony it was Beethoven's intention
from the outset to include the second subject in the development, as
the sketches reveal. By concentrating on the motivic possibilities of
the third and fourth bars he is able to overcome the usual problem,
especially as these two bars are rhythmically similar to the corresponding bars of the main theme. Throughout this section the
thematic and harmonic handling is more assured and supple than in
the First Symphony. The coda, too, is richer in content; the sketches
show the gradual emergence of the final concept, in the course of
which the composer rejects various new treatments of earlier
material and incorporates a new idea altogether.

In its colour and lyricism the A major *Larghetto* far surpasses its
predecessor. The opening of the first theme is derived from a sketch
of a theme in G, which also gave birth to the theme of the trio in the
third movement:

Ex. 7
a: sketch

b: second movement

c: third movement, trio

Throughout the movement there is a wealth of melodic invention
which, as Tovey rightly observed,[1] was plundered by Schubert.

[1] Cf. Donald Francis Tovey, *Essays in musical analysis*, I (London,
1935), pp. 27–8.

And the orchestration is equally inspired. Trumpets and drums are omitted. Clarinets, used sparingly in the First Symphony, come gloriously into their own in the ninth bar and continue to play a self-confident part in the movement. Significantly, they are left out of the central tutti, as if Beethoven were determined to emphasize their new-found liberation from a continuo role. The other wind instruments, too, appear in constantly renewed combinations of colour.

By wilful fragmentation of the texture, rhythmic displacement, and contradiction of dynamic and harmonic expectations, Beethoven creates a scherzo which is both explosive and witty. The same qualities characterize the concluding *Allegro molto*. They did not arise spontaneously, as the sketches make clear. The memorable opening theme of the finale, for example, with its six bars unevenly divided between the violent head-motive and its more flowing consequent, originated in a prosaic eight-bar phrase, which the composer eventually compressed. Compression is also the basis of the development section, in which Beethoven achieves powerful effects by the dislocation of his material.

One of the outstanding features of the symphony as a whole is its orchestration. Beethoven employs the same orchestral forces as in his First Symphony: double woodwind, horns and trumpets, drums, strings. Yet the effect is quite different. Berlioz, a connoisseur, wrote with enthusiasm of the scherzo: 'To hear the different instruments disputing the possession of some portion of a motive, which no one of them executes entirely, but of which each fragment becomes in this way coloured with a thousand different tints in passing from one to another, one might easily indulge the fancy of being present at the fairy gambols of the graceful spirits of Oberon'.[1] Not only here, but in the other movements also, Beethoven uses his technique of motivic orchestration to relate structure and colour.

The Third Symphony, the 'Eroica' (E flat major, Op. 55, 1803-4), marks an expansion of musical scale which is without precedent in instrumental composition. How far this expansion is directly due

[1] Hector Berlioz, *A critical study of Beethoven's nine symphonies*, trans. Edwin Evans (London, n.d.), pp. 36-7.

to the non-musical associations of the work is impossible to decide. It is most improbable that Beethoven thought of the symphony as a connected series of tableaux, each related in its programmatic content to some aspect of heroic endeavour. On the other hand, two of the movements have programmatic associations, one explicit, the other implicit. So it may be that Beethoven's natural tendency at this stage to expand his musical forms was supported by his reflections upon his original subject. At all events he displays a breadth of vision and a mastery of design which are altogether Napoleonic. The first movement, *Allegro con brio*, establishes the majestic scale of the work with its unprecedented span of 691 bars. Such an expansion demands new techniques of thematic and harmonic structure. A greater amount of thematic material is needed. The themes must be flexible and 'open-ended' to avoid too frequent cadencing, and also easily identifiable. Consequently none of Beethoven's themes in the exposition is a self-contained lyrical melody; and all are so rhythmically distinctive that they may be identified by their rhythm alone:

To see how Beethoven's thematic technique has developed we may compare the opening of the movement with the corresponding passages in the earlier symphonies. In the First Symphony the first theme leads to a tutti statement of a new theme. In the Second Symphony the tutti begins as a restatement of the first theme, and then moves in a new direction. In the 'Eroica' the opening theme occurs three times, the third time as the full tutti (this fanfare-like climax, at bar 37, in which all the wind proclaim the opening figure, lends support to Schmitz's view that the theme is a form of military signal).[1] So Beethoven has at once expanded his form and made it more thematically coherent.

A comparison of the tonal structures of the development section of the first three symphonies is also revealing. In the first two the overall tonal curve may be represented thus: ⌣, with flattening in the first part, and movement to the sharp side in the second. This is applied in a simple form in the First Symphony. In the Second Symphony new thematic material (possibly derived from the second subject) is introduced just before the recapitulation, in the 'sharp' key of F sharp minor. This idea germinated in the composer's mind, and the sketches of the Third Symphony show that from the earliest stages Beethoven intended to introduce a new lyrical theme, in the 'sharp' key of E minor, towards the end of the development. The tonal curve here is similar in general outline to that of the Second Symphony—a flattening from D minor through the circle of descending fifths to the subdominant, A flat major, and a subsequent rise to E minor. It is, however, extended at each end: first, by the initial plateau on C which begins the development, and the transition to D minor; second, by the continued tonal development which occurs after E minor is reached, and by the prolonged dominant preparation for the return to the home key. In the first two symphonies the 'false' dominants before the recapitulation deprive it of some of its effect as the resolution of the tonal movement. In the third, the tension of expectancy built up by the dominant finds overwhelming release in the resolution. (The premature entry of the second horn, also an early inspiration of Beethoven's, is psychologically entirely plausible in its context.) The recapitulation is followed by a coda of enormous dimensions. In it Beethoven continues to 'develop' his material. But the effect is one of stabilization,[2] and some events of the development are now absorbed into the home tonality and transformed in significance.

The march as a category interested Beethoven throughout his life, from the early Variations on a March by Dressler of 1782 to the

[1] Cf. Schmitz, op. cit., p. 101.
[2] Cf. also above, p. 222.

Alla marcia in the A minor String Quartet, Op. 132, of 1825.
Examples appear in a wide range of works: opera, mass, oratorio,
incidental music, piano variations, symphonies, chamber music. Of
the fifty or so marches or march sections, only three are specifically
labelled funeral march: the *Marcia funebre sulla morte d'un eroe* in
the Piano Sonata in A flat, Op. 26, of 1800; the *Marcia funebre* of
the 'Eroica'; and the *Trauermarsch* for *Lenore Prohaska* of 1815.
Ernst Bücken suggested that the funeral march in C minor from the
opera *Giulio Sabino* (1781) by Giuseppe Sarti may have been a
model for Beethoven.[1] But a more likely, if still hypothetical,
precursor is Sarti's pupil Cherubini. A taste for funeral marches
developed in France during the Revolution, and one example which
became widely known was the slow march which begins the *Hymne
funèbre sur la mort du Général Hoche* by Cherubini, written in 1797.
Cherubini's march is an extended composition in D minor in which
the solemn orchestral phrases are separated by short drum rolls.
The melodic line, although naïve in its rhythmic monotony, has
some points of contact with Beethoven's theme:

Ex. 8

[1] Cf. Ernst Bücken, *Ludwig van Beethoven* (Potsdam, 1934), p. 79.

Whether or not Beethoven's initial impulse came from a knowledge of Cherubini's piece, he transcends the limited form of his contemporary. He extends the ternary design of march and trio by cutting short the reprise, adding a fugato episode, a full, re-orchestrated return of the main section, and a coda. This produces a structure akin to a rondo in thematic content and to an expanded ternary form in its tonal layout:

March			*Fugal episode*		*March*	
C minor —C major—C minor			F minor	C minor—(A flat—C minor major)		
a	b	a	c	a	(d)	a

Such interlocking of the sections allows Beethoven to achieve a wide range of emotional expression without any loss of unity. Further unity is created by the motivic connection between the several themes, deriving from the opening interval of the rising fourth. The rhythmic dissolution of the main theme on its final appearance, so appropriate in its symbolism, was, in fact, a late inspiration, arrived at after Beethoven had attempted a variety of more conventional endings. The scherzo, too, apparently so spontaneous in its rush of energy, reached its final form after much alteration. The constant factors throughout the creative process were the melodic phrase beginning in the seventh bar, and the thematic use of the three horns. In the final version the melody provides much of the thematic material, appearing as it does in a variety of keys; and the trio is dominated by the horn group. The other important element in the movement, the note alternation B flat–C in the first four bars, was a late discovery. The momentum it creates within a triple-time metre is a major factor in creating the impetus of the movement.

It seems at least unlikely that Beethoven, in his choice of material for the finale, was indifferent to its earlier associations. He had used the theme on three previous occasions, an occurrence remarkable in itself; as a contredanse, as the theme for a set of piano variations, Op. 35, and as part of the final dance in his ballet *The Creatures of Prometheus*, Op. 43. The official theatre bill described Prometheus as 'an exalted spirit, who found the men of his time in a condition of ignorance, and who refined them through science and art and brought to them civilized customs'. Such a figure, closer to the divinely inspired artist than to the politician or general, embodied for Beethoven, as for many of his idealistic contemporaries, the highest form of heroic action. As he had, in the second movement, transformed the funeral march into a full-scale symphonic form, so here he creates an entirely new type of variation movement, one in which the maximum amount of freedom is achieved in relation to the original material consistent with overall coherence, so that the form might be described a variation fantasy. The widely varying sections—fugato, march, slow variation, as well as more directly related material—are welded together in a continuous whole. In the final *Presto* the horns, which have set their stamp on the whole work, burst into a blaze of exultation.

So organic is the growth of each separate movement, so powerful is the effect of overall coherence in the symphony, that writers have inevitably sought to define the source of unity in the 'Eroica'. Most attempts have concentrated on demonstrating thematic unity between the movements. These attempts are often interesting, usually ingenious, but rarely completely convincing. It is easy to show a general resemblance between most of the themes, for the obvious reason that they are based on arpeggio outlines; but it is much more difficult to establish specific criteria of relationships within the broad category of arpeggio-based themes. Moreover, the pre-existence of the 'Prometheus' material has been a stumbling-block to those who would like to see an organic thematic unity developing throughout the work. Alexander L. Ringer has dealt with this point in detail.[1] He draws attention to Beethoven's known admiration for the piano sonatas of Clementi, and points to specific passages in the Italian composer's work as sources for Beethoven's ideas. Two examples of parallel passages may be quoted —see Ex. 9 on page 294.

These and some of the other examples which the author adduces are undoubtedly convincing in establishing evidence of the influence, whether consciously or unconsciously absorbed, of Clementi upon Beethoven. But his further step, which is supported

[1] Alexander L. Ringer, 'Clementi and the *Eroica*', *Musical Quarterly*, XLVII (1961), p. 454.

by thematic analyses of the Rudolph Réti type, is less easily acceptable. 'The *Eroica*, then, owes its formal coherence not to the horizontal relationship of its various themes but to vertical connections between the Clementi material and all the themes individually. In other words, the symphony draws its life's blood from a motivic body that does not really belong to it but has been assigned to it, as it were, for continuous reference.'[1] Nevertheless, this attempt to widen the question of unity beyond the 'horizontal relationship of . . . various themes' is a valuable one. Another scholar, Ludwig Misch, has dealt with the same question in a wider context.[2] Misch draws a distinction between 'relationship of motive' and 'stylistic relationship'. Stylistic relationship may derive from

[1] Ibid., p. 464.

[2] Cf. Ludwig Misch, *Die Faktoren der Einheit in der Mehrsätzigkeit der Werke Beethovens* (Bonn, 1958).

melodic, harmonic, rhythmic, motivic, textural or colouristic elements. If a stylistic feature occurs frequently in different movements of the same work it acquires a unifying force in the context of that composition.

Misch supports his argument by a consideration of the Fourth Symphony (B flat major, Op. 60, 1806). He suggests that the prime unifying factor in the symphony is a harmonic one: the relatively frequent occurrence of the diminished seventh, and also of the dominant ninth and leading-note chords, throughout the work. Other unifying factors include rhythmic similarities and interconnections between themes; and the character of the instrumentation. All of these elements contribute to create the specific 'style' of the work. Although this concept of unity as arising out of a complex of relationships of different kinds, occurring almost at random through the work, has not the logical attraction of the thematic unity theory, it does correspond more closely to the composer's methods of composition. It is clear from the sketchbooks that at any time certain musical elements—thematic, rhythmic, harmonic—were germinating in Beethoven's creative mind. Each element could develop in a variety of ways (the emergence of two different themes from the same matrix in the Second Symphony is a case in point). These offshoots, which will often, but not necessarily always, be incorporated into different sections or movements of the same work, may show a generic likeness. But there is no evidence to suggest, at least in his early and middle periods, that Beethoven was consciously striving for thematic unity as an end in itself.

The introductory *Adagio* combines in a remarkable way the apparently contradictory functions of the two earlier introductions. Like that of the Second Symphony, it establishes the key-note firmly at the beginning. Like that of the first, it leads forward to a resolution in the fifth bar of the *Allegro vivace* by avoiding a cadence on to B flat, with the defining major third. The opening paragraph develops out of the first interval heard in the work—the chromatic one B flat–G flat. The harmonic course of the following paragraph as defined by the bass may be summarized thus:

Ex. 10

The chromatic G flat is thus employed cadentially in two ways: as the flattened sixth leading down to the dominant F; and as the root of the dominant chord of B (G flat=F sharp), which is resolved by an interrupted cadence on G. This musical pun is reversed in the *Allegro vivace*, at the return to the home key at the end of the development (bars 261 ff.). In the development section Beethoven again uses his favourite descending sequence leading to a strong subdominant statement. The main arpeggio theme gives birth at bar 221 to a lyrical counter-subject of great charm, which disappears during the shadowy transition, but returns in outline in wind and first violins at bar 351 in the recapitulation.

The *Adagio*, in E flat, resumes the lyrical vein of the Second Symphony, but with greater concentration and correspondingly richer meaning. The intensely expressive melodic line is set against an impersonal background conjured up by the martial drumlike figure heard in the first bar. Sometimes the dotted rhythm predominates, as when it leads into the dramatic central outburst. Elsewhere it is temporarily absent, and the lyrical flow is undisturbed, as in the clarinet's beautiful second subject. Just as the martial figure begins the movement, so, too, it has the last word. Its presence lends a poignancy to the music almost unequalled before the works of the last period. The texture is a delicate tapestry of instrumental colours, in which each strand is distinctly perceived, giving it the special quality of chamber music on an orchestral scale.

The third movement, also marked *Allegro vivace*, although different from its 'Eroica' predecessor in so many ways, shares with it the interplay of duple groupings within triple time as a source of rhythmic energy. Just as the dominance of the horns in the 'Eroica' trio symbolizes the character of the whole work, so, too, the trio of the Fourth, with its emphasis on the woodwind as graceful soloists and their interplay with lightly scored strings, sums up the spirit of the whole symphony, which is confirmed by the alternating exuberance and lyricism of the finale.

The Fourth Symphony is no less typical of Beethoven's many-sided personality than its immediate neighbours. But it is the Fifth Symphony (C minor, Op. 67, 1804–8) which has come to be regarded by many as embodying the essential Beethoven, the individual who struggled against and conquered a relentlessly hostile Fate. How far in reality Beethoven did attain the victory over adversity that he could envisage so clearly and express so movingly is not easy to decide. But there is no doubt that his vision of conflict resolving in triumph is the starting-point for the Fifth Symphony. It was a vision which was not peculiar to Beethoven in that war-torn age. Schmitz has pointed out that the French revolutionary composers aimed at arousing two states of mind in their military music: 'élan terrible' when the army was preparing for battle; and 'éclat triomphal' when victory was finally attained. The well-known story of the soldier from the Napoleonic guard who, on hearing the symphony for the first time, sprang to his feet at the beginning of the finale and proclaimed 'C'est l'empereur! Vive l'empereur!' gives point to the relationship of Beethoven's work to the military tradition. Schmitz [1] suggested a more specific link by drawing attention to a resemblance between the beginning of Beethoven's first movement and a passage in Cherubini's *Hymne du Panthéon* set to the words

> Sur votre cercueil héroïque
> Nous jurons tous le fer en main
> De mourir pour la République
> Et pour les droits du genre humain:

Ex. 11

[1] Cf. op. cit., pp. 104–5.

The first movement is, of course, remarkable for its concentration on rhythmic development, to the virtual exclusion of melodic and textural elaboration. Tonally, too, it is extremely tightly woven. In the first movements of earlier C minor works, such as the Piano Trio, Op. 1, No. 3, the String Trio, Op. 9, No. 3, the Piano Sonatas, Op. 10, No. 1, and Op. 13, and the String Quartet, Op. 18, No. 4, Beethoven moves to A flat major before approaching the relative major in the exposition. By so doing he gives the second key the relative 'sharpness' in relation to the preceding material which is normally implicit in a major-key work with the move from the tonic to the dominant key. (The exception to this practice, the C minor Piano Concerto, is a special and interesting case.) In this symphony he moves straight to the relative major, E flat, and furthermore he relates the second group as closely as possible to the first by his use of the thematic material. In this way he minimizes as far as possible the differences between the minor and the major areas of the exposition and thus achieves the maximum drive and continuity through the section. The development parallels the exposition. Beginning with the first-group material in the subdominant, F minor, he moves upwards through C minor and G minor. Then the horn call which introduced the second group in the exposition again leads to the major mode and to a falling sequence. The horn motive then disintegrates down to a two-note pattern, then to a single chord, and at the same time the secure sense of tonality dissolves. When, at bar 228, the motive re-forms in a new pattern related to the opening bars, so does the tonality also begin to acquire direction. This new pattern reappears at the beginning of the massive coda. Thus here, as in the two preceding symphonies, Beethoven is concerned to integrate new developmental ideas into the recapitulation or coda, even if the idea itself derives, as in this case, from earlier material.

The martial aspects of the *Andante con moto* and the importance of C major as an anticipation of the final resolution in the symphony need not be stressed. The main theme itself had its origins in this sketch:[1]

[1] On the sketches of this symphony see *NB*, pp. 10–11 and 62–4, and *NZB*, pp. 528–34.

Ex. 12 **Andante quasi Menuetto**

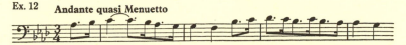

In the final version the accented appoggiaturas of bars 2 and 4 are removed. Hans Gál, referring to the melody as representative of Beethoven's mature style, defined the essence of Beethoven's 'absolute melody' as the avoidance of non-harmony notes on the main accents, and the restriction of ornamentation to diatonic passing and auxiliary notes, to the exclusion of suspensions and chromatic decorations.[1] He might have added that a further characteristic of the style, and one perfectly illustrated in this melody, is the prominence of the third, particularly the major third, of the harmony at crucial points of the melodic structure.

The third movement, *Allegro*, is a remarkable departure from Beethoven's usual approach to the scherzo and must be seen in relation to the violence of the first movement and the triumph of the finale. The extreme contrast between the shadowy *pp* figure rising from the depths of the orchestra, with its varied shapes, its apparently hesitant endings and its wayward tonality (B flat minor), and the answering *ff* horn call, its repeated notes recalling the rhythm of the first movement, seems to symbolize a mental rather than a physical conflict. In the extraordinary *pp* restatement of the first section the tonal uncertainty disappears and the horn call and its continuation dominate the thematic action. In the transition to the finale the device of suspending the sense of harmonic and thematic movement as a portent of coming resolution, which Beethoven uses *mutatis mutandis* in the first movements of this symphony and the preceding one, is now applied in a new and even more dramatic context. The brilliant finale, with its additional piccolo and trombones, resolves all uncertainties. The recall of the scherzo material before the recapitulation provides final evidence of the interrelationship of the movements. This is indeed, to use Paul Bekker's term, a 'finale-symphony', one in which the earlier movements lead up to the finale as the culmination of the work; with it the concept of the symphony is notably extended.

[1] Hans Gál, 'Die Stileigentümlichkeiten des jungen Beethoven', *Studien zur Musikwissenschaft*, IV (1916), p. 58.

The Fifth and Sixth Symphonies were both given their first performance at the same concert in December 1808. The fact that Beethoven worked simultaneously on two such diverse compositions emphasizes his ability to detach his creative expression from his immediate circumstances. Yet each work reflects a fundamental aspect of his philosophy. His love of nature was profound and of exceptional importance to his development. The artistic and spiritual refreshment which others might have found in religion, in intimate friendships or in contacts with fellow artists came to Beethoven through his solitary communion with nature. 'O God, what majesty in woods like these. In the heights there is peace—peace to serve Him', he wrote in 1815.[1] And the countryside awakened in him feelings of joy and stimulated him to increased creativity.

The conception of a programmatic work based on nature was not, of course, original, and it has been remarked that Beethoven has rarely been more open to recollections of other music than in his work on the 'Pastoral' Symphony (F major, Op. 68, 1807–8). Immediate precedents include a symphony by Justin Heinrich Knecht, 'The Musical Portrait of Nature' (1784), whose movement titles are very close to some of Beethoven's; a piano fantasia by Franz Jacob Freystädtler, 'Morning, Midday and Evening' (1791), from which Beethoven seems to have borrowed the introductory '*ranz des vaches*' of the last movement;[2] and, more generally, Haydn's oratorios and the so-called 'Toy Symphony' by Leopold Mozart, formerly attributed to Haydn. But popular and critical taste was reacting against musical imitation of natural sounds, and Beethoven himself was most anxious to formulate the relationship of his work to its source of inspiration in such a way as to exclude the charge of painting or 'Malerey'. After several attempts he eventually settled on the well-known and entirely appropriate phrase 'More an expression of feeling, than painting'.

Despite obvious differences, the twin symphonies have some

[1] On a scrap of paper formerly in the possession of the violinist Joseph Joachim.

[2] See Heinz Wolfgang Hamann, 'Zu Beethovens Pastoral-Sinfonie: Vorausnahmen eines Wiener Kleinmeisters aus dem Jahre 1791', *Die Musikforschung*, XIV (1961), p. 55.

points in common. Both first movements are in $\frac{2}{4}$ time, and they are almost the same length (No. 5 has 502 bars, and No. 6 has 512 bars). Yet where the Fifth is intensive and troubled, the Sixth is expansive and serene. Every aspect of the musical technique of the *Allegro ma non troppo* ('Awakening of happy feelings on arriving in the country') contributes to the creation of a mood of tranquillity. First, the almost total absence, not only of the minor key, but also of the minor triad. A minor triad occurs only four times in the whole movement, and never in the first or second group of themes. Second, the harmonic rhythm. The rate of harmonic change is so slow that in the development static chords replace key centres. Third, the importance of the relaxing subdominant, both as a chord and a key. It occurs frequently in the thematic structure as a I–IV or I–IV–I progression; the development begins in B flat major, and the return to the tonic at the recapitulation is through a IV–I progression. So B flat as the key for the second movement (*Andante molto mosso*: 'By the brook') comes as no surprise. Beethoven's struggles with the material of this movement, eloquently recounted by the sketches,[1] have been obliterated in the effortless flow of the final version. The repeated cadential extensions suggest a Schubertian involvement with the beauty of the individual phrase. The birdsong coda was a late addition, not, according to the composer, to be taken too seriously.[2]

The third movement (*Allegro*: 'Joyous gathering of country folk') is marked by a bucolic humour, expressed through abrupt modulations, uneven phrase-lengths, and evident parodying of village music-making. In the $\frac{2}{4}$ trio section the trumpets make their first entry in the symphony, with decisive effect. As in the Fifth Symphony, the return of the first part is considerably shortened and leads directly into the following movement (*Allegro*: 'Storm').

A piccolo and two trombones enhance the colourful score, whose agitation is resolved in the last movement (*Allegretto*: 'Shepherd's song; happy and thankful feelings after the storm'). In the Fifth

[1] Cf. *NZB*, pp. 369–78, on the sketches of this symphony, and on this movement in particular see Joseph Kerman, 'Beethoven sketchbooks in the British Museum', *Proceedings of the Royal Musical Association*, XCIII (1966–7), especially pp. 87 ff.

[2] Cf. *SB*, p. 145.

Symphony there is a spiritual progression; in the 'Pastoral' the mood of the opening, which has been disturbed by the advent of the merrymakers and by the subsequent storm, is restored in the finale. And there are many points of contact between the outer movements: the character of the melody; the broad harmonies; the importance of the subdominant. Two more specific comparisons may be made: the relationship between the two second subjects (see bars 67 ff. and 44 ff., respectively) and the similarity of these two passages, both near the end of their respective movements:

Ex. 13
a: first movement

b: finale

The Seventh Symphony in A major, Op. 92, was written in 1811 and 1812 and received its first performance, together with the 'Battle' Symphony, Op. 91, 'Wellington's Victory in the Battle of Vittoria', on 8 December 1813, under the composer's direction, at a charity concert for the benefit of Austrian and Bavarian troops wounded at the Battle of Hanau. The circumstances of its presentation and its general character have led to various speculations about its significance. Grove points out that, together with the 'Battle' Symphony and the 'Eroica', it was 'more or less closely associated with Napoleon'.[1] Schmitz relates it directly to the Fifth Symphony and to the French Revolutionary school, and compares a passage

---

[1] Cf. George Grove, *Beethoven and his nine symphonies* (London, 1896), p. 233.

in the finale with an extract from Gossec's *Le Triomphe de la Révolution*.[1] Interpretation has not been confined to military associations. Berlioz saw the *Vivace* as a 'Ronde des paysans'. Wagner called the whole symphony the 'Apotheosis of the Dance': one of the irresistible imaginary scenes in musical history is that of the elderly exponent of 'Tanz, Ticht und Ton' demonstrating his choreographic interpretation of the symphony to Liszt's accompaniment on the pianoforte.

The introduction to the first movement, *Poco sostenuto*, is the longest in the series. Beethoven expands the section by adapting procedures from sonata exposition: a double exposition of the opening theme, *p* then *ff*; a 'second subject' in C, later in F. As in the Fourth Symphony, the harmony of the introduction foreshadows tonal events in the *Vivace*; the development begins with a substantial passage firmly in C. The contrasts of harmony and texture in the introduction also adumbrate the *Vivace*. Like the first movement of the Fifth Symphony, the movement is dominated by a rhythmic figure. In the Fifth Symphony, however, the figure had the specific shape of a rhythmic unit, anacrusis-plus-accent:

. In the Seventh the figure is a pattern, not a rhythmic unit: . It can therefore be applied in a more flexible way. Thus, while there is no strong distinction between the ideas of the first and second group in the exposition, related as they are by the prevailing pattern, there are nevertheless sudden changes of harmony, texture and dynamic within each group. The recapitulation is again made the culmination of the development. The coda begins with a colourful move from A major to the chord of A flat, and a chromatic ostinato bass figure is used to build up to the final climax.

The poignant *Allegretto* achieved instant popularity and was one of the most influential of Beethoven's movements in the nineteenth century. Despite its tempo direction, and the absence of any more specific heading, its march-like character is unmistakable, and, in fact, it follows and develops the structural premisses of the 'Eroica' funeral march, as the overall form reveals (cf. p. 292 above):

[1] Cf. Schmitz, loc. cit.

March	Fugal Episode	March

A minor —A major—A minor	A minor	A minor—A major —A minor
a b a	c	a b a

Detailed points of resemblance include: the major trio sections, with their melodic flow, their triadic themes and their triplet accompaniments; the abbreviation of the first section on its re-appearances; and the 'disintegration' of the opening idea at the conclusion. But the form is extended by the adoption of another 'Eroica' feature—variation in which the bass is announced first, the melody being added subsequently. So the movement as a whole integrates march, rondo and variation form. Two other characteristics distinguish it from the earlier movement: the tonal unity, and the clear distinctions of instrumentation, the strings predominating in the minor sections, the wind in the major.

The *Presto* is in F major, a necessary change after the predominance of A in the first two movements. The tonal variety of the first movement is resumed. The first part of the main section moves to A major. The return of the opening material in the longer second part occurs, not in the tonic, but in the subdominant, B flat, with a following restatement in the home key (cf. the *Menuetto* of No. 8). The D major of the folk-style trio further expands the tonal relationships. As in the scherzo of the Fourth Symphony, Beethoven extends the movement by repetition of the sections to an A B A B A form.

The last movement, *Allegro con brio*, is related to the first by its rhythmic vitality and brilliant tutti scoring, and also by some points of harmonic treatment. The C sharp minor hinted at in the transition of the first movement now becomes the fully-fledged key of the second group, and C major again plays an important part in the development section. The powerful jubilation of the *fff* coda epitomizes the predominant character of the whole work.

At its first performance the Eighth Symphony (F major, Op. 93, 1811–12) suffered from a comparison with the Seventh, which was played earlier in the same programme, and it has still not attained the universal popularity of its companion, despite Beethoven's own comment that it is the better work. This is understandable. The

Eighth is essentially concentrated, almost elliptical in its structure, and as such demands a more sophisticated response from the listener than any other symphony in the series. It has been referred to as witty. Certainly two of the essentials of wit, namely brevity and unusual treatment of the familiar, characterize the first movement, *Allegro vivace e con brio*. The opening bars may serve as an illustration:

The head-motive (*x*), which forms the basis of the development, is not heard again in the exposition, a treatment without precedent in the symphonies. The whole twelve-bar phrase is composed thus: $a\ b^1\ b^2$. The true consequent of *a*, matching it in dynamic, orchestration, register and phrasing, is not, however, b^1, but b^2. Thus b^1 could be described as a pre-echo of b^2. At the point of recapitulation Beethoven regularizes the phrase structure by juxtaposing antecedent and consequent in the normal way. A similar transformation is applied to the tonality of the second subject on its return. The twelve-bar paragraph of the opening has its influence on the development, the first part of which is made up of twelve-bar sections, combining the head-motive with an octave figure derived from the closing bars of the exposition (this is one of the rare examples of a Haydnesque technique in the symphonies). The second part uses the head-motive and syncopated chords in a build-up of tremendous power, resolving in the *fff* recapitulation, which thus becomes the climax of the whole movement.

The coda in its original form was thirty-four bars shorter. Beethoven extended it, possibly after the first performance, to include material from the second group as well as the first. By so doing he undoubtedly achieved a better overall balance in the movement. In the following *Allegretto scherzando* the end comes with an almost perfunctory abruptness after the strong subdominant emphasis in the coda. This supposed tribute to Beethoven's friend Mälzel, the inventor of the metronome, is much the shortest of the slow movements. It is in a typically 'galant' form, sonata form without development. Beethoven compensates for the lack of development by varying the opening material on its restatement. The distinctive flavour of the movement is largely due to the orchestration; short antiphonal phrases on upper and lower strings against a quiet repeated-chord background create a texture of unusual effect. The *Tempo di Menuetto* is not so much a reversion to the eighteenth-century minuet as a reflection upon it. The orchestration and the character of the melodic line belong to Beethoven's maturity. So, too, does the detail of the form; the return of the opening of the minuet in the subdominant, followed by its restatement in the tonic recalls the identical procedure as applied to the second subject in the recapitulation of the first movement. The final *Allegro vivace* has been described by Tovey as 'one of Beethoven's most gigantic creations'.[1] It is a perfectly unified structure; yet it seems to be almost intentionally allusive. It recalls the first movement in its unexpected juxtapositions of key and dynamic; in the octave figure of the timpani which accompanies the first subject on its return; in the modulating second subject. The modulation to the subdominant at the end of the recapitulation resembles the similar move in the second movement, while the unexplained C sharp of the seventeenth bar, with its resolution on to F sharp minor in the coda, recalls the parallel key-relationship in the first movement of the 'Eroica'.[2] The coda is almost as long as the rest of the movement (234 bars out of 502) and crowns the whole work with its bursting vitality.

In 1812 Beethoven wrote to his publishers, Breitkopf & Härtel: 'I am composing three new symphonies, one of which is already finished'.[3] And among the sketches for the Seventh and Eighth Symphonies occur the phrases '2nd Symphony in D minor' and 'Sinfonia in D minor—3rd Sinf.' But it was not until 1817 that the

[1] Cf. Tovey, op. cit., I, p. 65.
[2] Also on the tonality of this movement see p. 159 above.
[3] See *LA*, letter 370.

composer began work on the first two movements of the projected composition. The sketches of that date[1] include a theme in D minor, intended for an instrumental finale; this theme was later used for the finale of the Quartet in A minor, Op. 132. Beethoven put aside the work for other things, but did not lose sight of it. In 1822 he decided to include a setting of part of Schiller's *Ode to Joy* in the symphony. He had been interested in Schiller's poem since his youth; in 1793 he intended to set it to music, and in 1812 he planned to incorporate parts of it in an overture. The bulk of the Symphony No. 9 in D minor, Op. 125, was composed in 1823, after the completion of the *Missa solemnis*, and the work was finished early in 1824. It received its first performance in May of that year, conducted by the composer.

The choice of key for the symphony, decided upon some years before any of the material had come into being, is significant. It is impossible to tell from the occasional remark made by the composer whether he had a consistent view of the emotional or colouristic quality of particular tonalities. But it is certain that works in the same key have a tendency to display family resemblances of technique and structure. The key-note D seems to have suggested to Beethoven the tonic major-tonic minor relationship. Out of fourteen extended instrumental works in D major, seven contain movements in D minor, and in many the alternation of tonic major and minor plays an important part within individual movements. On the other hand, there is only one other work of consequence in D minor, the Piano Sonata, Op. 31, No. 2. In this sonata B flat is the key of the central movement, and D minor that of the finale. The key scheme of the symphony would have followed that pattern if Beethoven had pursued his original intention. But the decision to end the work with the setting of the ode led to an overall key scheme which, except for the interversion of the second and third movements, is identical with that of the Fifth Symphony:

No. 5: C minor—A flat major (C major episode)—C minor (C major trio)—
C major

[1] The most recent study of the sketches for this symphony is the illuminating one by Antonín Sychra, 'Ludwig van Beethovens Skizzen zur IX Sinfonie', *Beethoven Jahrbuch*, 2nd ser., IV (1959–60), p. 85.

No. 9: D minor—D minor (D major trio)—B flat major (D major episode)—
D major

In both works the tonic major gradually emerges as a potent force in the second and third movements, before its full assertion in the finale. But the treatment of the tonic major-minor relationship is more complex in the first and last movements of the Ninth than in the corresponding movements of the Fifth. In the first movement of the Ninth, *Allegro, ma non troppo, un poco maestoso*, Beethoven achieves one of his most powerful returns after the development by resolving on to a *ff* D major chord. From then on major and minor vie for supremacy, the minor finally prevailing in the bleak ostinato march of the coda.

The unforgettable opening, with its shimmering empty fifth A–E and its disjointed arpeggio fragments, performs the function of an introduction within the main section of the movement, resolving as it does into the D minor arpeggio in bar 17. (The parallel with the D minor Sonata, which also begins on dominant harmony, resolving eventually into a D minor arpeggio, is worth noting.) Before the resolution the bassoons and the third and fourth horns move prematurely to the tonic D. A technique of harmonic anticipation is applied at different levels in the movement. The restatement of the main theme on the chord of B flat anticipates the key of the second group, while the D major chord in its first inversion at the beginning of the development foreshadows the recapitulation.

In his final period Beethoven tended increasingly to fuse elements from different structural techniques, and the gigantic proportions of the scherzo, *Molto vivace*, result from an amalgam of sonata, fugue and scherzo forms. The overall sonata form of the main section is treated with freedom; the second group is in the unusual key of the flattened seventh (C major), and the home key and main theme recur in the course of the development section. This theme was intended for fugal development from its first appearance in an 1815 sketchbook. The fugal treatment is itself integrated into the sonata-form structure. The first fugal exposition, which occurs after the eight-bar introduction, is regular, with alternating tonic and dominant entries at four-bar intervals. The four-bar phrase pattern thus evolved prevails throughout the sonata exposition. The second fugato, at the beginning of the development, in E minor, is freer and establishes a three-bar interval, specifically indicated by the composer's '*Ritmo di tre battute*'. There follows a two-bar imitation and, finally, successive entries on the horns of the one-bar figure before the restatement. So the counterpoint becomes literally absorbed into the homophonic texture. The major trio recalls the trio in the Second Symphony through a similarity in the main themes. But in scale of working-out and in imaginative treatment of the instrumentation it belongs to a different world.

The *Adagio molto e cantabile* in B flat is based on the double-variation principle, used by the composer in the Fifth Symphony, and subsequently in the *Heiliger Dankgesang* of Op. 132. The second theme appears twice, in D and G, while the first theme has two figured variations and forms the basis for the extensive coda. The continuity of Beethoven's thought throughout his life is graphically illustrated by a sketch for the first theme, with its unmistakable relationship to the *Adagio cantabile* of the 'Pathétique' Sonata, Op. 13. In the final version the similarity of the melody is obscured, but the bass of the first four bars remains identical:

Ex. 15

a: Op. 13

Adagio cantabile

b: Sketch for Op. 125

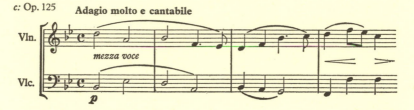

c: Op. 125   **Adagio molto e cantabile**

The intensity of emotion which Beethoven attains in his melodic style of the final period is wonderfully exemplified in this movement. It is achieved in part by a return of the ornamental aspects of melody excluded during the middle period, without loss of the powerful underlying structure. A comparison of the figuration technique used in the Ninth with that employed in the Fifth Symphony reveals the evolution of style. In the later work Beethoven adds suspensions and chromatic auxiliary notes to heighten his already expressive line. Suspensions and accented appoggiaturas are a predominant feature of the second theme, which consequently needs no further embellishment on its return, although it is differently scored. As well as displaying Beethoven's genius for melodic variation (Tovey has described the second variation as 'the richest ornament achieved in music since Bach'),[1] the *Adagio* testifies to the composer's constantly evolving concept of orchestral colour. The woodwind echoes of the strings in the main theme change the character of the whole passage. The warm unison of the violas and cellos in the second theme is modified by the varying octave additions of the woodwind. The predominance of clarinets and horn, supported by pizzicato strings, in the C sharp major episode enhances the romantic mystery of this transition, which resolves into the unclouded light of B flat major, with violins and oboe. And never has heterophony—the simultaneous presentation of a melody and its ornamentation—been more beautifully conceived than in this movement.

No aspect of the composer's work has given rise to such controversy as the choral finale. Critical opinion has ranged from condemnation to the extreme advocacy of Tovey, who asserted: 'There is no part of Beethoven's Choral Symphony which does not,

[1] Cf. Tovey, op. cit., II (London, 1935), p. 33.

310

become clearer to us when we assume that the choral finale is right; and there is hardly a point that does not become difficult or obscure as soon as we fall into the habit that assumes that the choral finale is wrong'.[1] Those who have accepted it have been concerned to demonstrate that it forms the logical culmination to the three preceding movements. Some have done this by demonstrating thematic or motivic unity between the separate movements. Others, wary of the finale's extra-musical connections, have been anxious to assimilate its structure to some purely abstract form. Schenker wrote: 'An offence against musical logic—in an absolute sense, fully independent of programme or text—was in his nature simply impossible, and so here again, as he embarked upon the setting of Schiller's text, he allowed himself to be guided only by the laws of absolute musical form ('Gestaltung')'.[2] Schenker's own solution, a ternary form, with a short middle section and complex sub-divisions of the outer ones, including a cadenza and a final stretto, is hardly satisfactory. Ernest Sanders claims that 'sonata form shapes both the music and the poetry of the Finale'[3] and arrives at a pattern containing a double exposition, a development, recapitulation and coda. Other interpretations have related variation and rondo forms.

All such attempts are based on the assumption that the structure of the last movement must be of the same order as those of the other movements of the work. But it is perverse to ignore the fact that Beethoven *was* setting a text, with the different criteria for formal coherence that this implies. Antonín Sychra[4] has established a fundamental distinction between Beethoven's approach to the finale and his method of work in the earlier movements:

In the first, second and third movements Beethoven experimented freely with the themes; he explored their varied possibilities and allowed himself to be borne along by the stream

[1] Ibid. Also cf. below, pp. 388–90.

[2] Cf. Heinrich Schenker, *Beethovens Neunte Sinfonie* (Vienna and Leipzig), 1912, p. 245.

[3] Ernest Sanders, 'Form and content in the finale of Beethoven's Ninth Symphony', *The Musical Quarterly*, L (1964), p. 71.

[4] Cf. Sychra, op. cit.

of his fantasy . . . and then from among all his ideas he selected the most quintessential, the most adequate, the most communicative. In the finale the procedure takes on a different guise. From the very beginning, from the shaping of the theme, he is seeking an adequate, suitably fitting realization in sound of completely concrete concepts; he does not allow himself to be distracted by chance inspirations, be they never so beautiful and enticing.[1]

Sychra lists the basic elements as follows:

1) the introductory dramatic fanfare for the full orchestra.
2) the baritone recitative.
3) the *Hymn to Joy*—the main theme.
4) the orchestral march designed as a ritornello.
5) the chorale 'Seid umschlungen, Millionen'.
6) the middle section of the chorale, 'Ihr stürzt nieder, Millionen'.
7) the combination of the chorale with the theme of Joy.
8) the climax of the theme of Joy in the line 'Und der Cherub steht vor Gott'.
9) the climax of the entire finale with a heightening of the instrumentation by the addition of piccolos, and especially with the fanfares in the *Maestoso*.

Thus, as Sychra rightly observes, Schiller's poem is at the heart of the finale, and the movement is a programmatic composition based upon it.

Schiller's *Ode to Joy* antedated the French Revolution by five years.[2] Nevertheless, despite its imperfections (the author later dismissed it as 'a bad poem'), it expresses as does no other German literary product of the time the intoxicating sense of universal brotherhood which played such a part in that blissful dawn. It was, in fact, the nearest German equivalent to the hymns and odes to brotherhood, liberty and humanity set to music by the revolutionary

[1] Ibid., p. 96 (author's translation).
[2] Attractive though it is, the story repeated by several writers that Schiller originally wrote his ode to Freedom ('Freiheit') instead of Joy ('Freude') is not supported by any historical evidence. Indeed, the particular circumstances of the poem's composition make it improbable.

composers in France. These settings ranged from the slight to the grandiose involving multiple choruses and orchestras. Characteristic features included extended instrumental introductions, a soloist (*coryphée*) who exhorted the people, represented by the chorus; a simple choral melody varied on its repetitions. Despite the limitations of the musical idiom, the best of them, such as Méhul's *Chant national du 14 Juillet 1800*, in D major, are direct, and dramatically powerful in their impact.

In his last years, the ageing and deaf Beethoven reverted increasingly to the musical experiences of his youth and drew upon them for compositions whose depth and range obscure their modest antecedents. As Warren Kirkendale has shown,[1] the monumental *Grosse Fuge* is an exposition of the types of fugal treatment enumerated by Beethoven's early teacher Albrechtsberger. And the finale of the Ninth, embracing as it does a vast range of techniques—fugue, variation, chorale, recitative, military march—transforms the revolutionary ode into something undreamt of in the musical philosophy of Lesueur, Méhul and Cherubini. So Beethoven's last statement through the medium of the symphony is a sublime reaffirmation of the youthful idealism which remained unshaken by thirty disillusioning years.

THE OVERTURES

Apart from the early overture to *Prometheus* (1801), Beethoven's overtures may be divided for convenience into two groups: the five written before 1810 and the five later ones. The latter include *The Ruins of Athens* and *King Stephen*, both composed rapidly for a pair of festival plays by the prolific dramatist Kotzebue; *Fidelio*, Beethoven's prelude for the 1814 revival of his recast opera; the ceremonial and dull *Namensfeier* and the neo-baroque *The Consecration of the House*. Those of the first group have much more in common and demand more detailed consideration. They are the three *Leonore* overtures; *Coriolan*, for a play by Collin; and *Egmont*, part of the incidental music for Goethe's great drama.

Despite the unconventionality of its opening chord progression

[1] Cf. Warren Kirkendale, 'The "Great Fugue" Op. 133: Beethoven's "Art of Fugue"', *Acta Musicologica*, XXXV (1963), p. 14.

(comparable to that of the First Symphony), *Prometheus* is firmly rooted in the techniques and outlook of the eighteenth century. It has no special relevance to the dramatic action of the succeeding ballet; and in it Beethoven shows no particular desire to break away from established sonata-form design or to venture into new realms of orchestration. But the following overtures reveal a different approach, one that could be summed up as an attempt to reconcile programmatic elements with abstract musical structure. A major factor in this change of outlook was the impact upon Beethoven of contemporary French opera, especially of the work of Cherubini.[1] Four of Cherubini's operas, *Lodoïska, Les deux Journées, Médée* and *Elise*, were produced in Vienna during 1802, and awakened in Beethoven a life-long admiration for their composer. The overtures introduced to him a more flexible type of formal structure and encouraged him to experiment with the form of his own overtures. Except for *Médée*, each begins with a substantial and colourful introduction. The *allegro* sections have elements of sonata form, but sonata form treated with the utmost freedom of tonal and thematic disposition. In fact, this freedom has its roots in a structural uncertainty; Cherubini's formal patterns remain arbitrary, and the whole is never more than the sum of the parts. But the detail is of exceptional interest and originality in the context of its time. The dramatic orchestral gestures in particular impressed Beethoven, who absorbed their essence and gave it new and always more vital expression.

The mysterious descent to a remote harmonic region at the beginning of *Les deux Journées*:

Ex. 16
a: Cherubini

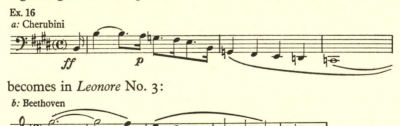

becomes in *Leonore* No. 3:

b: Beethoven

[1] For more on this subject see Chap. 9 below.

The syncopated chords and high violin figuration of *Elise* also
appear in *Leonore* No. 3; the following example shows the syncopated chords:

Ex. 17

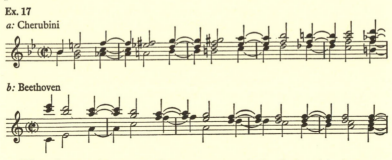

The clearest instance of a more extended relationship between
works of the two composers occurs in *Médée* and *Egmont*, both in F
minor. In the first group Beethoven follows Cherubini with a
descending theme in the lower strings:

Ex. 18

which is succeeded by a crescendo passage built on a repeated
rhythmic figure over a dominant pedal (Cherubini's figure being
; Beethoven's),
leading to a *ff* thematic statement in the home key. In the second
group both composers exploit a rising quaver scale:

Ex. 19

In the short development sections both move in sequence from A flat major to B flat minor and then on to C.

At every stage Beethoven improves upon his predecessor. His theme is more extended and wide-ranging, consequently more expressive. His rhythmic figure is used more purposefully, counter-pointed towards the climax by a moving bass. He brings in the same theme at the *ff* climax, where Cherubini returns to an earlier one. His repetitions of the scale are made cumulative by octave transpositions and doublings. When he reaches C in the development he treats it as the dominant of the home key. Cherubini arrives in C minor and is obliged to cancel its effect at some length before reintroducing F minor. To point out Beethoven's superiority is not to belittle Cherubini; it is to establish the difference between a pioneer of very great talent, and a genius. The fact remains that Beethoven's debt to Cherubini was a major one.

The attraction of the French 'free' form may be seen in different degrees in the three *Leonore* overtures. In all three Beethoven introduces Florestan's aria, and in Nos. 2 and 3 the trumpet call announcing the dénouement of the drama. In No. 1 he begins with an introduction not related thematically to the opera or to the following *Allegro*. But he substitutes an *Adagio* based on the aria for the development. And the exposition departs from convention in its tonal structure. In No. 2 the aria forms the basis of the introduction and of the second group of the *Allegro*. He dispenses with a recapitulation, the trumpet call at the end of the development leading instead to a reappearance of the aria, followed by a coda. This is the most extreme example in the overtures of Beethoven's subordination of musical form to programmatic content, and it evidently disturbed his profound sense of musical architecture, for in No. 3 he reaches a more satisfying form without excluding his two references to the opera. By so doing he creates the first, and perhaps the greatest, tone poem.[1]

Coriolan and *Egmont* posed very different problems. In Collin's drama the frustrated rage of the hero leads to his own destruction. There is no more explosive and violent music in Beethoven;

---

[1] For a full account of the *Leonore* overtures cf. Joseph Braunstein, *Beethoven's Leonore-Ouvertüren* (Leipzig, 1927).

even the lyrical second subject turns quickly to the minor and then into an *ff* outburst. Only at the end do the furious gestures of the coda subside into the symbolic dissolution of the main theme.

In *Coriolan* there is one predominating emotional drive. *Egmont* is about political struggle, defeat and ultimate triumph, and the overture is based on the conflict between the 'pleading' and the 'resisting' principles, as is the development section of *Leonore* No. 3. It seems reasonable to assume, as some have done, that the opening theme, with its sarabande rhythm, represents Spanish intransigence as personified by the Duke of Alba, and the main *Allegro* theme (Ex. 18*b*) the Netherlands drive for freedom, embodied in Egmont. The Spanish theme appears in the coda, depicting the hero's execution, and is followed by the music of the 'Victory symphony' in F major, from the end of the play. Egmont's vision before his execution, like that of Florestan in the dungeon, is the ultimate reality. In *Egmont*, as in *Leonore* No. 3 and *Coriolan*, Beethoven achieves a representation of the dramatic theme translated into purely musical terms. And so these overtures take their place beside the symphonies as statements about the human condition, whose significance transcends the particular circumstances of their origin.

EIGHT

The Concertos

BASIL DEANE

BEETHOVEN'S FIRST VENTURE into the realm of concerto composition gave little promise of things to come. The Piano Concerto in E flat (WoO 4; 1784), of which only the solo part with reductions of the orchestral tuttis has survived, is a competent essay in the galant style of J. C. Bach and the South German school, without being in any way remarkable. More significant in its adumbration of later works is the fragment of the first movement of a Violin Concerto in C (WoO 5), dating from the early 1790s.[1] Although the surviving text breaks off at the beginning of the development, the first part of the movement shows Beethoven intent on reconciling symphonic development with traditional concerto form. The opening tutti, nearly a hundred bars long, contains strong contrasts of material, abrupt modulation in the transition, and a distinct second group in the dominant key, and concludes with a fully orchestrated statement of the opening fanfare in the home key. The tendency of the opening tutti to assume a full symphonic life of its own, before the appearance of the soloist, was to play an important part in Beethoven's later work. The solo writing, too, foreshadows that of the later Violin Concerto, in its lyrical use of the upper compass, and its declamatory power in the semiquaver figuration:

---

[1] A facsimile of the ten-page fragment may be found in Ludwig Schiedermair, *Der junge Beethoven* (Bonn and Leipzig, 1925), appendix.

318

The confident handling of the surviving material lends support to the view that the movement was probably completed.[1] And it is conceivable that one or both of the two Romances for violin and orchestra (Op. 40 in F; Op. 50 in G) may have been intended originally as a slow movement for the concerto. They are scored for the same orchestral forces: flute, two oboes, two bassoons, two horns and strings; their tonalities are closely related to C major; their date of composition may be in advance of that of publication (1802) by several years, and there is nothing in the style or scale of either piece that would not accord with the concerto fragment. The writing shows the same awareness of the nature of the instrument; the emphasis is again on the upper register, but the composer is alive to the richness of the lower compass, used sparingly but with telling effect. There are other instances in contemporary violin literature of a Romance serving as a slow movement. Johann Franz Xaver Sterkel, a composer well known to the young Beethoven, had included a Romance as the slow movement of an 'accompanied sonata' for piano and violin, in his Op. 17 set. Sterkel's sonatas evidently made a strong impression upon Beethoven, as a comparison of these two extracts from his Op. 13 with passages from Beethoven's Violin Concerto and Third Piano Concerto respectively will show:

[1] Cf. *KH*, p. 434.

319

It was inevitable that Beethoven should return to concerto composition for the pianoforte during the early years of his sojourn in Vienna, when his reputation as an oustandingly original pianist had spread from the aristocratic salons to a wider public, and at his first public appearance as a virtuoso, in March 1795, he performed a concerto of his own composition. Almost certainly this was the Piano Concerto No. 2 in B flat, Op. 19, which, according to Beethoven's own evidence,[1] was written before No. 1 in C, Op. 15, and is scored for the same orchestra as the violin concerto fragment. It would be hard to refute his view that the B flat Concerto is 'of course not *one of my best compositions*'.[2] The influence of Mozart is strong, and not entirely digested; it is apparent in the overall forms, in the melodic figuration and often in the phrase structure. In other ways, however, Beethoven impresses his own personality on the material; so there is a stylistic conflict which remains unresolved. The opening bars of the first movement, for example, show Beethoven in Mozartian vein; but in the development the stable subdominant section, the dogged insistence on a rhythmic figure, and the very emphatic dominant preparation for the *ff* return are part of Beethoven's own symphonic conception. In the *Adagio* Beethoven reveals himself towards the end. The gracefully elaborated melodic line is abandoned, and in simple, broken phrases, marked '*con gran espressione*', the soloist engages in a subdued dialogue with the orchestral strings—a brief but significant pointer towards later developments. The concluding rondo is essentially a light-hearted, unproblematic movement with deftly handled scoring and modulation, and brilliant writing for the soloist. The Rondo in B flat for piano and orchestra (WoO 6; *c.* 1795) may have been intended as the original finale. If so, Beethoven's decision to

[1] Cf. *LA*, letter 48.   [2] Loc. cit.

replace it was a sound one: the central *Andante* in E flat does not, despite its charm, help the overall impetus of the movement.

The greater importance of the Concerto No. 1 in C, Op. 15 (*c.* 1796), is marked by an increase in the size of the orchestra: two clarinets, two trumpets and timpani are added. The opening of the first movement, *Allegro con brio*, shows how Beethoven has learned how to tailor convention to his own ends. The first paragraph is a regular statement in 'ceremonial' C major style. But the very first bar, in fact, assumes great motivic significance, both melodically and rhythmically, in the course of the movement. Beethoven's concern with organic development is evident later in the tutti; he represents the second subject at bar 49 with its antecedent only, reserving the consequent for the soloist's exposition, and then he combines elements from both subjects in a contrapuntal working-out starting at bar 72. The breadth of his formal conception is seen in the relationship of the main sections. After the active exposition the middle section is relaxed, and the *ff* return to the home key, preceded by a long but quiet dominant preparation, forms the climax to the movement: as elsewhere, Beethoven is aware of the importance of the point of return in the overall structure. The *Largo* in A flat has the intimacy of a chamber-music composition, with the clarinet matching and answering the cantabile phrases of the piano. In the sparkling rondo the indication '*scherzando*' is fulfilled in the treatment of the themes and in the modulations.

The Third Concerto, in C minor (Op. 37, 1800–2), is at once more ambitious and more problematic than its predecessors. The minor tonality presented Beethoven with both opportunity and a challenge: opportunity to express the turbulent, darker side of his personality, and a challenge to solve in the concerto context the special structural problems inherent in the minor mode. Of the strength of impulse behind the concerto there can be no doubt. The opening sixteen-bar paragraph, with its direct, unadorned thematic statement, rhythmic emphasis, and hammered *ff* cadence, conveys both energy and structural force. But the intensity of impact is lessened in the following passage by the immediate modulation to the relative-major key and the subsequent move to C major. From then onwards the interplay of major and minor modes is the distinctive factor in the tonal structure. The predominance of major in the double exposition is compensated for by the minor development section; and the recapitulation, again largely major, is brought back to the minor in the coda. The thematic treatment of the motive in bars 3 and 4, both in the development section and in the coda, where it is reiterated by the timpani, is an outstanding aspect of the movement. The *Largo* is in the distant key of E major. The contrast of tonality is striking, even disjunctive. Rarely does Beethoven juxtapose two such unrelated keys. In the F minor String Quartet, Op. 95, whose second movement is in D major, the latter tonality is anticipated in the course of the first movement. In the case of the concerto E major strikes the ear without preparation; its relationship to the tonic C minor is made clear only in retrospect in the finale.[1] The richly ornamented style of the solo writing is also in great contrast to the first movement. In the central transition, however, Beethoven achieves a strikingly sombre effect of harmony and texture, with alternate phrases on bassoon and flute, against a background of deep piano sonorities and pizzicato chords on the upper strings.

The development of Beethoven's ideas during the working-out period may be seen by comparing the rondo theme in its final form with an early sketch:

Ex. 3

---

[1] For a fuller treatment of the implications of this relationship and of other enharmonic relationships in Beethoven see Roger Bullivant, 'The Nature of chromaticism', *Music Review*, XXIV (1963), pp. 97 and 279.

Significantly, the first two notes, G–A flat, remain unchanged. Since A flat is the enharmonic equivalent of G sharp, the major third in the tonic chord of the slow movement, a connection between the two tonalities is implied; it becomes more explicit later in the movement, when a repeated A flat becomes G sharp and leads to a statement of the main theme in E major. The *Presto* coda to the movement, in a different mode and tempo (C major; $\frac{6}{8}$), again recalls the F minor Quartet. In both cases the end seems to be more of a postlude than a genuine resolution.[1]

The Triple Concerto for piano, violin and violoncello, Op. 56, dates from 1803–4. Beethoven's combination of solo instruments is an unusual one. Even in France, where the popularity of the *sinfonia concertante* was greatest, there seems to have been no instance of this particular combination. It remains Beethoven's least-known concerto, and performances of it are relatively infrequent. There are obvious difficulties, financial and artistic, in assembling three equally matched soloists. Moreover, the division of interest and difficulty within the solo group is uneven. Neither the piano nor the violin part would present any special problems for the artist capable of playing Beethoven's solo concertos; but the solo cello part was written with an Olympian disregard for the convenience of the player, and the work is one of the most taxing in the cello repertoire. These obstacles, however, can be, and often are, overcome, and still the concerto has not won general acceptance. The cause must lie, at least in part, in the quality of the music itself. In the first movement the material of the exposition is melodic in character and is subjected to restatement within the solo group. The middle 'development' section also relies on repetition of previously heard material. The basis of the movement, then, is lyric statement and restatement, not motivic development. Unfortunately the themes themselves do not have sufficient intrinsic interest to justify the repetition. The *Largo*, on the other hand, has a Schubertian melodic grace and makes striking use of the cantabile qualities of the string soloists, playing together in tenths. With it Beethoven abandons modulatory form in favour of varied

[1] For Dr. Simpson's more favourable view of the coda of Op. 95 cf. above, p. 264. (Eds.)

repetition of lyric melody and provides a link which leads directly to the finale, a *Rondo alla polacca*, whose most remarkable features are the sprightly main theme itself and its derivations in the coda.

If the Triple Concerto, at least in its outer movements, is one of Beethoven's least memorable compositions, the Violin Concerto in D, Op. 61 (1806), is one of his most sheerly beautiful (though his arrangement of 1807 of the solo part for piano is less satisfactory). It was apparently composed in a very short time. Certainly inspiration seems to be at work in every bar. The greatness of the concerto lies in the integration of lyricism with symphonic structure on the largest scale. In the first movement Beethoven finally achieves a complete reconciliation of concerto and sonata-form principles. The overall form of the movement is:

Bars:
1–88   Tutti, D major (D minor)
89–220   Solo exposition, D major–A major
221–283   Tutti, A major (A minor)–C major
284–364   Development, C major–G minor
365–535   Recapitulation, D major

The opening tutti, although harmonically coloured, does not depart from the tonality of D. The second tutti extends the tonality of the exposition by restating the second-group material in the dominant key, but at a *ff* dynamic. The result is two large sections in tonic and dominant respectively, equivalent to a full-scale sonata exposition:

1–126   First group, D major
126–143   Transition
144–262   Second group, A major

Three other points are worth special mention. First, the use of tonic major and minor alternation, and the association of this with the orchestral colour, the wind announcing the theme in the major, the strings or solo violin repeating it in a minor version (bars 43–51; 118–26). Second, the use which is made of the opening five-beat timpani figure as a developmental element. The figure takes on various melodic guises and plays a crucial part in the evolution of the movement, as for example in the second tutti, when a reiterated A sharp becomes B flat, inducing the tonal swing from A to C major. Finally, the richness of the orchestral colouring, in which the ever-varied combinations of solo violin and woodwind are of great importance.

The *Larghetto* follows the precedent of the Triple Concerto by renouncing modulatory form altogether. It consists of five statements of a ten-bar phrase in G major, interlinked with another phrase contributed by the soloist. Once again the movement derives its beauty, in part at least, from the orchestral colour and from the ethereal embroidery of the solo violin. As in the Triple Concerto and the last two piano concertos, the movement is linked to the rondo, which again makes play with the major-minor relationship and, like the first movement, has a central episode in G minor.

The first performance of the Piano Concerto No 4 in G, Op. 58, took place in March 1807, after that of the Violin Concerto, although it was begun before the companion work. The Fourth Piano Concerto is also associated with a very different composition: the Fifth Symphony. Sketches for the first movements of both works exist side by side, and Nottebohm's question, though ultimately unanswerable, is relevant: 'Would Beethoven have written the first movement of the G major concerto in its actual form if he had not also written the Fifth Symphony?'[1] In a real sense the two movements are complementary. Both use as the principal motive the same rhythmic figure: In the symphony the motive dominates the entire movement, and is consequently announced at the beginning as an isolated element, before being built up into a paragraph. In the concerto it is heard as an organic part of a complete phrase and, while it recurs frequently in different contexts, it does not exclude the introduction of contrasting rhythmic material.

One of Beethoven's problems in the earlier concertos arose from the fact that the symphonic development in the opening tutti tended to weaken the expectation of a solo entry. As we have seen, Beethoven maintains expectation in the Violin Concerto tutti by

[1] *NB*, p. 13.

keeping to the home tonic. In the case of the G major Concerto the second theme in the tutti is inherently a modulating one, and thus development is suggested. Beethoven's solution, one of genius, is to introduce the piano at the outset. Although it contributes only five bars, its absence throughout the rest of the tutti is a positive factor in the total musical experience. At its re-entry it asserts its importance with a cadenza-like passage before allowing the thematic argument to proceed. As in the Violin Concerto, the solo instrument in the exposition contributes ornamental embroidery in its highest register to the orchestral material:

Ex. 4

The quiet but stark opening of the development solo, with the piano's F natural contradicting the major third of the orchestra's D major chord (bar 192), is a remarkable dramatic stroke, leading eventually to the remote harmonic region of C sharp minor. Once again the return to the home key forms the climax of the development, and the magnificently sonorous restatement of the opening by the soloist, unsupported by the orchestra, is an original, but strictly logical, inspiration.

It would be difficult not to feel in the E minor *Andante con moto* the confrontation of two worlds, in which the aggressive rhythms of the unison orchestral strings are answered and finally overcome by the pleading phrases of the muted piano. Such confrontation is often implicit in Beethoven, but never elsewhere in the instrumental music is it so explicitly stated, and Liszt's view that the movement represents Orpheus taming the Furies is a credible programmatic interpretation. Its poignancy is unique and quite indescribable. The concluding rondo, following without a break, has a joyously wayward character, established by the lopsided harmony of the main theme, which begins emphatically on the subdominant chord, C major (an effect foreshadowed by the beginning of the G major rondo in the Cello Sonata, Op. 5, No. 2).[1] This involves the unusual procedure of treating the tonic chord of the movement as the dominant leading to the later statements. The theme provides a variety of material for development, and it reappears in simplified form, while the lyrical mood of the first two movements is recalled by the second subject.

Beethoven's last Piano Concerto, No. 5 in E flat, Op. 73, known in some countries as 'The Emperor', is also his largest in scale and represents a culmination of tendencies in his previous works; it dates from 1809. The synthesis of concerto and sonata principles achieved in the two preceding concertos serves as a secure base for further evolution. He expands his form without loss of coherence; and he makes an unprecedentedly bold assertion of the virtuosic rights of the soloist, without impairing the essential balance between the protagonists. At the beginning of the first movement the soloist establishes his pre-eminence at once, not, as in the Fourth Concerto, with a quiet phrase, but with *ff* elaborations of the chords in the progression I–IV–V–I: virtuosity indeed, but virtuosity with clear harmonic direction leading into the orchestral tutti. Here the orchestra makes its own distinctive contribution to the style of the work. The 'Eroica' Symphony is recalled in the breadth of the material and in the E flat minor passage with its subsequent resolution into the fanfare-like E flat major theme on the horns. The formal boundaries of the movement are extended in the solo exposition by a widening of the tonal range. The soloist restates the second-group material in B minor and C flat major, before reaching the dominant, B flat major. The importance of C flat is re-emphasized at the central climax in the development section by heavy repeated chords of C flat major on both orchestra and piano. At the return the soloist enlarges, with new figuration, upon the opening chords, and these

[1] Cf. above, p. 212.

327

quasi-improvisatory passages, together with the overall brilliance of the solo part, maintained to the end of the movement, make a conventional cadenza inappropriate. The *Adagio un poco mosso* takes up the tonality of C flat major, this time in its enharmonic form of B major. The soloist's comments on the quiet string melody again suggest improvisation, but now in the spirit of serene meditation, a mood which persists through the subsequent restatements of the theme, both by the soloist in an ornamented version and by the flute accompanied by gently persistent semiquaver figuration on the piano and off-beat chords on the strings.

The link to the last movement is one of Beethoven's most dramatic, in its harmonic shift and nebulous piano phrases. The main rondo theme is the peer of its predecessors; it expresses its individuality in its exuberant rising arpeggio and subsequent chromatic descent. The harmonic relationship tonic–flat submediant, developed in the first two movements as E flat–C flat (B), recurs in the middle section as a tonal sequence C–A flat–E natural. In other respects the movement is formally straightforward and provides a finale of bounding energy and pianistic bravura.

In sum, Beethoven's contribution to the concerto was of outstanding importance. He started with the Mozartian concept of co-operative interplay between soloist and orchestra in the thematic presentation, adapted it to his own particular kind of dramatic symphonic expression, and finally made of the concerto a vehicle for extreme virtuosity, without in any way detracting from its musical content or lessening the importance of the orchestra. He arrived at a more open conception of the first movement, with early participation of the soloist. He sought, and found, alternatives to the 'set-form' slow movement. He related his movements to each other, not only by linking passages between movements but also by interrelated tonal events. He left a legacy which influenced profoundly, both for good and bad, his nineteenth-century successors.

V

The Operatic and Vocal Music

NINE

Beethoven and Opera

WINTON DEAN

INTRODUCTION

THE UNIQUENESS of Beethoven's contribution to the operatic repertory must be ascribed to temperament rather than environment. The man who produced his single opera in three versions and equipped it with four overtures, yet complained of the same work that he found it far harder to rethink himself into an old composition than to begin a new one, was clearly not a born opera composer, least of all in the conditions obtaining at the turn of the nineteenth century. Nevertheless he was far from considering himself a one-opera man. He continued for the greater part of his life to invite librettos and plan fresh operas, only to abandon them in the early stages or allow them to lapse through inanition. His potential collaborators included such men of literary distinction and experience as Goethe, Grillparzer, Kotzebue, Collin, Rochlitz and Rellstab. *Fidelio*, whatever its faults, is a great opera and a work of theatrical genius. Yet not even a mouse followed the birth of the mountain. One might attribute the constant search for librettos to the spur of Beethoven's environment, and its regular frustration to some hidden force in his creative personality. But only a careful study of the opera he did write can suggest an answer to the question what that force was.

The circumstances of Beethoven's life, both in Bonn and Vienna, might have been expected to encourage rather than inhibit an operatic career, or at least an attempt at it. It is true that in neither city during his residence—and especially in his impressionable years—was a composer of the first or even the second rank writing for the stage. But there was plenty of opera; old and new works, home-grown and imported, were constantly on view. In Bonn, where his father was a tenor singer, albeit a drunken one, Beethoven must have learned much of the current repertory in his childhood. In 1783 and 1784, at the age of twelve and thirteen, he was employed as cembalist in the Elector's theatre orchestra under the Kapellmeister Christian Gottlob Neefe. This service was interrupted by the disbandment of the orchestra on the death of the Elector in April 1784. Even so, the next four years saw a number of visiting companies in Bonn, one of which (in 1785) may have introduced Beethoven to Gluck's *Orfeo* and *Alceste*.[1] Two years later, on his first visit to Vienna, he had a few lessons from Mozart. In the winter of 1788 the Elector Maximilian Franz, brother of the Austrian Emperor, established a new opera company at Bonn that gave regular winter seasons lasting several months. Until his departure for Vienna in November 1792—that is, for four full seasons and part of a fifth—Beethoven played the viola in the orchestra. The repertory consisted almost entirely of light works, whether Italian *opera buffa* (Cimarosa, Paisiello, Sacchini, Salieri, Sarti, Martín y Soler), French *opéra-comique* (Grétry, Monsigny, Dezède, Dalayrac) or South German *Singspiel* (Dittersdorf, Benda, Schuster, Schubaur, Umlauf). But it included Gluck's *Die Pilgrime von Mecca* and three operas by Mozart, *Die Entführung aus dem Serail* in 1788–89 and 1791–92, *Don Giovanni* (three performances) and *The Marriage of Figaro* (four performances), both in 1789–90. Practical experience of these scores can scarcely have failed to make a permanent impression on the young Beethoven.

His first ten years in Vienna brought little direct contact with the stage. Although several theatres were in operation, this was not a period of Viennese operatic glory. At the Court Theatre (Kärnt-

---

[1] There are curiously few references to Gluck in the Beethoven literature. Czerny says Beethoven played through *Iphigénie en Tauride* for some French officers in 1805. His letters never mention Gluck's name; the only two allusions are problematical. In February 1808 he lent Collin an *Armide* that did not belong to him; about the same time he borrowed an *Iphigénie* from Zmeskall and lost it (see *LA*, letters 163, 263 and 264). But he must have been familiar with Gluck's music.

nertor), largely confined to Italian opera, the favourite composers were Martín y Soler, Salieri, Cimarosa, Paer and Zingarelli. It did produce the most successful German opera between *Die Zauber-flöte* and *Der Freischütz*, Winter's *Das unterbrochene Opferfest* in 1796; but this singular association of a wildly exotic plot with music of demure domesticity, packed with Mozartian echoes but deficient in structure and characterization, in which a short-winded *volkstümlich* melody may eject without warning a rocket of extravagant coloratura, had little to offer Beethoven.[1] The popular German theatres, Marinelli's Leopoldstadt and Schikaneder's Theater auf der Wieden, specialized in farces and fairy stories, often with an oriental background. These were all *Singspiele* with copious dialogue; indeed, the scenic spectacle and the coarse buffooneries of the spoken text usurped the province of the music, which seldom attempted to impose any unity of structure or atmosphere. The leading composers were Wenzel Müller, Weigl, Sussmayr, Hoffmeister, Schenk and Kauer. Only *Die Zauberflöte*, which continued to draw audiences, can have won Beethoven's respect, and he was not tempted to emulate it, though he did compose two arias for insertion in a revival of Umlauf's *Die schöne Schusterin* in 1796. Apart from this and the ballet *Prometheus* (1801), his only tangible links with the Viennese theatre at this period are the titles of the operas from which he chose themes for variations, among them Grétry's *Richard Cœur de Lion*, Müller's *Die Schwestern von Prag*, Wranitzky's *Das Waldmädchen*, Paisiello's *La Molinara*, Winter's *Das unterbrochene Opferfest*, Weigl's *L'Amor marinaro*, Salieri's *Falstaff* and Sussmayr's *Soliman II*.

In 1802 occurred an event that changed this picture decisively. On 23 March Schikaneder produced Cherubini's *Lodoïska* at the new Theater an der Wien, which had replaced the Theater auf der Wieden in the previous year. This was the first major opera of the French Revolution school to reach Vienna; it was also one of the

---

[1] According to Alfred Loewenberg, *Annals of Opera* (2nd rev. ed., Geneva, 1955), col. 553, the last finale of Winter's *Marie von Montalban* (1800) is supposed to have influenced *Fidelio*. This claim will not bear inspection. Beyond the fact that Winter's finale contains a rescue and ends in C major there appears to be no resemblance.

best, with a solidity of technique, a pulsating energy and a flavour of contemporary realism that must have startled Viennese conservatives. Its success was immediate. Baron Braun, Deputy Director of the Court Theatre, went to Paris to obtain more French operas, 'all of which will be performed here most carefully according to the taste of the French'.[1] This journey led to Cherubini's commission to compose *Faniska* for Vienna. Meanwhile Schikaneder, encouraged it is said by Mozart's brother-in-law Sebastian Mayer, an actor and bass singer who was to be Beethoven's first Pizarro, decided to abandon pantomime and fairy stories for more serious fare. In the event *Les deux Journées* was produced by both managements under different titles on consecutive nights (13 and 14 August 1802). All Cherubini's other post-Revolution operas followed, *Médée* at the Kärntnertor on 6 November, *Elisa* at the Theater an der Wien on 18 December, *L'Hôtellerie portugaise* on 22 September 1803. They were the forerunners of an avalanche of French operas, many of which became more popular in Vienna than in Paris. Dalayrac (whose earlier work had long been successful in Germany), Méhul, Gaveaux, Boïeldieu, Isouard, Berton and a little later Spontini conquered the Austrian capital as easily as the armies of Napoleon. Of the more adventurous operas, Lesueur's *La Caverne* appeared at two theatres within ten days in June 1803, and Méhul's *Ariodant* followed on 16 February 1804.

Such was the background against which Beethoven's fitful career in the opera house began. Although its early course was inauspicious and in some respects obscure, two things are certain: the agent who established the link was Schikaneder, and the torch that fired Beethoven's imagination was the French opera—or rather *opéra-comique*—of the Revolution. His opinion of Cherubini is well known. When the two composers met in July 1805, while the one was working on *Fidelio* and the other on *Faniska* (produced at the Kärntnertor on 25 February 1806), both in collaboration with Joseph Sonnleithner, Beethoven treated Cherubini with marked respect. In March 1823 he wrote to him: 'I value your works more highly than all other compositions for the theatre.' Two months later he sent Cherubini via Louis Schlösser 'all kinds of amiable

[1] *AMZ*, quoted in *TF*, p. 326.

messages' and an assurance that 'my most ardent longing is that we should soon have another opera composed by him'. His expressions of esteem, often repeated,[1] were not always qualified by restriction to the theatre: he regarded Cherubini as the greatest living composer. Nor was Cherubini the only member of the French school admired by the fastidious Beethoven. On 18 February 1823 he asked Moritz Schlesinger for music by Méhul and in thanking him for an unidentified score pronounced it 'so worthy of him'. Of Spontini he said in 1825: 'There is much good in him; he understands theatrical effects and the musical noises of warfare thoroughly.' He rated the French librettos as high as the music. While he constantly complained that 'the Germans cannot write a good libretto' and told Rellstab in 1825 that he could never compose operas on subjects like *Figaro* and *Don Giovanni*, which he found frivolous and indeed repugnant, he declared in conversation with Julius Benedict in 1823 that the best librettos he knew were those of *Les deux Journées* and *La Vestale*.

There is a certain irony in the part played by Schikaneder. No evidence appears to support Emily Anderson's statement[2] that as early as 1801 he offered Beethoven his libretto *Alexander* with which he planned to open the Theater an der Wien (Teyber's setting inaugurated it on 13 June). But he did engage him to compose an opera early in 1803, and on most favourable terms, which included free lodging in the theatre. This commission is first mentioned in a letter of 12 February from Beethoven's brother Johann to Breitkopf & Härtel and thus preceded the concert at which the oratorio *The Mount of Olives* was first performed on 5 April. The latter may have been a by-product of the same set of circumstances (Beethoven said he wrote the music in a fortnight); it was taken as evidence of his fitness for theatrical composition. He moved into the theatre in the spring; on 2 August

---

[1] They were not wholly reciprocated. Cherubini said of *Fidelio* that Beethoven paid too little heed to the art of singing, and he found the modulations in the overture (*Leonore* No. 2) so confusing that he could not recognize the principal key. See *TF*, p. 399.

[2] 'On the road to Fidelio (1814)', in *Opera*, February 1961, p. 82, and 'Beethoven's operatic plans', *Proceedings of the Royal Musical Association*, LXXXVIII (1961–2), p. 62.

Die Zeitung für die Elegante Welt published an announcement, under the date 29 June, that 'Beethoven is composing an opera by Schikaneder'. The libretto was *Vestas Feuer*, and Beethoven worked on it for some time, though not very assiduously;[1] production was planned for March 1804. Towards the end of the year he discarded it in disgust, as he explained in an interesting letter to Rochlitz (4 January 1804), adding: 'I have quickly had an old French libretto adapted and am now beginning to work on it.'[2] This was the genesis of *Fidelio*. In the same letter he rejected the first act of a libretto by Rochlitz because its subject was connected with magic. The public were now as prejudiced against such a theme as they had formerly been enthusiastic in its favour: Schikaneder's 'empire has really been entirely eclipsed by the light of the brilliant and attractive French operas'.

That Beethoven was attracted more by the operatic idea than by Schikaneder's libretto emerges from Georg August Griesinger's report to Breitkopf & Härtel (12 November 1803) that though still at work on *Vestas Feuer* 'he told me himself that he is looking for reasonable texts'.[3] *Vestas Feuer* is not a reasonable text. It is a ponderously heroic affair set in ancient Rome (though the names of the characters suggest Parthia or India) and replete with tedious intrigue.[4] Schikaneder had lapsed from pantomime into the stagnant backwash of Metastasio while retaining (in Beethoven's words to Rochlitz) 'language and verses such as could proceed only out of the mouths of our Viennese apple-women'. Beethoven set the opening scene, in which the father of the heroine, inflamed by the dark counsels of a slave and the fact that his would-be son-in-law is the child of an old enemy, at first denounces the lovers, but is won over by their devotion and heroic bearing. The principal movements are a love duet of Mozartian grace and a trio of reconciliation for soprano, tenor and baritone. Eighty-one pages of

[1] He wrote to Alexander Macco on 2 November 'I am only now *beginning to work at my opera*.' See *LA*, letter 85.

[2] *LA*, letter 87a.

[3] Quoted in *TF*, p. 340.

[4] For a summary see Willy Hess, *Beethovens Bühnenwerke* (Göttingen, 1962), pp. 32–4. Hess published the complete libretto in *Beethoven-Jahrbuch*, 2nd ser., III (1957–8), pp. 63–106.

autograph survive, but the wind parts are incomplete.[1] The most interesting features of this fragment are the linking arioso passages (it was a grand opera, not a *Singspiel*), which have no exact equivalent elsewhere in Beethoven, the striking parallel with *Fidelio* in the progress from spiritual darkness and conspiracy to the light of joy and reconciliation,[2] and the fact that Beethoven used the material of the trio in the same key for the duet 'O namenlose Freude'.[3] Although the music is characteristic and mature in style, there are no grounds for lamenting the loss of a masterpiece. Beethoven could scarcely have transcended the slough of Schikaneder's later scenes.[4]

His contract was conveniently invalidated by the sale of the Theater an der Wien to Baron Braun on 14 February 1804. By this time he was fully committed to *Fidelio*; in March he was urging Sonnleithner to finish his task by the middle of April, so that 'the opera can be produced in June at latest'.[5] His letter to Rochlitz, already quoted, implies that he himself chose the subject, and this may well be true despite Georg Friedrich Treitschke's statement that the initiative came from Sonnleithner.[6] Baron Braun gave Beethoven a new contract, allowing him to retain his rooms in the theatre, an event that Treitschke places at the end of 1804. This is

[1] The score has been completed and edited by Hess (Wiesbaden, 1953; vocal score, Kassel, 1957). Gustav Nottebohm discussed the fragment in *NB*, pp. 82–99, and the sketches, which are associated with those for the 'Eroica' Symphony and the opening scenes of the 1805 *Fidelio*, in *Zwei Skizzenbücher von Beethoven aus den Jahren 1801 bis 1803*, ed. Paul Mies (Leipzig, 1924), pp. 56–7. See also Anderson, 'Beethoven's operatic plans', pp. 63–6.

[2] Before the discovery of the complete libretto Nottebohm, followed by Ernest Newman in *More opera nights* (London, 1954), p. 254, and others, mistook the fragment for a final scene. They should have been alerted by the occurrence in the sketches, after the trio, of a vengeance aria for the slave, which Beethoven never completed.

[3] For parallel quotations, see below, p. 355. The second strain ('Mein Mann an meiner Brust') had been set to the words 'Gute Götter, blickt herab' in *Vestas Feuer*.

[4] *Vestas Feuer* was subsequently set by Weigl and produced at the Theater an der Wien on 10 August 1805.

[5] *LA*, letter 88.

[6] Treitschke's personal knowledge was confined to the 1814 revival, and he is not always accurate about that.

337

probably an error, like his assertion that the libretto was chosen after the production of Paer's opera on the same subject (3 October 1804). It is not clear what caused the delay between the spring of 1804 and the summer of 1805, when the bulk of the work was done. The performance, planned for 15 October, was held up by the censorship, which demanded changes in the libretto (the back-dating of the action to the sixteenth century dates from this time) and evoked from Sonnleithner a declaration that the Empress 'found the original very beautiful and affirmed that no opera subject had ever given her so much pleasure'. The ban was soon lifted, but the delay was disastrous. On 13 November the French army occupied Vienna, which had been vacated by the nobility and most of Beethoven's friends. The opera was produced at the Theater an der Wien on 20 November before an audience full of French officers, and repeated to empty houses on the two following nights. The cast was:

Leonore	Anna Milder
Marzelline	Louise Müller
Florestan	Fritz Demmer
Pizarro	Sebastian Mayer
Jaquino	Caché
Rocco	Rothe
Don Fernando	Weinkopf

The conductor was Ignaz von Seyfried. Beethoven wished to call the opera *Leonore*, but since Paer had used this title and had close connections with the Kärntnertor Theatre the directors insisted on a change. It appeared on the bills as *Fidelio oder Die eheliche Liebe* and in the 1805 libretto simply as *Fidelio*.

The press was far from enthusiastic. The commonest complaint, not wholly without justification, was that the music, though beautiful in places, was 'ineffective and repetitious', especially in the treatment of words.[1] Beethoven's friends recognized this. In December, after he had withdrawn the opera, they organized a complete run-through with piano at Prince Lichnowsky's palace with the intention of persuading him to cut three numbers, the

---

[1] For quotations see *TF*, p. 387.

trio for Rocco, Marzelline and Jaquino ('Ein Mann ist bald genommen'), the duet for Leonore and Marzelline ('Um in der Ehe') and Pizarro's aria with chorus at the end of the original Act II. According to J. A. Röckel it took them six hours to overcome Beethoven's resistance. These pieces, though they disappeared later, were not cut in 1806. Instead, without consulting Sonnleithner, who was busy with *Faniska*, Beethoven brought in Stephan von Breuning to tighten up the libretto. When asking Sonnleithner's permission to print the result under his name (early March 1806) Beethoven added: 'To make the opera move more swiftly I have *shortened everything* as much as possible, the *prisoners'* chorus, and chiefly numbers of that kind.'[1] As will be seen, this was a misleading statement; the 1806 changes were by no means confined to cuts.

Beethoven made another attempt to restore his original title, and the new edition of the libretto appeared as *Leonore oder der Triumph der ehelichen Liebe*;[2] but the directors once more overruled him. The opera was revived on 29 March and repeated on 10 April with the original cast, except that Röckel replaced Demmer as Florestan. Although Beethoven was so late in finishing his score that only one orchestral rehearsal was possible—which no doubt explains his furious complaints in two letters to Mayer[3] that the chorus made dreadful mistakes and many of his dynamic marks were ignored—the reception was much more favourable than in 1805. There are two accounts of what followed. According to Breuning a cabal in the theatre prevented further performances; Röckel, who is more likely to be correct, said that Beethoven, fancying himself cheated of his share of the receipts, demanded his score back just when a lasting success seemed assured. In May there was talk of a private performance at Prince Lobkowitz's palace. It is not known if this took place; but plans to produce the opera in Berlin and later (1808) in Prague came to nothing.

[1] *LA*, letter 128.
[2] The 1810 vocal score, arranged by Czerny, over which, of course, the theatre had no control, also bore the title *Leonore*. This was the 1806 version without the overture and the two finales. Three numbers had been published separately in 1807.
[3] *LA*, letters 129 and 130.

Fidelio slumbered till the beginning of 1814, when Beethoven, to his evident surprise, learned that three singers[1] wished to revive it at the Kärntnertor for their benefit. He agreed on condition that he was permitted to make changes. This time the revision of the libretto was entrusted (with Sonnleithner's permission) to Treitschke, an experienced man of the theatre. Beethoven worked at the score from March until 15 May. He found it an arduous task: 'I could compose something new far more quickly than patch up the old . . . I have to think out the entire work again . . . this opera will win for me a martyr's crown' (to Treitschke, April).[2] The new overture was not ready in time for the first performance (23 May), when that to *The Ruins of Athens* was substituted. It made its début on the second night (26 May).

The cast was:

Leonore	Anna Milder
(Madame Hönig was the first choice)	
Marzelline	Mlle Bondra
Florestan	Radichi
Pizarro	Johann Michael Vogl
(replaced on 18 July by Anton Forti)	
Jaquino	Frühwald
Rocco	Carl Friedrich Weinmüller
Don Fernando	Saal

The conductor was Ignaz Umlauf. The seventh performance on 18 July was for Beethoven's benefit; his advertisement stated that 'two new pieces have been added'.[3] From this revival, followed on 21 November by Weber's production in Prague, the success of the opera was assured.

GAVEAUX'S 'LÉONORE'

J. N. Bouilly's libretto *Léonore ou L'amour conjugal*, set by Pierre Gaveaux and produced at the Théâtre Feydeau in Paris on 19

---

[1] The Pizarro, Rocco and Don Fernando of the 1814 cast, listed below.
[2] *LA*, letter 479.
[3] See below, pp. 371–2.

February 1798, was, like his *Les deux Journées* of two years later, based on a historical incident during the Reign of Terror.[1] Bouilly, serving in an official position at Tours, found himself in the role of Don Fernando; it is strange to reflect that the real-life Léonore and Florestan may have survived and even witnessed their translation to operatic fame. To prevent precise identification Bouilly moved the action to Spain, but acknowledged its authenticity by adding the words 'fait historique' to the title.[2]

The work is an *opéra-comique* in two acts with thirteen musical numbers (apart from the overture) and much spoken dialogue. Roc, Marceline and Jacquino talk in dialect. The general outline of the plot remains unchanged in Bouilly's libretto and Beethoven's three versions and is too familiar to need summarizing here; but there are significant shifts of emphasis. While Bouilly's act-division corresponds to that of the 1814 *Fidelio*, the course of events, the placing of the musical numbers and the dialogue are closer to 1805. Five of the seven numbers in Bouilly's first act—Marceline's *couplets*, her duet with Jacquino, Roc's *chanson*, the duet for Marceline and Léonore in which the former looks forward to the birth of their first child while the latter dissembles, and the prisoners' chorus—were retained by Sonnleithner with little change. The other two he combined in a single movement. Léonore has two consecutive solos, a *romance* in which she is sustained by conjugal love and addresses her lost husband, and an air apostrophizing hope; they are separated by dialogue in which she learns from Roc of Pizare's orders that the prisoner is to be killed for reasons of state and to preserve the honour of one of the noblest families in Spain. Pizare has not revealed this to the audience; he whispers to Roc and briefs him offstage. Léonore has an awkward moment after the duet with Marceline, who has heard her talking in her sleep; she has to pretend she is looking for her lost father. Although Marceline speaks of letting the prisoners out for their daily exercise, it is Léonore who does this on Roc's orders, as a cover

---

[1] Bouilly tells the story in his memoirs (*Mes Récapitulations*, Paris, [1836], II, pp. 81 ff.).

[2] This was common practice during the revolutionary period, when realism in all the arts was a matter of pride. The score has 'fait historique espagnol'.

for their descent to dig the grave. The prisoners' chorus contains a solo, but none of the named characters takes part or is on the stage.

Sonnleithner also kept the first four numbers in Bouilly's second act: a recitative and *romance* for Florestan, the grave-digging duet for Léonore and Roc (during which she resolves to rescue the prisoner whoever he may be), their trio with Florestan, and the duet for husband and wife. There is no quartet in Gaveaux's opera; the important action here, including the trumpet call, takes place in dialogue. Pizare is heavily disguised and has to change into uniform to receive the Minister. Roc, whose orders were to admit a masked man, is at first ignorant of his identity as well as his motives. Léonore reveals herself before Pizare, who after unmasking tosses Roc a second purse of gold. When Pizare's assault on Léonore has been frustrated by her pistol and the trumpet call, Roc snatches the pistol and goes out with Pizare, closing the door on the lovers. Léonore, her weapon gone, collapses in despair. During the duet Florestan, still bemused, calls her, but cannot reach her on account of his chains. She revives slowly, taking some time to grasp that he is indeed her husband. The movement ends in mutual rapture. As Léonore explains how she entered the prison an offstage chorus is heard demanding vengeance. This is combined with a second duet in which the lovers, convinced that their last hour has come, resolve to die together. The dénouement reverts to dialogue. Roc after exculpating himself restores the pistol to Léonore and throws both purses at Pizare's feet: he is cured of his lust for gold. Dom Fernand recommends the women in the audience to take Léonore as an example.

Bouilly tells an intensely dramatic story in clear straightforward terms. The compound of realism, low life and earthy humour on the one hand (Roc is a close-fisted French peasant with an eye on the main chance) and heroic endeavour, a last minute rescue and an elevating moral on the other is typical of French opera in the revolutionary decade. So is the confined space and darkness of the setting. *Léonore* contains many premonitions of romantic opera. It is as far as possible removed from the stagey conventions almost universal in contemporary German and Italian opera, whether serious or comic. Therein lay part of its appeal to Beethoven.

Gaveaux's *Léonore*, like many of the *opéras-comiques* of Grétry and his school, is as much a play with songs as an opera. The fact that Pizare is a spoken part[1] is enough to prevent the drama permeating the score. Nevertheless the music, influenced as much by Cherubini as by Grétry, is not negligible. The introduction to Florestan's recitative and air in the dungeon has a feeling for atmosphere; the horns are directed to play the opening bars '*les Pavillons l'un contre l'autre*', a favourite device of Méhul:

Ex. 1

Of particular interest are the strong indications that Beethoven knew Gaveaux's score, which had been published in Paris.[2] Half a

[1] He is listed as second tenor, but has not a note to sing.

[2] Gaveaux's *Le petit Matelot*, a great success in Germany, had been produced at the Theater auf der Wieden in 1801.

343

dozen movements seem to contain the germs of ideas that Beethoven brought to full flower; this, not chance thematic resemblance, is the significant debt that genius owes to the second-rate. Among such passages are the headlong string scales in the coda of the overture, strikingly prophetic of *Leonore* Nos. 2 and 3, though more symmetrical; the alternating minor and major strains of Marceline's *couplets* (an interesting early experiment in local colour marked '*Tempo di Minuetto Seguidilla*'); the cut of the melody of Roc's *chanson*:

Ex. 2

Sans un peu d'or, un peu d'ai-san-ce, Re - te - nez bien cet-te le - çon

the use of a solo horn to introduce Léonore's *romance*; the combination of ostinato and repeated chords in the accompaniment of the grave-digging duet; and most of all the treatment of the prisoners' chorus. As in Beethoven, the slow-moving harmony, long pedals and gradual climb in pitch and volume from an initial *pianissimo* express the wonder of the prisoners as they creep out of their cells and peer into the light:

Ex. 3

THE OPERAS OF PAER AND MAYR

Between the inception and the performance of *Fidelio* two other operas based on Bouilly's libretto, both in Italian, came to birth. The libretto of Paer's *Leonora ossia L'amore conjugale* (Dresden, 3 October 1804), probably by the singer Giacomo Cinti, preserves much of the detail of the story at the expense of its spirit. The part of Marcellina is expanded, evidently for a favoured singer boasting a top D and E flat. She has two substantial arias in the first act as well as several ensembles; like Gaveaux, Paer seeks to establish the locality, setting her initial aria in bolero rhythm. Her ambitions are thrust inappropriately into the foreground not only in the first finale but in the dungeon scene, where she appears catastrophically (having stolen the key from Rocco) between Pizarro's exit and the reunion of the lovers. She brings news of the Minister's arrival and refuses to budge without specific and repeated assurances of Fedele's love. Leonora is forced to comply in an extended duet in the presence of her husband. He is the only prisoner; there is no chorus, and Pizarro (a tenor) has no solo, though he sings in ensembles. On the other hand, the librettist does attempt to construct viable musical numbers from Bouilly's dialogue. There is a *buffo*[1] trio for Marcellina, Giacchino and Rocco (both basses) at the point corresponding to Beethoven's 'Ein Mann ist bald genommen', and another trio when Pizarro, watched by Leonora, orders Rocco to follow him to receive secret instructions. Paer has a quartet in the second act, beginning when Leonora reveals her identity, but not in the first.

His score is more ambitious than Gaveaux's, but has less character. The style might be described as sub-Mozart; the duet for Marcellina and Giacchino is heavily indebted to *Figaro*. The dramatic scenas for Leonora in Act I and Florestan in Act II are on an enormous scale, bigger indeed than those in Beethoven's opera. Each has several linked movements comprising recitative, cavatina and cabaletta; Leonora's contains a motive used in the

---

[1] The opera belonged to the *semiseria* category, which sought to combine the old *seria* and *buffa* styles. It was an important stage in the development of romantic opera.

overture. The introduction to Florestan's, thirty-eight bars long, shows Paer at his least insipid:

Ex. 4

Richard Engländer in an emphatic article[1] has argued that
Beethoven and Sonnleithner knew Paer's opera and that all three
versions of *Fidelio* are considerably indebted to it. Beethoven
certainly possessed a copy of the score, though there is nothing to
indicate when he acquired it. Engländer conjectures that it was
Paer, on a visit to Vienna early in 1803, who brought the subject to
his attention, and claims his Dresden *Leonora* as a vital link between
Gaveaux and *Fidelio*. It is true that Paer's and Beethoven's
librettos share certain features not found in Bouilly, for example
the trio for Marzelline, Jaquino and Rocco near the beginning,
Pizarro's angry return in the first finale, and the dungeon quartet;
but these are predictable moves for any librettist anxious to
strengthen the links between music and drama. The one unquestionable point of contact concerns the 1814 version of *Fidelio* and
is mentioned below. Engländer's musical parallels are for the most
part period clichés and quite unconvincing. An exception is the
resemblance between the chorus 'Wer ein holdes Weib' (Ex. 5*b*)
and a theme in Paer's finale (*a*):

Ex. 5
a

Suon di gio-ia in si bel gior-no [etc.]

b

Wer ein hol-des Weib er-run-gen, stimm' in un-ser'n Ju-bel ein

This is certainly striking, and it is conceivable that some visitor
from Dresden whistled—or bellowed—a little Paer outside Beethoven's window. On the other hand, the sketchbook shows him
hammering out his melody by the usual laborious process,[2] and the
date '2 June' among the sketches for this finale probably refers to
1804 (before the production of Paer's opera) rather than 1805.
Paer's *Leonora* did not reach Vienna until March 1806, when it was

[1] 'Paers "Leonora" und Beethovens "Fidelio"', *Neues Beethoven-
Jahrbuch*, IV (1930), p. 118.

[2] Not until the last of the seven incipits quoted by Nottebohm does it
begin to resemble either its eventual form or Paer's.

347

given privately at the Lobkowitz palace. Beethoven attended its first public performance (in German) on 8 February 1809.

Simone Mayr's *L'Amor conjugale*, a one-act *farsa sentimentale* (a cross between Italian *farsa* and French *opéra-comique* with the *buffo* element played down), saw the light at Padua early in 1805.[1] The librettist, Gaetano Rossi, transferred the action to Poland, doubtless under the influence of *Lodoïska*, which Mayr had already set twice in Italian. His text reduces the realism and potency of Bouilly's plot to a caper with the conventions. The political content vanishes: Pizarro's motive is love for Leonora, who is rescued by the fortuitous arrival of her brother-in-law.[2] Jaquino does not appear, nor do the prisoners; Rocco patronizes the bottle (Mayr, unlike Paer, keeps the gold aria). In place of the grave-digging duet Leonora sings a strophic romance in popular French style, hoping that Florestan will recognize her voice. Unlike Gaveaux and Paer, Mayr binds together the closing scenes in continuous music, beginning with a quartet when Rocco signals to Pizarro that the grave is ready. The climax of this is delayed by a slow *cantabile* in E flat, typical of Mayr and his Italian successors, including Rossini, after which the pistol and the trumpet signal restore the tempo. The finale contains an angry aria for Pizarro, very like Dourlinski's in Act III of Cherubini's *Lodoïska*, which gives it a collateral relationship with Beethoven:

Ex. 6

Ah per-chè non t'ap - ri, O ter - ra, sot - to a miei tre -
- man - ti pas-si ro - vi - na - te, or - ren - di mas-si,
m'in-vo - la - te al mio fu - ror

---

[1] See Ludwig Schiedermair, *Beiträge zur Geschichte der Oper* (Leipzig, 1907), II, pp. 39–50.

[2] In this summary I have retained the familiar names of the characters rather than confuse the reader with their Polish equivalents.

Mayr's style is not unlike Paer's; he, too, concentrates on big dramatic monologues for Leonora and Florestan. Again the introduction to the latter is as memorable as anything in the score:

Ex. 7

When Florestan begins to think of his wife, two cors anglais (a favourite instrument) introduce a melody that oddly anticipates the main theme of Beethoven's 1814 overture. As usual Mayr is most individual in his treatment of the orchestra, especially the solo wind instruments. His function in the history of music was to provide a bridge between Mozart on the one hand and Rossini and Donizetti on the other. No one has suggested that Beethoven knew his opera.[1]

---

[1] By a curious coincidence Mayr was invited to set a German libretto by Schikaneder in April 1803, just when Beethoven was about to take up *Vestas Feuer*. See the interesting letter from Hubert Rumpf to Mayr (Schiedermair, op. cit., II, p. 191) informing him, among other Viennese theatre gossip, that Schikaneder is working on an opera 'mit, und für Pethoven' [*sic*].

THE 1805 VERSION OF BEETHOVEN'S OPERA

Beethoven's opera is by far the closest to the letter and the spirit of Bouilly. Sonnleithner's libretto is largely a translation with additional musical numbers. He divided Bouilly's first act into two, with no change of scene until the second finale, which he moved from the prison courtyard to another part of the fortress. Act I has three inserted numbers, a trio ('Ein Mann ist bald genommen') in which Rocco and Marzelline dash Jaquino's hopes of marriage, the canon quartet, and the trio for Rocco, Leonore and Marzelline (No. 5 of the 1814 score), after which the curtain falls. The first three numbers in Act II, the March, Pizarro's aria with chorus and his duet with Rocco, are new. Pizarro posts the trumpeter before his aria and briefs Rocco on stage in the duet, but is not overheard by Leonore. Sonnleithner retains the long scene for Leonore and Marzelline, including the duet (without the passage, redolent of Papageno and Papagena, in which they speculate whether their child's first words will be 'Maman' or 'Papa') and the dialogue about Leonore talking in her sleep. The recitative before Leonore's aria ('O brich noch nicht, du mattes Herz!') is translated from Bouilly and very different from 1814; the apostrophe to hope is not in the 1805 libretto, but was probably inserted before performance. The scene changes at the end of the aria, and the finale follows at once. Marzelline lets the prisoners out in the ordinary course of her duties. Sonnleithner extended their chorus into a substantial finale. Rocco orders them back to the cells before telling Leonore the outcome of his interview with Pizarro. The Governor's wrath, warning of which is brought by Marzelline alone, is provoked not by the release of the prisoners but by Rocco's delay in digging the grave. He hustles the jailer and his assistants out and ends the act with a second aria, supported by male chorus, that involves much sabre-rattling, but does not advance the plot.

Act III follows the model closely, apart from the insertion of the quartet and the connection of Bouilly's last two numbers with the intervening dialogue in a continuous movement. The final section of Florestan's aria, as in Bouilly, is addressed to Leonore's portrait. Pizarro enters masked and disguised, but he reveals

himself before Leonore and does not offer Rocco a second purse.
The dialogue linking the quartet to the lovers' duet becomes a
recitative. In the finale the chorus denounce Pizarro's sentence as
too lenient, and Don Fernando decides to leave the decision to the
King (was this one of the changes demanded by the censorship?).
Pizarro is silent throughout. Leonore does not mention Marzelline's dowry, and there is no homily to the audience from Fernando
or anyone else. These two details are essentially French, the
former of all time, the latter characteristic of the Revolution period
(compare Bouilly's ethical conclusion to *Les deux Journées*: 'Le
premier charme de la vie, C'est de servir l'humanité'). Perhaps in
compensation Sonnleithner (or Beethoven) introduced a slightly
modified quotation from Schiller's *Ode to Joy* in the couplet beginning 'Wer ein holdes Weib errungen', thereby linking the opera
with the finale of the Ninth Symphony. Both works carry the same
message; it is even possible that the one put the other into Beethoven's head.

Sonnleithner's chief aim was to increase the opportunities for
expressing drama by musical means. In this he is often successful,
especially in the two quartets and the development of Pizarro's
part. The finales of the second and third acts, though not wholly
satisfactory, are moves in the right direction. What is effective in
Bouilly he preserves. The obvious flaw is the enormous expansion
of the first and less dramatic half of the story. The exposition of the
Marzelline subplot, leisurely in Bouilly, is further retarded by the
new musical numbers. The first act merely outlines a situation;
the action has yet to begin. Of the three central characters, Leonore
does not appear until half-way through Act I, Pizarro until Act II,
Florestan until Act III. Up to Pizarro's first exit Sonnleithner
has deployed nine musical numbers (excluding the overture),
several of them developed at considerable length by Beethoven,
against Bouilly's three. After this the drama sags again in the
superfluous scene for Leonore and Marzelline; nor does the second
finale draw all the threads together. The lightweight opening in
the jailer's household, whose function is to set the scene, has
usurped the prominence of the main plot. When the last act begins
it is too late to redress the balance.

351

This defect is accentuated by Beethoven's music.[1] Though never dull, its regular periods are geared to abstract musical design rather than dramatic pace; consequently it lags behind the action and seems on occasion diffuse and repetitive. This must be ascribed to lack of practical experience in the theatre. The movements are all longer—some of them much longer—than in the 1814 score,[2] and there are more of them. The trio 'Ein Mann ist bald genommen' in Act I and the duet 'Um in der Ehe' in Act II are dramatically otiose, especially the latter, which enlarges on a false situation of which we have already had more than enough and disperses the tension when it has at last begun to accumulate. The old-fashioned concertante layout with solo violin and cello, for all

[1] The 1805 version, reconstructed after great labour from scattered manuscripts, many of which had been used by Beethoven for his revisions, was edited by Erich Prieger under the title *Leonore* (full score, six copies only without critical apparatus, Leipzig, 1908–10; vocal score 1905, 2nd edn., 1907; neither score contains the spoken dialogue). This material was used for the Berlin revival under Richard Strauss on 20 November 1905, the centenary of the first performance. In 1967 Willy Hess brought out a new full score in two supplementary volumes (XI and XII) to the complete Beethoven edition, with a scholarly critical commentary that identifies all the sources. The basis of this score is a reproduction of Prieger's; although many corrections have been made to the text, others could not be incorporated and must be supplied from the notes. Hess's preface promises a later supplement containing the 1806 version, which has never been published in full, although as early as 1853 Otto Jahn attempted a vocal score (published by Breitkopf & Härtel), indicating the 1805 text where it differed. This was a fine achievement for its date, but later scholarship has modified some of Jahn's conclusions. Certain details remain in doubt; it is not always possible to distinguish Beethoven's changes before the first performance from those for the 1806 revival. Other disputable points are mentioned below. The best account of the various versions is Hess's *Beethovens Oper Fidelio und ihre drei Fassungen* (Zürich, 1953), which includes a line-by-line comparison of the 1805 and 1806 librettos. Adolf Sandberger, in *Ausgewählte Aufsätze zur Musikgeschichte*, II (Munich, 1924), reprinted the Bouilly and Sonnleithner librettos and compared them in detail with Treitschke, but ignored 1806 and consequently attributed some of Breuning's work and even Sonnleithner's to Treitschke. There is no reliable account in English. Ernest Newman's in *More opera nights*, pp. 253 ff., is misleading in several important particulars.

[2] With the single exception of the March, which (apart from a different treatment of repeats in 1814) remained unchanged throughout. Treitschke's statement that it was composed in 1814 is wrong.

its charm, belongs to a more leisurely type of pre-Revolution rescue opera, that of Mozart's *Die Entführung*. In recommending the omission of these two numbers and Pizarro's second aria, the weakest music in the score, Beethoven's friends showed sound judgement, as he tacitly acknowledged when he followed their advice in 1814. The musical idiom, especially in the early scenes, is much more Mozartian in 1805 than in 1814. The 1805 overture, *Leonore* No. 2, might be criticized for its lopsided construction, especially when compared with its successor; but Beethoven's intention seems to have been to supply a graphic summary of the action rather than a formal overture. The result is a piece of programme music that ranks as a mighty forerunner of the symphonic poems of Liszt and Strauss.[1]

The original third act is a different matter. Although this, too, contains passages, especially in the finale, where the music clogs the wheels of the drama, it is less a primitive attempt at what Beethoven achieved in 1814 than a volley at a different target. This change of aim is discussed below. Meanwhile the music that did not survive 1805-6 demands comment. The *Andante un poco agitato* F minor conclusion to Florestan's aria, though it lacks the radiance of his F major vision in 1814, has a defiant stoicism that is not only most movingly expressed but enlarges our view of Florestan's character. Anyone can see his beloved in a trance; it takes a hero to look back on his past happiness and accept his fate. There is some doubt whether the *Melodram* before the grave-digging duet formed part of the 1805 score. Prieger and Hess include it; Jahn ascribes it to 1814. Certainly its surviving form cannot belong to 1805, for it quotes the F major (1814) section of Florestan's aria when he stirs in his sleep. Yet there are sketches dating from 1804 as well as 1814. The most likely solution is that it was performed in 1805 in a version since lost, and rewritten in 1814. The sketches prove that the allusions to the $\frac{6}{8}$ section of the Leonore-Rocco duet in the previous finale ('Wir müssen gleich zum Werke schreiten') were part of Beethoven's original plan.

---

[1] Beethoven subsequently shortened it, possibly for the second or third performance. For a full account of the overtures see Josef Braunstein, *Beethovens Leonore-Ouvertüren* (Leipzig, 1927).

353

From the end of the quartet onwards the 1805 score (following Bouilly) has a dramatic tension and a vividness of characterization, both fully realized in musical terms, that are almost entirely absent from 1814. When Pizarro goes out, in response to the more florid trumpet call of the No. 2 overture, Leonore throws herself at Rocco's feet with a spoken appeal against the closing bars of the orchestral ritornello. Rocco snatches the pistol from her and disappears; the quartet ends with a *fortissimo* diminished seventh as she utters a piercing cry and falls senseless. The long recitative in which Florestan tries to reach her, she slowly recovers, and each at last grasps the truth is a superb stroke of musical drama. Based on a beautiful melody for solo oboe:

Ex. 8

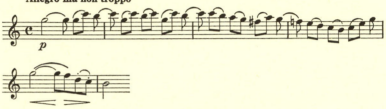

it builds up gradually over seventy-six bars to the passionate discharge of the duet 'O namenlose Freude'. The music has a quality of dawning suspense paralleled only by that which introduces the finale of the Fifth Symphony. It launches the duet with a tremendous impact, reinforced by the fact that both voices enter together and the melody is carried up to the top B. This may be instrumental vocal writing (the words are a much poorer fit than in *Vestas Feuer*), but it releases the full emotional content of the situation. Of Beethoven's three versions of this melody the second is by far the most exciting in its context because it has been so thoroughly prepared (see Ex. 9).

Moreover the whole ambience of the duet is transformed by the fact that the lovers have no reason to believe themselves out of danger. They have lost their only weapon and naturally take the distant cries of vengeance, supported by trombones behind the scenes, as directed against them. These and the incursion of the

Ex. 9
a: Vestas Feuer

b: 1805

c: 1814

whole tumultuous crowd into the dungeon produce another splendid theatrical climax, which may well have reminded early audiences of the storming of the Bastille. The finale contains some rather
commonplace rejoicing, though Fernando's solos have a Sarastro-
like nobility, and is undeniably static. The F major *Andante assai*,
twice as long as in 1814, is a tribute to the continuity of Beethoven's
development: its principal theme comes from the *Cantata on the*

death of the Emperor Joseph II, composed in Bonn as early as 1790. The original words are significant, and may have suggested the borrowing; but the simple dance-like accompaniment shows no sign of the later polyphonic resource.

Ex. 10

This is perhaps the point to mention the sketches and a number of drafts rejected before the first performance. The former have been studied by Nottebohm[1] and more briefly by Jahn.[2] Beethoven sketched the movements for the most part in the order in which they occur in the opera. As usual this was a prolonged labour. The first ideas are often primitive and feeble, with little or no relation to the ultimate form—for example in the prisoners' chorus and Pizarro's entrance music in the Act II finale, which suggests an elderly *buffo* rather than a tyrant. The Act I quartet was planned from the start as a canon, but it took Beethoven at least thirteen shots to evolve the melody. He drafted Florestan's aria in three

[1] Cf. *Zwei Skizzenbücher von Beethoven aus den Jahren 1801 bis 1803,* and 'Ein Skizzenbuch aus dem Jahre 1804', in *NZB,* p. 409.

[2] *Gesammelte Aufsätze über Musik* (Leipzig, 1867), pp. 236 ff.

sections, the second of which, *Moderato* in F major with flute obbligato, was suppressed. Röckel's story that the aria originally consisted of the *Adagio* only, with a sustained top F for the tenor at the end, may be explained by the existence of two sketches of the *Adagio* running straight into the *Melodram*; but this seems to have been an abandoned later project. It is, however, possible that an early version of the aria has disappeared. The 1806 libretto has eight additional lines (of which no setting is known) after the *Adagio*, and no complete manuscript of the 1805 version survives.[1]

The sketches for the grave-digging duet are of particular interest; only after prolonged wrestling did Beethoven find a satisfactory accompaniment figure and a verbal declamation that distinguished the two characters. Two rejected accompaniment figures were:

Ex. 11

One sketch shows an almost Straussian realism in tone-painting as Rocco and Leonore struggle to raise the heavy stone:

Ex. 12

[1] See the preface and critical commentary of Hess's full score.

The minims followed by rests towards the end are explained by a stage direction in the libretto 'They draw breath' and the word 'Athemholen', which Beethoven wrote twice against the corresponding bars in another sketch. This passage is different in all three performing versions. Beethoven seems to have conceived the straining bass figure of Ex. 12 in connection with Leonore's and Rocco's attempts to move the stone. By 1805, however, he must have associated it (in place of the minims and rests) with their breathlessness after the event, for he reserved it for the pause when the voices are silent; but there is no check in the movement:

Ex. 13

358

In 1806 he cut the voices short and added a fermata:

Ex. 14

In 1814 he inserted the semiquaver figure for double bassoon and string basses (at the moment when the stone is moved) and emphasized the effort involved with two fermatas, one before (underlined by a sforzando) and one after, and only then admitted the 'breathless' figure in the bass:

Ex. 15

The fact that the sketches for Leonore's recitative and aria occur out of sequence after the Act III finale led Nottebohm to conjecture that a different aria in F was sung in 1805. This receives superficial support from the 1805 libretto, which gives two eight-line stanzas without a recitative and without the 'Komm, Hoffnung' quatrain. But it seems more likely that the text was changed at a late stage in 1805 after the libretto had been printed.

The best known of the rejected pieces is the *Leonore* No. 1 overture, whose one point in common with its successors is the quotation from the *Adagio* of Florestan's aria. Schindler's statement that it was tried out privately at Prince Lichnowsky's in 1805 and found too slight is now generally accepted.[1] There are three early versions of Marzelline's aria, all related in material; probably the third was sung in 1805.[2] The first, in C major throughout, is

[1] For a full discussion of the evidence, see Braunstein, op. cit., pp. 4–23.

[2] Jahn printed all three in vocal score in his edition referred to in n. 1 on p. 352; the full scores of the first two are in the second supplement to the complete Beethoven edition. Including the shortened form sung in 1814 and a further truncation without coda (see Hess, *Beethovens Oper Fidelio*, p. 254), there are altogether five versions of this aria.

somewhat ornate and does not convey the undercurrent of anxiety in Marzelline's mind. The second and third both adopt the C minor-major alternation with coda. The second, with a plaintive seven-bar initial ritornello, borrows the theme of the first for its sections in the major and shortens it; the third restores its full length, but reduces the ritornello to two bars. In the appendix to the complete-edition score Hess prints an earlier, slightly longer and differently scored version of the grave-digging duet with no major variants, an abandoned opening of Leonore's recitative and aria, which argues against Nottebohm's conjecture of a previous setting in F, and the rejected orchestral coda to the trio 'Euch werde Lohn'. Jahn attributed this last change to 1806.

THE 1806 VERSION

The changes made in 1806 are generally dismissed as hasty cuts to serve a temporary emergency. This does less than justice to Beethoven and Breuning. Although some of the excisions are crude and were later restored, it is clear that the authors had a shrewd idea what was the matter with the opera. They reduced it to two acts by combining the original Acts I and II, but made a change of scene at the old act-break. They altered the order of movements and events in the new first act. Rocco's aria was omitted, but not before Breuning had supplied it with new words;[1] when it was eventually restored, the text was a fusion of these and Sonnleithner's. Pizarro now posts the trumpeter *after* his aria (a good touch). Leonore enters in great agitation immediately after the Rocco-Pizarro duet; she has observed their conference, but is uncertain whether Rocco has obtained permission for her to enter the dungeon. Her recitative and aria (No. 11 in 1805) follow; then the scene with Marzelline, including the duet 'Um in der Ehe' (No. 10), *preceded* by the conversation about Leonore talking in her sleep. Jaquino overhears the end of the duet. Leonore, seeking a pretext to escape, asks if it is not time to let the prisoners out for their exercise and hurries off. Jaquino flies into a jealous rage, leading to the trio with Rocco 'Ein Mann ist bald genommen' (No. 3), which like the other trio (No. 6)

[1] Jahn prints both sets with the 1805 music.

361

is followed by a change of scene. Leonore enters with keys, delighted to release the prisoners and wishing she could do the same for Florestan. But Rocco does not send the prisoners back to the cells after their chorus; they go into the garden, as in 1814, and we do not witness their return. It will be seen that several improvements usually attributed to Treitschke date from 1806.[1] Breuning also clarified a number of points in the dialogue and stage directions.

In Act II he added the direction about shifting the stone during the duet and made the words of the trio 'Euch werde Lohn' more graphic. Leonore's reference to her beating heart and Florestan's observation that the boy as well as the man seems moved are new. In the quartet Pizarro opens his cloak instead of taking off his mask. Leonore's first half-conscious words in the recitative before 'O namenlose Freude' were changed from 'Gebt ihm mir!' to 'Todt! Dahin!' There were several amendments to the finale. Just after Don Fernando raises Leonore to her feet Jaquino has a brief exchange with Marzelline. His hopes revive on the instant, and she encourages him too readily with a reference to the trio in which she refused him in Act I. This cannot be called good psychology, and it disappeared in 1814 in favour of Marzelline's single cry of distress. The long section in which Don Fernando pronounces sentence on Pizarro, Leonore and Florestan appeal for mercy, the chorus demand greater severity and Don Fernando decides to refer the matter to the King was replaced by a short recitative: Fernando disposes of Pizarro with a terse 'Hinweg mit diesem Bösewicht!'[2] Breuning had to supply Leonore with a new quatrain in the closing ensemble. In 1805 she was mute for the last 132 bars of the opera. Beethoven carved a top line for her out of the choral soprano part and rewrote Florestan's music here in more florid form.

[1] The confusion is partly due to the fact that Jahn, when he prepared his score, had not seen the 1806 libretto and was unaware of the changed order of movements. Elliot Forbes falls into the same trap in *TF*: see his footnotes to p. 572. *KH* is also wrong about the 1806 order.

[2] A mysterious (and superior) second setting of this and the three following lines was copied in a score of the 1814 version prepared for Dresden in 1823 (see Hans Volkmann, *Beethoven in seinen Beziehungen zu Dresden*, Dresden, 1942, p. 106). The lines belong only to 1806; but they were in the original 1814 libretto from which Beethoven worked, and he may have set them again in that year.

Rocco's aria and the *Melodram* were the only movements to disappear entirely. But most of the others were shortened, some of them drastically.[1] Both trios in Act I suffered something approaching mutilation, and so did the opening of Florestan's scena: the recitative was rewritten, by no means for the better, and the *Adagio* deprived of its ritornello.[2] Leonore's aria lost fourteen bars in the coda, including an elaborate and taxing cadenza. An interesting change here was the insertion of the words 'O Hoffnung, O komm', marked *sprechend oder singend*, against the ritornello of the *Adagio*. The orchestral introduction to the grave-digging duet was shortened by seventeen bars, but the double bassoon was added to the score.[3] Beethoven rewrote the trio 'Euch werde Lohn' in much terser form, modifying the anacrusis of the main theme, removing a long roulade for Florestan on the word 'Dank!' (bar 94 of the 1814 score) and transplanting the next section, where all three voices sing together just before the change of tempo, back into the middle of Florestan's first solo, where it replaced the earlier statement of the same material. This destroyed the balance of the movement at both points; Beethoven rectified it in 1814. He severely compressed 'O namenlose Freude' and its recitative, reducing a total of 291 bars to 185, but lengthened and improved the orchestral coda, which reached its 1814 form in 1806. Leonore's part in the duet was eased by the removal of two slow chromatic-scale passages climbing to top C, possibly at the request of Milder. Both finales were considerably shortened, the first by 122 bars, the second by 154. This affected all their principal movements. The prisoners' chorus was pruned of much repetition. In the second finale the

[1] The exceptions appear to have been Marzelline's aria, both quartets, the March and the Pizarro-Rocco duet. Some of these were changed in detail.

[2] Jahn did not print the 1805 version. Hess restored the recitative and ritornello from fragmentary sources, but the 1805 *Adagio*, if it differed from that of 1806 (as is very likely), is lost. Hess's score diverges from Prieger's more sharply here than elsewhere because Prieger back-dated to 1805 alterations made in 1814.

[3] The double bassoon in Hess's score, like the direction for scaling down the dynamics of the whole duet (also added in 1806), is an uncancelled relic of Prieger's.

offstage chorus lost its trombones[1] and the F major section its long opening quintet for the soloists. A more positive change was the substitution of the No. 3 overture for No. 2 and the consequent simplification of the trumpet calls in the quartet. Tempo alterations suggest that several movements were taken too slowly in 1805. The prisoners' chorus was marked up from *Allegretto* to *Allegretto con moto*, Pizarro's second aria from *Allegro ma non troppo* to *Allegro con brio*, the trio 'Euch werde Lohn' from *Andante con moto* (leading to *Più mosso*) to *Allegro* (leading to *Un poco più allegro*), the dungeon quartet from *Allegro* to *Allegro con brio*, the opening of 'Wer ein holdes Weib' from *Maestoso* to *Maestoso vivace*.

While the effect of these alterations must have been beneficial in speeding up the action, they did not go to the root of the problem, the undue prominence of Marzelline, and some of them were ill-judged. It is not surprising that Beethoven returned to the attack eight years later.

THE 1814 VERSION

Treitschke's statement that he rewrote the dialogue 'almost wholly anew, succinct and clear as possible' is disingenuous; he preserved a great deal of both Sonnleithner and Breuning, though he made cuts and a few small insertions. His changes were, however, radical in several important respects. He tackled Marzelline firmly, omitting the trio and duet shifted in 1806 and the conversation about Leonore talking in her sleep. He transposed the order of the first two numbers, obtaining a more effective launch into the drama. He abolished both changes of scene in this act. Leonore now overhears Pizarro's duet with Rocco and reacts to it in the new recitative 'Abscheulicher!' This is the one episode in *Fidelio* that undoubtedly echoes Paer's libretto, where the corresponding scene begins (in the German translation): 'Abscheulicher Pizarro! Wo gehest du hin? Was denkst du? Was hast du vor?' and the aria contains the line 'Des Meers empörte Wogen'.[2] It is at Leonore's special request

[1] So did Pizarro's 'Ha! welch ein Augenblick!'—but it appears to have gained a second pair of horns, which were removed in 1814.

[2] This may explain Beethoven's reference to the libretto of *Fidelio* as 'a French and Italian book' in conversation with Benedict in 1823.

that Rocco lets out the prisoners. Treitschke worked much more action into the finale. At the bass prisoner's solo 'Sprecht leise' a sentry appears on the wall and goes off to inform Pizarro. Jaquino as well as Marzelline brings warning of the Governor's wrath, which is more formidable because more strongly motivated than in 1805. Rocco takes a less abject stand. His excuses include the subtle one that since Pizarro's particular prisoner is to die the others can surely be allowed to enjoy the sunshine and celebrate the King's name day. He has, however, to recall them from the garden and lock them up. This makes room for their second chorus and the ensemble based on it.

There are few changes in the first half of Act II, except that Florestan, instead of addressing Leonore's portrait, has a delirious vision of her as an angel summoning him to freedom in heaven. (Treitschke left a vivid account of Beethoven improvising the music of the new F major section as soon as he received the words; nevertheless it appears in its proper place among the sketches.) The quartet is interrupted after the second trumpet call by the arrival of Jaquino and soldiers, to the unconcealed delight of Rocco. This effectively circumscribes Pizarro's movements, but destroys the effect of Beethoven's modulation. At Pizarro's exit Rocco, instead of disarming Leonore, seizes her hand and Florestan's, presses them to his breast and points to heaven before hurrying out. In the dialogue that replaces the recitative Leonore assures Florestan that all their troubles are over. Rocco returns after the duet and informs them, in dialogue, that Florestan's name is not on the official list of prisoners; his detention was therefore illegal. The scene changes to the parade-ground, where the chorus, including the prisoners, acclaim the long-awaited day of justice. Don Fernando brings from the King a pardon for all the prisoners and makes a political speech: tyranny is at an end, let brother seek the hand of brother. He is astonished when Rocco produces Florestan and Leonore (Rocco does not throw down the purse, and he tells Don Fernando a good deal that we already know). Pizarro asks permission to speak, but is refused and led off *before* the removal of Florestan's fetters.

Treitschke's treatment of Act I merits unstinted applause. The drama begins to move earlier, gathers momentum from Pizarro's first appearance, and retains a tightening grip until the end. The changes in Act II produce exactly the opposite effect. Rocco's character is sentimentalized. The lovers' secure confidence saps the excitement of the duet, which in the absence of the recitative makes a standing instead of a flying start. The spoken conclusion (generally omitted today) is feeble in the extreme. The change of scene, which Treitschke regarded as the healing of 'a great fault' in Sonnleithner's libretto, fails to achieve one of the most resounding anticlimaxes in the history of opera only because Beethoven capped it with a hymn to freedom of surpassing nobility.

We must, however, recognize that this was the result of deliber-ate choice. Sonnleithner, like Bouilly, concentrates on the personal drama of Leonore and Florestan; the other prisoners are little more than a background. The moral is not emphasized, but allowed to emerge through the action. Treitschke and Beethoven raise it from the particular to the universal and ram it home so hard that the hollow reverberations of a thumped tub are all but discernible. (In a letter of April 1814, already cited, Beethoven told Treitschke that he was setting the text 'exactly in the way you have altered and im-proved everything, an achievement which every moment I am recognizing more and more';[1] but it must be assumed that they had already agreed on the main trend.) The prisoners, no longer re-stricted to a single chorus, play a much larger part and obviously symbolize for Beethoven the whole of suffering mankind. The finale with its general amnesty becomes a pattern of the day of judgement. Moreover the change of scene gives the opera a neatly symmetrical plan: Act I moves from light into darkness, Act II from darkness into light. But although this idealized content finds ample utterance in the music, it does not spring convincingly from the plot; the symbolism is stretched beyond its implications. We have little reason to suppose that all the prisoners had been unjustly incarcerated, or that their crime was political (though Pizarro's anonymous letter does hint that Florestan may not be the only

---

[1] *LA*, letter 479. This was not always his opinion. On 19 April 1817 he wrote to Charles Neate that 'the book and the text left much to be desired': cf. *LA*, letter 778.

innocent victim); they could be a set of thieves, murderers and delinquents. In delivering this mighty pæan Beethoven comes closer still to the spirit of the Ninth Symphony;[1] but he drains his characters of individuality and smudges the portrait of the hero and heroine so movingly drawn in 1805. They become personifications, and since Pizarro alone stands for evil the mottled personality of Rocco must be whitewashed into benevolent conformity.

The musical changes in 1814 nearly all bear witness to richer maturity. The splendid new E major overture supplies a more fitting introduction to the light tone of the first scene than *Leonore* No. 3, whose massive stature throws much that follows into shadow. The key may have been chosen to pick out the E major of Leonore's aria. The 1805–6 versions have a clear C major home tonic; the first and last vocal movements each move from C minor to C major, and the words of Marzelline's aria, 'O wär' ich schon mit dir vereint', announce at the outset one of the central ideas of the story. The rearranged order and the new overture indicate a different tonal plan. Beethoven made further changes in all the numbers he retained. Many of them are small cuts, involving the elision of idle bars and florid ornamental passages, especially at cadences. Their cumulative effect is considerable, and reflects a powerful urge, typical of late Beethoven, to break down exact symmetry of phrase; at the same time they accommodate the expression and declamation of the music more strictly to the ebb and flow of the drama. Hess, though full of complaints that Beethoven destroyed the perfection of his 1805 design, rightly points out that in such movements as the duet in which Pizarro and Rocco plan the murder he took a substantial stride towards the flexible methods of Wagner. There are numerous improvements in detail. These, like the sketches,[2] throw much fascinating light on

[1] The words, too, take a step nearer, especially in the two lines repeated by Don Fernando: 'Es sucht der Bruder seine Brüder, Und kann er helfen hilft er gern' ('Brother seeks out his brothers and gladly helps whom he can').

[2] Sketches survive for all the new music of the 1814 score except the fifty bars before the second prisoners' chorus. They are discussed in *NZB*, pp. 293–306. At one time Beethoven thought of using the trumpet call in the new overture.

Beethoven's creative processes; only a few can be mentioned here. It is clear that he did indeed rethink the whole score from the beginning. While he accepted most of the 1806 cuts, in three movements, the two surviving trios and the recitative and ritornello of Florestan's aria, he made a partial return to the longer text of 1805, though not in identical form.

The canon quartet, slightly modified, lost a single bar. Pizarro's aria was improved by the insertion of sixteen bars with a bold new modulation and a new rhythm at the first entry of the chorus. Leonore's aria, apart from its more striking recitative, emerged in much terser and more concentrated form. The ritornello was shortened, the voice part simplified and pruned of adornments, the first twenty-two bars of the *Allegro con brio* with an arresting passage for horns cut altogether, thereby altering the whole balance of the aria, and the *Più lento* mark added at the words 'in Fesseln schlug'. Milder told Schindler that she had severe struggles with Beethoven over 'the unbeautiful, unsingable passages, unsuited to her voice' in the *Adagio* and finally refused to sing it in the old form. This did the trick. A comparison of the final bars indicates what she achieved:

Ex. 16
a: 1805

b: 1814

Beethoven made an interesting change—or rather two successive changes—to the tenor prisoner's solo in the chorus 'O welche Lust'. In 1805 he set the third and fourth lines thus:

Ex. 17

The pause of nearly two bars, punctuated by shy staccato arpeggios on the woodwind, gives a touching emphasis to the words 'wir werden frei', as if the singer scarcely dare utter them. In shortening the whole passage for 1806 Beethoven reduced this to a momentary hesitation, emphasizing 'frei' with a sforzando:

Ex. 18

wir wer-den frei,— wir— fin – – den Ruh'!

In 1814, though the accompaniment is virtually unchanged, he modified the declamation and dynamics:

Ex. 19

Die Hoff - nung flüs – tert sanft — mir— zu: wir wer-den
frei,——— wir fin - den Ruh', wir fin - den Ruh'!

'Frei' carries more weight, but the pause has gone, and it is impossible not to feel that something has been lost. The later part of the finale from shortly after Pizarro's return, including the exquisite chorus 'Leb' wohl, du warmes Sonnenlicht', is all new. The formal and the tonal balance are strengthened: the 1814 finale, though it makes an impression of greater spaciousness and mass, is the shortest of the three.

Florestan's aria has many differences in addition to the restoration of the ritornello and the new F major conclusion. The introduction and recitative were refashioned for the second time, and the *Adagio* extended. The only musical alteration to the grave-digging duet (the words were touched up towards the end) was the new semiquaver bass figure for the shifting of the stone (Ex. 15). Beethoven again rewrote the trio 'Euch werde Lohn', bringing it much closer to 1805 than to 1806. There were many changes to the vocal lines of the quartet, especially in Pizarro's part, and to the scoring of the last section. Leonore's top note at 'Tödt erst sein *Weib*!', which had been B natural (despite the accompanying harmony) in 1805, became B flat,[1] and her top B flat at 'und du bist *todt!*' an octave above the trumpet entry fell to a low F below it. The second trumpet call was now unaccompanied, and two introductory bars were added after the spoken interruption, perhaps to help the voices. In 'O namenlose Freude', the one movement unmistakably weakened, the voices sing the modified melody in succession instead of together. Whereas in 1805 the duet expresses the joy of reunion and the A major episode of the finale the sense of release as the spiritual light of freedom bursts into the dungeon, in 1814 the duet has to carry a double response to reunion and rescue, and the A major music (with new words) is played in full daylight after all is over. Nevertheless the new finale is musically a great improvement. The opening chorus and Don Fernando's solo are new; from the A major section onwards everything is rewritten on the old material. The F major *Andante assai*, now *Sostenuto assai*, begins not with a quintet (as in 1805) or a chorus (as in 1806), but far more movingly with solos for Leonore and Florestan expressing wonder. Beethoven had second thoughts about several of the tempos altered in 1806: the first prisoners' chorus is now *Allegro ma non troppo*, the trio 'Euch werde Lohn' *Moderato*, 'Wer ein holdes Weib' *Allegro ma non troppo* (*Presto molto* instead of *Allegro con brio* in the coda).

A certain mystery surrounds Beethoven's advertisement of two new pieces for his benefit on 18 July. One of them was Rocco's aria, not heard since 1805. Treitschke conflated two versions of the words; Beethoven slightly shortened the $\frac{6}{8}$ sections, removed the trumpet and drum parts and changed the tempos from *Allegretto moderato* ($\frac{2}{4}$)—*Allegro non molto* ($\frac{6}{8}$) to *Allegro moderato—Allegro*. The other insertion was a new aria for Leonore; Beethoven reported to Treitschke early in July that 'Milder got her aria a fortnight ago'.[2] Treitschke says it held up the action and 'was again omitted' (after one performance?); the *Allgemeine Musikalische Zeitung* also considered the act had 'become unnecessarily long'.[3] Despite

---

[1] Thus reversing the tendency of the 1804 sketches, where Beethoven began with B flat and a mild dissonance. The 1810 vocal score has B flat. Possibly the singer found it difficult to keep the B natural in tune.

[2] *LA*, letter 483.

[3] Quoted in *TF*, p. 588.

certain inconsistencies in the press notices this was almost certainly the aria we know today. But if so, what had Milder sung at the first six performances? A dated manuscript libretto in the theatre archives, unquestionably prepared for the 1814 revival, contains a different version of the 'Abscheulicher' recitative (eight lines, the last four quite unconnected with the seven that took their place),[1] followed by the words of the *Allegro con brio* in the 1805–6 setting (beginning 'O du, für den ich alles trug'); no sign of 'Komm, Hoffnung'. (A later hand has inserted the familiar words, and those of Rocco's aria.) This agrees precisely with Treitschke's statement that the aria 'received a new introduction, and only the last movement, "O du, für den ich alles trug", was retained'.[2] It seems likely that an earlier 'Abscheulicher', from which the entire 'Komm, Hoffnung' section was struck out, was sung six times and subsequently lost. Some support for this conjecture may be found in another manuscript libretto[3] of very recent discovery, which also omits Rocco's aria and has the earlier form of 'Abscheulicher'. Its margins are covered with Beethoven's annotations (words, music, indications of scoring and tempo), which clearly reflect his first thoughts on receiving the text early in 1814, before sketching began. Against the last two lines of 'Abscheulicher' he wrote 'Corni $^6_8$', an indication that corresponds with no surviving version.[4] It is true that there is no sign of a lost aria in the sketches; but those for the first finale before the chorus 'Leb' wohl, du warmes Sonnenlicht', which would have immediately followed any such aria composed in the spring of 1814, are likewise missing. The sketches for the familiar 'Abscheulicher' come very late, after those for the overture, which was not ready for the first night.

In 1925 Hans Joachim Moser suggested the construction of a

---

[1] Printed in *NZB*, p. 304.

[2] Much of Treitschke's account is in *TF*, pp. 572–4.

[3] Described in Sotheby's sale catalogue, 29 April 1969, lot 204A.

[4] This fascinating libretto has many further points of interest. Beethoven himself altered the title from *Leonore* to *Fidelio* and made changes in the words. Many of the ideas rapidly (and not always legibly) noted were subsequently adopted, but not all. He seems to have considered a new recitative before 'O namenlose Freude'. Pizarro was still to be on stage during the removal of Florestan's fetters.

fourth version of the opera, combining all that is best in the first and third. This is neither practicable nor desirable.[1] But there is no need to regard the later version as a replacement of the earlier; both are viable, and the labours of Jahn, Prieger and Hess have made 1805 as accessible as 1814. Our preference can remain a matter of taste. It is perhaps worth commenting on the custom, begun by Mahler and followed by Toscanini, Klemperer and other conductors, of interposing the No. 3 overture between the dungeon and parade-ground scenes. This cannot be defended on the score of authenticity; but neither can it be condemned as dramatically injurious, for the drama is dead. The overture repeats in summary what we have just witnessed; it scarcely affects Beethoven's pæan to liberty. And it may bridge an awkward lacuna while the scenery is changed.

INFLUENCES ON 'FIDELIO'

Beethoven's opera, though timeless in its appeal, is a product of the French Revolution and of the school of Cherubini in particular. The principal models were *Lodoïska* and *Les deux Journées*, especially the former, and the librettos exercised as pronounced an influence as the music. The *opéra-comique* or *Singspiel* form, the background of domestic realism tinged with comedy,[2] the super-imposition of a heroic or patriotic story involving violence and

[1] Moser's plan (*Neues Beethoven Jahrbuch*, II, 1925, p. 56) may be quoted as a morphological curiosity. It was to have three acts, Act I in the 1805 version, Act II (from the March) in that of 1814. Act III was to follow 1814 with the following exceptions: the F minor (1805) *Andante un poco agitato* of Florestan's aria inserted between the A flat and F major sections of 1814; the 1805 recitative introducing the 1814 duet; the opening of the 1805 finale, accompanied by a visible scene-change after the *Parsifal* manner, leading from the revenge chorus to the 1814 finale with its orchestral introduction cut; the F major *Sostenuto assai* ('O Gott, O welch' ein Augenblick!') restored to its 1805 form.

[2] Ernest Newman's argument (*More opera nights*, pp. 268–9) that subsidiary characters of a lower social order were required by stage convention to serve as a fill-up until the real action began misses the point. They have the vital function of emphasizing the closeness of the story to real life. This is also the artistic justification of the *Singspiel* form, at any rate in serious opera.

often a spectacular catastrophe, a happy end produced not by a *deus ex machina* but by an act of superhuman courage, a strong ethical content tending to divide the characters into sheep and goats: this was the pattern of the rescue opera. That Beethoven adopted it lock, stock and barrel (though with Bouilly he eschewed the more lurid type of dénouement) can be attributed to his choice of libretto; but he imitated Cherubini's practice with remarkable assiduity. The powerful overture presenting the kernel of the drama in symphonic form, the use of *Melodram* and recitative as well as spoken dialogue, the very wide range of musical design— simple quasi-strophic airs and duets alongside others of concentrated symphonic development, trios and quartets that look now backward to Italian tradition, now forward to romantic opera, enormous finales involving a succession of large-scale movements for chorus and principals—are the regular ingredients of Cherubini's operas. The intense energy of Cherubini's style, with its pounding rhythms, constant sforzandos, cross-accents and dynamic contrasts, massive treatment of the orchestra, and still perceptible though partly transformed influence of the Neapolitan *opera buffa*, left a palpable mark on *Fidelio*. If the duet for Pizarro and Rocco suggests *Médée*, it seems probable that Pizarro's musical character was modelled on Dourlinski in *Lodoïska*, one of the few baritone villains in French opera of the Revolution. Their vengeful outbursts are expressed in strikingly similar terms. The rhetorical vocal line and the whole orchestral layout—busy first violin figuration, tremolando second violins and violas, heavy wind chords and contrasted dynamics—are common to several passages in both operas. Example 20 on page 375 shows the opening of the septet in Act II of *Lodoïska*.

For the treatment of the trumpet calls there was an equally close model in Méhul's *Héléna* (on another Bouilly libretto), produced in Vienna on 22 August 1803 less than six months after its Paris première. In this opera the arrival of 'le Gouverneur' in the first finale is signalled by backstage trumpets, and the whole episode is anticipated in the overture. Not only the sudden fanfare in a strange key but its repetition and the slow-moving harmony combined with pedal and string ostinato produces an effect so like the

Ex. 20

- ran - ce, c'est sur vous seu - le dé - sor -

- mais, c'est sur vous seu - le dé - sor -

mais   que   tom - be tou-te ma ven-

- gean - ce

one in *Fidelio* as to rule out coincidence; the following example illustrates the appearance of this material in the overture:

Ex. 21

We can hardly condemn as maladroit the destiny that on 20 November 1805 filled the Theater an der Wien with French officers.

The other important influence on *Fidelio*, equally transmuted by Beethoven's genius, was of course Mozart. This was essentially musical rather than dramatic. It scarcely affected the design of the opera but so permeated and enriched the texture as to render it capable of expressing an infinite variety of inflexion and emphasis. Beethoven had no use for Mozart's Italian librettos and considered *Die Zauberflöte* the best of his operas, a judgement that may explain his own willingness to collaborate with Schikaneder, though the ethical potency of the opera is due far more to Mozart's music than to the text. Edward J. Dent described *Fidelio* as 'the natural sequel to *The Magic Flute*; Florestan and Leonore are Tamino and Pamina born again as real human beings, facing as realities what they had previously seen only as symbols'.[1] This was the likeliest point at which Beethoven could make operatic contact with Mozart.

[1] Introduction to his translation of *Fidelio* (London, 1938), p. xiv.

He was interested in characters less as individuals than as standard-bearers of the human spirit. His psychological need to indulge in hero-worship (it was at this period that he gave his third symphony the title 'Bonaparte')[1] was presently dissatisfied even with the heroic end of the 1805 score: it had to be reinforced in 1814 by Don Fernando's explicit enunciation of the principles of the Revolution. The more Beethoven revised the opera, the more deeply he impregnated it with the spirit of 1789.

If any other Mozart opera left a mark on *Fidelio*, it was *Idomeneo*, which was still current in the early years of the nineteenth century, Treitschke providing a German translation for a Viennese revival on 13 May 1806, and which itself reflected an earlier French influence through Gluck. The striking rhythmic resemblance between the *Allegro con brio* melody of Leonore's aria (Ex. 22*b*) and a theme in Electra's first aria (*a*) could be an unconscious echo, especially as both are presented over a long pedal and a similar accompaniment figure:

Ex. 22

This rhythm, or slight variants of it, runs like a coloured thread through the score of *Idomeneo*: see, for example, the *Allegro molto* of Idomeneo's aria 'Vedrommi intorno' in Act I, the quartet (at the words 'morte cercando altrove') and Electra's last aria, 'D'Oreste, d'Ajace'. Beethoven's blindness to the quality of Da

[1] Alan Tyson ('Beethoven's heroic phase', *Musical Times*, CX, 1969, p. 139) has associated his growing preoccupation with heroic subjects during the first years of the century, in the *Prometheus* ballet and *The Mount of Olives* as well as the symphony and the opera, with his reactions to the onset of deafness. This may well be so; but such matters are notoriously complex, and his social and political views undoubtedly played a part.

Ponte's librettos was a matter of temperament and extended to other works of the Italian school. No one who has studied the vernacular German *Singspiel* of the last quarter of the eighteenth century, especially in Vienna, can be surprised that it offered no valid alternative. If Beethoven needed a stimulus, it had to come from elsewhere. The new French operas in 1802 found something like a spiritual vacuum in Viennese operatic life, and they filled it with a sonic boom that resounded through the romantic theatre.

ABORTIVE OPERAS

The failure of *Fidelio* in 1805–6 was far from discouraging Beethoven's new-found enthusiasm for opera. In December 1807 he submitted a memorandum to the directors of the Imperial Theatre offering to compose at least one grand opera a year in return for a fixed salary, throwing in an occasional *Singspiel* gratis. He showed himself fully aware that the task would demand all his time and inhibit any other major activity. It is interesting to speculate on what would have happened if this remarkable offer had been accepted. In the event he and his friends continued earnestly to hunt for suitable librettos, a search that threw up an extraordinary profusion of suggestions during the next eighteen years. Among the projects that never left the ground were a comedy recommended by Schindler (March 1807), *Memnons Dreiklang*, on an Indian story by the orientalist Hammer-Purgstall (March 1809), *The Return of Ulysses* (Beethoven suggested this early in 1812 to the young poet Karl Theodor Körner, soon to be killed in battle), *Mathilde ou Les Croisades* (Karoline Pichler, 1814; Beethoven acknowledged that the libretto was 'very beautifully written', but rejected it), *Brutus* (Bauernfeld, winter of 1814–15), *Die Ankunft der Pennsylvanier in Amerika* (Johann Baptist Rupprecht) and *Libussa* (Grillparzer), both in January 1820, *Bacchus* (Jeitteles, 1821), *Alfred der Grosse*[1] (Marianna Neumann), *Die Apotheose im Tempel des Jupiter Ammon*[2] (Johann Sporschil) and *Wanda, die Königin der Sarmaten.*

---

[1] *TF*, p. 842. Hess (*Beethoven Bühnenwerke*, p. 71) gives the title as *Alexander der Grosse.*

[2] This libretto survives and has been published by Volkmann, *Neues über Beethoven* (Berlin, 1904), pp. 67–72.

381

These last three (late 1823) were among many proposals inspired by the successful revival of *Fidelio* at the Kärntnertor on 3 November 1822 and the offer of a commission from the theatre. Other subjects canvassed at this time were Schiller's *Fiesco*, Voltaire's tragedies, a poem by one of the Schlegels, *Macbeth* (see below) and *Romeo and Juliet*. In the spring of 1825 Rellstab sent Beethoven his libretto *Orest*. On an empty page of his letter Beethoven's brother jotted down a list of books suitable for operatic treatment, among them Scott's *Kenilworth*. Rellstab gave him another list, including Attila, Antigone and Belisarius. The last subject mentioned, in 1826, was Goethe's *Claudine von Villa Bella*, which Friedrich August Kanne, editor of the *Allgemeine Musikalische Zeitung*, was deputed to adapt. This brings the story full circle, for Beethoven had set an aria from this work for someone else's opera in Bonn about 1790.

Few if any of the above schemes were seriously considered. Others made a little more progress, and in two or three instances Beethoven sketched some music. In 1808 Heinrich Collin embarked on a *Macbeth* libretto, about which Beethoven (according to Röckel) was very enthusiastic. Nottebohm[1] printed two sketches for the witches' music in the first scene, planned to follow the overture without a break. One of them, as is well known, grew into the slow movement of the D major Trio, Op. 70, No. 1. But Collin abandoned the libretto in the middle of the second act for the pusillanimous reason that 'it threatened to become too gloomy';[2] he printed the first act in 1809. Soon afterwards he produced a libretto on the Alcina story, *Bradamante*. Beethoven thought the subject too familiar and disliked the magic element 'because it has a soporific effect on feeling and reason', but promised to set it all the same.[3] Collin, however, offered it to Reichardt, whose version was produced in concert form at Lobkowitz's palace on 3 March 1809. Beethoven's manifest desire to work with Collin was frustrated by the latter's death in 1811.

Incompatibility of temperament seems to have undermined a

---

[1] *NZB*, pp. 225–7.
[2] Quoted in *TF*, p. 441.
[3] See *LA*, letters 175 and 185.

collaboration with Goethe over *Faust*, first broached in 1808, when Cotta's *Morgenblatt* announced Beethoven's interest, and mentioned as late as 1823. When the two giants met at Teplitz in July 1812 Beethoven was repelled by the courtier in Goethe. He told Breitkopf & Härtel (24 July) that Goethe 'has promised to write something for me',[1] and two years later (29 August 1814) Count Heinrich Otto van Leoben reported that Beethoven had induced Goethe to arrange *Faust* for music.[2] But nothing came of it; at least two of Beethoven's three sketches for vocal pieces from *Faust* date from before 1800.

In the spring of 1811 Beethoven invited Treitschke to arrange a French melodrama, *Les Ruines de Babylone*, and protested vigorously when he heard that an actor intended to revive the original for his benefit. In the same letter (11 June)[3] he told Count Pálffy, a director of the Imperial Theatres, that since the previous year he had turned down twelve or more librettos that he had paid for out of his own pocket. In July he asked Treitschke for 'plenty of recitatives and dances.'[4] This was the same subject as *Giafar*, which Varnhagen von Ense talked of adapting for Beethoven, only to find that he had been anticipated.[5]

On 28 January 1812 Beethoven made a direct approach to Kotzebue, offering to set anything he cared to propose. 'Whether it be romantic, quite serious, heroic, comic or sentimental, in short, whatever you like, I will gladly accept it. I must admit that I should like best of all some grand subject taken from history and especially from the dark ages, for instance, from the time of Attila or the like.' On 25 May 1813 we find Beethoven asking Ignaz Franz Castelli for 'one or two of the opera libretti you promised me'. About 1814 he told his first Leonore, Anna Milder, that when his circumstances improved 'my task will be to write an opera for our *one and only*

---

[1] Ibid., letter 379.

[2] *TF*, p. 602. Leoben is not mentioned in the exasperatingly inadequate index.

[3] *LA*, letter 312.

[4] Ibid., letter 317.

[5] See his letters to Rahel Levin quoted in Thayer, *Life of Beethoven*, ed. Henry Edward Krehbiel (New York, 1921), II, pp. 204–5. They are excluded from *TF*.

Milder'. Her success as Leonore in Berlin revived this ambition two years later, when (6 January 1816) he asked her to obtain from Baron de la Motte Fouqué 'a subject for a grand opera which would also be suitable for *you*'.[1]

Meanwhile the 1814 revival of *Fidelio* had evoked another libretto from Treitschke. This was *Romulus*, which according to *Der Sammler* of 13 December Beethoven had 'contracted to compose'. In January 1815 he told Treitschke he was so engaged and would 'begin to write it down one of these days'.[2] Almost immediately a hitch occurred. One J. E. Fuss published a notice that he had composed a *Romulus und Remus* for the Theater an der Wien. Then the directors made difficulties about terms. Beethoven wrote to Treitschke on 24 September: 'I would have begun your Romulus long ago, but the Directors refuse to grant me for a work of this kind anything more than the *takings for one night*'.[3] He was still hopeful of having the opera ready by February or March 1816 if he could obtain decent terms. He told Cipriani Potter in the summer of 1817 that he was working on it. Sketches for a classical opera of about 1815–16 were printed by Nottebohm,[4] but they are thought to belong to *Bacchus* by Rudolph vom Berge, the libretto of which Karl Amenda sent to Beethoven on 30 March 1815. They contain references to the god Pan and the intriguing note: 'Perhaps the dissonances should not be resolved throughout the whole opera, for in those primitive times our highly developed music would not be the thing. Yet the subject must be treated in a pastoral way.'[5] Another note, 'it must be evolved out of the B.M.', led Riemann to conjecture a Bacchus motive.

The last serious candidate for collaboration, early in 1823, was the dramatist Grillparzer, a nephew of Sonnleithner. Although he was unhappy about the treatment of the voice in Beethoven's recent work and doubted if he was still capable of composing an opera, he submitted two proposals, *Drahomira*, described by Thayer as 'a

---

[1] The letters quoted in this paragraph are in *LA*, Nos. 344, 423 and 595.
[2] Ibid., letter 525.
[3] Ibid., letter 559.
[4] In *NZB*, pp. 329–30.
[5] Cf. Thayer, *Life of Beethoven*, ed. Krehbiel, II, p. 315, n.1.

semi-diabolical story drawn from Bohemian legendary history',[1] and *Melusine,* another legend. Beethoven was enthusiastic. When Grillparzer delivered the libretto of *Melusine* in the spring of 1823 he insisted on a formal contract. He had several long discussions with the poet, who offered to remove a hunting-chorus at which Beethoven seems to have jibbed and suggested the use of 'a recurrent and easily grasped melody', first heard in the overture, 'to mark every appearance of Melusine or of her influence in the action'.[2] On 17 September Beethoven wrote to Spohr that he had begun the music and hoped to return to it. Grillparzer understood that it was 'ready'. In fact, little if anything seems to have been written down, though the subject cropped up as late as 31 May 1826, when Beethoven told the publisher Adolf Martin Schlesinger that Count Brühl, the Berlin intendant, wanted him to make another choice owing to the similarity between *Melusine* and de la Motte Fouqué's *Undine,* Hoffmann's setting of which had been produced at Brühl's theatre in 1816.[3]

How seriously did Beethoven consider any of the operatic projects after *Fidelio* ? His professions of enthusiasm were undoubtedly sincere. No man of his temperament would have bothered to make lightly the wide-ranging request to Kotzebue or the 1807 offer to the theatre directors. The *Macbeth* and *Bacchus* sketches are proof of more than indifference. Yet if we exclude all peripheral suggestions, the schemes that came nearest to fruition, though in many respects heterogeneous, have one thing in common. Every one of them was concerned with a distant or legendary period; all were equally remote from the climate of *Fidelio.* Beethoven expressed a preference for the dark ages; was he unaware that *Fidelio* drew its strength from its contemporary realism ?

Probably his attitude was ambivalent. He was strongly attracted to opera (and his experiences with *Fidelio* could have increased rather than diminished this); yet he may half-consciously have sought reasons to avoid a final commitment. No composer was ever more certain of his strength, or more willing to stretch convention in

---

[1] Ibid., III, p. 118.
[2] Cf. *TF,* p. 862.
[3] Letters referred to in this paragraph are in *LA,* Nos. 1240 and 1487.

order to give utterance to his ideas. Had his genius impelled him to tackle another opera, he would have overcome every impediment in its way. There was no inadequacy in his equipment. It is easy, in admiring the grandeur of *Fidelio*, to overlook the sheer operatic technique it enshrines. The composer who in 'Mir ist so wunderbar' could express the contrasted emotions of four characters with absolute conviction in the same music, and who could create the extraordinary dramatic intensity of the dungeon scene in the 1805 version, had few potential equals in operatic history. Yet there was something that took precedence over drama and character and ensured that the pull, when it came (and it repeatedly did), was never quite strong enough to carry the field. Humanity was of more importance to Beethoven than the individual. *Fidelio* was successfully achieved because it satisfied one of the psychological needs of his existence, the search for the ideal woman. He found her in art where he failed in life, and placed her on a pedestal. No wonder he wished to call the opera *Leonore*. But in yielding to the urge to raise the height of the pedestal he partly dehumanized her. The most conclusive evidence that Beethoven was not a predestined opera composer is provided by his treatment of *Fidelio* in 1814. It is impossible to imagine Mozart or Verdi sacrificing their characters to the expediency of a moral, however elevated.

TEN

The Choral Music

DENIS McCALDIN

BY EIGHTEENTH-CENTURY STANDARDS the list of Beethoven's choral works is surprisingly small. Apart from some minor occasional pieces, there are scarcely a dozen of any real significance, and of these only the Ninth Symphony and the *Missa solemnis* enjoy much popularity today. The explanation for this is bound up with the changes that occurred in Austrian society during the composer's lifetime. Whereas musicians working in Vienna a generation before Beethoven had found themselves obliged to write every kind of music as part of their duties towards their aristocratic patrons, by 1800 the situation had begun to alter. Public concerts became increasingly important, gradually taking the place of private musical evenings at the homes of the nobility and catering for a new type of audience. For them Beethoven was of interest less as a composer than as a brilliant concert artist, a virtuoso pianist and improviser; though there was consequently a demand for his instrumental music, it was some years before he was commissioned to write a large-scale choral work.

The more important secular items will be discussed first and are listed below:

1790 Cantatas for the Emperors Joseph II and Leopold II
1808 Choral Fantasia, for piano, chorus and orchestra
1811 *King Stephen* ⎫ for the opening of a new theatre at
1811 *The Ruins of Athens* ⎭ Budapest
1814 *Der glorreiche Augenblick* ('The Glorious Moment'), cantata for the Congress of Vienna

1814–15 *Meeresstille und glückliche Fahrt* ('Calm Sea and Prosperous Voyage')

1822 *The Consecration of the House* (a revision of *The Ruins of Athens*), for the opening of the Josephstadt Theatre, Vienna

1822–4 Symphony No. 9 in D minor, finale

The most striking feature of these pieces, taken as a whole, is their unevenness. From the two earliest cantatas to the Ninth Symphony it is clear that Beethoven's natural response is to the dramatic elements in his texts and not to the lyrical ones. Moreover, whereas his predecessors had been primarily interested in the voice, and above all in opera, the new generation found themselves more attracted to the expressive powers of purely instrumental music. Consequently Beethoven's treatment of the chorus is often uncertain; sometimes it is used as part of an orchestrally conceived texture, while on other occasions it is more conservative and follows the well-tried formulae of his teachers Albrechtsberger and Salieri.

Of the music in the two early works, written in Bonn, the final chorus of the *Cantata on the accession of the Emperor Leopold II* is immediately impressive, and the soprano aria with chorus, 'Da stiegen die Menschen', in the *Cantata on the death of the Emperor Joseph II*, which reappears in richer form in *Fidelio*, is surprisingly mature (see Ex. 10 in Chapter 9 above). The orchestral and choral textures in both works are full of variety, and there is a judicious blend of homophonic and contrapuntal writing for the voices. Some years later, in 1808, Beethoven composed his Choral Fantasia as the grand finale to a memorable concert at which both the Fifth and Sixth Symphonies received their first performances. Mention has often been made of the similarities between this work and the finale of the Ninth Symphony,[1] and Beethoven himself compared the

---

[1] As the sketchbooks frequently indicate, there was often a long period between Beethoven's initial conception of a work and its completion. In addition, experiments begun on one piece often appear to be consolidated in a second which builds upon the experience of the first. Thus the Choral Fantasia is related to the Ninth Symphony and the Mass in C to the *Missa solemnis*. Elsewhere the connection takes the form of self-borrowing, as in the case just mentioned above.

two pieces in letters of 10 March 1824.[1] As the precursor of the later masterly set of symphonic variations, the Choral Fantasia seems very lightweight indeed. The score calls for solo piano, orchestra, soloists and chorus, and consists of a number of simple variations on a modified version of Beethoven's early song *Gegenliebe* (1794 or 1795). The likeness between this theme (Ex. 1*a*) and that of the finale of the Symphony (*b*) has often been noted; their most obvious similarities are that they both move mainly by stepwise motion and have second phrases which are almost identical:

Ex. 1

There are other parallels, too: the text of the Choral Fantasia is in praise of music, while that of the symphony is derived from Schiller's *Ode to Freedom* (as conceivably it should be called),[2] and both are sets of variations in which the chorus is used as a final climactic resource rather than as an equal partner with the orchestra.

Following the piano improvisation and orchestral introduction the soloist announces the principal theme alone, after which a very simple set of instrumental variations gradually builds up to a full orchestral tutti and coda. The analogy between the variation treatment here and in the symphony is clear and can be taken further to include the march that follows the two more expansive variations in C minor and A major. At this point the music breaks off in anticipation of the appearance of the chorus; in both scores Beethoven's aim is to introduce the voices with the minimum of artificiality. Initially in the Fantasia, for example, the singers' presence was to be indicated by the words 'Hört ihr wohl'. The final solution in each case was to employ a solo recitative-like link; in the earlier piece it is given to the piano and in the symphony to the baritone. Once the

---

[1] *LA*, letters 1269 and 1270. Also see below, p. 420.
[2] But see n. 2 on p. 312 above. (Eds.)

voices have entered, Beethoven's treatment of them in the two works is quite different and reflects the enormous change that took place in his technique between 1808 and 1824. The balance of the whole movement is much better served by the extended treatment given to the voices in the Ninth Symphony than in the Fantasia, where their contribution adds up to less than one-quarter of its total length. Moreover, the use of the soloists is quite different in the two scores. There is nothing either idiomatic or virtuosic in the earlier piece; Beethoven uses them as he uses the solo woodwind and strings in the orchestra, that is simply as an alternative to a tutti. Moreover, the demarcation between soloists and chorus is minimal, whereas the maturer structure and textures of the symphony are the fruit of the greater understanding that Beethoven gained from the composition of the *Missa solemnis*. The Fantasia contains no contrapuntal sections, the main function of the full choir being to expand the orchestral tuttis in a predominantly chordal manner. The final *presto*, based on the last phrase of the preceding section, has a taxing soprano part, which Beethoven might well have altered had his experience of vocal composition been greater. As it is, the penultimate bar is always untidy—partly because of the angular line, but also because of the ungrateful word-setting (see Ex. 2). The Fantasia ends with a series of exchanges between piano and orchestra while the singers look silently on. This refusal to allow the chorus to continue to the end of the movement is curious and occurs again and again in Beethoven's music. Even in the Ninth Symphony and the *Missa solemnis*, where the partnership between voices and instruments is much more complete, it is always the orchestra alone who are entrusted with the last word, never the choir as well.

Ex. 2

froh die Ga - ben, die Ga - ben— schö - ner Kunst,

The opening of a new theatre at Budapest in 1812 was the occasion for the composition of both *King Stephen* and *The Ruins of Athens*. They formed the prelude and finale to the celebrations and had texts by Kotzebue, whom Beethoven described for some extraordinary reason as possessing 'unique dramatic genius'.[1] Some of the music from *The Ruins of Athens* is still occasionally heard; it is perhaps significant that it is the simpler sections, such as the choral song 'Wir tragen empfangliche Herze', with its mood of quiet pastoral calm, that succeed best.

The Glorious Moment, written in 1814 for the Congress of Vienna, is interesting for two reasons. One concerns the initial B flat *allegro* section scored for chorus, solo soprano and solo violin. Beethoven seems to have been particularly attracted by this textural combination, since it occurs again in the incidental music to *The Consecration of the House* and still later, in a modified form, in the 'Benedictus' of the *Missa solemnis*. The other point relates to the finale, which marks a distinct step forward towards a more consistent handling of the chorus and orchestra. It begins as a gentle strophic song and ends as a fugue. The first part follows a familiar formula; the chorus is divided into three groups of voices (men, women and children), each of whom, divided into two parts, sing a verse on their own before the independent strands are combined for a final climactic statement. It is quite apparent that Beethoven did not yet consider the word-setting with the care that he was to exercise later in his treatment of the text of the *Missa solemnis*, since the effect of all three pairs of voices singing their own set of words simultaneously at this point is very bewildering. Beethoven's interest in fugal textures, dormant since he completed the Mass in C in 1807, reappears in the final section of the cantata. In some ways the exposition is a model of the traditional style based on the principles of species counterpoint, since, while the subject moves principally in crotchets, the counter-subject proceeds in minims. Albrechtsberger would also have approved of his pupil's treatment of the orchestra, which initially follows his principles meticulously.[2] The movement fails to achieve real distinction only because of the five-bar subject itself, which directs the tonality too strongly towards the subdominant, so that each entry of the answer (necessarily in the dominant area) sounds abrupt and unconvincing:

[1] *LA*, letter 344.

[2] Cf. Johann Georg Albrechtsberger, *Methods of Harmony, figured base, and composition*, ed. Ignaz von Seyfried, trans. Arnold Merrick (London, [1834]), I, p. 262.

Ex. 3

A year later Beethoven set two poems by Goethe in the form of a short choral work known as *Calm Sea and Prosperous Voyage,* and in 1822 he rearranged the music of *The Ruins of Athens* for the celebrations at the Josephstadt Theatre in Vienna, where it was performed as *The Consecration of the House.* For this version he added a new overture and one other number, a tripartite piece for chorus, solo soprano and solo violin known as 'Wo die Pulse'.

The last and greatest example of Beethoven's secular choral style is the Ninth Symphony, which he completed in 1824.[1] Mention has already been made of the similarities between this work and the Choral Fantasia, but not of its vastly greater spiritual range. The treatment of soloists, chorus and orchestra is now entirely dictated by Beethoven's response to the text in the light of his experience with the *Missa solemnis,* completed in 1823. In such music there can be no valid distinction between sacred and secular influences; Beethoven's last works unite the church tradition with the symphonic, forging a unique and moving language which is both expressive and highly personal.

Many critics have discussed the progress towards this late style through the instrumental music, but very few have examined the composer's religious works with the same thoroughness. The number of such pieces is small: two settings of the Catholic mass—the Mass in C and the *Missa solemnis*—and the early oratorio *The Mount of Olives (Christus am Oelberge)* (1803). Both this last work and the opera *Leonore,* which followed in 1805, explore the theme of suffering. The libretto is by Beethoven himself (in collaboration with Franz Xaver Huber) and concerns Christ's agony in the garden, his arrest, the despair of his disciples and his confrontation with Peter,

---

[1] See above, pp. 306–13, for a fuller discussion of this work.

with a final chorus of praise to the Almighty Deliverer. The similarities between this plot and that of *Leonore/Fidelio* are considerable,[1] though musically the oratorio is not as strong as the opera. In spite of his knowledge of Haydn's *Creation* and *Seasons*, Beethoven does not seem to have been drawn to this type of musical drama in *The Mount of Olives*, which instead looks back to a more old-fashioned style. If a parallel is to be made, it should perhaps be with *The Return of Tobias*, which Haydn composed some thirty years earlier. Both works are in the style of the Neapolitan opera and cantata and are clearly the work of young men more versed in instrumental than in large-scale vocal composition. Neither is consistent stylistically; the best music is in the dramatic or atmospheric sections and often involves the chorus. *The Mount of Olives* begins well, with a prelude in E flat minor that conveys just the right atmosphere of threatening uncertainty needed for the drama. This mood carries over into Christ's first recitative and aria but is not sustained because of the intervention of the Seraph, a character extraneous to the original drama and often an embarrassment to composer and listener alike. After the serious beginning it is hard to imagine a more incongruous item than the *allegro* section of her first number, which takes the form of a bright *buffo* aria-with-chorus, complete with perky woodwind parts and spirited coloratura. It was this mixture of styles that critics objected to at the first performances and which Beethoven tried to eliminate from the score before its publication in 1811. Unfortunately his attempts were only partially successful. The best choral item is the finale, which succeeds because of its conservatism. It opens with a grand orchestral section, based on a typical double-dotted rhythm, to which the voices add homophonic support. Then follows a fugal *allegro*, which sheds some light on Beethoven's attitude to this type of composition in 1803. The shape of the fugue subject (Ex. 4a), which is closely related to that of the 'Et vitam venturi' in the C major Mass (b), and the treatment of the first exposition, with its

[1] Cf. Alan Tyson, 'Beethoven's heroic phase', *Musical Times*, CX (1969), p. 139, 'Beethoven's oratorio', ibid., CXI (1970), p. 372, and 'The 1803 version of Beethoven's *Christus am Oelberge*', *Musical Quarterly*, LVI (1970).

characteristic orchestral doublings, are features of the old Viennese church music tradition. The subsequent stretto, counter-exposition and dominant pedal point all reinforce this impression. However, Beethoven now releases himself from any textbook restraint by proposing two fresh quasi-expositions, which, far from enhancing the total effect of the fugue, delay the final cadence for a further forty bars and severely weaken the overall design.

Nottebohm[1] blames Albrechtsberger for the inconsistent quality of much of the composer's fugal writing: 'There is no doubt,' he states, 'that Beethoven failed to receive a thorough training in the

---

[1] Cf. Gustav Nottebohm, *Beethovens Studien* (Leipzig and Winterthur, 1873), quoted in Paul Nettl, *The Beethoven Encyclopaedia* (London, 1957). p. 65.

form of the fugue from Albrechtsberger.' While this may well be true, there also seems to have been a basic conflict between his pupil's unusually strong musical personality and the accepted fugal style of the period. It was a problem that was to remain with Beethoven for the rest of his life and to which he found many different solutions. Nowhere is this more apparent than in the two Mass settings, which must now be considered in turn.

Beethoven's first Mass, in C, Op. 86, was commissioned by Prince Nikolaus Esterházy for the celebration of his wife's name day at Eisenstadt in 1807. It had become the tradition to hear a new festive setting of the mass on these occasions, and between 1796 and 1806 Haydn had provided six such works and Hummel three. Although Beethoven had already written his first four symphonies and a good deal of other large-scale music by this date, he had composed very little in the church style. He maintained an interest in it throughout his life, however, and the inventory for probate shows that his library contained a number of works by Palestrina, Victoria, Handel and Mozart, as well as at least two of Haydn's masses—the 'Nelson' and the *Heiligmesse*. It seems likely that Haydn had some say in Prince Esterházy's decision to commission the Mass in C from his ex-pupil, and there is convincing internal evidence that Beethoven went to some pains to follow the Eisenstadt tradition. The opening movement is very restrained and oddly reminiscent of the Kyrie in Haydn's 'St. Nicholas' Mass, written thirty-five years earlier. Both works begin with melodic fragments outlining a minor sixth and are harmonized in thirds over an implied plagal bass (I–IV–I):

Ex.5

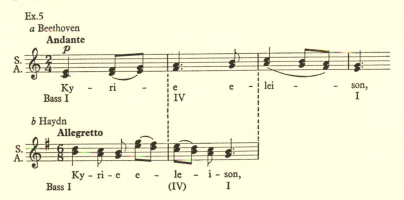

a Beethoven

b Haydn

There is no slow introduction to either work; each begins instead with peaceful but not too slow music, which is maintained for the whole of the 'Kyrie'–'Christe'–'Kyrie' text. In Beethoven's setting, an *andante*, the pastoral mood is heightened by the orchestration, which in this movement lacks flute, trumpets and drums. As might be expected, he goes further than Haydn in exploring the implications behind the text. The ternary symbolism of the Trinity, for example, is made very apparent by the clear-cut ABA form and by the use of conjunct thirds in the instrumental parts. Key relationships based on the interval of a third were a continual fascination to Beethoven throughout his life, particularly from his middle years onwards, so it is not unexpected to find the first 'Kyrie' set in C, the 'Christe' in E and the second 'Kyrie' in C again.

The 'Gloria' has the typical tripartite structure derived from the *missa brevis* form; in the outer *allegro* movements the chorus carry most of the text, which is treated in a predominantly homophonic manner. As yet those personal and subjective interpretations of the liturgy, which Beethoven assigns to the solo quartet with such poignant effect in the *Missa solemnis*, are hardly apparent. The second section, in the subdominant, F minor, has some affinity with Haydn's 'Nelson' Mass, both in the treatment of the 'Miserere' text as a choral refrain and in the use of certain solo instrumental lines. The 'Cum sancto' fugue also follows tradition with its broad exposition, chromatic counter-subjects and abrupt changes in dynamic before the final jubilant cadence. The reappearance of the 'Quoniam' text, though liturgically unjustified, is good evidence of Beethoven's symphonic outlook, anticipating as it does the elaborate coda that appears in the parallel position in the *Missa solemnis*.

The 'Credo' could be said to owe something to the sixteenth-century motet style in that each textual idea has its own musical counterpart. Beethoven makes repeated use of a quaver figure in the orchestral bass line in an endeavour to unify the opening section, and draws on a number of simple pictorial devices to illustrate the meaning of the words: semiquavers for 'visibilium', isolated pizzicato chords for 'invisibilium' and a falling phrase on the solo clarinet to suggest the descent of the Holy Spirit at the beginning of the 'Et incarnatus'. This central section (up to 'passus et sepultus est') was traditionally treated with great care, so it comes as no surprise to find Beethoven introducing the solo quartet for the first time in the movement at this point, while observing another old custom by giving the actual announcement 'et homo factus est' to the tenor soloist. The notion of Christ's crucifixion as the responsibility of all mankind is illustrated by the return of the chorus, and his suffering and burial are graphically described first by the soloists and then by the chorus as they stutter out the final phrase 'et, et, et sepultus est'. Beethoven has often been criticized for these repetitions, which according to the strictest liturgical view are forbidden. However, in the light of the many other improper practices that flourished at the time, such as the polytextual treatment of this text in the Austrian *missa brevis*[1] and the notorious 'Credo' by Alessandro Capuana[2] fashioned from the music of Mozart's *Don Giovanni*, these criticisms pale into insignificance. The final section opens and closes with fugal textures, briefly for the 'Et resurrexit' and more expansively for the 'Et vitam venturi', whose subject, as we have seen, bears a marked resemblance to that of the finale of *The Mount of Olives* (cf. Ex. 4). Once more Beethoven finds himself with the problem of marrying his symphonic attitudes to the more formal aspects of the Viennese church style, but in this case the union is more successful. The whole paragraph is a good deal less self-conscious than usual, and the coda, with its delicate wind textures and strong dynamic contrasts, is a charming inspiration. The tonality of the 'Sanctus', A major, shows Beethoven again exploring the relationship of a third (this time below) with the principal key of the mass. The setting is short and therefore liturgically appropriate, as is the use of the timpani to enhance the solemnity of the text.

The problems involved in setting the remainder of the Ordinary seem to have occupied Beethoven a good deal, both here and in the *Missa solemnis*. The liturgy requires the sequence 'Osanna'–'Benedictus'–'Osanna'–'Agnus Dei'–'Dona nobis pacem' at this

[1] Cf., for example, Haydn's Little Organ Mass in B flat and his brother Michael's Mass No. 38 in G.

[2] Cf. Arthur Hutchings, *Church music in the 19th century* (London, 1967), p. 78.

point, but composers generally made little or no attempt to establish unity between its different sections. Haydn again showed a different way in his *Heiligmesse* and *Paukenmesse*, and 'Theresa' and 'Creation' Masses, where the second 'Osanna' is completely absorbed into the music of the 'Benedictus', thus avoiding the abrupt change of mood found in almost every other Viennese mass of the time. Along with many others, including Hummel and Joseph Eybler, Haydn also attempted to mirror the mood of the finale of a symphony by casting the 'Dona nobis pacem' as a cheerful, hopeful section rather than as an extension of the prayerful atmosphere of the 'Agnus Dei'. That Beethoven was quick to appreciate the implications of these innovations can be seen in both his masses. In the earlier work the music proceeds directly from the first 'Osanna' to the text of the 'Benedictus', which begins with the solo quartet singing *a cappella*. Beethoven thus rejects the long rambling introduction typical of earlier settings, in order to allow the drama of the mass to proceed with as little hindrance as possible. Soloists and chorus are treated rather in the manner of a sixteenth-century motet for double choir, and the absence of elaborate wind accompaniments is a striking departure from contemporary Viennese practice. The 'Agnus Dei' is treated more conventionally, with a good number of appoggiaturas to emphasize the yearning quality of the text. A link to the 'Dona nobis pacem' is provided by the prominent clarinet part, which bridges the two sections with a characteristic triplet figure and which persists into this final section.[1]

It must be admitted that in performance the effect of these movements on the listener is somewhat disappointing. The necessary feeling of conviction and finality that is needed in these last few pages somehow eludes the composer, and the expansive assurance that promises so well at the beginning of the work is sadly lacking towards the end. Almost as if echoing these feelings himself, Beethoven reintroduces the music of the 'Kyrie' in an attempt to round off the work. But even this device, used with such charming effect in other works, is not wholly successful here, since the new

[1] Cf. Haydn's 'Creation' Mass (Henle complete edition, XXIII, 4, Munich and Duisburg, 1967, p. 188).

mood is scarcely established before it is interrupted by the final cadence.[1]

It is not difficult to see why Prince Esterházy and his court were perplexed by the Mass in C. Beethoven had accepted the commission with some trepidation,[2] and the combination of disastrous rehearsals and a misunderstanding at the reception after the first performance made the occasion anything but a happy one. Yet the work has many good features, and his approach to the problems of mass composition is already very individual. His interest in symphonic structures prompts him to use a wider range of tonalities than Haydn: in particular, those based on the subdominant (F major and minor) and those related to C major by the interval of a third, i.e. E ('Christe'), E flat ('Et incarnatus') and A ('Sanctus'). Furthermore, the treatment of the chorus as the main protagonists follows his often-stated opinion that in church music the vocal parts must always be the most important.

Several features of the instrumentation also deserve comment. The orchestra is slightly larger than usual for these occasions and has double woodwind—a luxury that Haydn never enjoyed. Also peculiar to the Eisenstadt tradition is the absence of trombones, which were generally used in church music of this period, if only to strengthen the three lower parts of the chorus.[3] Although the actual size of the orchestra is a little larger than before, Beethoven, who had only recently been censured for the brutal dynamics of the 'Eroica' Symphony, uses it with surprising delicacy. The textures are far less dependent on the string choir than they are in the works of other composers of the time, and the formalized ritornellos and busy accompanying patterns of the old baroque style are gone for good.

'With his C major Mass, Beethoven entered a new era in the composition of masses, very different from that of Mozart and Haydn.' Like many comments on the work, this remark by Her-

[1] The recapitulation of the music of the 'Kyrie' for the 'Dona nobis pacem' was very common in eighteenth-century settings of the *missa brevis*, e.g. the *Missa S. Caroli* by Georg von Reutter and Haydn's 'St. Nicholas' Mass.

[2] See *LA*, letter 150, of 26 July 1807.

[3] Cf. Mozart's Requiem, Schubert's Masses in E flat and A flat, etc.

mann Kretzschmar[1] is only partially true; for while there is certainly some evidence of the composer's preoccupation with the deeper and more personal aspects of the text of the mass, there is still a good deal of dependence on more traditional formulae. The quotation can be much more appropriately applied to the *Missa solemnis*,[2] which must now be considered in detail.

Beethoven began work on the Mass in D, Op. 123, in 1819. It was to have been performed at the enthronement of Beethoven's pupil and friend Archduke Rudolph of Austria as Archbishop of Olmütz, but the labour of composition proved too great and it was not ready in time. He did not intend it to be his last essay in this form. One of the sketchbooks of 1822 has a memorandum saying 'the *Kyrie* in the second mass with wind-instruments and organ only', and further on there are six bars of a 'Dona nobis pacem' with the rubric 'Mass in C sharp minor'.[3] Almost certainly Beethoven hoped to offer one of these other masses to the Emperor as evidence of his ability to replace Anton Teyber, who had died in November 1822, as composer to the Imperial Court. A letter of 23 February 1823 from Count Moritz Dietrichstein to Count Lichnowsky on the subject is very revealing in this context:[4]

> . . . I am also sending you herewith the score of a mass by Reutter which Beethoven wished to see. It is true that H.M. the Emperor is fond of this style, but Beethoven, if he writes a mass, need not adhere to it . . . have a care only that the mass be not too long or too diffiuclt . . . a *tutti* mass [with] only short soprano and alto solos in the voices . . . but no tenor, bass or organ solos . . . If he wishes he may introduce a violin, oboe or clarinet solo.
>
> His Majesty likes to have fugues well worked out but not too long; the *Sanctus* and *Osanna* as short as possible, in order not to delay the transubstantiation, and . . . the *Dona nobis pacem*

[1] *Führer durch den Konzertsaal*, II (Leipzig, 1888–90), p. 60.

[2] Technically speaking, the term '*missa solemnis*' can be used to describe any setting of the *missa longa* that is particularly expansive or grandiose, but since its composition the name has been reserved more and more for Beethoven's D major Mass only.

[3] See *TF*, p. 793.

[4] Printed in ibid., pp. 840–1.

connected to the *Agnus Dei* without marked interruption, and soft. In two masses by Handel (arranged from his anthems), two by Naumann and Abbé Stadler, this makes a particularly beautiful effect.

Beethoven never wrote such a mass, nor does it seem likely that he ever could have done. He finally completed the *Missa solemnis* in 1823, and, bearing in mind that this letter dates from the same year, it is difficult to see how he could possibly have turned back to a style such as that favoured by the Imperial Chapel.

At first sight the Mass in D looks impossibly long and inappropriate for church use, and this has been the focus of a good deal of hostile criticism towards it right from the beginning. Further examination, however, reveals that Beethoven took considerable trouble to design the work so that, although monumental, it would still be suitable for worship. Initially, he had planned to provide all the music for the installation service—Mass, Gradual, Offertory and Tantum ergo—but this proved impossible. All the same he never lost sight of this idea. Inspired by the ideals of the French Revolution, and in contact with the views of thinkers such as Schiller, Goethe and Kant, it is not surprising that he should interpret the mass text in the light of his own highly personal faith. The *Missa solemnis*, for all its grandeur, avoids the empty verbosities of the Neapolitan cantata style and concentrates on the subjective elements. There are certain obvious idiosyncrasies: the repeated interjections of 'o' and 'non', and of the 'Quoniam' text at the end of the 'Gloria'; the return of the music for the word 'Credo' during the course of that movement; and the elaborate structure of the 'Dona nobis pacem'. Beethoven took such liberties with the text, it is true, but they are not particularly extravagant ones. Haydn, Albrechtsberger and Schubert were all guilty of more obvious offences, sometimes omitting whole clauses from the 'Credo' or else allowing different lines of text to be sung simultaneously in each of the vocal parts.

The overall design of the work has a superficial resemblance to the cantata masses of Caldara, Hasse and many other Italianate composers of the eighteenth century, because the text is divided into a number of separate movements. However, whereas in those works there is little or no attempt to interrelate the various sections, Beethoven manages both to follow the diversities of the text and still to weld the different musical elements into a convincing whole. Forced into a more spiritual view of the world by his increasing deafness and his many other difficulties, he sets the text of the mass as a huge five-movement symphony—a work which is therefore the logical outcome of the Viennese classical tradition and yet needed a Beethoven to achieve it.

The 'Kyrie' follows the same ternary structure as in the Mass in C, but here the symbolism of the Trinity is more detailed. As if in imitation of liturgical practice, the 'Kyrie' is intoned three times by the choir (people) and answered three times by a soloist (priest) in a majestic opening section in D. The music then modulates to the relative minor. Again following the example of previous centuries, and reflecting the care Beethoven took over the appropriateness of his setting, the 'Christe' is more subdued and is initially entrusted to the soloists. It is a remarkable passage, and one which consciously pays tribute to Palestrina in its narrow vocal range and freely flowing lines of conjunct crotchets. The second 'Kyrie', more closely derived from the first section than is commonly the case, completes the noble arch form.

The structure of the 'Gloria' poses several problems. The simple fast-slow-fast design that Beethoven adopted for his C major Mass is both effective and appropriate for church use. An alternative scheme, however, would be to ignore the implicit unities in the text and to set the whole section as a series of independent numbers, following the traditions of the Neapolitan cantata style.[1] Beethoven's search for diversity within unity, which occupied so much of his creative thought in his later years, seems to have prompted him to yet another solution. At the opening there is a brilliant flourish for the phrase 'Gloria in excelsis', and this texture is used as a motto which returns at suitable points in the movement. It is subsequently heard at the words 'laudamus te', 'benedicimus te', 'glorificamus te' and 'Domine Deus, rex coelestis' and in a final *presto* section

[1] Cf. Haydn's 'St. Cecilia' Mass, etc.; and, of course, Bach's Mass in B minor offers a familiar earlier example of such a structure.

where it could be considered liturgically unjustified, but where it is musically very satisfying. Interspersed with this recurring material are some highly arresting incidents, such as the shift to B flat major for the 'Gratias agimus tibi' and the whole of the 'Qui tollis'. Towards the end of the movement Beethoven almost destroys this quasi-symphonic structure, on which he had worked so carefully, by his choice of a very expansive subject for the customary final fugue on the words 'In gloria Dei Patris'. Often the high point of the Gloria, as in Haydn's late masses, Beethoven's treatment again underlines the conflict between the elements of fugue and other principles, which he repeatedly attempted to resolve in so many of his later works. As in the finale of *The Mount of Olives*, this example becomes less convincing the more it proceeds. After the formal working-out and its prolongation at a slightly faster tempo than the original *Allegro ma non troppo e ben marcato*, anything further might quite understandably be seen as something of an anti-climax. Nevertheless, in an attempt to give the entire movement even greater unity, Beethoven now brings back the opening phrases of the 'Gloria' as a coda to a coda. Unhappily, while one can admire the concept in principle, in practice the result is neither completely satisfying artistically nor liturgically justified.

Beethoven's attempt to organize the 'Credo' into a similarly unified design is more successful. The text is very long, and it is clear from his treatment of it that he attached more significance to some lines than to others.[1] The words 'Et in unam sanctam catholicam et apostolicam ecclesiam', for example, which a more orthodox believer such as Haydn set in majestic octaves in five of his masses, are here tucked away in the middle of the vocal texture and are therefore generally inaudible.[2] Faced once more with the difficult task of interrelating the diverse elements of the given text, Beethoven adapts and extends the motto principle that he used for his setting of the 'Gloria'. In this third movement of the mass, he chooses a simple but memorable theme for the word 'credo', which he then uses to bind the different sections of the text together. The

[1] See Martin Cooper, *Beethoven: the last decade, 1817–1827* (London, 1970), pp. 240 ff., for an interesting analysis of this problem.
[2] In Schubert's settings they are omitted altogether.

device can hardly have been unknown to him: Jommelli's D major Mass of 1766, which was popular all over Europe, makes use of the same idea, as do two of Mozart's early masses, K.192 and K.257. More important, perhaps, is the influence of Cherubini, whose music Beethoven is known to have admired and in whose Mass in F (1809) both the 'Gloria' and 'Credo' are organized in this manner.

The wide range of tonalities used by Beethoven in his symphonic works also has its parallel in the *Missa solemnis*. Up to this time the 'Credo' was generally in the tonic key of the mass, but Beethoven departs from general practice by using the third-related tonality of B flat. Once again nearly every phrase of the text is scrutinized and its meaning underlined in musical terms. After the opening jubilant bars, establishing the central importance of the word 'Credo', the motet-like treatment returns; 'consubstantialem patri' is given a contrapuntal character, suggesting perhaps the timeless power of the Almighty, and finally a move flatwards to the darker tonality of D flat heralds the mystery of Christ's appearance on earth. With the 'Et incarnatus' Beethoven leads us into his own mystical world, a world he was to explore again later in the last string quartets. The use of the Dorian mode (and of the Mixolydian in the 'Et resurrexit' that follows) is significant.[1] The text is first given to the soloists, who throughout this work can be seen to stand for Man as an individual, and then to the chorus, who represent Mankind as a whole. The orchestration is also wonderfully imaginative, with a solo flute vividly suggesting the idea of the omnipotent Holy Spirit coming 'in the likeness of a dove',[2] while the chorus recite on a monotone the words 'Et incarnatus est de spiritu sancto ex Maria virgine' in free speech-rhythm. Building, perhaps, on the example in Haydn's 'Kettledrum' Mass, the tenor soloist now repeats the word 'et' of the phrase 'et homo factus est' as though to underline the spiritual implications more completely.

[1] In the eighteenth century the modes were closely identified with the idea of the supernatural, so their use here, and of the Lydian mode in the slow movement of the A minor Quartet, Op. 132, was of great significance to Beethoven's contemporaries.

[2] Cf. Donald Francis Tovey, *Essays in musical analysis*, V (London, 1937), p. 172.

At this hopeful prospect the tonality changes, only to return to the minor again for the tragic outcome of Christ's descent to earth— the Crucifixion. Though it is known that Beethoven studied Bach's setting of these words in the B Minor Mass, there is little similarity between the two versions. Bach transforms the traditional baroque lament, with its chromatically descending ground bass, into a formal song of mourning, whereas Beethoven's 'Crucifixus' is more individual and is shot through with stabbing, off-beat accents and discontinuous textures. The semitonal inflections in the violin line at 'passus et sepultus est', on the other hand, have many parallels both in Bach and elsewhere.[1] If the comparison between Bach and Beethoven is carried further, as it is by Tovey, there are other striking differences. Bach's setting of the 'Et resurrexit' is one of his most brilliant and highly-developed choruses and makes a fine contrast to the previous section. In Beethoven the antithesis is even stronger, since his 'Et resurrexit' is only six bars long and is for un-accompanied chorus. A really satisfactory explanation for this is hard to find. Perhaps Beethoven was deliberately setting out to make this passage as unconventional as possible; certainly no other orchestral mass of the period has such a passage for *a cappella* choir at this point. The rising scale for the words 'et ascendit' shows a return to the musical symbolism of the past and is followed by a highly effective entry on solo trombone which heralds the 'Judicare'. This whole central section of the 'Credo' ends with the phrase 'non erit finis', followed by three repeated cries of the word 'non', which link it to the last part of the movement in truly Beethovenian style. The 'credo' motto now returns, and the remaining sentences of the text are declaimed against it. Finally, as a pendant to all that has gone before, the time-signature changes for the mighty double fugue 'Et vitam venturi'.

The argument of the music here is more coherent than in the 'Gloria' and consists of two large paragraphs with the usual coda. The fugue opens quietly, with the two subjects presented immediately by the sopranos and tenors. In the first part the voices are supported by a combination of woodwind and lower strings, a

[1] See the 'Agnus Dei' of Mozart's Requiem and of Haydn's 'St. Nicholas' Mass.

texture that Beethoven had already used with telling effect in the
'Sanctus' of the C major Mass. The notorious B flat entry for
the sopranos (at bar 328), which Beethoven declined to alter for
the first performance,[1] also occurs here. The exposition of the fugue
continues with the twin subjects presented in inversion as the
music moves towards flatter key centres. Suddenly, at the climax
of this first section the train of thought ceases abruptly, a foretaste
of the many similar occurrences that are to appear in the last string
quartets. The violins, which up till the previous bar have been
silent, begin afresh with a diminished version of the subject which
fits against both the original idea (still in minims) and the new
counter-subject:

Both this and the first exposition still show vestiges of Beethoven's
studies with Albrechtsberger and Haydn in their use of certain
elements of species counterpoint. Tradition is again served by the
pedal point (at bar 399) over which Beethoven piles up a noble
volume of sound; then, just when the movement seems to be drawing to its close in a majestic *grave*, the texture evaporates a second
time, leaving the four solo voices to set their own personal seal
upon the music that has gone before. This coda is the most successful in the work—partly because it is the simplest, but also because
it is the least self-conscious. Its gently rising scales are not emphatically related to any of the ideas heard previously; instead, it is as
though in these last few pages Beethoven is trying to convey some
kind of pictorial image, such as that of man's spirit leaving the
earth and ascending to heaven.

For the 'Sanctus' the tonality returns to D, the principal key of
the work. Bach's B minor Mass, originally written for Lutheran

[1] Cf. *TF*, p. 907.

use, has here a grand ceremonial quality which contrasts strongly with the hushed, prayer-like atmosphere of this short, typically Catholic, setting. Though it seems quite appropriate, therefore, for the soloists to sing this particular passage alone, it is hard to understand why Beethoven wanted them to do battle with the full orchestra in the 'Pleni' and 'Osanna' that follow. The evidence of the autograph and early prints makes this intention quite clear, though most modern conductors find it more practical to assign the last two sections to the full choir.

The problem of unifying the remaining portions of the mass text, already discussed in connection with the Mass in C, understandably receives a more elaborate solution in the *Missa solemnis*. A sense of logic is imparted to those movements which lead up to the transubstantiation by means of tempo indications that increase with each succeeding paragraph: *adagio* for the 'Sanctus', *allegro pesante* for the 'Pleni' and *presto* for the 'Osanna'. Then follows one of Beethoven's finest inspirations, the beautiful instrumental Praeludium to the 'Benedictus'. The scoring is for flutes, clarinets, bassoons, lower strings and organ pedals, and the predominantly dark textures of these instruments provide the perfect foil to the two high flutes and solo violin with which the movement proper begins. In spite of the brevity of the text, Beethoven's 'Benedictus' constitutes a complete symphonic movement in which he is able to fuse together a number of different musical elements to form 'a kind of aria-concerto of violin, voices, and orchestra'.[1] Indeed, so important are the formal considerations to him that he prefers to incorporate the text of the second 'Osanna' into the fabric of the movement, just as Haydn had done in his 'Theresa' and 'Creation' Masses, rather than disrupt the mood of humble supplication by returning in the conventional manner to the music of the first 'Osanna'.

The remaining part of the *Missa solemnis*, the finale, as it were, of this mighty choral symphony, is again built on traditional procedures. The 'Agnus Dei' has an unusually clear tripartite design, which in some respects looks back to the symbolic treatment favoured by Renaissance composers, and is in B minor—a

[1] Cf. Tovey, op. cit., V, p. 181.

key which Beethoven considered to have particularly dark overtones. This is linked directly to the 'Dona nobis pacem', whose
first page bears the inscription 'prayer for inward and outward
peace'.

Just as Beethoven introduces voices in the last movement of his
Ninth Symphony in order to complete and intensify his conception
of the whole work, so is the 'Dona nobis pacem' of the *Missa
solemnis* cast in the form of a symphonic finale with the same end in
view. Basically the design is that of a free sonata-rondo, consisting
broadly of the following sections: A B A¹ C Coda—where A
represents the 'prayer for inward peace', while B and C represent
the desire for 'outward peace'. The first paragraph (A) is elaborate;
it opens with a double fugue which then blossoms out into this
final phrase:

Ex.7

The sudden disappearance of the orchestral accompaniment at this
point, and the conspicuous interval of a falling sixth in the soprano
line, help to make it one of the most memorable moments of the
entire work. A brief fugato now leads to the second part of the 'A'
structure, which takes the form of a set of characteristically contrasting ideas. Of these the first element consists of an exchange between
the upper and lower voices of the choir, backed by delicate staccato
scales in the orchestra (at bar 131). Having firmly established the
dominant key of A major, Beethoven then emphatically negates it
with a mysterious F natural on the timpani, and this initiates the
first episode, B. Fanfares on trumpets and drums (played *pianissimo*) vividly portray the sounds of battle that can come to disrupt
the 'outward peace' of the finale, just as they had done at the same
point in Haydn's 'Kettledrum' Mass written some twenty-seven
years earlier. Against this background the soloists and chorus return

to the prayer 'Agnus Dei, qui tollis peccata mundi' in an even more passionate plea for peace. The music of the opening now recurs in the key of F major (Section A^1) and modulates freely before the second group of ideas are recapitulated; first the *a cappella* phrase, then the fugato built on the same falling sixth and this time strongly reminiscent of a section from the 'Hallelujah Chorus' in Handel's *Messiah*. The second episode (C) is marked '*presto*' and takes the form of a remarkable orchestral fugato based on the rising scale of the first vocal fugue. This again reflects back to the first episode (B) in its overt turbulence, though here the effect is achieved by more extreme means, including some extraordinary modulations and a good deal of discontinuous scoring. The true function of this interlude is not easy to assess. It may be that the material the composer wanted to explore was only suitable for an instrumental ensemble or that he wanted to rest the voices of the choir before calling on them again for the final pages. It is possible, too, that, having made one unconscious reference to Handel's *Messiah*, Beethoven also half-remembered the effect of the instrumental section in the final 'Amen' chorus of that oratorio and decided to introduce a similar episode into his own score. As the tonality shifts towards B flat the warlike trumpet and drums reappear, nearer and more insistent than before, sweeping the choir towards the coda and the central key of D. The supple $\frac{6}{8}$ metre, which began the movement, now returns, bringing with it the consoling prospect of 'inner peace' once again, and gradually the tension relaxes. The phrase with the falling sixth (Ex. 7) reappears, accompanied by a final threatening mutter on the timpani. This in its turn is silenced by the choir repeating their previous cadence on the word 'pacem'. Finally the entire phrase is heard *forte e ben marcato*, after which the orchestra bring the work to a triumphant close with a brief flourish.

So ends one of Beethoven's greatest compositions, a work that took over four years to complete, in which every note seems to have been carefully pondered and for which revisions continued right up to the time of publication. The path towards its creation was never easy, and one has only to look back over some of the earlier works to appreciate the true nature of Beethoven's achievement.

The vocal writing no longer follows the conventional formulae of the period but is now entirely subservient to the subtlest textual implications. Simple homophony, as in the Choral Fantasia, for example, gives way to a much more elaborate treatment of the chorus, in which the spacing and sonority of every chord are carefully calculated in relation to the total texture. Like the late piano sonatas and string quartets, the *Missa solemnis* is one of the landmarks of musical history, both the culmination of one tradition and the beginning of another. Prince Nicolas Galitzin clearly recognized this when he wrote to Beethoven after the first performance in St. Petersburg in these words:[1] '. . . this whole work in fact is a treasure of beauties; it can be said that your genius has anticipated the centuries and that there are not listeners perhaps enlightened enough to experience all the beauty of this music; but it is posterity that will pay homage and will bless your memory much better than your contemporaries can'.

[1] Quoted in *TF*, p. 925.

ELEVEN

The Songs

LESLIE ORREY

IF WE SET on one side the 150 arrangements of folk and national songs of these islands that Beethoven made for the Scottish publisher George Thomson,[1] we are left with a heritage of some eighty original songs, some with Italian words, some in orchestral settings, but the great majority in German and with piano accompaniment. It is a legacy that has been too much overshadowed on the one hand by his own instrumental works, and on the other by the richer variety of the songs of Schubert. In linking these two names together one must remind oneself that, however much or little Schubert's song style is indebted to Beethoven, any contrary influence is out of the question. Beethoven had virtually put song behind him by 1816: a good half had been written by 1811, the year of Schubert's first extant song; and many were written before Schubert was born. In the world of *Lieder* Beethoven rather than Schubert was the pioneer, groping towards a satisfactory solution with few precedents to build on; and the unevenness of his output reflects this.

Of the several musical influences bearing on the art-song of the time, that of Italian opera must by no means be overlooked. Musicians nurtured in this atmosphere unconsciously acquired a grace and felicity of melodic phrase, a clarity and shapeliness of

---

[1] See Cecil Hopkinson and C. B. Oldman, 'Thomson's collections of national songs, with special reference to the contributions of Haydn and Beethoven', *Transactions of the Edinburgh Bibliographical Society*, II, 1 (1940).

outline that could triumph over harmonic poverty. It was in the opera-house, too, that men learnt the dramatic, emotional and pictorial value of the instrumental background, and the forerunners of Schubert's typical accompaniments are to be traced to the theatre rather than to the unpretentious song collections of the time.

Even piano technique, which was developing in fields other than song, could not escape this influence. The slow movement of a sonata, for example, is a descendant of the operatic air. In pianistic terms this means a melody played by the right hand, the left hand providing the background and support; but the evolution from such textures to an independent piano accompaniment, which, balanced and complete in itself, would yet not overpower the voice nor distract the listener, did not come at once, nor of itself. Among Beethoven's songs there are some, such as *Mollys Abschied, Marmotte, Das Blümchen wunderhold,* that read exactly like some of his easier piano movements, while more ambitious songs go to the other extreme and offer an elaborate, almost concerto-like part with a vocal obbligato (*Der Wachtelschlag, Lied aus der Ferne*).

There can be little doubt, too, that the widespread publication of operas in vocal score proved immensely suggestive, was far more influential in opening composers' eyes to the piano's possibilities than the simpler song books and fostered a demand for 'operatic' songs. Such a song is Mozart's *Erzeugt von heisser Phantasie,* K.520—through-composed, employing motives at once illustrative and structural, and clearly operatic in conception.

In contrast to this the folk-like songs of the North German school show a frugal, almost puritanical simplicity. Their song books were put out on two staves only, and under such conditions an accompaniment in the modern sense was clearly impossible. The example quoted below, by Schulz, is typical; it comes from his *Lieder im Volkston, bey Clavier zu singen* (1782):

Ex.1

Johann Abraham Peter Schulz (1747–1800) may be cited as representative of this North German school of song-writing. They leant towards simplicity of utterance; they favoured a *volkstümlich* style, with the minimum of elaboration in the piano part. Of the forty-eight songs in this 1782 book the last ten are in a separate section entitled 'Etliche Theatergesänge'; they differ from the others in length rather than in style. The settings, to words by Bürger, Friedrich von Stolberg, Hölty, Claudius and others, are mostly very short and simple, eight or sixteen bars in length. The treatment is syllabic or near-syllabic; the bottom stave very rarely has anything but a bass line, sometimes in octaves, though *Liebezauber* (Bürger) has some chords and a couple of bars of Alberti-type bass. Another Bürger setting, *Der Ritter und sein Liebchen*, offers an example of the tedious jogtrot of mainly repeated notes that the North German composers so often used for narrative. One more quotation may be permitted. In *Seufzer eines Ungeliebten* Schulz allows himself the luxury of a slight chromatic 'expressiveness' at the word 'allein':

Ex.2

Schulz had a vein of true lyricism, for the most part admirably mated with the quiet and unadventurous poetry he was setting. The production of songs of *volkstümlich* character was obviously spurred on by Herder's *Volkslieder,* and besides the volumes by individual composers such as Johann André, Johann Gottlieb Naumann, Johann Friedrich Reichardt and many others, a number of collections appeared. The biggest of these was the Mildheim song book.[1] The music to this first came out in the following year, and then later under the title *Melodien zum Mildheimisches Lieder-buche für das Pianoforte oder Clavier* (Gotha, 1790). It was printed on two staves only, the songs are all strophic and the general level is not very remarkable. The composers included Reichardt (strongly represented), Zelter, Neefe, Hiller, Benda and many others.

Of these composers Johann Adam Hiller (1728–1804) is associated with the *Singspiel*: he wrote a dozen or more for the theatre at Leipzig. But he is also remembered in connection with the history of music periodicals: he founded two musical weeklies, the

---

[1] *Mildheimisches Lieder-Buch von 518 Lustigen und ernsthaften Gesängen über alle Dinge in der Welt und alle Umstände des menschlichen Lebens, die mann besingen kann. Ges. für Freunde erlaubter Fröhlichkeit und ächter Tugend, die den Kopf nicht hängt von Rudolph Zacharias Becker.* 1782. ('The Mildheim Songbook of 518 songs, grave and gay, on everything in the world and all the affairs of mankind, that can be sung about. Collected for friends of seemly jollity and worthy virtue by Rudolph Zacharias Becker.')

The Songs

Wöchentlicher musicalische Zeitvertreib ('Weekly Musical Pastime')
and *Wöchentliche Nachrichten und Anmerkungen, die Musik
betreffend* ('Weekly Notes and News concerning Music'). The
former ran for only about a year, during 1759, but the second,
which was occupied by articles on music rather than by the music
itself, ran for longer. It contained a novel, *Die Geschichte der Miss
Fanny Wilkes*, by J. T. Hermes (1738–1821), which, in the fashion
of the times, included several lyrics which Hiller set to music. A
second novel, *Sophiens Reise von Memel nach Sachsen*, ran during
the years 1769–73; it contained a greater number of lyrics, and
Hiller's settings of these appeared in 1779.[1] A typical example of
Hiller's songs, quoted below, is *Das aufhobener Gebet*, taken from
his first weekly. It is a duet between Phyllis and Damon, with
violin or flute and figured bass; these few bars from the opening
ritornello show clearly the stylistic relationship with the Italian
school:

[1] Three were also set by Mozart (K.390–2).

415

Also typical is *Aeol*, from his *Vierte Sammlung kleiner Clavier- und Singstücke* (Leipzig, 1774). Apart from the fact that the figuration is now in the right hand of the clavier part instead of on the solo violin or flute, there is no difference in style.

Italian as this music is when compared with Schulz's, that of Christian Gottlob Neefe (1748–98) is still more so. Like Hiller, whose pupil he had been, he wrote for the Leipzig theatre, but later toured the Rhineland with a theatrical company, the Seyler company, and eventually in 1779 he settled in Bonn, to become one of Beethoven's teachers. His *Serenaten beym Clavier zu singen* published in Leipzig in 1777 are not so much songs as scenas, almost cantatas, in the Italian manner, often with rapidly changing moods, varying from arioso to recitative and back again, in fact following a form familiar to us in some of Purcell's extended arias, and foreshadowing the ballads of Zumsteeg, which were to exert such a dangerous fascination on the young Schubert. In at least one of these, the sixth, to a text possibly by Neefe himself, the clavier part is written out on two staves, the voice part on a third. The opening words not unexpectedly give rise to a boisterous unison passage in semiquavers; notice, too, the expressive chromaticism on the word 'einsamer':

Ex. 4

(The rain pours down; the storm has arisen. Forsaken I lie here in the lonely night.)

Perhaps even more interesting and prophetic is the treatment found in Neefe's *Die frühen Gräber*. Klopstock's poem, which received many settings (that of Gluck is particularly noteworthy), is addressed to the moon. There are three stanzas, the first two set to identical music; the clavier part is a good deal nearer the consistent piano accompaniment we find in later song composers. The third stanza begins in the relative minor, somewhat slower, and there is a short but effective postlude based on an expressive little motive in thirds.

The almost universal strophic form served not only for the simple lyric of two or three stanzas but also for lengthy narrative poems of the ballad type. Bürger's famous ballad *Lenore*,[1] for instance, has no fewer than thirty-two stanzas. It was set strophically by several composers, including Johann Philipp Kirnberger in his *Gesänge am Clavier* (1780). To complain of the monotony of such treatment is to miss the point. The music of such songs was essentially 'neutral', and it was left to the singer to invest this

[1] Translated by Scott as *William and Helen*.

neutral 'carrier wave' with the variety of declamation appropriate to each stanza. That Beethoven was not above this somewhat obvious treatment is evidenced by such trifles as *Urians Reise um die Welt*, with fourteen stanzas, and *Der freie Mann*, with seven.

How much of this abundant musical fare came Beethoven's way in his formative years in Bonn is hard to say;[1] he must, one supposes, have been familiar with some of it, if only through Neefe. The repertory of operas at the court theatre was varied, with French leanings[2] that are noticeable in at least one song, *Marmotte*. The words are by Goethe, from a Shrovetide play, *Fastnachtspiel*; Beethoven's setting, written about 1790-2, possibly for a revival of the play, has something of the lilt of an Alsatian folk-song. The first published song, and one of the very earliest of his works to be seen in print, appeared in 1783 in a weekly music magazine, *Blümenlese für Liebhaber*.[3] This was *Schilderung eines Mädchen*; it and another publication the following year, *An einen Säugling*, reflect the beneficent influence of Neefe, who had begun to give him lessons probably some time in 1780. The lightness of touch in these and other songs from the Bonn period such as *Prüfung des Küssens* or *Elegie auf den Tod eines Pudels* will surprise only those who cling tenaciously to the idea of the 'Olympian' Beethoven.

A different approach to song composition is seen after he left Bonn for Vienna in 1792, and during the next two or three years he wrote several that merit closer attention: *Opferlied*, to words by Matthisson; *Seufzer eines Ungeliebten* (words by Bürger); *Adelaide* (words again by Matthisson); and the concert aria with orchestra,

---

[1] The song books current in Vienna are listed in Irene Pollak-Schlaffenberg, 'Die Wiener Liedmusik von 1778 bis 1789, *Studien zur Musikwissenschaft*, V (1918), pp. 98–100, and Editha Alberti-Radanowicz, 'Das Wiener Lied von 1789–1815', *Studien zur Musikwissenschaft*, X (1923), pp. 38–42. A small and not particularly representative selection is in *Das Wiener Lied von 1778 bis Mozarts Tod*, ed. Margarete Ansion and Irene Schlaffenberg, *Denkmäler der Tonkunst in Österreich*, XXVII, 2 (Vienna, 1920), and *Das Wiener Lied von 1792 bis 1815*, ed. Hermann Maschek and Hedwig Kraus, op. cit., XLII (Vienna, 1935). Mozart's songs were first collected and published by Breitkopf & Härtel in 1799.

[2] For some details of the repertory see *TF*, pp. 150–2.

[3] Probably the earliest English publication of any Beethoven work was also a song, *La Tiranna*, written about 1788 and published soon after 1800.

Ah! perfido!, to a text by Metastasio, as well as a number that remained unfinished, including an attempt at *Erlkönig*. The four songs and a duet subsequently published in 1811 as Op. 82 may also have been written about this time.[1] Of the songs mentioned, *Opferlied* is linked in mood to the Gellert songs,[2] but the other three are plainly operatic in style and can no doubt be related to his studies with Salieri. *Seufzer eines Ungeliebten* is, in fact, paired with *Gegenliebe*, to make up a recitative and bipartite aria corresponding to the typical cavatina-cabaletta of Italian opera. The piano writing is entirely different from that of the other aria-like songs we are about to examine and suggests a piano transcription of an orchestral score. The prototype can be seen in Mozartian opera, or in the song K.520 we have already noted, its more elaborate realization in *Ah! perfido!* written probably for the Countess Josephine von Clary and first performed in Prague by Josefa Duschek on 21 November 1796. The two songs have so many features in common that it is tempting to regard *Seufzer* as a preparatory study for *Ah! perfido!*

For one thing the poetic contents are very similar. Both sing of thwarted or unfulfilled love—a constantly recurring theme in Beethoven's songs. The recitative of *Seufzer*, it is true, is only nine bars long, in contrast to that of *Ah! perfido!* which, very much more elaborate, extends to sixty-one bars of fairly involved musical treatment, highly dramatic and ranging from fury to despair. The ensuing arias, however, are remarkably similar. Both are in E flat, both in $\frac{3}{4}$ time, both exemplify the 'formal-instrumental' type of composition we shall have frequent occasion to notice in later songs. They are almost identical in length, seventy-seven bars of *andantino* in *Seufzer* as against seventy-two bars of *adagio* in *Ah! perfido!* (the latter is followed by an *allegro assai* of symphonic proportions). Both arrive at a formal perfect cadence in the dominant at almost exactly the same time—bar 26 in one, bar 27 in the other. In neither instance is the new key held, and in each song the return is by way of a series of descending $^6_3$ chords—a little motive that plays a significant structural part in both arias. The emotional and musical range of the second song, it is true, is

---

[1] *KV* puts them slightly earlier, *c.* 1790.
[2] See below, pp. 421–2.

enormously wider—notice particularly the move to C flat major in bar 53; and there is, of course, no comparison between the enormous concluding *allegro assai* with its wealth of material and the companion song to *Seufzer*, attractive though that is.[1]

This 'formal-instrumental' style is equally noticeable in *Adelaide*, Op. 46, written in 1795 or 1796.[2] It is a long song, 181 bars, in the same bipartite operatic aria form. Matthisson's words, which suffer a good deal of repetition at Beethoven's hands, are somewhat conventional, with the familiar nightingales, murmuring streamlets, evening breezes and so on of the nature poets. The setting has always been popular with singers, since it demands a certain virtuosity; but its virtues are formal and musical rather than poetical. The diversified figurations in the accompaniment, for instance, stem from a musical urge towards variety rather than from any poetic compulsion. The symphonic treatment of the motive:

Ex.5

in the D flat section satisfies our demand for musical unity. There is some poetic justification for this modulation, which is in any case of the mediant type (from B flat via F) that Beethoven turns to more and more frequently, and also for the accompaniment pattern

[1] There is a family likeness between *Gegenliebe* and the theme of the last movement of the Ninth Symphony, and there is a curious connection between them. For in 1808, when he came to write the Choral Fantasia, Op. 80, itself in a way a preparation for the Ninth, this melody was pressed into service. Cf. above, pp. 388–9.

[2] The first edition was in 1797 and was dedicated to the poet, who, however, did not thoroughly approve; in fact, he remarked that of all the settings he knew Beethoven's was the one wherein the poem was most overshadowed by the music. See Paul Nettl, *The Beethoven Encyclopaedia* (London, 1957), art. 'Matthisson'; also Henri de Curzon, *Les Lieder et airs détachés de Beethoven* (Paris, 1905), p. 21.

(illustrating the word 'Abendlüftchen'—'evening zephyrs'). There is, however, none for the sudden tonic minor (B flat minor) in the last section at the *repetition* of the words 'Einst, O Wunder!' (bar 114). Nor can the augmented sixth chord in bar 62, at the words 'Wellen rauschen', be justified poetically, though musically and formally it is unexceptionable: the progression used here, augmented sixth on the flattened submediant moving to the dominant, had become one of the accepted conventions of the Haydn-Mozart symphonic style, and in doing so it lost its emotive connotation and became a purely formal element. The contrast with the same chord used *poetically* in *An die Hoffnung*, Op. 94 (discussed below), is instructive.

It is interesting to turn to another long song, *Lied aus der Ferne* to words by 'that rascal Reissig',[1] written much later, in 1809. A composition in strict ternary form, its opening ritornello is of almost concerto-like proportions and does, in fact, expound nearly all the material for the singer's first stanza. There is no special poetic reason for this, though the material is apt enough; the piano writing can be matched in many an instrumental movement, and one would not be surprised to find it as the opening of, say, a rondo for violin. The new accompaniment pattern in bar 53 at the beginning of the middle section is understandable, but the modulation from B flat to D flat is less poetically justified and probably reflects the fact that by this date Beethoven was using such mediant modulations quite naturally in his instrumental works. And though the augmented sixth in bar 81 (at 'Ich opfre dir alles') and the increased excitement of the last stanza can certainly be ascribed to a poetic stimulus, the song as a whole is more instrumentally biassed than any so far discussed.

The six songs by Gellert, Op. 48 (May and June 1803), reveal a different approach. The *Geistliche Oden und Lieder*, from which these six are taken, were published in 1757 and in the following

---

[1] Christian Ludwig Reissig (*c.* 1783–1847) makes several appearances in Beethoven's letters, mainly in association with nephew Karl. His collected poetry, *Blümchen der Einsamkeit*, appeared in 1809 and 1815. No fewer than forty composers set his words, including Himmel, Hummel, Reichardt, Weber and Zelter.

year appeared with music by C. P. E. Bach. The words express in simple terms a firm, confident faith in the goodness of God, a belief in his almighty power testified by the universe around us; they extol brotherly love and express humble penitence—ideas that were in accord with Beethoven's own religious views. His settings are strophic—most, indeed, are settings of a single strophe—and with the exception of the last, *Busslied*, are of a hymn-like simplicity comparable with Bach's own settings. If the piano part does little more than support the voice, it has at times (e.g. in *Die Ehre Gottes aus der Natur*) a considerable harmonic and tonal range. There is an occasional flash of Handel (*Gottes Macht und Vorsehung*), but on the whole little trace of the sublime Beethoven in the first five songs.

In the sixth, *Busslied*, he seems to have been moved to abandon this all too naïve style: the result is a song that is certainly below the level of his best but with many points of interest. The first section, *poco adagio*, in A minor, is more chromatic than usual, justifiably so. The upward-thrusting diminished seventh in bar 7 on the word 'Fluch' ('curse') is understandable, its reappearance in bar 30 somewhat less poetically convincing: bars 29–31 are a repetition of bars 6–8, transposed, and set to different words. The new accompaniment figure in bar 16 is there for both musical and poetic reasons, but the sforzando syncopations in bars 37, 39 and 51, thoroughly typical of the composer as they are, have less poetic than musical meaning. On the other hand the following, major, section is a disappointment. It contains three stanzas set to a melody that is shapely enough but of no great distinction, no better, in fact, than those to be seen in any Victorian anthem book. The piano accompaniment to these stanzas is little short of astounding—academic exercises in 'free counterpoint' such as any competent student could turn out with no trouble at all. This is a sad let-down after the promise of the first section.

Nevertheless this section does display one interesting feature which Beethoven was later to develop—the idea of strophic variation. But before following that up it will be instructive to examine the song *An die Hoffnung*, Op. 32, and compare it with his second thoughts, Op. 94. Op. 32 dates from 1805 and is thus contemporary with *Leonore*, the first version of *Fidelio*; sketches for it and the opera are found in the same sketchbook. The words, by Christian August Tiedge (1752–1841), come from a long poem, *Urania über Gott, Unsterblichkeit und Freiheit,* written in 1801 and drawn upon frequently by composers. The three stanzas are set strophically to a melody that matches suitably the sentiments of the first stanza: see, for example, the melisma on 'Seele quält'—'quälen' meaning 'to torture'—and the bright upward swing to E natural on the word 'Hoffnung'—'hope'—in bar 15; and this scheme does no violence to the remaining stanzas. But the extension of the musical phrase over a dominant, with $^6_4$–$^5_3$ harmony, at the words 'ein Engel seine Thränen zählt', followed by an interrupted cadence (bars 20-2), is a compositional device that we owe entirely to instrumental practice. The last two lines of poetry are at once repeated, to music that clearly grows out of the previous passage; and this time the $^6_4$–$^5_3$ progression is presented with slightly more elaboration—a musical extension that again is determined more by instrumental musical logic than by any poetic compulsion. The whole passage is quoted here:

Ex.6

- ho - ben, den Dulder ah - nen, dass dort o - ben ein En-gel

sei - - ne—Thrä - nen zählt!

(. . . an angel may record his tears! O hope! Let the suffering one hope
that, lifted upwards by you, an angel there above may record his tears!)

The accompaniment, simple though it is, shows similar traits.
There is an artistic variety of texture, from simple chords to chords
in alternate hands, repeated chords, triplet broken chords, all
musically rather than poetically inspired. The triplets arise naturally
from the opening prelude, itself a purely instrumental type of
figuration. The musical unity of the song is helped along by the
reappearance of this, first as an interlude, and later as a postlude.

In his second setting, dating from 1813—conceivably as a result
of discussion with the poet, whom he met in Teplitz in 1811—
Beethoven abandons this strophic form in favour of a recitative and
aria, through-composed but with the first stanza repeated. The
recitative begins in B flat minor, an unusual key for him; the words,
beginning 'Ob ein Gott sei?', were not used at all in Op. 32. The
first stanza is in G, and instead of the simple and unassuming but
rather appealing melody of the earlier song the words are now set
much more elaborately, with some chromaticism and rhythmic
variety. The up-curve at 'O Hoffnung' is preserved, but with less
intensity (bars 33–4), the climactic upward sweep being held back
for a few bars until in bar 36 the music soars aloft through an
arpeggio to a high G on the words 'den Dulder ahnen, dass dort

oben'. The interrupted cadence at 'Thränen zählt' and the attendant extension are also retained, the latter being intensified to become eight bars of $\frac{4}{4}$ time (the tempo is *Larghetto*), and with the word 'Thränen' ('tears') given an expressive chromatic stress. Ex. 7 shows bars 36–45:

Ex. 7

zählt, ein En - gel— sei - ne Thrä - nen zählt!

This reliance on the text for inspiration is redoubled in the setting of the second stanza, illustrated by the darker key, E flat— the key of the first setting, and an instance of the flat submediant modulation so common in Beethoven—for 'Wenn längst verhallt' ('when the echoes of dearly loved voices have died away'); by the more cheerful C major of the next section (bars 52 ff.), similar in treatment to the corresponding passage in Op. 32; and by the shuddering diminished seventh chord, *pp*, at the word 'Mitternacht' ('midnight'). The accompaniment here uses figurations or patterns similar to those in a corresponding passage in the first setting, but they now make poetic as well as musical sense.

A short passage in bare octaves at the words 'sich auf versunk'ne Urnen stützt' ('supporting himself on half-buried urns') rapidly expands into harmony and moves via an augmented-sixth chord to the leading-note key, D minor, for the third stanza, 'Und blickt er auf . . .'. Beethoven here uses what might be termed the 'exaltation' technique of repeated chords, a technique that was to become a mannerism with the later romantic writers. After a climax at the words 'letzten Strahlen' the music relaxes to a short *adagio* in B major, moving after three bars to C major, the tension thereafter increasing rapidly until at the word 'Sonne' the climax of the song is reached with the voice stranded on a top A with a dramatic 'cut-off' on a *fortissimo* dominant seventh in the home key.

It will be seen that after the too simple strophic setting Beethoven has here gone to the other extreme, underlining the imagery of the poem with vivid and varied musical illustration. These two stanzas are an example of superb dramatic writing, but the note-for-note repetition of the first stanza at the end has little or no poetic justification: Beethoven the formal-instrumental composer has taken over.

This search for a more exact, purely poetic realization is pursued in a number of smaller songs written, and sometimes rewritten, at about this time. He did a setting of *An die Geliebte* (words by J. L. Stoll) in 1811; a second setting, published in 1814, is vocally almost identical, the minute changes (in bars 6, 8, 10, 15, 19–21 and 23–5) of the later version all directed towards a more natural declamation of the words. The accompaniment, however, while preserving the same harmonic basis except for one tiny alteration at the end, was completely recast. Instead of the merely decorative accompaniment (an undulating triplet figure that did no more than give adequate support to the vocal line) we now have a supple, almost Schumannesque piano part. It mostly consists of no more than an alternation between the two hands; but the chords are carefully spaced, and the dynamic directions (completely absent in the first setting) have obviously received studied attention and are as worthy of examination as those in Op. 94. The typical Beethoven syncopation in bar 22, with a sforzando, is here completely justifiable, conjured up by the word 'Schmerzen'; and the one harmonic alteration can be traced to the same word. The accompaniment is now right psychologically as well as musically; Ex. 8 shows the first version (*a*) and the second (*b*):

Ex. 8

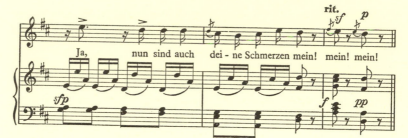

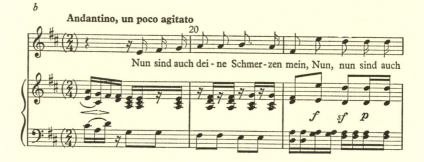

(Your sorrows are now also mine.)

Mastery in a yet higher degree is shown in the setting of the much-composed *Wonne der Wehmuth*, the first of the three Goethe songs of Op. 83 (1810). Slight in dimension, the poem sums up in its two short stanzas the whole self-immolatory, masochistic conception of romantic love. It is hardly possible to imagine a setting where poetic and musical ideas are fused together more perfectly; it is far superior to Schubert's setting. The tears that refuse to be stilled are sublimated into a musical idea that sounds dry enough, even crude, when described as a scale in detached demisemiquavers, but in performance it is pictorially apt, eloquent and wonderfully moving.

It is important to note that while Beethoven is clearly aware of the emotional force of harmony *per se*, as shown for example in the chords of the first two bars or in the setting of the words 'wie todt die Welt ihm erscheint!', he was rarely content to rely on this alone, as later composers were so apt to do. His musical ideographs are rhythmically alive, so that we never experience that stasis that affected nineteenth-century German music more and more as the century grew older. The intensification in the second stanza, in E minor, is demanded by the new urgency in the text ('unglück-licher Liebe'), and the melisma on the latter word in bar 15 is a particularly happy example of Beethoven revitalizing an old formula. It had long been the custom in the operatic *da capo* aria for the singer to improvise embellishments at the point of return, on a dominant pause. The ornament here is of just such a nature; but it is equally dictated by the poem (the word 'Liebe'), which is likewise the justification for the extension, by way of the interrupted cadence of bar 19, and the tiny epilogue.

None of the other Goethe songs approaches the high standard of excellence of this one, which in truth looks forward to the pregnant tone-pictures of Schumann and Wolf. The early *Mailied*, for instance, seems to me to catch only the surface of the meaning. The poem is one of the Sesenheimer lyrics (1771), written by Goethe the young romantic; it expresses the boundless, irrepressible, wondering joy in the beauties of nature around us; without hyperbole, with no glowing or involved poetic imagery but in simple words and short ecstatic phrases it sings of those sights and sounds and those upsurging emotions that create the world afresh for every lover. Such a poem is almost impossible to set to music. To express ecstasy the musician needs space, he must have ample room and long phrases. But the poet need not; and indeed here the short phrases with few syllables are essential to the mood of breathless enchantment that suffuses the poem. That the music is not indissolubly wedded to Goethe's words is attested by the fact that Beethoven used the melody for an aria, or rather strophic song, 'O welch' ein Leben', inserted in a *Singspiel* called *Die pucefarbenen Schuhe*, or *Die schöne Schusterin*, by Ignaz Umlauf, probably at its revival in Vienna in 1796.[1]

The two other Goethe songs of 1810 are no more than elegant trifles. *Sehnsucht* ('Was zieht mir das Herz so ?'), Op. 83, No. 2, is a light-hearted, varied-strophic song, and the last of Op. 83, *Mit einem gemalten Band*, has a nimbleness of gait that reminds us that Vienna was a city of Italian opera. The poem, like *Mailied*, is an early one, and the setting is successful in capturing the Anacreontic quality of the verse.

A little earlier Beethoven had wrestled with another *Sehnsucht*, 'Nur wie die Sehnsucht kennt' (WoO 134), a poem that has tempted many composers without eliciting a definitive version. This is one of Mignon's songs from Goethe's novel *Wilhelm Meisters Lehrjahre*: Beethoven's four settings, composed in 1808, seem almost like sketches for a final solution he never achieved. The difficulty here is that Mignon being a child must sing like a child, yet the words that Goethe puts into her mouth tempt the sophisticated composer into a language that is foreign to her innocence. It is the kind of problem Mozart might have solved, had he been alive when *Wilhelm Meister* was published (in 1795–6). Beethoven clearly recognized the need for simplicity, as is seen immediately by a glance at the accompaniments. The vocal lines are equally simple, with a compass (except in No. 3) of at most a diminished seventh. Comparing Nos. 1, 2 and 4, all in G minor, we notice a number of interesting parallels and contrasts, and the melodic outlines, the choice of chords, the types of accompaniment and the use made of melismata are all indicative of the closest attention to detail. By contrast

[1] See *TF*, p. 194.

Sehnsucht III (*Poco adagio*, E flat, $\frac{3}{4}$ time), though the simplest harmonically, betrays a sophistication lacking in the other three. The wider compass of the vocal line, a tenth, and the typical $\frac{6}{4}-\frac{5}{3}$ cadence on 'Freude' coupled with the ornamentation at this point suggest the *bel canto* of the operatic air. But the proportions are wrong: music of this type needs more space to develop than can be offered by this tiny lyric, and after the first seven bars, with their suggestion and promise of amplitude, the immediate repetition of the first phrase comes as a shock. The other three settings are to be preferred and catch successfully something of the simplicity of 'the most ethereal of all Goethe's characters', as Mignon has been described.

A year or so later, in 1809, Beethoven set another of Mignon's songs, *Kennst du das Land*. Here Goethe voices the envious yearnings of those living in northern climes for the warm Mediterranean, with its oranges, symbols of nature's clemency, its architecture and sculpture standing as present witnesses of an age-old civilization. The setting, in the sunny key of A major (the key of his own Seventh Symphony and of Mendelssohn's 'Italian' Symphony), is strophic, with some slight variation in the last stanza. Lacking the pictorialism of Liszt's setting, it yet does convey the excitability of the child as her imagination re-creates those far-off scenes of her dimly remembered childhood. Beethoven had surely pondered over Goethe's description of Mignon as she sang this song (in Book III, chapter 1): 'She began every verse in a stately and solemn manner, as if she wished to draw attention towards something beautiful, as if she had something weighty to communicate. In the third line, her tone became deeper and gloomier; the words "dost now?" were uttered with a show of mystery and eager circumspectness; in "'tis there! 'tis there!" lay an irresistible longing; and her "let us go!" she modified at each repetition, so that now it appeared to implore, now to compel and persuade' (Carlyle's translation). Goethe, by the way, did not approve of Beethoven's setting.

The years between 1810 and 1815 were devoted largely to instrumental works, and apart from *An die Hoffnung*, Op. 94, discussed above, the few songs, such as *Merkenstein* and *Der Bardengeist* (both referred to again below), are quite insignificant. Then,

possibly as a result of the final revision of *Fidelio* in 1814, comes a
new interest in vocal music. Still brooding no doubt over the
problems of song composition, his mind perhaps went back to that
experiment in the last of the Gellert songs. If that attempt at
strophic variation may be counted only a partial success at most,
another *Sehnsucht*, to words by Reissig (1815–16), offers a most
beautiful example. The poem, in three stanzas, is another of those
familiar expressions of heartache, of unfulfilled longing; it is not so
much, however, the yearning of the poem as a whole that stirred
Beethoven as the image in the first stanza of night enfolding the
countryside, the glassy lake, the silence. The 'theme' as presented
here has the majestic simplicity of many of the late Beethoven
themes, and it is interesting to compare this melody, with its
astonishingly small compass of a seventh, with the equally simple
but far less eloquent melodies of Op. 48. But another, subtler,
comparison suggests itself, for in mood, key, tempo and rhythm,
and to some extent in the curve of the vocal line, it so closely
anticipates the last movement of the Piano Sonata, Op. 109—itself
an example of the typical introspective variation form—that one
might almost imagine it to be a first draft for that theme:[1]

Ex. 9

[1] Beethoven apparently took extraordinary pains over this song; there
are no fewer than sixteen versions of the first few bars of the vocal line in
the sketchbooks: see *NZB*, pp. 332–3. The two fragments printed here
reinforce the similarity with the sonata.

(Silent night casts cooling shades over valley and peak!)

Abendlied (1820), a setting in the same key, E major, of a poem by Goeble, expresses similar sentiments in the first stanza, though the theme of the poem as a whole is quite different; and here the variation technique is used with a closer regard for the fluctuating moods of each stanza. It is a song of aspiration, with a consolatory message of peace and fulfilment in another world beyond this—a pendant, as it were, to the Gellert poems. In stanzas 1, 2 and 4 the third lines refer to stars, or to upward striving, and so in each stanza at this point the 'exaltation' technique is used.[1] But in the third stanza this idea comes in the second line, reinforced: 'Wo der Sternenrichter thront' ('Judge enthroned in starry splendour'), and the heightened emphasis is reflected in the more impassioned accompaniment, semiquavers replacing triplet quavers. Also in the third stanza, the words 'though the earth by tempest shaken' suggested the stormy piano figuration, and 'fear' and 'might' gave rise to the agitated dotted rhythm. The treasure in heaven that is the recompense for earthly pains is reflected in the serene postlude, which anticipates Liszt's 'seraphic' E major practice with chords high in the treble register.

This variation technique is nowhere used to better advantage than in the song-cycle *An die ferne Geliebte*, Op. 98 (1816), the

[1] Cf. the discussion of Op. 94 on p. 426.

first great example of the form and one in which, exceptionally, the
music is continuous. The words are by Alois Jeitteles (1794–1858),
a doctor who later settled and practised in his birthplace, Brünn;
they come from a collection, *Gedichte in Selam*, published in 1815.
Selam was the name of an almanac, one of the many circulating at
that time; its editor, Ignaz Castelli, was a playwright, translator and
man of the theatre, whose memoirs help to shed light on the
Viennese scene. Both he and Jeitteles belonged to the curiously-
named 'Ludlamshöhle'—an odd sort of club whose members,
besides the expected conviviality, indulged in the same kind of
fanciful nicknames that Schumann later bestowed on his Davidites.
Other members included Grillparzer, Gyrowetz, Salieri, Weber,
Benedict, Rellstab and many others.[1] Beethoven was an occasional
visitor and may have met Jeitteles there.

The theme of the cycle is the ever-recurring one of love's yearning, the treatment a conventional one in terms of the familiar
natural phenomena of hill and dale, flowers, birds, brooks—a
chaplet of nature poems. Beethoven sets them all strophically
except the last, which, giving a hint to Schumann,[2] harks back to
the music of the first song; and all but one of these strophic settings
have some form of variation technique applied to them. They make
an interesting study, with the formal-instrumental and the poetic-
expressive held nicely in balance. Thus in the first song, 'Auf dem
Hügel', the variations, apparently instrumentally inspired, seem to
intensify the heartache rather than conflict with it, and the two-bar
interlude between each stanza, as typically a Beethoven hallmark
as the similar passage in Op. 48, No. 5, has the syncopations here
softened by the absence of the sforzandos and ceases to be felt as an
intrusion. The last three stanzas of the third song, 'Leichte Segler'
(in A flat), are set in the tonic minor, not, as in *Adelaide*, merely for
tonal variety but of poetic necessity. The diverse figures of the
accompaniment of the same song spring from the same need, as
does the sudden incursion of the triplet figure in the last song, 'Nimm

[1] See Ignaz Castelli, *Memoiren meiner Lebens* (Vienna and Prague, 1861),
passim.

[2] It is not the only one. There are several quotations from *An die ferne
Geliebte* in Schumann's music: cf. Eric Sams, *The Songs of Robert
Schumann* (London, 1969), *passim*.

sie hin', at the words 'und sein letzter Strahl . . .' ('the last glow of evening fades away')—an 'exaltation' motive such as we noticed in *Abendlied*.

The sparseness of chromatic harmony in the cycle is noteworthy. In the second song, 'Wo die Berge so blau', the stab of dissonance in the third stanza, at the words 'innere Pein', is thrown into sharper relief by the contrast with the blue-skied serenity of the rest of the song. Almost the only other striking chord progression, the 'pathetic' augmented sixth—dominant cadence, occurs in the link between No. 4, 'Diese Wolken', and No. 5, 'Es kehret der Maien', in a classical cliché that robs it of its force.

Whether the Distant Beloved is to be identified with the Immortal Beloved remains a matter for conjecture. The famous letter[1] was written in 1812, and the dedication of the song-cycle four years later to Prince Franz Joseph von Lobkowitz offers no clue.

The variation technique so far noticed has been in the piano part. Variation in the vocal line is more of a rarity. In a few places a phrase heard first in simple form is repeated in a slightly ornamented version. The ornamentation is as a rule not very elaborate, most frequently taking the form of slurred quavers or semiquavers, a pair to a syllable, as in, for example, the early *Gegenliebe*. This pairing being a feature of an earlier style we naturally expect to see it in youthful songs such as the Mozartian *Der Abschied* (1797–8, author unknown), or the *Lied* of 1793 or before, to words by Lessing. But there are later examples—the two Reissig settings, *Der Jüngling in der Fremde* (1809) and *Des Kriegers Abschied* (1814). It is noticeable that certain words, phrases or ideas—love, joy, the freedom and dignity of man—seem to move Beethoven to this particular type of expression. Thus the *Lied*, a tiny strophic song whose central theme is that a life without love is incomplete, is packed with them; in *An die ferne Geliebte* they are virtually restricted to the coda, where the words 'liebend Herz' call them forth. A comparison with the solo quartet variation in the last movement of the Ninth symphony is instructive.

It has already been remarked how often Beethoven's love songs dwell on the idea of distant lovers, parted lovers and unrequited or

[1] *LA*, letter 373.

unattainable love. This theme understandably forms the core of much of the love poetry of the world. It was also, ostensibly, Beethoven's own personal tragedy that his own passionate nature was to suffer an intense longing for womanly affection, but never to experience its fulfilment. The question arises, why such a strong personal emotion in so highly charged a musician should have produced so few love songs of the highest class. One answer has often been put forward, namely, that his genius lay in the instrumental field, that he handled words with difficulty. He is indeed supposed to have confessed to Rochlitz that he did not like composing songs. We have, in fact, noted several successful songs where the success is heavily indebted to his formal-instrumental technique; but it has been equally apparent that the right poem, for instance, *Wonne der Wehmuth*, could on occasion inspire him to great heights.

But it may be that he was not as deeply stirred by the man-woman love relationship as he thought he was. Certain universal themes such as the idea of brotherly love, man's emancipation and the freedom of the individual, the contemplation of nature (linked in his mind with the contemplation of God), the Creator, the Infinite—these gave rise to some of his most sublime musical thoughts, including, as we have seen, some of the finer songs such as *Abendlied* and the Reissig *Sehnsucht*. If we turn now to the love songs pure and simple we find that on the whole the level of inspiration is much lower.

A number of them have already been discussed. Of those that remain—songs such as *An die fernen Geliebten* (1809, words by Reissig); *Als die Geliebte sich trennen wollte* (1806, words by his friend Stephan Breuning); and *Der Jüngling in der Fremde* and *Der Liebende* (both written in 1809 to Reissig's words)—not one rises above a good average. Whatever their merits, passion and deep feeling are not among them, and indeed sometimes seem to be deliberately avoided. There could hardly be a more painless parting than *Der Abschied* or a much less ardent protestation of love than *Ich liebe dich* (1797, words by Herrosee); and if *Der Liebende* makes some outward show of emotion it remains only a semblance.

All these songs are in a curious way looking back over their shoulders to a past age, to the artificial Arcadian poetry of nymphs and shepherdesses; and it is not the least of the surprises awaiting the student of Beethoven's songs to find a number that could be set beside the entertainment songs of our own Vauxhall and Ranelagh Gardens without any incongruity. There is *Der Kuss*—written, or at least sketched, in 1798—an arch little story about Chloe (the name is sufficiently significant), who, threatened with being kissed, vows she will scream, and does—but long afterwards. The words are by C. F. Weisse, whose talent for light and attractive verse was as responsible as Hiller's music for the success of the *Singspiel* and who provided Mozart with the texts of three songs (K.472–4) that link together to form a pre-Beethoven song-cycle. There is *Gretels Warnung*, a setting of Gerhard Anton von Halem of 1798 or earlier, a cautionary tale in $\frac{6}{8}$ time and A major, warning the village lasses against the dangers of the local Lothario, Christel. There is *Der Bardengeist* (1813, text by Hermann), an echo of Thomas Moore, a sad E minor threnody on Germany's past glories. There are patriotic songs such as the Friedelberg settings *Abschiedsgesang* (1796) and *Kriegslied der Oesterreicher* (1797), and *Kriegers Abschied* (1814, words by Reissig); while *Urians Reise um die Welt*, written in 1793 in Bonn to Claudius's words, provides us with a world tour somewhat in the manner of the *Scottish Student's Songbook*, with little in the way of adventure and, for moral, the conclusion that home's best.

It will be noticed that not all of these were early songs, and indeed several other later songs could be added to the above list, such as *Merkenstein*, a setting of Rupprecht dating from about 1814, and *Der Mann von Wort* (1816), the words by no less a worthy than the Viennese chief of police, F. A. Kleinschmidt. Most of these songs made their appearances in one or other of the many almanacs of the time. Thus *Der Bardengeist* was printed as a music supplement to Johann Erichson's *Musen-Almanach für das Jahr 1814*; the more distinguished *Abendlied* appeared in the *Wiener Zeitschrift für Kunst, Literatur, Theater und Mode* for 28 March 1820. *Resignation* (words by Haugwitz) had seen the light in an earlier issue of the same magazine, on 31 March 1818; *Ruf vom Berge* (words by Treitschke) was printed as a music supplement to *Gedichte von*

Friedrich Treitschke; and the Reissig *Sehnsucht* appeared as one of three songs 'aus Reissig's *Blümchen des Einsamkeit*' in company with Gyrowetz and Ignaz von Seyfried.

If one is inclined to dismiss some of these rather obvious, too hearty, boisterous songs as unworthy of our attention it must be remembered that this convivial, good-humoured, unsophisticated type of communal entertainment was deeply ingrained in the Germany and Austria of Beethoven's time. It was as much part and parcel of the musico-social history of Teutonic countries as Purcell's tavern music is of ours, indeed more so. For these *Vaterlandslieder, Soldaten- und Jägerlieder, Studentenlieder* (I quote them as they appear in Erk's popular collection, *Deutscher Liederschatz*), besides enlivening the company at the Ludlamshöhle and other places of good cheer, also find their way into the more serious music of Schubert, Weber and the eclectic Schumann, to be later parodied by Wolf and Mahler. On the literary side, too, they enjoyed the sanction of no less a person than Goethe, who was certainly not above writing *Tischlieder* and *Bundeslieder* for convivial purposes. In this perspective we shall perhaps see the great tune in the last movement of the Ninth symphony with new eyes, as the grandest *Tischlied* or *Bundeslied* of them all.

One or two questions remain to vex us. For example, who sang the songs? Vienna had a rich concert life, both private and, especially after 1800, public; but while instrumental and operatic performances are reasonably well chronicled, details of song performances are much scarcer. The solo recital had not yet been invented, and there seems to have been no one to do for Beethoven's songs what Vogl and Anna Milder did for Schubert's. We seem indeed to have little information as to performances during his lifetime; one of the few references is to a concert given under Schuppanzigh's direction in 1796, when besides the wind and piano Quintet, Op. 16, an aria was sung, by Madame Willmann. No title is mentioned, but it could have been *Adelaide*. As for *An die ferne Geliebte*, Max Kalbeck claims[1] that the performance by Heinrich Schmidt, the tenor of the Leipzig Stadttheater, to Mendelssohn's accompaniment, was the work's first hearing as a

[1] In *Johannes Brahms*, I (Berlin, 1904), p. 424.

cycle, though surely it must have had at least an impromptu run-through in the Lobkowitz palace on publication in April 1816?

Glancing through the songs again one is impressed by their range and diversity, by their unconventionality. No doubt because he was working in untried fields Beethoven was forced to think each problem out for himself; the result was a series of compositions unlike anything that had appeared before. The rough humour of *Flohlied*, the onomatopoeia of *Wachtelschlag*, the rapture and sub-limity of *Resignation* and the 'Innigkeit' of *Wonne der Wehmuth* really have no precedents. He brought a new seriousness to song-writing. The four versions of Goethe's *Sehnsucht*, the ceaseless striv-ing for the perfect mating of words with music revealed by the sketches for Reissig's *Sehnsucht*, indicate an approach far removed from the ideals of the eighteenth century and point beyond Schubert towards the more nervous music of Schumann and Wolf.

For Schumann *An die ferne Geliebte* was, as Eric Sams says,[1] 'a favourite source-book', and there are few devices in either the vocal or piano parts of later nineteenth-century writers that are not suggested in Beethoven's songs: with only a hint here and there to go on he virtually created the German *Lied*. It is a remarkable tribute to his genius that, working in a medium that by his own confession was not entirely congenial to him, he should have pro-duced a handful of works that, uneven in quality as they admittedly are, yet remain as an adumbration of a century's work in the field of German song.

[1] Cf. op. cit., p. 174.

VI
Practical Matters

TWELVE

Sketches and Autographs

ALAN TYSON

> I make many changes, and reject and try again until I
> am satisfied. Then the working-out in breadth, length,
> height and depth begins in my head, and since I am con-
> scious of what I want the underlying idea never deserts
> me.
>
> —Beethoven in 1823,
> as noted down by Louis Schlösser.

I

ANYONE WHO BEGINS to explore in detail the course of Beethoven's
life and the origins of his compositions will soon come across
references to two types of documents that are peculiar to him: his
conversation-books and his sketchbooks. The conversation-books
were a social necessity: by 1818 his deafness had progressed to a
degree that prevented friends from being able to communicate with
him even when he was using an ear-trumpet, and he therefore
adopted the habit of keeping by him notebooks in which his
visitors could write down what they wished to say. Since Beethoven
usually replied orally, his own contributions to the conversation
must for the most part be inferred from the context.[1] The sketchbooks were evidently a necessity of a rather different kind: they
were, or they became, indispensable to his creative processes. There
can be few composers who have not made some use of sketches
when engaged in planning and drafting a work or more generally in

---

[1] Cf. Luigi Magnani, *I quaderni di conversazione di Beethoven* (Milan
and Naples, 1962), and Donald W. MacArdle, *An index to Beethoven's
conversation books* (Detroit, 1962).

443

ordering their ideas. What surprises us in Beethoven's case, and appears to set him apart from his colleagues, is the extent of his reliance on sketches—the systematic place that he assigned to them in his daily life and that made them as essential to his hours of solitary work as the conversation books were to his hours of company.

What did the sketchbooks mean to Beethoven? Such a question might well daunt us at any time, and certainly as long as the detailed contents of so few of them are available for study in facsimile or in transcription.[1] But that they were private and personal documents there can be no doubt. From time to time Beethoven gave away an autograph to a friend or visitor,[2] but he seems never to have parted with any of the sketchbooks; they evidently remained with him, an increasingly bulky collection, and accompanied him in all his many changes of residence in town. Sketchbooks from every period of his life were with him when he died, and over fifty of them were included in the auction of his *Nachlass* (they realized some of the lowest prices in the sale).[3] There is therefore some irony in the fact that today the sketchbooks,

[1] At present only two sketchbooks have been published both in facsimile and in transcription: the 'Wielhorsky' sketchbook of 1802–3, now in Moscow (ed. N. L. Fishman, Moscow, 1962), and the 'Kafka' miscellany of *c.* 1786–99 in the British Museum (ed. Joseph Kerman, London, 1970). Two others have been published in facsimile: a Moscow sketchbook of 1825 (commentary by M. Ivanov-Boretsky, 1927) and the 'Engelmann' sketchbook of 1822–3 (Leipzig, 1913). Four transcriptions have appeared: the 'Landsberg 7' sketchbook of *c.* 1801 (ed. K. L. Mikulicz, Leipzig, 1927), and three published by the Beethovenhaus, Bonn: these contain sketches of the *Missa solemnis* (ed. Joseph Schmidt-Görg, 1952), the Choral Fantasia and other works (ed. Dagmar Weise, 1957), and the 'Pastoral' Symphony and the Op. 70 Trios (ed. Weise, 1961).

[2] The autograph of the 'Appassionata' Sonata, Op. 57, was given to the pianist Marie Bigot, and a copyist's score of the Violin Concerto, Op. 61, to Charles Neate. In 1810 he complained that he possessed hardly any manuscripts (*LA*, letter 281). Cf. also F. G. Wegeler and Ferdinand Ries, *Biographische Notizen über Ludwig van Beethoven* (Coblenz, 1838), p. 113, quoted in the next chapter, p. 468. In the same work (p. 77) Ries states that Beethoven gave him the autograph (now lost) of the Second Symphony.

[3] Cf. Georg Kinsky, 'Zur Versteigerung von Beethovens musikalischem Nachlass', *Neues Beethoven-Jahrbuch*, VI (1935), p. 66.

or fragments of them, are scattered among the libraries of the world.[1] The careful hoarding by Beethoven of these arcane volumes, in some cases for half a lifetime, suggests that they performed a special function for him in maintaining his morale as well as in facilitating his creative processes and that he preserved them so scrupulously, as Joseph Kerman has suggested, 'in order to look back over them in times of need or in times of doubt.'[2] He evidently could not be parted from them for long; indeed, they were a part of his daily régime, as his contemporaries did not fail to note: 'He was never to be seen in the street without a small notebook, in which he jotted down whatever occurred to him at the moment. Whenever conversation turned to this, he would facetiously quote the words of [Schiller's] Joan of Arc: "Without my banner I dare not come", and he stuck to this self-imposed rule with singular firmness.' The observation comes from Ignaz von Seyfried,[3] with whom Beethoven was on friendly terms throughout his Vienna years. He is probably writing of the early 1800s, but precisely the same behaviour could have been noted in the later Beethoven. As time went on, in fact, Beethoven spent more and more time in sketching; it is no mere accident of preservation that the sketches for the last works, even when due allowance is made for their vastly increased scale, are among the most extensive of all.

2

We are perhaps only marginally better placed at present to attempt an answer to a second question: *What happens in the sketchbooks?* Accounts by Beethoven's contemporaries show that they were puzzled and amused by his seemingly bizarre way of seeking inspiration and by the wholly miscellaneous nature of what he appeared to write down. Even Schindler, who was a witness to

[1] For the most recent census of the sketchbooks and their fragments, see the comprehensive account by Hans Schmidt, 'Verzeichnis der Skizzen Beethovens', *Beethoven-Jahrbuch*, 2nd ser., VI (1965–8), pp. 7–128.

[2] Kerman, *The Beethoven quartets* (London, 1967), p. 65.

[3] Ignaz von Seyfried, *Ludwig van Beethovens Studien in General-Basse, Contrapuncte und in der Compositions-Lehre* (Vienna, 1832), Appendix, p. 20.

much that happened in Beethoven's last years, makes him seem capricious rather than purposeful:

> In both winter and summer it was Beethoven's practice to rise at dawn and go immediately to his writing desk. There he would work till two or three o'clock, the time of his midday meal. In the course of the morning he would usually go out of doors once or twice, where he 'worked as he walked'; then he would return home after half an hour or an hour with new ideas and write them down. Just as the bee gathers honey from the flowers of the meadows, so Beethoven gathered his sublime ideas while roaming the open fields. These sudden excursions, and the equally swift returns home again, took place at every season of the year.[1]

Doubtless Schindler was neither tempted nor encouraged to examine the contents of the sketchbooks—which were not intended to be accessible to anyone other than their compiler.[2] Interest in them started only with Beethoven's death. Thayer wished it to be placed on record that he had been the first to consult them for purposes of chronology;[3] but our systematic knowledge of their nature and contents starts with the pioneering investigations of Gustav Nottebohm, who began over a century ago to describe a large number of them in detail.[4] Many of the features to which

[1] Anton Felix Schindler, *Biographie von Ludwig van Beethoven* (Münster, 1840), p. 259. The passage is somewhat different in the third edition (Münster, 1860), Part 2, p. 192; *SB*, p. 385.

[2] But J. W. Tomaschek cast at least a glance at some sketches of *Der glorreiche Augenblick*, Op. 136, when he visited Beethoven on 10 October 1814: 'On the keyboard lay a lead pencil, with which he sketched out his works; beside it on a scribbled sheet of music paper I found ideas of the most diverse sort jotted down without any connection, with the most heterogeneous items put next to each other just as they may have sprung to his mind. This was the material for the new cantata.' *Libussa* (1846), p. 359. Reprinted in A. W. Thayer, *Ludwig van Beethovens Leben*, trans. and ed. Hermann Deiters, completed by Hugo Riemann, 3rd ed., 5 vols. (Leipzig, 1917–23), III, p. 432.

[3] Cf. *TF*, p. viii (letter of Thayer to Deiters of 1 August 1878).

[4] There are two extended accounts: *Ein Skizzenbuch von Beethoven* (Leipzig, 1865) (the 'Kessler' sketchbook of 1801) and *Ein Skizzenbuch von Beethoven aus dem Jahre 1803* (Leipzig, 1880) ('Landsberg 6', the 'Eroica' sketchbook). In *NB* and the posthumous *NZB* a large number of sketches are referred to.

Nottebohm was the first to call attention have now become commonplaces: the profusion of unilinear drafts, the constant repetition of passages in a slightly altered form until the final, finally satisfying version is 'found' (Nottebohm's word); the linear sketches of a whole section of a movement; the simultaneous work on several movements or even several different compositions; the sketches for unknown (i.e. never realized) works.

In retrospect, indeed, Nottebohm's writings may be regarded as having had a somewhat inhibiting effect on later study of the sketchbooks. Such was the authority that he justly derived from his command of the material, his skill in deciphering the sketches and the satisfying concept of the composer at work which he presented, that for a hundred years his evaluation of their nature and significance has been taken largely on trust and has served scholars as well as popularizers. And naturally it is the most immediately accessible parts of Nottebohm's accounts that have touched the common imagination; thus, despite the attention that he paid to sketches of a movement's overall design—most notably, perhaps, those for the first movement of the 'Eroica' Symphony—one might almost be excused for concluding that for Beethoven the main function of sketches was melodic refinement, the raising of a theme from banality to sublimity.

3

The sketchbooks themselves are of more than one type, and the diversity reflects differences in their functions. Best known, perhaps, are the books consisting of some forty to a hundred uniformly ruled oblong sheets. The two sketchbooks described in Nottebohm's monographs, and also the ones transcribed by Mikulicz, Fishman and Weise, are of this kind; the earliest survivors are two sketchbooks of 1798 and 1799 now in Berlin ('Grasnick 1' and 'Grasnick 2'). They seem for the most part to have been made up of gatherings or fascicules of uniform paper stitched together;[1] whether they were bound before use is uncertain, though the 'Kessler' sketchbook of 1801 seems to have been tightly stitched

---

[1] 'Wielhorsky', for instance, is uniform throughout; 'Landsberg 6' is of uniform 16-stave paper except for 36 sheets of 18-stave paper. But some, e.g. 'Landsberg 7', contain sheets of great diversity.

before use, and we might take this as evidence that by that date Beethoven had systematized his recourse to sketching. These books were too large to be carried around on walks; they must instead have remained on his desk at home and have been used for the main part of his steady work on the compositions in hand. Not unexpectedly, therefore, the great majority of the entries are in ink. The portable notebooks, on the other hand, to which Seyfried refers directly and Schindler indirectly, were necessarily of a different format. Many of them seem to have been made by folding over a small number of the large oblong sheets, to produce a not-too-thick booklet of about eight by five inches; this would slip into an ample coat pocket.[1] Quite naturally, the great majority of what Beethoven noted in such pocket sketchbooks is in pencil. And it is likely that the content of these books will prove on examination to be somewhat different in kind from the continuous elaborations of the desk sketchbooks: the short, disjointed, tentative ideas—the honey that the bee had gathered in the meadows—were worked upon more systematically after the return to the hive.[2]

In both the above types of sketchbook one would hope to find some unity if not of subject-matter at least of time: the sketches all come from the same period—and in some cases their juxtaposition (by showing unsuspected connections) enhances their interest.[3] But another class of 'sketchbook' contains sketches evidently dating from widely different periods of Beethoven's life. In these cases the paper is not uniform and the books were not bound before use. Indeed, it is highly likely that such an assemblage owes nothing to Beethoven and that the miscellaneous pages were brought together only after his death by some zealous collector or library. But to this presump-

[1] This description is taken from Kerman, 'Beethoven sketchbooks in the British Museum', *Proceedings of the Royal Musical Association*, XCIII (1966–7), p. 78.

[2] Pocket sketchbooks from the period before about 1815 do not seem to have survived, and it is possible that they were destroyed by Beethoven after he had transferred the entries that he wished to preserve to the larger books at home.

[3] In his commentary on the 'Wielhorsky' sketchbook Fishman (pp. 147–8) draws attention to resemblances between the theme of the minuet of the Sonata, Op. 31, No. 3, and some of the sketches for the Op. 35 Variations—two works in E flat sketched in succession in 'Wielhorsky'.

tion there is almost certainly one important exception. The earliest sketchbook that we possess, the so-called 'Kafka Notirungsbuch' (British Museum Add. MS 29801, Part 2), is a collection of 124 leaves of a completely miscellaneous sort; the paper varies widely in shape, size and texture, and although it is bound as an oblong book some of the pages have had to be turned on their sides. The earliest drafts that it contains apparently date from about 1786, but it also includes sketches from the end of the 1790s. There is no doubt that a bundle of papers, carefully hoarded by Beethoven in his Bonn days and brought with him to Vienna in November 1792, must have formed the nucleus of this heterogeneous collection; fair copies of completed early works, pianoforte exercises and passage-work figures, and contrapuntal studies are intermingled or juxtaposed with sketches in the stricter sense, i.e. compositional drafts.[1]

Apart from the various kinds of sketchbooks, there are many scattered leaves that contain sketches of an analogous kind; doubtless the bulk of these are, in fact, from partially or totally dismembered sketchbooks, and it may be possible in some cases to reassemble them or to assign them to their original site.[2]

4

In fact, the sketchbooks contain more than drafts in musical notation for emergent compositions. Quite often we find short memoranda, in words, which Beethoven addressed to himself about the nature or design of a movement: those for the 'Pastoral' Symphony ('all painting in instrumental music fails if it is pushed

---

[1] This is discussed in great detail in Kerman's introduction to the first volume of his edition of the miscellany (cf. above, p. 444, n. 1). The above remarks apply equally to a smaller miscellany of fifty-six leaves in the Berlin Staatsbibliothek (Stiftung Preussischer Kulturbesitz), catalogued there as 'autograph manuscript 28' and sometimes known as the 'Fischhof' miscellany. From their contents it seems certain that 'Kafka' and 'Fischhof' were once part of the same portfolio.

[2] Thus, twenty-eight leaves known to have been cut out of the British Museum's 'Pastoral' Symphony sketchbook have now been located in a Berlin miscellany, 'Landsberg 10'; and some leaves from the 'Wielhorsky' sketchbook have been found in Bonn and Modena.

too far'; 'people will not need titles to recognize the whole as a matter more of feeling than of painting in sounds', etc.) are perhaps the most widely known. There are drafts, too, of difficult letters, and of title-page dedications; lists of errata; fair copies of short passages, presumably for his copyist to transcribe; sums and calculations; and pianistic figuration and exercises which were probably intended for practice, or as memoranda for his famous improvisations, or even, as recently Kerman has ingeniously suggested,[1] as 'improvisations on paper', a form of abstract study, rather than for insertion into a sonata or concerto.

It would, however, be very misleading to suggest that the vast majority of sketchbook pages were filled with anything other than compositional sketches. It is rather the other way round: work for Beethoven was so bound up with the immediate noting down of ideas, the planning and replanning of the structure of movements, and the progressive refinement of his thematic material, that he seems to have been unable entirely to confine the sketching process within the books that he had reserved for it. Drafts of musical ideas, at any rate, and thematic scraps and other visible signs of the reworking of passages spilled on to the other sheets of paper that were on Beethoven's table: on to the backs of letters, for instance, and the pages of the conversation-books.[2] And they appear even to have crept into the margins or blank lower staves of scored-up completed works. There, however, they can be shown to be fulfilling a somewhat different function from the rest of the sketches, as is explained below (see pp. 456–8), and perhaps they deserve a different name.

5

It is only to be expected that all the major sketchbooks contain, besides short fragments, passages developed to some length that form no recognizable part of any completed work. Most of these

[1] In the introduction to the first volume of his edition of the 'Kafka' miscellany.

[2] Cf. *Ludwig van Beethovens Konversationshefte*, IV, ed. Karl-Heinz Köhler and Grita Herre (Leipzig, 1968), p. 299, for a sketch of a passage in the finale of the Ninth Symphony, in a conversation-book filled between *c.* 29 November and 6 December 1823.

obviously represent drafts of works which Beethoven subsequently abandoned[1] (although a few may be discarded ideas for extant movements that were later worked out in a totally different manner). But in the case of the works whose history does not end in the sketchbooks there must have come a time at which he turned to the writing out of a score. When was this? Surely it must have been after he had not only gained a good picture of a movement's overall design but had satisfied himself concerning many of the details. And in general the sketchbooks bear this out: that is to say, the process of sketching can often be seen to continue until something like the continuous melodic line (essentially the *Hauptstimme*) of at any rate a large section of the movement as we know it is reached.

But there is another way in which the change from sketching to writing out a score may be described: it marks a change from private writing to public writing. For the sketchbooks, as we have seen, are documents of an intimate and personal kind. And this private status is reflected in the obscurity of the handwriting and in the neglect of the normal conventions of notation. The entries were (with negligible exceptions) not intended to be intelligible to anyone other than Beethoven; and therefore clefs are often lacking and indications of key and metre usually so.[2] Deciphering the writing—determining the exact notes and interpreting the shorthand devices and abbreviations—is often a discouraging and at worst an unrealizable task.

The autograph score, on the other hand, is a public document. We can see this both from the writing itself—which is, if we take elementary precautions to understand its economical and expressive notation (and provided that we do not insist on neatness), perfectly legible—and from the presence of other features that someone who is not the composer himself has a right to expect (cf. pl. 9*a*). At the beginning, for instance, Beethoven usually writes the work's title (either at the top of the music or on a preliminary page serving as a

---

[1] He did not always abandon them for ever. A sixteen-bar 'tedesco' in the 'Wielhorsky' sketchbook, evidently written there in 1802, was expanded in 1822 to form the Bagatelle, Op. 119, No. 3 ('à l'allemande'), and published a year later.

[2] For a good discussion of this see Kerman's introduction to the second volume of his edition of the 'Kafka' miscellany.

wrapper), and often the date as well. On the first page of an orchestral work he provides the staves to be used with the clefs and key-signatures appropriate to each instrument—the actual names of the instruments are usually, though not invariably, added—and the metre and tempo indications. There is an excellent facsimile of the autograph score of the Fifth Symphony[1] which shows many of the typical features of Beethoven's orchestral scores written during this period of his life. The format is oblong, like that of most of his autograph scores and the non-portable sketchbooks. Here there are sixteen ruled staves to the page. This was a number which varied from score to score and sometimes within a work, but it was not likely to be less than twelve for an orchestral piece or sixteen for a concerto, whereas eight was the commonest choice for a piano work.[2] The order in which the instruments are placed in the score of the Fifth Symphony is also typical: from the top downwards, first and second violins and violas, then flutes, oboes, clarinets, bassoons, horns, trumpets, timpani, violoncellos (a stave filled in only when the cellos have an independent part) and basses.[3] This order has to be memorized, since Beethoven ordinarily omits the names of the instruments, and even their clefs and key-signatures, after the first page of each movement unless a rearrangement of the score is called for or there is a change in the number of the ruled staves on the paper.[4] A line down the left-hand margin of the staves terminating

[1] Berlin, 1942 (with introduction by Georg Schünemann). See also Schünemann's *Musikerhandschriften von Bach bis Schumann* (Berlin and Zürich, 1936), Plates 59–63.

[2] For an interesting discussion of Beethoven's choice both of format and of number of staves see Lewis Lockwood, 'The Autograph of the First Movement of Beethoven's Sonata for Violoncello and Pianoforte, Op. 69'. *The Music Forum*, II (New York, 1970), p. 22. The late choral works required over twenty staves. Cf. Beethoven's letter to Haslinger of 27 May 1824, requesting that some 22-stave paper be ruled for him (*LA*, letter 1293, where—as in all editions of this letter—the number of staves is wrongly given as '202'). Paper with over twenty staves on it could scarcely be oblong.

[3] After about 1812 Beethoven tended to place the violins and violas low down in the score, above the basses.

[4] Cf. Schünemann, *Musikerhandschriften*, Plate 55 (Fifth Piano Concerto, first movement, bars 104–6): the instruments are named, since at this point the paper changes from sixteen staves to fourteen staves.

in a flourish indicates the limits of the 'system' (the staves in use) on each page. It will be seen that in the first movement of the Fifth Symphony the system comprises twelve of the sixteen staves, the lowest four being blank; in the last movement, however, where a piccolo, three trombones and a double bassoon are added to the orchestra, all sixteen staves are utilized, and where the double bassoon has a part that differs from that of the basses it has to be scrawled in the lower margin of the score.

6

To follow Beethoven as he sets to work on an orchestral score, we must imagine that there lies before him not a large bound volume but a gathering of some four or eight double sheets, already ruled with its twelve or sixteen staves, but otherwise bare except for the first-page indications just described and—in a good number of instances—for three vertical ruled lines dividing each side into three large bars. With his working surface thus prepared, Beethoven seems to have started on a determined effort to write out the score from start to finish, with regard for neatness if possible, but even more for intelligibility. Proceeding laterally from the first bar, he seems to have written down the main continuous melody for about a page at a time. Next he turned to its basic accompaniment, usually filling in the bass-line and the strings on their appropriate staves. As he proceeded he made alterations. On the early pages, at any rate, the commonest changes were in scoring: details of the instrumentation of a passage are hardly ever to be found in the sketchbooks, and although Beethoven may have had a clear idea of the scoring that he wanted while working in terms of linear drafts (where a solo instrument was sometimes identified by a single word), it must often have looked rather different when it was down on paper. (It is part of the rationale of sketching, after all, that things will look rather different when they are written down.) Occasionally there were other changes to be made, as notes were entered in error on the wrong staves, or accidental omissions or other slips of the pen had to be corrected. Wrong entries were simply crossed out (in very neat scores they were sometimes scraped out) and the corrected version was put in their place—or rather, just to their side. We can now see the reason for the generous allocation of paper on the three-bar page: those great bars permitted two or even three false entries to be written down and then on reflection deleted while still allowing bare room for a final version to be inserted. Where Beethoven was reasonably sure of how he was going to proceed, or where the scoring consisted essentially of the continuation or repetition of passages that had already been worked out, he could afford to save paper by subdividing the large bars by means of extra vertical bar-lines drawn in freehand. Most pages of the Fifth Symphony, for instance, have six or seven bars to the page, and there are places where confidence has encouraged him, or mis-calculation has compelled him, to fit in as many as nine or ten bars on one page.

We begin, too, to realize why so many pages of the sketchbooks were devoted to recording the continuous melodic line of large sections of a movement. Until he had gained an overall view of the forward motion in every bar, and of the lengths of the various sub-divisions (of the coda, for instance, or the transition to the second subject), it would have been foolhardy to embark on a full score. He needed a conspectus; and the sketchbooks are in this respect a record of his experiments in determining the length that he needed to say what he had to say. The sectional drafts for the first movement of the 'Eroica' Symphony (by far the longest movement he had written up to that time), which Nottebohm published in 1880, have already been referred to; a recent discussion by Kerman of the sketches for the development section of the slow movement of the 'Pastoral' Symphony places particular emphasis on the composer's experiments with the sequence of keys.[1] With the underlying continuity secured by the sectional sketch Beethoven could afford to press forward with the scoring, changing and correcting and improv-ing as he went along and occasionally leaping ahead to a new section and leaving a gap of a calculated length to be returned to and filled in later. Not unexpectedly—since calculations can be mis-calculations—we find in the orchestral scores blank, unwanted bars, half pages and even full pages that have to be ruled through, as well

[1] Kerman, 'Beethoven sketchbooks in the British Museum', pp. 87–94.

as pages where extra bars have had to be crammed in between the bars already scored or in the margins.

7

When pages became unserviceable, whether because of the extent of the corrections he had made on them or because of a change of the direction in which he planned to proceed, a number of possibilities were open to Beethoven which are conveniently illustrated by the Fifth Symphony facsimile:

1. He could simply cross out the repudiated pages and continue with the amended version after them (with a 'vi–de' to bridge the gap). This was a convenient method if the pages following were not scored up: e.g. if the correction was made at the end of a movement or before anything further had been written. When a twenty-two bar ending to the first movement of the Fifth Symphony was rejected in favour of the present three-bar ending, all the music after bar 499 on pp. 83–5 was simply struck through.

2. At the beginning of a movement it was probably easier to remove the unwanted pages and to substitute new ones. The first four sides of the scherzo (pp. 145–8) are on a different type of paper from the rest of the score; and these bars, which show few corrections, may well have been recopied.

3. If the offending page was in the middle of a completed score, a revised version of it could be glued or stuck with sealing-wax or stitched over it. The stitches were sometimes removed by a later generation, with the result that both versions can now be seen. Tiny holes in the margins of pages 233/4 and 235/6 in the finale indicate that these two sheets had once been sewn together: 236 is obviously a replacement for 234 (235 is blank). A similar, but more complicated, instance in the Andante involves pages 123/4 and 125/6, also formerly sewn together. Here page 125 was begun as a revision and rescoring of 123 (a marginal sketch for the rescoring is to be found at the foot of 121). But Beethoven completed his revision by abandoning 125 and returning to 123 for further changes there; and finally 124 and 125 were 'buried' with the stitching together of the sheets.

Major changes, however, could also be made on the score without paste-overs or stitching or the replacement of pages. A very clear instance can be seen in the first movement of the Op. 69 Cello Sonata, excellently discussed in the recent article by Lewis Lockwood. The facsimile of the autograph (accompanying the article) shows that whereas the exposition and recapitulation were written down in what was, despite many alterations, essentially their final form, this was not true of the development section. The alterations there are massive; and Lockwood has been able to unravel two full-length versions of the section. The roles assigned to the cello and piano in the first version are totally recast and exchanged in the second version. Here it is easy to see that a compositional process of great importance (and of considerable length) has taken place within the autograph score rather than in a sketchbook. Sketches involving three or four staves at the same time—what might be called 'short-score sketches'—are by no means uncommon in the sketchbooks; and it would not be surprising to find that Beethoven had regressed to the use of sketchbooks *after* he had begun to write out a full score. But he seems also to have welcomed the structure provided by a written-up score even when he suspected that the changes were going to be radical, as in the cello sonata. Doubtless it was for the same reason that he used a copyist's score as a foundation in revising the 1805 version of his opera *Leonore* for performance in 1806, and later in preparing the 1814 version, even though in places hardly a note of the earlier versions was allowed to remain.[1]

8

In orchestral works we sometimes find on a blank stave running below the system a line of jottings resembling a well-spaced-out sketch. The writing, that is to say, is 'private' like that of the sketchbooks, and so the entries cannot be mistaken for the occasional bar or two of 'public' writing, also to be found from time to time on those staves, which represent fair copies of passages *within* the system obscured by repeated corrections and which are almost

[1] Schunemann, *Musikerhandschriften*, Pl. 56—though this in fact shows drastic revisions made on a copyist's score in preparing the *1805* version.

always linked to the place within the system from which they are an overspill by a sign such as the word 'vi–de'. Yet these jottings cannot be sketches in the ordinary sense, for a little study reveals that they are intimately connected with the formal score standing above them—which they appear to have preceded. They seem in fact to be a kind of précis of the formal score, so that if they do correspond to anything in the sketchbooks it can only be to the sectional sketches for a large portion of a movement already referred to, the *Hauptstimme* passages.

Did Beethoven simply transfer the *Hauptstimme* of the sketch-books to the blank staves below an orchestral score? This would have the advantage of giving him a ground-plan over which the formal score could be built, and he may have chosen this method in a few instances.[1] But if it were his regular procedure we should, I think, expect to see far more of these cues written in the blank lower staves of scores.[2] In an extended form they are comparatively rare; and they seem to be commonest where Beethoven decided to see what he could do *without* much further sketching. Thus they may be a substitute for sketching rather than an example of it. My impression is that they occur most frequently in codas and finales and in movements with simple episodic forms such as rondos— precisely the places that might tempt him to proceed *currente calamo* without a ground-plan that had been already worked out to the last detail within the sketchbooks.

These below-the-score linear aids to continuity do not occur— to judge at any rate from the published autograph facsimiles—in the piano works. His preference for eight-stave paper in the piano sonatas, giving four two-stave systems, excluded blank staves and left little enough room between the systems for corrections. Nevertheless, as in the orchestral works, revisions and alterations abound. Some bars were evidently replaced immediately; others, by means of a 'vi–de', were corrected on a lower system or an adjacent page or at the end of the work. We also find paste-overs and stitched-on strips. Most remarkable of all, perhaps, is the auto-

---

[1] Cf. Lockwood's account of the 'cue-staff' in Beethoven's unfinished piano concerto of 1815, *Acta Musicologica*, XLII (1970), pp. 45–7.

[2] A few may have been erased or cut off.

graph of the Op. 110 Piano Sonata.[1] Beethoven evidently embarked on the fugue confident that his preparations and his élan would carry him through. But he soon got into difficulties; a whole series of 'vi–de's' and asterisks lead from one deleted passage to another, and it was only after he had exchanged his pen for a pencil and had filled a page or two of the autograph with sketches in his 'private' writing that he was able to sail into the comparatively calm waters of the G minor *Klagende Gesang*. The autograph has here taken on some of the functions of a sketchbook. But this is merely a rather striking example of the way in which, quite generally, compositional processes begun in the sketchbooks are continued in the autograph scores.

[1] Cf. the facsimile, ed. K. M. Komma, 2 vols. (Stuttgart, 1967).

THIRTEEN

Steps to Publication – and Beyond

ALAN TYSON

> Perhaps the only touch of genius which I possess is
> that my things are not always in very good order,
> yet no one but myself is able to deal with them.
>
> —Letter to Hoffmeister, 22 April 1801

I

A CONSIDERABLE PROPORTION of Beethoven's surviving correspondence consists of letters to publishers, offering new works for publication or discussing, often in great detail, problems that arose in the process of bringing them out. This is not unexpected: from the time that his deafness forced him to give up all thoughts of a career as a virtuoso and to withdraw from society he had no occupation apart from composing. His hopes of contact with a wider public, and of the financial security that he needed for writing music, appeared to depend on satisfactory mastery of the complexities of publication. Although from 1809 the basis of his economic position was the annuity of 4,000 florins guaranteed to him by three of his aristocratic friends (Prince Kinsky, Prince Lobkowitz and the Archduke Rudolph), Beethoven never abandoned the view that he depended for his livelihood on the sale of his works to publishers. 'You know,' he wrote to his English friend Charles Neate on 19 April 1817, 'that I am obliged to live entirely on the profits from my compositions. Since the onset of my illness I have been able to compose only extremely little and therefore have been able to earn only extremely little.'[1] This was a theme to

---

[1] *LA*, letter 778.

which he returned in letter after letter, often with a pun relating the notes of music to his needs (in German: 'Not'). In the last decade of his life his concern about the necessity of obtaining the best possible terms for the sale of each work, and his devious behaviour towards its prospective purchasers, became more marked; and it reached a new and somewhat ridiculous intensity in the case of the *Missa solemnis*, which at various dates between 1820 and 1824 he was offering to seven different publishers. It is scarcely surprising, perhaps, that another favourite pun connected publishers with embarrassment ('Verleger'-'verlegen').

There were several reasons for the increasing anxiety, and the consequent lack of straightforwardness, that make his later letters to publishers so much less engaging than the warm and open-hearted exchanges with Franz Anton Hoffmeister (1800–2), the chatty correspondence with Breitkopf & Härtel (1808–12) and the mock-military banter with Steiner and his assistants (1815–17). One reason is alluded to in the letter just quoted: the growing amounts of time that were spent on a sick-bed, interrupting the labour on most of his last works. Another was (as he says in 1816 in another letter to Neate) 'the additional burden of maintaining a poor orphan'[1]—his nephew Karl, of whom he became co-guardian with the boy's mother upon the death of his brother Caspar Carl in November 1815. A third reason, which had come to the fore somewhat earlier, was the bankruptcy of the Austrian state as a result of the Napoleonic wars; this imperilled the annuity in 1811, and although the deficiency was made up to Beethoven there were further delays in payment after the death of Prince Kinsky (the largest contributor) in 1812. To all of which may be added two more general, characterological reasons: increasing suspiciousness about those around him, to which his deafness doubtless contributed and in which his intimate friends and well-wishers were liable to be caught up, and a special fear that the middlemen of the artistic world were battening on his talents: 'greedy brain-pickers', he once called publishers in a memorandum which luckily remained unpublished. 'The human brain in itself is not a saleable commodity',[2] and to those for whom quartets and symphonies were in

---

[1] *LA*, letter 636.   [2] Cf. *LA*, Appendix I (6).

the last resort merchandise the artist felt that he owed little consideration. This is part of the background against which his dealings with publishers must be judged.

2

It should be borne in mind that all Beethoven could hope for in the sale of each work was a single cash payment. Royalties were unknown. So was international copyright—a principle in support of which Hummel canvassed Beethoven on his death-bed[1] and which obtained some legal sanctions only in the 1830s. What a publisher therefore looked for was a quick initial sale on publication, for a popular work was likely to be copied (pirated)[2] by foreign publishers; in a few weeks or at most months imported copies of their editions could then flood the home market and (as no fee had been paid to the composer) undercut the original publisher's price. Since neither composer nor publisher stood to gain from the slow acceptance of a work of classic stature, it was a system that fostered the proliferation of ephemera (which at all times form the bulk of musical publication). Letters written by Gottfried Christoph Härtel to Beethoven as early as 1802 contain a very exact appreciation of the risks of being exposed to piracy;[3] and it deserves to be said of his Leipzig firm, as of the brothers Schott in Mainz and Steiner in Vienna, that they accepted the risks and the responsibility of bringing out Beethoven's larger and unfamiliar works.

There was at any rate no time at which Beethoven had much difficulty in getting his music accepted by publishers. In this respect his experience in Vienna was different from that of Mozart in the 1780s and Schubert in the 1820s. Only a year after his arrival in Vienna, in apologizing to Eleonore von Breuning for dedicating a slight and small-scale work to her, he claimed that people in

[1] Cf. *LA*, Appendix I (8) (after 8 March 1827).

[2] The word 'pirated' is convenient, but sounds over-censorious when applied to a practice which all publishers adopted from time to time and which was not illegal.

[3] Cf. Wilhelm Hitzig, 'Die Briefe Gottfried Christoph Härtels an Beethoven' *Zeitschrift für Musikwissenschaft*, IX (1926–7), pp. 323–4 (letters of 10 June and 3 November 1802).

Vienna had been pestering him to publish it.[1] And in 1801—the year that he disclosed the secret of his deafness to his closest friends—he was able to present his financial situation in a very favourable light. Not only had Prince Lichnowsky started to set aside 600 florins per annum for his use until he should obtain an appointment, but his works were selling steadily: 'My compositions bring me in a good deal; and I may say that I am offered more commissions than it is possible for me to carry out. Moreover for every composition I can count on six or seven publishers, and even more, if I want them; people no longer come to an arrangement with me, I state my price and they pay. So you see how pleasantly situated I am.' The same claim is made around this time in other letters.[2] But although publishers often competed for his works, Beethoven may have been less successful than he indicated in raising the prices. Certainly not all his works were accepted at the fees first demanded; there were evidently limits above which publishers, unprotected against piracy, could not afford to go. Comparisons with the prices that other composers demanded and obtained are of interest here; it is perhaps noteworthy that when Beethoven's brother Caspar Carl wrote to Breitkopf & Härtel in January 1803 to offer a number of works by the composer Antonín Reicha (who had lately come to Vienna from Paris and had entrusted the negotiations to him) the fees asked for were of the same order as those at which he had recently offered some of Beethoven's compositions.[3]

3

It is clear that, whatever the price obtainable, Beethoven preferred to see his works published rather than remain unpublished. The only exceptions were some very early compositions that he had left far behind him, and—for a time at any rate—showpieces such as piano concertos, which could be kept as a surprise for concerts:

[1] *LA*, letter 7 (2 November 1793).

[2] The quotation is from *LA*, letter 51 (29 June 1801); cf. also letters 53 (1 July 1801) and 62 (18 October 1802). It should perhaps be added that Beethoven sometimes offered publishers works that he had not yet written.

[3] Cf. A. W. Thayer, *Ludwig van Beethovens Leben*, trans. and ed. Hermann Deiters, completed by Hugo Riemann, 3rd ed., 5 vols. (Leipzig, 1917–23), II, p. 616.

'Musical policy,' he wrote to Breitkopf & Härtel on 22 April 1801, 'demands that one should keep one's finest concertos to oneself for a time.'[1] A small work like the *Rondo a capriccio*, Op. 129, which Beethoven never published, may have been kept for concert use and then overlooked when he had outgrown it and had lost interest in it; but there are few other examples of music of any maturity and significance remaining unpublished. At the sale of Beethoven's *Nachlass* on 5 November 1827, some of the keenest bidding was between the publishers Haslinger, Diabelli and Artaria for the autographs of unpublished compositions; but in fact the pickings were small, as almost all the items were incomplete, immature or occasional works.[2]

To have an important work unpublished for a long time seems indeed to have made Beethoven uncomfortable—although his claim (in a letter to Breitkopf & Härtel of 18 April 1805) that delays in publication had frequently damaged his 'standing as a composer' is without plausibility.[3] In his negotiations with publishers we can observe a tendency to offer a number of miscellaneous works for a round sum; and perhaps he suspected that if he did not do this items of an uncongenial genre would be left on his hands. Piano sonatas and variations could always be sold; orchestral works offered in proportion to their size somewhat lesser rewards, but the greatest difficulty was evidently found with religious works. His first mass of 1807—of which he thought highly—did not get accepted for a long time, and the oratorio of 1803, *The Mount of Olives* (*Christus am Oelberge*), had to wait even longer. When Breitkopf & Härtel told him that there was no demand for church works, he replied that the firm must accept the publication of the mass or else they could not receive 'the other works'—which included the Fifth and Sixth Symphonies.[4] But in the end he had

---

[1] *LA*, letter 48.

[2] Cf. Georg Kinsky, 'Zur Versteigerung von Beethovens musikalischen Nachlass', *Neues Beethoven-Jahrbuch*, VI (1935), p. 66. For a general discussion of Beethoven's policy of not holding on to unpublished work—which, however, contains inaccuracies in details—cf. F. G. Wegeler and Ferdinand Ries, *Biographische Notizen über Ludwig van Beethoven* (Coblenz, 1838), pp. 124–6.

[3] *LA*, letter 111.   [4] *LA*, letter 168 (*c.* 8 July 1808).

to make a present of the mass to Breitkopf & Härtel in an arrangement whereby they purchased the oratorio as well as the symphonies and some chamber works. In this way Beethoven rid himself of a backlog of unpublished music. As for his withholding a work from publication because it was too advanced for his audiences, this was not really his way. We may note, however, that the F minor String Quartet of 1810—the 'quartetto serioso', Op. 95, a somewhat isolated work that anticipates many of the features of the third-period style—was not offered to any publisher until 1815; a year later Beethoven explained to Sir George Smart that it was written for a small circle of connoisseurs and was never to be performed in public.[1]

4

There were other ways besides simply pressing publishers for higher fees in which Beethoven attempted to gain a greater financial reward from his compositions. One was by fulfilling private commissions. The usual arrangement was for the work to remain the property of the music-lover who had commissioned it for six months or a year (sometimes longer); at the end of that time the rights of ownership reverted to the composer, who was then free to make whatever terms he could with a publisher. In this way Beethoven was able to obtain two fees for the same work. Most of the commissions came from aristocratic circles; the institution appears to have been regarded as a form of gracious patronage, and on publication the work was normally dedicated to its sponsor. Certainly there is nothing about the works themselves—they include the Op. 29 Quintet, the Fourth Symphony and the String Quartets, Opp. 127, 130 and 131—to distinguish them from ones of a different origin. Indeed, if Beethoven's brother is to be believed, most of the early works were commissioned.[2]

[1] *LA*, letter 664 (*c.* 11 October 1816).
[2] Cf. the (admittedly tendentious) letter of Caspar Carl to Breitkopf & Härtel of 5 December 1802 (Thayer-Deiters, op. cit., II, pp. 614–15), and Beethoven's letters to Hoffmeister of 8 April 1802 and to Galitzin of late July 1825 (*LA*, letters 57 and 1405).

There was a certain risk to Beethoven in allowing an unpublished work to pass out of his hands, even for a few months, and those who received music that they had commissioned had to undertake to keep it to themselves. This was not always done. In the case of the Op. 29 Quintet it appears that its recipient, Count Fries, was tactless enough to supply a manuscript copy to Artaria in Vienna some time before Breitkopf & Härtel, to whom Beethoven had sold the work, brought it out in Leipzig. Beethoven, unable to suppress the Viennese edition, connived at it, and even corrected some proofs, but it nearly cost him the Leipzig publishers' fee.[1] Unscrupulous copyists were another means by which manuscripts found their way into the wrong hands; Beethoven's anxieties here were shared by Haydn.[2] When the *Missa solemnis* was being copied he even took the precaution of removing the first and last pages of the 'Gloria' from his autograph.[3]

There was another form of arrangement with publishers which became very important to Beethoven in later years, though also very troublesome. Although, as has been said, international copyright was unknown, a publisher's rights of ownership within a country were often protected or respected. There were advantages, therefore, in having the same work published at the same time in more than one country. The composer stood to obtain two or more fees and could therefore afford to ask a more manageable price from the several publishers, each of whom would have the sole rights to the work in his own country. This was not a new device: from the 1780s onwards it had been tried by Haydn, many of whose later works were published at more or less the same time in both Vienna and London. Success or failure in such ventures largely turned on matters of timing. Since publishers were often willing to forfeit potential sales of an edition abroad in return for a guarantee that they would not be anticipated elsewhere, *simultaneous publication* in two or more countries on an agreed date appeared to be the most efficient arrangement. A letter to Simrock in Bonn of 25 May 1803

[1] Cf. Thayer-Deiters, op. cit., II, pp. 587–609 and 614–16; and Hitzig, op. cit., pp. 324–6.

[2] *LA*, letter 301 (end of March 1811), and Haydn's letter to Frau von Genzinger of 2 March 1792.

[3] Cf. *LA*, letter 1244 (13 December 1823).

from Beethoven's brother Caspar Carl already suggests an ambitious plan: publication of a work simultaneously in London, Leipzig, Vienna and Bonn.[1] Although nothing as comprehensive as that was ever achieved, a substantial number of important works were published independently and at more or less the same time in two cities, of which one was London and the other either Vienna or Leipzig.[2]

Beethoven's correspondence supplies many of the details of his efforts to sell his works in more than one country, to draw up the appropriate contracts, to determine a suitable timetable for publication (with dates fixed some time in advance) and to arrange for the manuscripts to be delivered on time at their remote destinations. But it often shows how things went wrong too. Even if he had been a more systematic correspondent, and even if wars and blockades had not so often interrupted the exchange of letters, it might have been hard for him to achieve the desired synchronization. As it was, negotiations were sometimes broken off when a publisher heard—or, what was worse, saw—that a work had already appeared elsewhere.[3] Yet we must grant Beethoven a fair amount of success in his efforts at simultaneous publication; certainly his earnings from the authentic English publications were far from negligible.

5

What could a publisher expect to receive from Beethoven? The choice lay between Beethoven's own autograph and a manuscript of the work made by a copyist. For both parties each had its advantages and disadvantages. The autograph, being wholly from the composer's pen, might be presumed to be wholly from the composer's brain. But there were obvious difficulties. Beethoven, as we have seen, did a proportion—occasionally a very considerable proportion—of the later phases of composition on the open score, and although his intentions in the much-revised passages are

[1] Cf. Thayer-Deiters, op. cit., II, p. 398.

[2] Cf. Alan Tyson, *The authentic English editions of Beethoven* (London, 1963).

[3] Cf. Wegeler and Ries, op. cit., p. 123, for the story of Ries, Boosey and the Diabelli Variations.

almost always clear, a little experience of his handwriting and more than a little patience are needed if complete fidelity to his intentions is to be achieved.[1] It is unclear why Beethoven did not make a fair copy at least of the most problematical passages: all we can say is that this, the obvious solution, seems to have gone against the grain. Perhaps he suspected that in recopying the work he would be tempted to make further changes, or that to embark on a mechanical and uncongenial task was likely to set the stage for errors and slips of the pen.

This drudgery was eliminated when a copyist produced a manuscript copy of the score direct from the autograph under Beethoven's supervision (cf. pl. 9*b*). There were further advantages. For the publisher it meant that his engraver worked from a 'clean' copy, and one written in a standard way: Beethoven's handwriting (like that of most composers) was idiosyncratic in a way that no copyist's could afford to be. For Beethoven it meant that he could retain his autograph while dispatching the manuscript copy, with obvious advantages (especially at the proof stage). What were the disadvantages? The chief difficulty was that good copyists were not always available when they were needed. Some were careless, and the misinterpretation of Beethoven's messy scores was simply set back a stage earlier—admittedly to a stage where error was in theory easier to correct.

Surrendering an autograph score to a publisher, instead of merely supplying a copyist's manuscript, was naturally more of a problem for Beethoven in the years from 1801 onwards, when he began to offer new works to publishers in Leipzig and elsewhere.[2] In the 1790s, when all his works of consequence came out in Vienna, it is likely that the *Stichvorlage* (the score from which the

---

[1] Yet on 26 July 1809 Beethoven wrote to Breitkopf & Härtel of 'the confirmation of my experience that the most correct engravings have been of those compositions of mine which were written out in my own handwriting' (*LA*, letter 220). And in his diary for 1812–18 he wrote: 'A score is never so correctly written out as when the composer himself does it.' Quoted in Ludwig Nohl, *Die Beethoven-Feier und die Kunst der Gegenwart* (Vienna, 1871), p. 57.

[2] Beethoven resisted the idea that a publisher who had bought a work was entitled to the autograph as proof of ownership: see *LA*, letter 1180 (shortly after 17 May 1823).

edition was engraved) was the autograph. Almost all these autographs are lost: of the first fourteen works published with opus
numbers nothing has survived but a score of the Op. 3 String Trio.[1]
Thus there is every reason to believe the account of Ries, his pupil
in the years 1801–5:

> Beethoven attached no value to his autograph scores: once they
> had been engraved, they usually lay in an adjoining room or else
> on the floor in the middle of the room along with other items of
> music. I have often put his music in order, but when Beethoven
> was looking for something everything was turned upside down
> again. At that time I could have carried off the original auto-
> graphs of all the compositions that had already been engraved,
> and if I had asked him for them I am sure he would have given
> them to me without a moment's hesitation.[2]

One might suspect that the systematic use of a copyist to prepare
the *Stichvorlage* was a consequence of the difficulties that Beethoven began to experience once works were sent for publication
outside Vienna; and the tally of the surviving autographs and
scores made by copyists supports this notion to some extent. Even
so, there were many exceptions, particularly with piano works. It
seems, for instance, to have been the autograph itself of the three
Piano Sonatas, Op. 31, and not a copy, which Beethoven sent to
Nägeli of Zürich and which resulted in an edition with 'really
extraordinarily numerous and serious mistakes'; and the important
Piano Variations, Op. 34 and Op. 35, were likewise engraved by
Breitkopf & Härtel from the autographs. It is less surprising that in
Vienna itself Beethoven allowed autographs to go to the engraver:
the Sonatas, Op. 28, Op. 53 and Op. 57, the Op. 33 Bagatelles, and
at least one orchestral work, the Op. 50 violin Romance, were all
engraved from autographs (they were all published by the same
Viennese firm, the Bureau des Arts et d'Industrie). In none of
these cases is there evidence that Beethoven himself was hoping for

---

[1] An autograph page has survived containing a second trio to the scherzo
of the String Trio, Op. 9, No. 1. But these fifty-one bars seem never to have
been intended for publication but for inclusion in a special performance.

[2] Wegeler and Ries, op. cit., p. 113.

simultaneous publication in another country; and so there was really no need for any score apart from the easily retrievable autograph.

6

The role that copyists played in helping Beethoven to produce a score fit for the publisher has already been referred to more than once and must now be discussed in more detail.[1]

It should not be forgotten that in the eighteenth century, and for some way into the nineteenth, most of the sheets of music from which players performed were still copied out by hand; and the professional copyist, working by himself or as part of a team in a music-copying establishment, or in the employment of a court or a theatre, was a familiar feature of the musical scene.[2] Occasional references to outlays for copying are found in the diary that Beethoven kept of his day-to-day needs and expenses during his first years in Vienna;[3] and some impression of the demands that he was capable of imposing on copyists even at that time may be gained from Wegeler's account of the preparations for the first performance of the C major Piano Concerto:

> Beethoven did not write the rondo . . . till the afternoon of the day but one before the concert. He was suffering at the time from fairly severe abdominal pain, a frequent complaint. I helped him in little ways as much as I could. Four copyists sat in the room outside, and he gave them the pages one by one as they were finished.[4]

A glance at the surviving autograph of the concerto, and particularly

[1] For a fuller account, with illustrations of the handwriting of several of these copyists, see my article in the *Journal of the American Musicological Society*, XXIII (1970).

[2] In his *Dictionnaire de Musique* (Geneva, 1767; Paris, 1768) Jean-Jacques Rousseau, who himself had worked as a copyist, gives under the word 'Copiste' a subjective and entertaining account of the skills required of a good copyist in the middle of the eighteenth century.

[3] Cf. Thayer-Deiters, op. cit., I, p. 325, and Theodor von Frimmel, *Beethoven Studien*, II (Munich and Leipzig, 1906), p. 5.

[4] Wegeler and Ries, op. cit., p. 36.

at its last movement, supports the accuracy of the anecdote so far as the rapidity of composition is concerned.[1]

In the course of time there was one man who found a place as Beethoven's regular copyist and on whom the composer came to rely heavily. This was Wenzel Schlemmer (1760–1823). We do not know when he first came in contact with Beethoven, or how; rather typically, perhaps, we learn of Schlemmer's importance to him less from any positive expression of gratitude or praise than from the undercurrent of complaints or excuses that he put forth whenever Schlemmer's services were interrupted by illness or pressure of other work and the copying had therefore to pass to less experienced (and perhaps less sympathetic) scribes. This relationship ended only with Schlemmer's death on 6 August 1823.[2] Writing half a century later, Gerhard von Breuning reported that Beethoven had had the same copyist for thirty years—which would put the start of the relationship in Beethoven's earliest years in Vienna.[3] (The information appears to have come from Breuning's mother.) The figure is a round one, and it would be unwise to take it literally. But Schlemmer's hand can probably be identified in manuscripts of works by Beethoven dating from the end of the old and the beginning of the new century: for instance, in some portions of the parts to the early version of the String Quartet in F that Beethoven inscribed for his friend Karl Amenda in June 1799.[4]

On the larger assignments Schlemmer did not work alone but employed clerks whose labour he supervised.[5] These were naturally trained to model their style closely on his; no doubt Schlemmer revised their work and corrected oversights and omissions. The

[1] Although Wegeler states that the concerto was the C major one, there are chronological difficulties (connected with the dates when he was in Vienna), and he may have confused it with the B flat Concerto.

[2] Cf. *Ludwig van Beethovens Konversationshefte*, IV, ed. Karl-Heinz Köhler and Grita Herre (Leipzig, 1968), p. 336, n. 40.

[3] Cf. Gerhard von Breuning, *Aus dem Schwarzspanierhause* (Vienna, 1874,) p. 49.

[4] Cf. Hans Josef Wedig, 'Beethovens Streichquartett op. 18 nr. 1 und seine erste Fassung', *Veröffentlichungen des Beethovenhauses in Bonn*, II (Bonn, 1922).

[5] Cf. for example *LA*, letters 152 (22 September 1807) and 301 (end of March 1811), and Breuning, loc. cit: 'he had trained men working under him' ('geschulte Unterarbeiter').

conscious attempt to achieve stylistic unity in the scripts, and the presence within the same score, and even on the same page, of writing by more than one similar hand, must inevitably lead to uncertainty over what was copied by Schlemmer and what was copied by his clerks; and in the past too many manuscript copies have been attributed without discrimination to 'Schlemmer'. His stylistic characteristics seem nevertheless to have remained throughout his life remarkably constant, from the pages in the quartet just mentioned to a small portion of the Diabelli Variations—pages 59–62 of the copy destined for England, now in the Beethovenhaus at Bonn—which was possibly the last task that he attempted to carry out for Beethoven before his final illness.

Schlemmer's skill in deciphering Beethoven's troublesome musical handwriting and the scrupulous accuracy with which he reproduced what he found before him have come in for praise in recent times;[1] but Beethoven's dependence on him and his helplessness during Schlemmer's frequent illnesses are even more eloquent.[2] Schlemmer was willing to visit Beethoven and to copy music in his rooms; he may have been one of the copyists that Tomaschek found at work on *Der glorreiche Augenblick* when he visited Beethoven on 24 November 1814: 'In the middle of the room I found two copyists, who were copying his cantata . . . in the greatest haste; in the second room every table and chair was covered with fragments of scores which Umlauf [the conductor] . . . was probably correcting'.[3] This was a concert which

---

[1] Cf. Hubert Unverricht, *Die Eigenschriften und die Originalausgaben von Werken Beethovens in ihrer Bedeutung für die moderne Textkritik* (Kassel, 1960), p. 40 (concerning a copy of Op. 111). Another testimonial to Schlemmer's care comes from Georg Schünemann's introduction to the facsimile of the autograph of the Fifth Symphony (Berlin, 1942), p. 7. But after studying photographs of a few pages of the (now lost) copyist's score of the symphony I am not convinced that in either case the copyist was Schlemmer.

[2] Cf. *LA*, letters 108, 116, 359 and 892 for references to Schlemmer's illnesses in 1805 (presumably Schlemmer), 1812 and 1818. From 1819 till his death Schlemmer seems to have been in very poor health; his eyesight, moreover, was affected.

[3] J. W. Tomaschek in *Libussa* (1847), p. 430; reprinted in Thayer-Deiters, op. cit., III, p. 454. A bill for the copying of the cantata, signed by Schlemmer, is in the Deutsche Staatsbibliothek, Berlin.

Beethoven had to postpone three times, apparently because of the difficulty in producing accurate parts in time. From time to time he attempted to find other arrangements. In 1811 he was thinking of taking into his service someone who could copy music;[1] and, of course, from time to time everyone around him, his pupil Ries, his 'famulus' Schindler, friends such as Holz was pressed into tasks of copying and proof-reading.[2]

Schlemmer himself, though bound to Beethoven by regularity of employment, seems to have kept his independence; he worked in any case for others and was sometimes too busy to serve Beethoven.[3] Further information about their dealings with each other is hard to come by and is usually indirect. We know, for instance, that in 1807 Schlemmer was paid at the rate of ten kreuzer per sheet (*Bogen*— in effect, four sides) and that some other copyists charged more. By 1814 copyists were asking for fifteen kreuzer per *Bogen*, and in 1823 the rate was over twenty.[4] It is not clear what part the depreciation of the currency played in these changes, or what adjustments, if any, were made for the additional amount of copying involved in Beethoven's late works with extra-large instrumental forces. From the conversation-books it appears that Schlemmer was owed money by Beethoven at the time of his death in 1823 and that his widow continued to farm out the work to other copyists for a while.[5]

'I have no intelligent copyist,' wrote Beethoven to the brothers Schott on 17 December 1824; 'the copyist I had and upon whom I could depend has been in his grave for eighteen months; but so excellent a copyist must first be *trained*.'[6] In his last years Beet-

---

[1] *LA*, letter 340.

[2] Cf. Wegeler and Ries, op. cit., p. 82; Anton Felix Schindler, *Biographie von Ludwig van Beethoven*, 3rd ed. (Münster, 1860), Part 2, p. 17 (*SB*, p. 240); and *LA*, letter 1219 (July 1823).

[3] Cf. *Konversationshefte*, II, ed. Schünemann (Berlin, 1942), p. 349 (February 1823), where Ferdinand Piringer writes: 'Herr Kreutzer is having his opera *Libussa* copied by Schlemmer'; and Beethoven's letter (*LA*, letter 1019) of 23 April 1820 to Simrock: 'My usual copyist happened to have too much to do for our Court.'

[4] *LA*, letters 152 (22 September 1807) and 477 (April 1814) and *Konversationshefte*, II, p. 379.

[5] *LA*, letter 1219 (July 1823), and *Konversationshefte*, IV, p. 336, n. 40.

[6] *LA*, letter 1325.

hoven found no true replacement for Schlemmer, who here—posthumously and a shade obliquely—is acknowledged to have been 'excellent'. Instead, he had to rely on a series of rather unsatisfactory copyists at the very time that the idiosyncrasies of his handwriting were being increased by intermittent illness.[1] The most experienced of these was probably Wenzel Rampl. Born in 1783, he seems to have been an old friend of Schlemmer (who was witness to his first marriage in 1811) and to have worked for him for a time.[2] Other names, many of them (like 'Wenzel') of Bohemian origin, are encountered in connection with Beethoven's difficulties in getting the late works, including the *Missa solemnis* and the Ninth Symphony, accurately copied: e.g. Peter Gläser, Paul Maschek, Ferdinand Wolanek, Mathias Wunderl.[3] To Gläser Beethoven wrote politely, though on occasion reproachfully ('I asked you to copy exactly what I had written . . . I most earnestly request you not to inflict on me a third and fourth task').[4] But Wolanek was imprudent enough to return unfinished work to Beethoven and to allude in a covering letter to Beethoven's difficult temperament; by virtue of the torrent of indignation and abuse ('Stupid ass! Slovenly copyist! . . .') poured by Beethoven over both sides of the letter he is preserved from oblivion.[5] Some of Rampl's deficiencies in copying the parts of the A minor Quartet, Op. 132, are alluded to in a letter to Karl Holz of August 1825; fourteen months later, on completing his last quartet, he wrote to the Paris publisher Maurice Schlesinger (for whom it was destined) that he had had to copy out the four parts from the score himself, since he could find no copyist in Gneixendorf.[6] By then he had no doubt realized that there were times when it was the lesser of two evils to be his own copyist.

[1] *LA*, letter 1402 (18 July 1825): 'In regard to the copying of the quartet you may tell him that I write quite differently now, much more legibly than during my illness.'

[2] *Konversationshefte*, IV, p. 351, n. 197.

[3] Cf., for Gläser, *Konversationshefte*, IV, p. 337, n. 44, and for Wunderl, ibid., p. 349, n. 176, and *Musical Times*, CXI (1970), p. 26.

[4] *LA*, letter 1275 (April 1824).

[5] *LA*, letter 1463.

[6] *LA*, letters 1421 (August 1825) and 1538 and 1538a (*c.* 30 October 1826).

7

Although other forms of music printing, such as lithography and printing from movable type, were occasionally employed in the period covered by Beethoven's lifetime, the vast majority of his works first came out in 'engraved editions'—that is, in editions that were printed from engraved metal plates. This method of production had certain consequences for the composer and therefore merits a short description. The engraver was employed by the publisher.[1] It was his task to rule the staves on the plates and then, working partly free-hand and partly with punches, to engrave the music so that it corresponded with the manuscript—the *Stichvorlage*—before him. When the engraving was completed the plate's surface was a mirror-image of the music; the engraver had therefore to be skilled in working 'backwards' (in mirror-fashion). Perhaps something like tracing paper was used, and the position of the notes, running from right to left, lightly marked before the plate was attacked with stylus and punch. If an error was made, it could only be corrected by first restoring the surface of the plate to its original condition at that spot; the faulty incision was eliminated by hammering on the opposite side of the plate and by filing and smoothing the surface.

The plates remained with the publisher and were used to print off copies of the work in question as they were needed, in batches. In the case of some of Beethoven's works the business records of Breitkopf & Härtel show us the size of the batches (impressions).[2] The two Piano Trios, Op. 70, for instance, each had a first impression of a hundred copies.[3] When a work had a small but steady demand the plates continued to be used for many years. In the case of the Fifth Symphony we find that up to 1828 there were seven

---

[1] He was paid more than a copyist: in *Konversationshefte*, II, p. 349 (February 1823), Piringer remarks that an engraver earned eight gulden a day, a copyist only three gulden. For engraving the score of the Op. 130 Quartet Hodick (see below) was paid forty-eight kreuzers per plate (cf. *NZB*, p. 365).

[2] Every batch constitutes an *impression*; the term *issue* is used for an impression which is textually distinct.

[3] Günther Haupt, 'Gräfin Erdödy und J. X. Brauchle', *Der Bär* (1927), p. 77.

impressions, with a total printing of 700 copies in all, and in the years up to 1862 a further 350 copies were printed from the plates.[1] Since the cost of the plates themselves and of their engraving was, apart from the fee paid to the composer (which a pirated edition naturally evaded), the most costly part of preparing an edition, publishers were often tempted to go on using the same plates even after they had become badly worn or cracked. The life of a plate was measured not by time but by use, and although figures are hard to obtain it seems that in the early nineteenth century a Viennese plate began to deteriorate badly after about a thousand copies had been impressed from it.[2]

The way that an engraver could immediately correct an error he had made on a plate has already been described. But plates could also be changed after a specimen set of pages had been printed and shown to the composer—this we should call a proof—and indeed at any subsequent point of time between the printing of batches. These plate-changes would, of course, be embodied in any copies subsequently printed from the plates. It was feasible to correct the plates at any time that an error was discovered, whether this was before or after publication day (the date that copies of the earliest batch were put on sale). Indeed, some plate-changes were evidently made years after an edition was first published. It is important to realize that not all copies of an edition will necessarily be identical and that the copies from the later batches or issues may be the more correct ones; while the plates of an edition tended to deteriorate physically with the passage of time, textually they sometimes improved.[3]

Many of the French eighteenth-century engravers had signed their work. Their successors in Vienna and Leipzig worked for the

[1] *KH*, p. 159. The first printing of the Piano Sonata, Op. 81a, was 500 copies; but that edition was not engraved but lithographed (ibid., p. 217).

[2] There are various approaches to this problem. Copies of the earliest issues, for instance, of Schubert's Opp. 1–7 and 12–14, published by subscription, were initialled and numbered by the composer and give some impression of the rate at which plates deteriorated.

[3] These conclusions, not always welcome to editors of Beethoven, are nevertheless important. Cf. Tyson, 'Beethoven in Steiner's shop', *Music Review*, XXIII (1962), p. 119 (with examples from the F minor Quartet, Op. 95, and *An die ferne Geliebte*, Op. 98).

most part anonymously, though the efforts of a particular man can sometimes be recognized by his style. We know the names of a few of those who engraved editions by Beethoven. Johann Schäfer, for example, who evidently worked for a number of Viennese firms, signed his name on the first page of the Piano Sonata, Op. 27, No. 1, published by Giovanni Cappi in March 1802. He had earlier done signed work for Artaria (e.g. Haydn's Op. 76 Quartets in 1799); and the unsigned edition of Beethoven's Variations for piano on 'La stessa, la stessissima', WoO 73, which Artaria published in February 1799, is probably also by Schäfer. And on grounds of style it is reasonable to attribute to him two Beethoven editions published by Hoffmeister in December 1799: the piano Variations on 'Tändeln und scherzen', WoO 76, and the rather beautiful one of the *Sonate Pathétique*, Op. 13. Other engravers whose names have variously come down to us, with the publishers for whom they were working, are Joseph Sigg (Diabelli Variations, Op. 120, for Cappi & Diabelli); 'Herr Fischer der jüngerer' (violin Romance, Op. 50, and the 'Waldstein' Sonata, Op. 53, for the Bureau des Arts et d'Industrie) and Hodick (Op. 130 Quartet and the *Grosse Fuge*, Op. 133, for Matthias Artaria). Title-pages, often engraved not on pewter (or some soft alloy) but on copper, were sometimes entrusted to a different engraver, e.g. Andreas Müller (nine works, Opp. 90–3, 95–8, 101, for Steiner) and A. Kurka (Op. 130 and Op. 133 for M. Artaria; Op. 103 and WoO 3 for Artaria & Co.).

Some of these craftsmen—Johann Schäfer, for instance—were elegant engravers. But since they stand between us and the composer we are likely to be less interested in their elegance than in their accuracy. This was a distinction of which Beethoven was acutely aware. Writing to Breitkopf & Härtel in June 1803 about the errors in the Zürich edition of the Op. 31 Piano Sonatas, he lamented: 'The edition is so beautiful that it is most unfortunate that it should have been launched into the world with that extreme slovenliness and lack of care . . . It is such an extremely unpleasant experience, particularly for the composer, to see an otherwise finely engraved work full of mistakes.'[1] It has to be said that the famous house of Artaria, the main publisher not only of

[1] *LA*, letter 79.

Beethoven's early works but of many of the mature ones of Haydn and Mozart, maintained low standards both in design and in accuracy; its Beethoven editions of the 1790s teem with errors.[1] No correspondence about this between Beethoven and the firm has survived, so we cannot tell if it is more than coincidence that he praised the engraving at this time of Simrock at Bonn and of Hoffmeister & Kühnel at Leipzig.[2] With his later publishers Beethoven was more fortunate—though one might not have guessed it from the letters: understandably, he had grown more fastidious as well. His expostulation on 6 May 1811 to Breitkopf & Härtel ('mistakes—mistakes—you yourself are a unique mistake') has often been quoted;[3] but a large part of his correspondence with Steiner & Co. is also concerned with the shortcomings of the firm in regard to the accuracy of its publications.

In the last resort the errors of the engraver could be eliminated by careful proof-reading. Beethoven's problems here must now be discussed in more detail.

8

How can a composer exercise control over the text of an engraved edition? First of all, he can ensure that the publisher receives an accurate version of the work that is to be published: either a legible autograph, or a score made by a careful copyist. Secondly, after the work has been engraved, he can insist on receiving proofs, which he must then read carefully. His corrections at this stage—not only the removal of the engraver's errors, but any other changes that on seeing his work again he now feels necessary, such as additional dynamics—will require the plates to be inspected by the engraver and altered at the appropriate places. After the work has been published (i.e. put on sale to the public) he can, if it is very faulty, repudiate the edition—a rather drastic step; or he can arrange for another firm (perhaps in another country) to publish a more correct version. Or, if he is still on amicable terms with his own publisher,

---

[1] Cf. also Haydn's scathing comments in his letter to Artaria of 10 December 1785.

[2] *LA*, letters 12 (2 August 1794) and 57 (8 April 1802).

[3] *LA*, letter 306.

he can press him to issue an errata slip, or encourage him to make corrections in pencil or ink at least in the unsold copies. Or he can get him to make corrections on the plates, which will ensure that subsequent issues at least will be free from error.

In Beethoven's case we find all these six methods of control being exercised or at least attempted. For a start, he tried to get good manuscripts to his publishers: the autographs (it has been suggested above) in the case of his earliest published works, and later on a score from the hand of a reliable copyist. Almost all these copyists' scores, of which a good number have survived (perhaps because they often remained in the publisher's archives after the work had appeared), bear evidence of having been corrected and revised by Beethoven, in some cases quite extensively.[1] There were other occasions on which Beethoven became alarmed that what had already been sent to the publisher contained errors which he had overlooked; in March 1819, for instance, he wrote in some agitation to Ries in London in case the manuscript copies of Op. 104 (the string quintet arrangement of the Op. 1, No. 3, Piano Trio) and the 'Hammerklavier' Sonata, Op. 106, that had been sent there for projected English editions contained serious errors, and his letters enclosed extensive corrigenda lists.[2] As for correcting the errors of engravers, that was something that preoccupied Beethoven for the whole of his working life, as we can see throughout his correspondence, from the letter of August 1793 concerning the violin and piano Variations, WoO 40, to the letter to the brothers Schott less than two months before his death with corrections to the Ninth Symphony and to the Paris and Mainz editions of the Op. 127 String Quartet.[3] How were these errors to be prevented? Curiously enough, it seems to have taken him some time to discover that orderly control of the proof stage, with refusal to permit publication of anything that he had not completely approved, offered the best solution. As late as June 1803 he was still writing to Breitkopf & Härtel as if he were asking a favour in requesting proofs at all: 'Since you have engraved my variations [Op. 34, and perhaps

---

[1] Cf. *LA*, letter 174 (shortly after 14 September 1808).
[2] *LA*, letters 938 and 939 (8 March, *c.* 20 March 1819).
[3] *LA*, letters 5 (August 1793) and 1548 (27 January 1827).

Op. 35] from my manuscript, I am also in a state of perpetual trepidation lest a number of mistakes may have crept into them; and I should very much like you to send me a proof copy beforehand.'[1] In the course of a strenuous and outspoken correspondence with the same firm in the years 1809–11 he continued to complain that his compositions were coming out with mistakes that had not been in the original manuscripts, and to request at least the right of being shown a copy of each edition before it was released to the public. Finally, in February 1811, he was able to write: 'At last you have adopted the sensible arrangement of sending me the proofs of the fantasia [Op. 80] to correct; and in general you should always adopt this procedure. But send me the second or third proofs, and you shall have them back as swiftly as an arrow.'[2] But his troubles were not really at an end; and it is this last sentence that gives the game away. For Beethoven was not a particularly good corrector of proofs—a fact that he acknowledged at times, once confessing (with a pun on the verb 'übersehen'): 'when he *looks over his own work* the composer really *does overlook* the mistakes'.[3] We can form an estimate of his efficiency as a proof-reader not so much from examining the few surviving sets of corrected proofs (such as those of the 'Archduke' Trio, Op. 97)[4] as from noting the number of errors that escaped him in editions that we know had been critically scrutinized by him. Certainly for some features he had a sharp eye: for missing accidentals, for instance, or for omitted changes of clef. Yet far grosser errors were on occasion overlooked. If we follow the textual progress of a work like the Violin Concerto on its journey from autograph to copyist's score, and then from that score to the first edition that was engraved from it, we can see how some errors originated in the autograph and were never eliminated, and how others crept in with the copyist or with the engraver and remained undetected in Beethoven's lifetime.[5] We are entitled, therefore, to

[1] *LA*, letter 79.

[2] *LA*, letter 297 (19 February 1811).

[3] *LA*, letter 220 (26 July 1809).

[4] Cf. Sotheby & Co.'s sale of 19 December 1960, lot 248a. There is a brief description in the sale catalogue.

[5] For some examples of each type of error cf. Tyson, 'The textual problems of Beethoven's Violin Concerto', *Musical Quarterly*, LIII (1967), p. 482.

remain sceptical before his constant lamentations that the inaccuracies of the editions of his published works were entirely due
to the incompetence of his publishers and their engravers and assistants. When Beethoven discovered that he had overlooked errors in
the proofs he tended to complain that he had not been provided with
the necessary 'second or third proofs'; and he claimed the right to
ask for changes to be made not only when he returned his proofs but
at any time up to the publication of the work—and (as we can see)
beyond.[1]

Besides looking through his proofs Beethoven sometimes checked
them for errors by having the work in question played through.
This encouraged him not merely to eliminate mistakes but to
introduce improvements as well. There is a good example of this in
the case of the Fifth and Sixth Symphonies. They were first performed on 22 December 1808; and on 4 March 1809, only a month
or so before the works were published and long after they had been
engraved, he excused himself for wanting further changes in a letter
to Breitkopf & Härtel: 'When I gave these works to you, I had not
yet heard either of them performed—and one should not want to be
so like a god as not to have to correct something here and there in
one's created works.'[2] The corrections to the Fifth Symphony,
which did not follow till 28 March, could not, of course, be included
in the hundred copies of the first issue; but the plates were changed
so that the second and subsequent issues included them.[3] But a
further, highly necessary correction to the scherzo, about which
Beethoven wrote on 21 August 1810—sixteen months after publication—was never attended to till Mendelssohn drew it to the
publishers' attention in 1846.

What of mistakes that were discovered in copies that had been
printed but not yet sold? It was unrealistic to expect the publisher
to destroy the copies; but Beethoven felt entitled to request that
they should be corrected in pencil or in Indian ink before sale, and

[1] The correspondence with the firm of Steiner & Co. in the years 1815-
17 provides ample evidence for these statements.

[2] *LA*, letter 199.

[3] Cf. Paul Hirsch, 'A Discrepancy in Beethoven', *Music and Letters*,
XIX (1938), p. 265.

in one letter to Steiner he suggested that his copyist Schlemmer could help in that task.[1] More drastic measures were necessary in the case of a really faulty edition that had been widely disseminated. The Zürich edition of the Op. 31 Sonatas had been given to the world unproof-read, and its publisher, Nägeli, had even introduced some arbitary changes of his own. Beethoven arranged for a corrigenda list to be published in the *Allgemeine Musikalische Zeitung*—for some reason it did not appear—but he also requested Ries to send Simrock of Bonn a similar list of mistakes and encouraged that firm to bring out its own corrected version of the sonatas, to be marked '*édition très correcte*'. This Simrock did.[2] The device of an errata slip was also proposed by Beethoven to deal with errors in Steiner's editions of the Seventh Symphony; and soon after he had written to the brothers Schott in January 1827 with a short list of faults he had found in the Ninth Symphony and in the String Quartet, Op. 127 (both published some months earlier), a printed sheet detailing the errors was slipped into the uncorrected copies.[3] The other possibility open to Beethoven—the tacit encouragement to another publisher to produce an amended version—was adopted in the case of the last two piano sonatas: when the editions of Op. 110 and Op. 111 published by the Schlesingers in Paris and Berlin were found to contain serious mistakes he secretly helped the firm of Cappi & Diabelli in Vienna to bring out its own corrected editions.

[1] *LA*, letter 675 (November 1816); cf. also letters 665, 691 and 1060.
[2] The relevant documents are: Caspar Carl's letters to Breitkopf & Härtel of 21 May 1803 (Thayer-Deiters, op. cit., II, p. 619) and to Simrock of 25 May (ibid., pp. 398–9); Beethoven's letters to Ries and to Breitkopf & Härtel in June (*LA*, Nos. 76–9); Härtel's letters to Beethoven of 2 and 30 June (Hitzig, op. cit., pp. 326–7); Ries's letters to Simrock of 29 June and 6 August (*Simrock Jahrbuch*, II, Berlin, 1929, pp. 23–4); and Ries's account in Wegeler and Ries, op. cit., p. 88. The statement that the sonatas had not been proof-read comes from Caspar Carl's letter of 21 May. Ries less plausibly states that the four bars that Nägeli had interpolated in the coda of the first movement of Op. 31, No. 1, were detected along with the other errors when Beethoven asked Ries to play through the proofs as a means of checking them.
[3] *LA*, letters 675 and 677 (November 1816); and cf. letter 1548. A score of the Ninth Symphony in the Royal College of Music, London, is among the ones to contain this errata list.

9

The title-page of an edition was in most cases the last to be prepared. Besides the title or description of the work itself it usually carried other information of practical interest, such as the price and the publisher's name and town, and two items that we must now consider: the opus number and the dedication.

In the eighteenth century opus numbers were often put on music by the publishers and not the composer: neither Mozart nor Haydn, for instance, did anything to control the opus numbers that were attached by publishers to the works of their maturity. With Beethoven from the start things were otherwise. At the beginning of his publishing life in Vienna he decided to reserve the series of opus numbers for his more important compositions; the lesser pieces, such as songs, ballroom dances and smaller piano works, were sent into the world without opus numbers, though one category of the latter, the sets of piano variations on popular themes of the day, was given *numbers*—not, however, *opus* numbers—to distinguish them. The very few exceptions to this rule are in themselves instructive. His Variations for violin and piano, WoO 40, the first work to be published in Vienna (in July 1793), originally appeared as 'Œuvre I'; but this, like the description of the violin part as being 'ad libitum' and not obbligato, may have been against Beethoven's instructions. Both points at any rate, as well as a sprinkling of misprints, were corrected in later issues, when the variations reappeared as 'No. 1'.[1] Beethoven reserved the dignity of being the 'real' Op. 1 for the work with which he intended to launch his public career as a composer. This, the three piano trios dedicated to his patron Prince Lichnowsky and accompanied by a subscription list of 123 names, appeared in the summer of 1795. Beethoven seems to have been reluctant to publish anything slight in the year before the publication of the Op. 1 Trios.[2] Shortly after they came out two of his most superficial sets of variations (WoO 69 and WoO 70) were issued by another publisher as 'Op. 2' and 'Op. 3'; and we may suspect that here again the

[1] Cf. *LA*, letter 5 (August 1793).
[2] Cf. *LA*, letter 10 (18 June 1794).

initiative came from the publisher, since these, too, were changed to 'No. 2' and 'No. 3' on reissue.

In the 1790s it was the sonata-form works that were honoured with opus numbers. A song like *Adelaide*, Op. 46, or a piano piece like the Rondo, Op. 51, No. 1, was excluded by its genre;[1] and the principle even extended to an impressive set such as the Gellert songs, published in 1803. But gradually the inner significance of a work began to count for more than its outward form. In December 1802 Beethoven asked Breitkopf & Härtel to include an explanatory note in his two latest sets of piano variations which they were publishing:

> As these v[ariations] are distinctly different from my earlier ones, instead of indicating them like my *previous ones* by means of a number (such as, for instance, Nos. 1, 2, 3 and so on) I have included them in the proper numerical series *of my greater musical works*, the more so as the themes have been composed by me.
>
> The Composer[2]

The variations accordingly appeared as Op. 34 and Op. 35 (though the composer's explanation was not, in fact, published). Most of the later vocal sets, and a few non-strophic songs, were given opus numbers: for example, *An die Hoffnung* (Op. 94) and the song-cycle *An die ferne Geliebte* (Op. 98). According to Schindler the publication of two short strophic songs as Op. 99 and Op. 100 was on the publisher's initiative; Beethoven's protests against such 'arbitrary and whimsical numbering' by Steiner & Co. are said to have been disregarded.[3]

In deciding which compositions were to be dignified by opus numbers, therefore, Beethoven can be said to have been self-conscious about the canon of his major works. To some extent he was deliberately defining his œuvre; the fact that most composers since him have followed his example should not lead us to overlook the historical importance of his stance. Even when several

[1] These opus numbers were acquired only later.
[2] *LA*, letter 67 (*c.* 18 December 1802).
[3] Schindler, op. cit., Part 1, p. 205 (*SB*, p. 176).

compositions were being published at more or less the same time it was important to him that the opus numbers should indicate the sequence of their composition. This is perhaps only a further manifestation of an attitude to his creations which made him ask for the 'Eroica' Symphony to be published in score rather than in parts,[1] and for some indication of absolute as well as relative chronology to be added to an edition: 'Would you agree to add the year as well? I have often wanted this, but no publisher would do it.'[2] We shall hardly be surprised to find that his disorderliness, when added to the inconsistencies of publishers, resulted in a distribution of opus numbers that fell short of the ideal. He confessed to Breitkopf & Härtel in 1811 that he did not remember his earlier opus numbers,[3] and at times he assigned numbers that were clearly 'wrong'.[4] As a result a few numbers were duplicated; many more remained unused. By the end of his life, or in the quarter century that followed, these gaps were filled up—almost always by works that had originally been published without an opus number; naturally the position that they occupy at the present time in the now 'traditional' series stretching from Op. 1 to Op. 138 bears no relation to their order either of composition or of publication.[5] And even in Beethoven's lifetime a change in opus number was occasionally brought about by comically trivial circumstances. Two violin sonatas had been planned to appear as his Op. 23. But the violin part of the first sonata was engraved in upright format, that of the second in oblong format; and shortly after publication it was decided to avoid this incongruity by reissuing the sonatas separately, as Op. 23 and Op. 24.

10

If Beethoven took opus numbers seriously, the same cannot quite

---

[1] *LA*, letter 96 (26 August 1804).   [2] *LA*, letter 1050 (7 March 1821).
[3] *LA* letter 297 (19 February 1811).
[4] *LA*, letters 199 (4 March 1809) and 662 (1 October 1816).
[5] This is sometimes forgotten. The mistaken view that the *Rondo a capriccio*, published posthumously as Op. 129, is a late work—in actual fact it was written by 1798—almost certainly derives from the high opus number. Cf. Erich Hertzmann, 'The newly discovered autograph of Beethoven's Rondo a capriccio', *Musical Quarterly*, XXXII (1946), p. 171.

be said of dedications; and only a few points will be touched on here. The majority of his important works were published with dedications, although a few—the Eighth Symphony, for instance, or the Piano Sonata, Op. 110—were undedicated. The custom, in fact, fulfilled a number of useful functions: it was a way of expressing loyalty, friendship, obligation, gratitude, or the hope of favours. Thus it was entirely proper for Beethoven to dedicate his Op. 1 to Prince Lichnowsky, his first real patron in Vienna, and his Op. 2 to Haydn, his first teacher there.[1] Other works were dedicated, as we have seen, to the persons—mainly members of the Viennese nobility—who had commissioned them. It is somewhat strange to find the Fifth and Sixth Symphonies, published separately though almost simultaneously, both dedicated to the same two noblemen—why not one symphony apiece? But Beethoven's dedications seem at times almost whimsical, not least in the changes of plan, prompted by a passing irritation or estrangement, or by the urgent need to favour a recent benefactor. In some of his dedications he shows a touching respect for his fellow artists, musicians like Kreutzer or Salieri (also one of his teachers), and poets and dramatists such as Matthisson, Collin or the revered Goethe.

When a work was being published abroad as well as in Vienna, Beethoven did not scruple at finding a second dedicatee. He authorized Neate to sell the dedications of the English editions of the Op. 96 Violin Sonata and the Op. 97 Trio. Neate did, in fact, find a lady who offered ten guineas for the dedication of Op. 97— but unfortunately the work had already appeared in London with its original Viennese dedication to the Archduke Rudolph.[2] Beethoven hoped to persuade Neate, and later Ries, to look after his publishing interests in London. To encourage them he gave Neate manuscript copies of the Op. 102 Cello Sonatas dedicated to him, and later sent Ries a manuscript copy of the Diabelli Variations with a dedication to Ries's wife; but in each case plans for an

---

[1] But according to Ries (Wegeler and Ries, op. cit., p. 86) he declined to describe himself on title-pages as 'pupil of Haydn', claiming that although he had had some lessons from him he had never learnt anything.

[2] Cf. *LA*, letters 636 (18 May 1816) and 683 (18 December 1816).

English edition were frustrated by the arrival of printed copies from the continent, those of the Diabelli Variations even bearing (to Ries's chagrin) a dedication to a different lady.[1]

II

We have now followed Beethoven, and have illustrated his continued concern for the exact form that each work should take, in the various stages from the first jottings in the sketchbooks to the completion of a definitive autograph score, and subsequently through all the processes of publication that further modified it for better and for worse. There was one final form of supervision over his œuvre to which he was strongly (though somewhat intermittently) attracted. This was via a collected edition of his works. It was doubtless the wide popularity of his early piano compositions that first made such a collection seem a tempting venture. On 2 June 1803 Härtel—whose firm had already embarked on the '*Oeuvres complettes*' of Mozart in 1799 and of Haydn a year later— suggested that a uniform edition of Beethoven's piano works would be welcome to the public, and referred in passing to one of the possible difficulties—the fact that the ownership of the pieces was distributed over a number of publishers:

> It is much more satisfying for music lovers to get the works of a composer that they admire from a single publisher and in a uniform edition than to have to assemble them laboriously from several different publishers and to own them in editions very diverse in their formats and in their engraving. And this simply encourages the pirates, and all the legitimate publishers suffer. These are the reasons why the admirers of your piano compositions will be delighted if ever you come to an agreement with the publishers of your earlier piano works and want to arrange for a new uniform edition. Those publishers who have already exercised their right would probably not put many difficulties in your way in this settlement; or you could perhaps make things easier for yourself by making the surrender to you of their rights

[1] Cf. Wegeler and Ries, op. cit., p. 123.

one of the conditions under which you let them have further new instrumental works. Should you find this idea feasible and attractive, you would find us very ready to offer you our help and agreeable terms . . .[1]

But Breitkopf & Härtel became discouraged on finding that a firm in Mainz (Zulehner) was already selling by subscription a uniform collection of piano works by Beethoven, all pirated. Beethoven could do little but put a disclaimer in the *Wiener Zeitung*, which at the same time stressed his interest in textual accuracy:

> I would never have proceeded to make a collection of my works, an undertaking which in itself I regard as premature, before discussing the matter with the publishers of the individual works and arranging to ensure that accuracy which is lacking in the editions of the various separate compositions.[2]

Seven years later it was Beethoven who took the initiative: in August 1810 he wrote to Breitkopf & Härtel about a 'great speculation' on which he was hoping to embark. This was 'an authentic edition of my collected works to be prepared by myself and, if we can come to some agreement, to be published first by your firm'. The Leipzig publishers would be associated with a Viennese and a Parisian one, and a 'privilege' (a form of copyright) sought for the Austrian states as a protection against piracy.[3] Härtel's lengthy examination (in his reply of 24 September 1810) of the reasons for regretfully declining the proposal should be studied by anyone concerned with the publishing trade in this period. Pirated editions of Beethoven had by that time become too widely distributed throughout Europe to make a new and authentic collected edition a paying venture, for apart from the individual works that had already appeared in 'France, England, Offenbach, Bonn, Mainz, Augsburg, Berlin, Amsterdam, Hamburg, Munich and in Leipzig too', collections had already begun to appear in some of those places.[4]

[1] Hitzig, op. cit., pp. 326–7.
[2] *LA*, Appendix H(3) (22 October 1803).
[3] *LA*, letter 273 (shortly before 21 August 1810).
[4] Hitzig, op. cit., pp. 334–8.

From time to time Beethoven tried to interest other publishers in a collected edition: Simrock in 1817 and 1820, Peters in 1822–3, Schott in 1825.[1] All these efforts were unsuccessful. Publishers were more interested in acquiring new works than in reissuing corrected versions of old ones (which—in their uncorrected form—they could pirate anyway).[2] One of Beethoven's more ingenious plans, first advanced in a letter to Peters in 1822, was to include a brand-new composition for each category of work that was to be republished; and so far as string quartets were concerned he seems to have come near to reaching an agreement of this sort with Maurice Schlesinger in Paris.[3]

We may find it ironical that it was only when Beethoven was no longer able to correct or revise his works that collected editions of them, conscientiously edited by his friends and admirers, began to appear in Vienna, Paris, London and elsewhere.[4] But his death allowed publishers at least to survey the extent of his output with some sense of finality. All in all, it seems to me to be a superficial view that regards Beethoven's dealings with publishers as anything other than successful. How ethical he was, and believed himself to be, in some of his transactions is a question which is deliberately avoided here, although the evidence presented must suggest that the faults are not on one side only. 'Everything I do apart from music is badly done and is stupid.'[5] This poignant aside from

[1] And, according to Schindler, op. cit., Part 2, pp. 38–9 (*SB*, pp. 254–5), Friedrich Hofmeister of Leipzig in 1816 (Schindler writes 'Hoffmeister').

[2] Beethoven's revisions might have been drastic. According to Schindler, op. cit., pp. 215–16 (*SB*, pp. 402–3) he spoke of removing the scherzos from some of his early four-movement sonatas, e.g. the Violin Sonata, Op. 30, No. 2.

[3] Cf. Tyson, 'Maurice Schlesinger as a publisher of Beethoven, 1822–1827', *Acta Musicologica*, XXXV (1963), pp. 186–91.

[4] Cf. Otto Erich Deutsch, 'Beethovens gesammelte Werke: des Meisters Plan und Haslingers Ausgabe', *Zeitschrift für Musikwissenschaft*, XIII (1930–1), p. 60, and Tyson, 'Moscheles and his "Complete Edition" of Beethoven', *Music Review*, XXV (1964), p. 136.

[5] Quoted by J. A. Streicher (in whose presence the remark was made) in a letter to C. F. Peters of 5 March 1825: cf. *LA*, letter 1324, n. 2.

the year 1825 came from a deaf, sick and lonely man who was nevertheless able to look after the thing which was most important to him—and for which we value him.

VII

The View of Posterity

FOURTEEN

The View of Posterity: an Anthology

ELSIE and DENIS ARNOLD

BEETHOVEN IS THE SUPREME example of the artist whose greatness was not only acknowledged during his lifetime but also acknowledged to the full in the years since his death. Individual works have gone in and out of favour; individual critics have condemned and misinterpreted; individual composers have found his music distasteful and best avoided. Even so, there has never been a time when the greater part of the musical public has not been aware of his achievement. The vagaries of his reputation are in many ways more revealing of the nature of the writer and his age than of Beethoven himself. In the first place it was, as Berlioz pointed out, the public rather than the musicians who found the real content of his music.[1] Such professional teachers of composition as Antonín Reicha ignored him completely—unless we can read positive disapproval in the sinister sentence contained in a discussion of the moderns:

The pretence that in the last resort everyone has the right to judge is not only ridiculous but indeed exceedingly pernicious for music . . .[2]

At the same time, Berlioz could report that:

. . . From the moment of its first appearance, the celebrated allegretto in A minor of the Seventh Symphony, which had been

---

[1] Hector Berlioz, 'A critical study of Beethoven's nine symphonies' from *A travers chants*, trans. Edwin Evans (London [1913]; repr. 1958), pp. 24 f.

[2] Antonín Reicha, *Traité de haute composition musicale* (Paris, 1824), II, p. 328. This and other unattributed translations in this chapter are by the authors. In quotations from English sources misprints have been corrected and minor changes of layout have been made.

inserted in the Second [Symphony] in order to help to pass off the remainder, was appreciated at its value by the public of the 'Concerts Spirituels'. The pit rose in a body with vociferous cries for its repetition; and, at a second performance, the first movement and the scherzo of the Symphony in D, which had not been much enjoyed on the occasion of the first trial, met with an almost equal success . . .[1]

Indeed, Londoners could feel positive superiority to lesser breeds merely because they had discovered Beethoven earlier than others:

The French seem just to have discovered the merits of Beethoven's symphony in C minor. At the first performance for the present season of the *Société des Concerts*, on the 21st of December, this stupendous composition was performed, and received with *transports of admiration, almost amounting to frenzy*. It met with nearly as warm a reception at the Philharmonic Concerts, no less than sixteen years ago, when, owing to the determined perseverance of one or two of its members, it was there performed, for the first time out of Germany. Some resistance was made to its introduction; even Salomon thought it 'mad and impracticable', and was only induced by the earnest entreaty of a friend he much valued, to consent to lead it at a rehearsal, by way of giving it a trial. But when the band had got through about one-third of the first movement, he stopped, and, with that candour which so strongly marked his character, exclaimed, 'This is the finest composition of Beethoven that ever I heard!'

The French orchestra, on the above occasion, *covered themselves with glory*, we are told; and, doubtless, they did it justice, for they have an abundance of skill, and their enthusiasm is unbounded. Nevertheless, if the audience were so affected at the performance of this composition by a band to whom it was new, how would they have felt had they heard it executed by the Philharmonic orchestra, to which it is almost known by heart?—Strait waistcoats would have been necessary.[2]

Nor do works which have been described as 'difficult' seem to have presented many problems to the public at large. A concert which

[1] Op. cit., p. 52.
[2] *The Harmonicon*, VII (February 1829), p. 38.

included three sections from the Mass in D *and* the Ninth Symphony might be fancied to be scarcely popular with an audience to whom they were entirely new. In fact, an English journal following an account from Vienna reported:

. . . The deep and general feeling which this concert, in honour of the great master of the modern art in Germany, excited, together with the disappointment experienced by many who were unable to obtain admission, induced the Director of the Theatre to make an offer to the composer, of a certain consideration, if he would condescend once more to appear in public, and assist at a repetition of the same music. With this request he complied, and in addition to the pieces before performed, he offered them a manuscript terzetto, with Italian words, which was accordingly performed, and considered by the numerous Italian amateurs in Vienna, as a kind of compliment paid by the composer to themselves.—The performance went off with still greater éclat than on the former occasion, and this new composition was hailed by all with no less enthusiasm than the other works.[1]

Even from so far away as New York, Beethovenian novelties were applauded without any feeling that the composer was in any way beyond his public:

. . . The first part of the performance closed with the sublime and majestic chorus from the oratorio of the *Mount of Olives* by Beethoven, which was another of the full pieces, that has never before been presented to the public in this city. The connoisseurs and critics, those present who *had* confidence in the ability of the society, and those who had not—were all waiting with considerable solicitude, to hear this splendid effort of genius, and which may be justly ranked among the first compositions of the present day. We believe we may assert with confidence, that the expectations of all were fully realized; and with regard to many of the audience, far exceeded—the effect was indeed grand, and was heightened by the trumpet of Mr J. Petrie, and the excellent drums owned by the *Handel and Haydn Society*, and which were politely loaned for the

[1] *The Harmonicon*, II (October 1824), p. 181.

occasion.—Our limits forbid our enlarging on this admirable chorus . . .[1]

It was, in fact, the critics with preconceived ideas who found most of the difficulties. The reviewer of a first performance of the Ninth Symphony in London clearly had his own ideas about what a symphony should contain:

The new symphony of Beethoven, composed for, and purchased at a liberal price by, this society, was now first publicly produced. In our last number we mentioned it, and we see no reason for altering the opinion we there offered. We must, however, correct our statement as to its duration. At a rehearsal, where so many interruptions occur, it is next to impossible to ascertain exactly the length of a piece: we now find this to be precisely one hour and five minutes; a fearful period indeed, which puts the muscles and lungs of the band, and the patience of the audience, to a severe trial. In the present symphony we discover no diminution of Beethoven's creative talent; it exhibits many perfectly new traits, and in its technical formation shews amazing ingenuity and unabated vigour of mind. But with all the merits that it unquestionably possesses, it is at least twice as long as it should be; it repeats itself, and the subjects in consequence become weak by reiteration. The last movement, a chorus, is heterogeneous, and though there is much vocal beauty in parts of it, yet it does not, and no habit will ever make it, mix up with the three first movements. This chorus is a hymn to joy, commencing with a recitative, and relieved by many *soli* passages. What relation it bears to the symphony we could not make out; and here, as well as in other parts, the want of intelligible design is too apparent. In our next we shall give the words of the chorus, with a translation; in the present number our printer has not been able to find room for them. The most original feature in this symphony is the minuet, and the most singular part, the succeeding trio,—striking, because in duple time, for which we are not acquainted with anything in the shape of a precedent. We were also much pleased by a very noble march, which is introduced. In quitting the present subject, we must express our hope that this new

[1] From an account of a concert given by the New York Choral Society in *The Harmonicon*, II (December 1824), p. 223.

work of the great Beethoven may be put into a produceable form; that the repetitions may be omitted, and the chorus removed altogether; the symphony will then be heard with unmixed pleasure, and the reputation of its author will, if possible, be further augmented.[1]

This discrepancy between critic and public is polarized still further in yet another review of this same performance:

There can be nothing so distressing to the feelings of a true artist as to see, and be obliged to notice, the partial failures of great men, whose productions have been the ornament of the art they cultivate. With such feelings we may suppose an artist to view a work of some mighty master, which, from the precision and finish displayed in parts of it, he would say, 'if this were the production of an aspiring artist for fame, it must be considered an extraordinary performance; but knowing it to proceed from the pencil of one, with whose former works I and the rest of the world have been delighted and astonished, I cannot but feel that it falls infinitely short of them, and consequently fails to satisfy the minds of his true admirers'. Such was the effect produced upon my mind, when the new grand symphony of Beethoven's was tried for the third time, at the Philharmonic, ushered into notice as it were by the flattering accounts from Germany of its magnificence and grandeur, supported by a most zealous and indefatigable conductor (Sir G. Smart), performed by a band, containing some of the most talented musicians in Europe accustomed daily to the music of this wonderful genius, incited by its novelty and reported excellence, and, lastly, rehearsing it before a select company of musicians and amateurs, who, impressed like myself with a sense of Beethoven's wonderful powers, anxiously awaited opportunities of bestowing that warm and energetic applause, which from such men should be given to those compositions only that unequivocally display the hand of the master. Before I enter into a brief detail of the beauties and defects of this symphony, it may be right at once to say, that its length alone will be a never-failing cause of complaint to those who reject monopoly in sounds, as it takes up exactly one hour and

[1] *The Harmonicon*, III (April 1825), p. 69.

twenty minutes in performance, which is not compensated by any beauty or unity of design, taking the composition as a whole.

. . . To say that the symphony was not loudly applauded would be to utter a direct untruth. The members of the Philharmonic were anxious to make it go off to the very best advantage, which heaven forbid they should not. There ought and ever will be different feelings and opinions on musical as well as upon political, scientific, or literary subjects, and I am the last to wish it should be otherwise. I merely give my candid and unbiased opinion. I am as zealous an admirer of the composer, as any one of those who would (how wisely remains to be proved) exalt this symphony above everything else he has written, as my opinions on subjects involving improvement are never connected with other feelings or views, and as I have long been in the habit of carefully comparing different great effects, I have come to a decision in my own mind, that until any one (and he must be a subtle logician indeed) can persuade me that bad is good or that black is white, I must ever consider this new symphony as the least excellent of any Beethoven has produced, as an unequal work, abounding more in noise, eccentricity, and confusion of design, than in those grand and lofty touches he so well knows how to make us feel—such as those of the symphony in C minor, in most of his splendid slow movements, and in the fine movement, the 'heroica' of the seventh symphony, which will remain an ever-during monument of his amazing genius.

One great excuse remains for all this want of perfection. It is to be remembered, that the great composer is afflicted with an incurable disorder (deafness), which to powers like his must be a deprivation more acute and distressing than any one can possibly imagine. May not this disturb a mind gifted with such extraordinary genius ? Age is stealing upon him, and every one must see from daily experience, that age, unaccompanied by domestic happiness, seldom improves the temper, and now the homage of the world is divided as it were between himself and Von Weber . . . More than this, Beethoven, we are told, reads of the world, although he sees and hears but little of it; he finds no doubt, as a man of penetration and sense, that throughout civilised society superficial education, manners, and habits are now generally adopted by the 'million';

he finds from all the public accounts, that noisy extravagance of execution and outrageous clamour in musical performances, more frequently ensures applause than chastened elegance or refined judgement—the inference therefore that we may fairly make is, that he writes accordingly. He writes to suit the present mania, and if this be so, he has succeeded in his purpose, for everywhere I hear the praises of his last work. The truth is, that elegance, purity and propriety, as principles of our art, have been gradually yielding with the altered manners of the time to multifarious and superficial accomplishments, with frivolous and affected manners. Minds that from education and habit can think of little else than dress, fashion, intrigue, novel reading, and dissipation, are not likely to feel the elaborate and less feverish pleasures of science and art . . .[1]

A few years later Mendelssohn was finding the situation much the same. Beethoven was obviously too highbrow for the provincial Munich public—that is, until this public had the chance to judge for itself:

I have often played to Goethe in the morning hours. He wanted to get an idea of how music has developed and wished to hear the music of different composers in chronological order. He seemed rather wary of Beethoven; but I could not spare him this acquaintance because he had to hear 'where sounds had turned to', and so I played for him the first movement of the C minor symphony which he liked very much . . . Here, in Munich, the musicians . . . believe that good music may be considered a heaven sent gift, but just *in abstracte*, and as soon as they sit down to play they produce the stupidest, silliest stuff imaginable, and when people do not like it they pretend that it was still too highbrow. Even the best pianists had no idea that Mozart and Haydn had also composed for the piano; they had just the faintest notion of Beethoven and consider the music of Kalkbrenner, Field and Hummel classical and scholarly. On the other hand, having played myself several times, I found the audience so receptive and open-minded that I felt doubly vexed by those frivolities. Recently, at a soirée given by a Countess, who is supposed to lead in fashion, I had an outbreak. The young ladies, quite able to perform adequate pieces very

[1] *The Quarterly Musical Magazine and Review*, VII (1825), pp. 80 ff.

nicely, tried to break their fingers with juggler's tricks and rope-dancer's feats of Herz's; when I was asked to play, I thought: well, if you get bored it serves you right, and started right out with the C-sharp minor sonata of Beethoven. When I finished, I noticed that the impression had been enormous; the ladies were weeping, the gentlemen hotly discussing the importance of the work. I had to write down a number of Beethoven sonatas for the female pianists who wanted to study them.[1]

And again, he found the critics and theorists behind the public:

You say, Fanny, that I should become a missionary and convert Onslow and Reicha to a love for Beethoven and Sebastian Bach. That is just what I am endeavouring to do. But remember, my dear child, that these people do not know a single note of 'Fidelio', and believe Bach to be nothing but a wig stuffed with learning. I played Onslow the overture to 'Fidelio' on a very bad piano, and he became quite distracted, scratched his head, added the orchestration in his mind, at last sang with me; in short went quite mad with delight. The other day, at the request of Kalkbrenner, I played the organ preludes in E minor and B minor. My audience pronounced them both 'wonderfully pretty', and one of them remarked that the beginning of the prelude in A minor was very much like a favourite duet in an opera by Monsigny. Everything went green and blue before my eyes.[2]

Today, it is usually assumed that the period immediately after an artist's death tends to be the nadir of his reputation. George Hogarth writing for a London audience probably orientated more to Italian opera and Mendelssohn than to philosophy of the German kind was nevertheless warmly appreciative:

Germany, during the seventeenth century, produced a great number of excellent musicians, several of whom once enjoyed high reputation, but their works are now utterly forgotten, and little more is known of them than their names, a catalogue of which

---

[1] From a letter to Carl Friedrich Zelter dated Munich, 22 June 1830, in Felix Mendelssohn, *Letters*, ed. G. Selden-Goth (London, 1946), p. 81.

[2] From a letter of Mendelssohn's to his family dated Paris, 20 April 1825, in ibid., p. 32.

would be wholly uninteresting. At that period, the music of the Germans was distinguished by learning and depth, rather than facility and grace; by intricate combinations of harmony, rather than flowing and expressive air. This, indeed, is in a considerable degree the character of the German music to this day, when compared to that of Italy. But the more recent German composers have drawn, from the fountain of Italian melody, draughts which have awakened their imagination and refined their taste; their music has gained beauty and simplicity, without losing the richness of its harmony. In saying this, we mean it to apply to those only who have studied the Italian models, for it is undeniable, that much of the German music is still dry and overlaboured, abounding in rugged combinations, and deficient in smooth and agreeable strains, partaking too much, in short, of the qualities of *saur-kraut*, to all but German tastes. We mean our remark to apply to all the music of Mozart, to most of that of Haydn, to those parts of all the greatest works of Beethoven, where the most enchanting strains of melody come upon the ear, through his wild and gloomy masses of sound, like gleams of sunshine through the clouds and darkness of an April sky; and, finally, to the best and happiest effusions of Weber and Spohr . . .

As a musician, Beethoven must be classed along with Handel, Haydn, and Mozart. He alone is to be compared to them in the magnitude of his works, and their influence on the state of the art. Though he has written little in the department to which Handel devoted all the energies of his mind, yet his spirit, more than that of any other composer, is akin to that of Handel. In his music there is the same gigantic grandeur of conception, the same breadth and simplicity of design, and the same absence of minute finishing and petty details. In Beethoven's harmonies the masses of sound are equally large, ponderous, and imposing as those of Handel, while they have a deep and gloomy character peculiar to himself. As they swell in our ears, and grow darker and darker, they are like the lowering storm-cloud on which we gaze till we are startled by the flash, and appalled by the thunder which bursts from its bosom. Such effects he has especially produced in his wonderful symphonies. They belong to the tone of his mind, and are without a parallel in the whole range of music. Even where he does not wield the strength of a great orchestra, in his instrumental concerted pieces, his quartets, his trios, and his sonatas for the piano-forte, there is the same broad and massive harmony, and the same wild, unexpected, and startling effects. Mingled with these, in his orchestral as well as his chamber music, there are strains of melody inexpressibly impassioned and ravishing; strains which do not merely please, but dissolve in pleasure; which do not merely move, but overpower with emotion. Of these divine melodies, a remarkable feature is their extreme simplicity. A few notes, as artless as those of a national air, are sufficient to awake the most exquisite feelings.

The music of Beethoven is stamped with the peculiarities of the man. When slow and tranquil in its movement, it has not the placid composure of Haydn, or the sustained tenderness of Mozart; but it is grave, and full of deep and melancholy thought. When rapid, it is not brisk or lively, but agitated and changeful—full of 'sweet and bitter fancies'—of storm and sunshine—of bursts of passion sinking into the subdued accents of grief, or relieved by transient gleams of hope or joy. There are movements, indeed, to which he gives the designation of *scherzoso*, or playful; but this playfulness is unlike as possible to the constitutional jocularity to which Haydn loved to give vent in the *finales* of his symphonies and quartets. If, in a movement of this kind, Beethoven sets out a tone of gaiety, his mood changes involuntarily—the smile fades away, as it were, from his features—and he falls into a train of sombre ideas, from which he ever and anon recovers himself, as if with an effort, and from a recollection of the nature of his subject. The rapid *scherzos*, which he has substituted for the older form of the minuet, are wild, impetuous, and fantastic; they have often the air of that violent and fitful vivacity to which gloomy natures are liable; their mirth may be compared to that of the bacchanalian effusion of the doomed Caspar. They contain, however, many of Beethoven's most original and beautiful conceptions; and are strikingly illustrative of the character of his mind.

The works composed by Beethoven in the latter years of his life are not so generally known or relished as his earlier productions. These earlier compositions are clear in design, and so broad and simple in their effects, that, when they receive justice from the performers, they at once strike everyone who is susceptible of the influence of music. In his more recent works, his meaning is obscure, and in many instances, incomprehensible. He has cast away all established models, and not only thrown his movements into new and unprecedented forms, but has introduced the same degree of novelty into all their details. The phrases of his melody are new; his harmonies are new; his disposition of parts is new; and his sudden changes of time, of measure, and of key, are frequently not explicable on any received principles of the art.

It is in his symphonies that the powers of Beethoven's genius are most fully displayed. The symphony in C minor stands alone and unrivalled; and the *Sinfonia Pastorale* is probably the finest piece of descriptive music in existence. Every movement of this charming work is a scene, and every scene is full of the most beautiful images of rural nature and rural life. We feel the freshness of a summer morning. We hear the rustling of the breeze, the waving of the woods, the cheerful notes of birds, and the cries of animals. We stray along the margin of a meandering brook, and listen to the murmuring of its waters. We join a group of villagers, keeping holiday with joyous songs and dances. The sky grows dark, the thunder growls, and a storm bursts on the alarmed rustics, whose cries of dismay are heard amidst the strife of the elements. The clouds pass away, the muttering of the thunder is more and more distant; all becomes quiet and placid, and the stillness is broken by the pastoral song of gratitude. Nothing can be more beautiful or more true to nature then every part of this representation. *It requires no key, no explanation—but places every image before the mind with a distinctness which neither poetry nor painting could surpass, and with a beauty which neither of these could equal.*[1]

And though there were those who scoffed at the later music as yet hardly known, even these could scarcely deny him his due:

. . . Since the time of Haydn, no composer has created so wide a schism in the musical public of Europe as Beethoven. The question at issue can of course be decided by posterity alone. Doubts have

[1] George Hogarth, *Musical history, biography, and criticism* (2nd ed., London, 1838), I, p. 94, and II, pp. 143 and 152, respectively.

been expressed, however, by many eminent professors, and among Beethoven's greatest admirers, as to whether some of his latter works will stand the test of time; nor are these doubts likely to be removed by the charge of 'paltriness' with which he threatened all such as should express their inability to comprehend these productions. There is reason to fear that Beethoven suffered the moodiness of his temper to affect the productions of his muse, and was thus induced to fill his music with crude innovations out of a morbid opposition to existing opinion. He never could bear to hear his early works admired, yet it may be confidently said that many of these are among his finest and most lasting productions. Beethoven was a great scoffer at the rules of composition, and has recorded his opinion of them in terms of unmeasured contempt. Sometimes, when in good humour and conversing with his professional friends on his delinquencies in this respect, he would rub his hands with delight, saying 'Aye, aye, I should like to see what you gentlemen with your treatises on harmony would say to that'. In this scorn of rules he has been followed by Rossini, who writes against the errors in his scores '*per saddisfazione de' pedanti*' (for the edification of the pedants).

Of Beethoven's music it may be said briefly and generally, that in melody, the soul of music, as Mozart called it, he is inferior both to him and to Haydn. There are few, we suspect, who will not acknowledge that the melodies in each of these latter writers, which have become 'familiar as household words' to us, far exceed in number, if not in quality, those furnished by Beethoven; but in the stern and massive grandeur of his harmonies he has certainly never been surpassed, perhaps never equalled, by any one but Handel.

If the scepticism we have alluded to respecting some of Beethoven's latter works should prove well founded, it may be fortunate for his reputation that he did not live any longer; but it has lately been asserted that the post-humous quartets, upon which there exists so great a difference of opinion, are not genuine; that is, that they have been put together by some enterprising publisher from detached scraps of manuscript found among Beethoven's papers.[1]

[1] *The Penny Magazine*, 11 January 1840, p. 14.

But adulation is more typical of the time, and the reviewer of the *Biographie Universelle des Musiciens* in *The Boston Quarterly Review* is one of those to begin the erection of the pedestal which was to dominate the 1840s:

His music is a true picture of his life. Each thought that dawned upon him was transferred to the note-book, which he held always in his hand; and in some inspired moment, when fancy wooed him, and the fullness of his heart forced him to expression, they were imprisoned upon the immortal pages of his music. Beethoven has done for his art, what Shakspeare[1] [*sic*] has done for literature, and Raphael for painting. The grandeur of Bach and Handel existed in him, but it is softened, and rendered entrancing, by the drapery of his vivid imagination. The music of the two great fathers of the art, like the stern and solitary figures of Michael Angelo, inspires us with awe;— Beethoven's harmony, like the bewitching grouping of Raphael, vanquishes by the power of its blended beauty. With a versatility like that of Shakspeare, he has arrayed the passions in the most powerful of epic imagery, dwarfing them not in outline, but with all the shading that is thrown over them by the varieties of human character; and with an eye for beauty, that roamed like a poet's over the world, he painted on to thin air, the fairest scenes of nature. No unmeaning straws, no idle vagaries deform the pages of his music; —he never relinquished the unity which he knew to be the soul of composition. No harmonist has ever penetrated so far into the unknown regions of sound; the gloomy, the mysterious, the fanciful, the pathetic, all ministered to the operations of the mighty spirit. Doomed by his infirmity to an existence of solitude, while the prison of his deafness was narrowing slowly around him, without companionship, save his own great thoughts, and his stringless piano, we cannot wonder that his conception became coloured by the sadness of his destiny; and as has been truly said, his imagination seemed feeding on the ruins of his sensitive organs.

[1] The comparison with Shakespeare has been made many times. A writer in *AMZ* (XV, 1813–14, pp. 806 f.) as early as December 1813 had made it with some interesting suggestions for Beethoven to compose some overtures on Shakespearean subjects, to be played at the theatre as interludes. The writer thought of *Macbeth, Romeo and Juliet* and *The Tempest* as especially suitable for 'the greatest romantic of music'.

505

This is used to preface a plea:

A love of music is incorporating itself into our national character; slowly, it is true, but surely; contending step by step with national peculiarities. It will never sway us, as it does the Italian, with the impetuosity of a passion; or inspire us with that tenderness of imagination and perseverance in embodying conception, which accompanies the musical enthusiasm of the German; but we shall in time experience it with calmness, and regulate it with judgment; and with that pride in the reputation of our country, which has never yet been wanting, we shall not suffer her to be indifferent to the works of true genius, under whatever form they may appear.[1]

The canonization was more or less complete with the Beethoven festival in Bonn in 1845, and the unveiling of the statue there on 12 August 1848. That early English Beethovenian, William Gardiner, was at the latter to hear the performance of the *Missa solemnis* conducted by Liszt:

The evening performance commenced with the Posthumous Mass, the most wonderful of all Beethoven's inspirations. It is cast upon a scale too vast for the ordinary service of the Catholic Church. He intended it for the solemn occasion of the crowning or death of a monarch. It opens with a grand burst from all the instruments. As this sound dies away, a soft breathing note steals from the voices of the females, as if it had begun on the other side of the Rhine. Into this, creeps a lower tone from the mezzo, followed by the mellifluous tenor; a combination of harmony so luscious, as to wrap the soul in forgetfulness—during which, for a time, it remains unconscious of everything, but the music of another world. To describe this magical work would be a vain attempt. Since I returned, I have met with a more sober description from the pen of Mr Hogarth:—

> The mass was generally regarded as an incomprehensible production, the depths of which (if they really were depths) it was impossible to fathom. This opinion, I confess, I adopted; but however mistaken, it was conscientiously formed. Nobody in England tried to perform it; and an examination of the score was the only means of judging . . .'

[1] *The Boston Quarterly Review*, III (July 1840), p. 332.

Such is the general case in England at this day, where the *Missa Solennis* is as completely unknown as on the day it was published. The Germans, however, have mastered it, and the performance of last night displayed it in all its grandeur and beauty . . . Like all great and original works of art, it will be slowly understood and appreciated; but the time will come (though I shall not live to see it) when the *Missa Solennis* of Beethoven will be regarded as we now regard the greatest works of Handel.[1]

By this time, Beethoven had become more than a musician; he was a symbol of modernity, a substitute even for conventional religious beliefs. Schumann in combating such adulation adds his own poetic attitude to the legend:

I had to laugh—Florestan began, as he launched into the A major Symphony—I had to laugh at a dry old actuary who found in it a battle of giants, and in the last movement their final destruction—though he had to pass lightly over the Allegretto because it didn't fit into his plan . . . But most of all my fingers itch to get at those who insist that Beethoven always presented in his symphonies the most exalted sentiments: lofty ideas about God, immortality, and the courses of the stars. While the floral crown of the genius, to be sure, points to the heavens, his roots are planted in his beloved earth.

Now about the symphony itself; this idea is not my own, but taken from an old volume of *Cäcilia* (though there the setting is changed to the parlour of a count, perhaps out of too great a diffidence for Beethoven—which was misguided) . . . it is a most merry wedding. The bride is an angelic child with a rose in her hair, but only one. Unless I am greatly mistaken, in the Introduction the guests gather together, greeting each other with inverted commas, and, unless I am wrong, merry flutes recall that in the entire village, full of maypoles with many-coloured ribbons, there reigns joy for the bride Rosa. And unless I am mistaken, the pale mother looks at her with a trembling glance that seems to ask, 'Do you know that now we must part?' And Rosa, overcome, throws herself into her arms, drawing after her, with the other hand, that of the bridegroom . . . Now it becomes very still in the village outside (here

[1] William Gardiner, *Music and Friends*, III (London and Leicester, 1853) p. 330.

Florestan came to the Allegretto, taking passages from it here and there); only a butterfly flits past or a cherry blossom falls . . . The organ begins; the sun is high in the sky, and single long, oblique rays play upon particles of dust throughout the church. The bells ring vigorously—parishioners arrive a few at a time—pews are clapped open and shut—some peasants peer into hymnbooks, others gaze up at the superstructure—the procession draws closer—first choirboys with lighted candles and censers, then friends who often look back at the couple accompanied by the priest—then the parents, friends of the bride, and finally all the young people of the village. And now all is in order and the priest approaches the altar, and speaks first to the bride, and then to the happiest of men. And he admonishes them about the sacred responsibilities and purposes of this union, and bids them find their happiness in profound harmony and love; then he asks for the 'I do' that is to last forever; and the bride pronounces it firmly and deliberately—I don't want to continue this picture, and you can do it your own way in the finale. Florestan thus broke off abruptly and tore into the close of the Allegretto; the sound was as if the sacristan was slamming the doors so that the noise reverberated through the whole church.[1]

It is not far from fanciful interpretation of this kind to the use of Beethoven's reputation as propaganda for other musical philosophies. Although Wagner was probably the greatest and most understanding of Beethoven's propagandists, it is difficult to acquit him of the charge of using Beethoven to further theories which he would never have nourished himself:

Young Beethoven . . . we see daring the world from the first with that defiant temper which kept him in almost savage independence his whole life through: a stupendous sense-of-self, supported by the proudest spirit, armed him at every hour against the frivolous demands addressed to Music by a world of pleasure. Against the importunities of an etiolated taste, he had a treasure of inestimable price to guard. In those same forms, in which Music was expected to merely shew herself a pleasing art, he had to proclaim the divinations of the inmost world of Tone. Thus he is at all

[1] L. B. Plantinga, *Schumann as critic* (New Haven and London, 1967), p. 67.

times like a man possessed; for to him in truth applies what Schopenhauer has said of the Musician in general: he speaks the highest
wisdom in a tongue his reason (*Vernunft*) does not understand.

The 'Vernunft' of his art he found in that spirit which had built
the formal framework of its outer scaffolding. And what a scant
Vernunft it was that spoke to him from that architectonic poise of
periods, when he saw how even the greatest masters of his youth
bestirred themselves with banal repetition of flourishes and phrases,
with mathematical distribution of loud and soft, with regulation
introductions of just so many solemn bars, and the inevitable
passage through the gate of just so many half-closes to the saving
uproar of the final cadence! 'Twas the Vernunft that had formed the
operatic aria, dictated the stringing-together of operatic numbers,
the logic that made Haydn chain his genie to an everlasting count-
ing of his rosary beads. For Religion had vanished from the Church
with Palestrina's music, and the artificial formalism of Jesuit
observance had counterformed Religion and Music alike. So the
thoughtful visitor finds venerable Rome disguised beneath the
Jesuit architecture of the last two centuries; so glorious Italian
painting turned to slops and sugar; so, and under the selfsame lead,
arose French 'classic' poetry, in whose spirit-slaying laws we may
trace a speaking likeness to the laws of construction of the operatic
Aria and the Sonata.

We know that it was the 'German spirit', so terribly dreaded and
hated 'across the mountains', that stepped into the field of Art, as
everywhere else, to heal this artfully induced corruption of the
European race. As in other realms we have hailed our Lessing,
Goethe, Schiller and the rest, as our rescuers from that corruption,
today we have to shew that in this musician Beethoven, who spoke
the purest speech of every nation, the German spirit redeemed the
spirit of mankind from deep disgrace. For inasmuch as Music had
been degraded to a merely pleasing art, and by dint of her ownest
essence he raised her to the height of her sublime vocation, he has
set open for us the understanding of that art which explains the
world to everyone as surely as the profoundest philosophy could
ever explain it to the abstract thinker. *And herein lies the unique
relation of great Beethoven to the German people,* which we now

will try to follow through the special features of his life and work, so far as known to us . . .

Nothing can yield us a more instructive answer as to the relation borne by the Artist's modus operandi to the synthetic operations of the Reason, than a correct apprehension of the course pursued by Beethoven in the unfolding of his musical genius. For it to have been a logical procedure, he must consciously have changed, or even overthrown the outward forms of music; but we never light upon a trace of that. Assuredly there never was an artist who pondered less upon his art. The aforesaid brusque impetuosity of his nature shews us how he felt as an actual personal injury, almost as direct as every other shackle of convention, the ban imposed upon his genius by those forms. Yet his rebellion consisted in nothing but the exuberant unfolding of his inner genius, unrestrainable by those outward forms themselves. Never did he radically alter an existing form of instrumental music; in his last sonatas, quartets, symphonies and so forth, we may demonstrate beyond dispute a structure such as of the first. But compare these works with one another; compare e.g. the Eighth Symphony in F with the Second in D, and marvel at the wholly new world that fronts us in wellnigh the identical form!

Here is shewn once more the idiosyncrasy of German nature, that profoundly inward gift which stamps its mark on every form by moulding it afresh from within, and thus is saved from the necessity of outward overthrow. Thus is the German no revolutionary, but a reformer; and thus he wins at last a wealth of forms for the manifesting of his inner nature, as never another nation. In the Frenchman this deep internal spring seems silted up: wherefore, when troubled by the outer forms of matters in his State or art, he fancies he must dash it into atoms, as though the new, the pleasanter form would thereafter leap into existence of itself.[1]

The Wagnerians naturally followed. Hans von Bülow even develops the nationalism inherent in his master's views quite blatantly in a speech after a concert by the Berlin Philharmonic Orchestra in 1892:

[1] *Richard Wagner's Prose Works*, trans. W. Ashton Ellis, V (London 1896), pp. 83 ff.

We need not seek farther whom we must put down on the title page of the *Eroica*. We musicians dedicate and consecrate with heart and brain, with hand and lips, the *Eroica* symphony to the greatest hero that has seen the light of day since Beethoven. We dedicate it to Beethoven's twin, the Beethoven of German politics, the Prince Bismarck. Prince Bismarck, hail![1]

Surprisingly, such views were less widespread than might be imagined in a period when nationalism became pronounced as a political force. In the Nazi era, Wagner was the arch priest, Beethoven apparently considered to be above such considerations. Furtwängler, writing a preface to yet another reappraisal of man and music, began:

Scarcely any other German name has been accorded such veneration through the entire world as that of Beethoven. If it is not in the same sense *volkstümlich* as are the creations of Wagner or Schubert, Beethoven's work yet possesses a spiritual power that Germany does not possess elsewhere in the art of music. Through no one else is the force and greatness of German perception and being brought to such penetrating expression.[2]

But in the end Furtwängler is less interested in the nationalist concept than Beethoven's overwhelming musicality. Perhaps, in fact, it was the reaction against Beethoven as a nationalist that had more effect on musicians. Verdi certainly felt the dangers of the Beethoven legend for the Italian composer at a time when the cult of the foreigner was probably quite strong in snobbish intellectual circles:

Twelve or fifteen years ago, I can't remember whether it was in Milan or somewhere else, they asked me to become the president of a String Quartet Society. I refused and said: Why not found a society for vocal quartets? This would be an Italian thing. The other is a German art. Perhaps this was blasphemous then as now, but an institution for the performance of vocal quartets would be able to hear Palestrina, the best of his contemporaries, Marcello, etc. etc, and would be able to keep alive in us the love of singing,

---

[1] *Hans von Bülows Leben in seinen Briefen dargestellt*, ed. Marie von Bülow (2nd ed., Leipzig, 1921), p. 548; quotation and translation taken from Jacques Barzun, *Pleasures of Music* (London, 1952), p. 496.

[2] Wilhelm Furtwängler's preface to Walter Riezler, *Beethoven* (Zürich, 1936; repr. 1966), p. 9.

the highest form of which is opera. Now everyone has a tendency towards instrumentation and harmonization. The alpha and the omega: the Ninth Symphony of Beethoven (sublime in its first three movements, bad as a structure in its last movement). No one will ever reach the heights of the first part of it; but they will imitate so easily the bad writing for the voice of the last one and, with the authority of Beethoven behind them, they cry: it must be done like this . . .[1]

Looking through the pages of the *Gazzetta Musicale di Milano* (the Ricordi journal which occupied a similar position in Italy to the *Musical Times* in England), it becomes clear that Beethoven was more honoured than played. Though the symphonies and some piano sonatas were heard, the predominance of the opera house prevented his music from becoming a central feature of Italian musical life. *Fidelio* was first given in Rome only in February 1886, to receive a not very encouraging review in the *Gazzetta Musicale*:

In Rome, the name of Beethoven has been surrounded by a kind of veneration. In all the orchestral concert programmes it has figured with all due honour. There has been, however, quite suddenly someone who has felt the need to expose it to an unpleasant examination, neither more nor less than if it was the name of a beginner from whom good or bad can be hoped. I do not know how Doctor Lamperti came to announce *Fidelio* on the programme of the Apollo Theatre; it must be that he had no exact idea of the work and of the necessary means to give it a worthy interpretation. The artistic education of our public has progressed a lot recently, but anyway, if one wants to make a work of art produce the desired effect, it is necessary to present it under its true colours and in its most favourable light.

I will leave aside the objections which can be made in the choice of the work. *Fidelio* has nothing to add to Beethoven's reputation. It is a most interesting work to those who wish to study the achievement of this great composer from all angles; in a theatre which possessed a great repertoire of old and modern scores, it should certainly be given; but it has been observed wisely that in

---

[1] *Giuseppe Verdi: autobiografia dalle lettere*, ed. Aldo Oberdorfer (Milan, 1941): letter dated April 1878, p. 325.

Italy, and especially in Rome, various other masterpieces unknown to the public should be staged before *Fidelio*. I have no intention to embark on a close analysis of the music, in which Beethoven's genius is certainly to be found everywhere; but at the same time it remains true that it confirms the view that the composer of the Ninth Symphony was uncomfortable in writing for voices, and was at a disadvantage working within the limits, however august, of a stage action. But leaving aside the infantile and fatuous libretto, the thin theatricality of *Fidelio* is obvious from the forms and the development of the musical pieces, very few excepted. What an immense distance, in this respect, between Mozart and Beethoven; and to think that in Rome they do not know Mozart's *Don Giovanni*, which has been heard for one night only, cut quite horribly, at the Apollo![1]

In France, the development of the concert societies obviated such difficulties; and the early enthusiasm of the musical public for Beethoven was continued even after the 1870 war with Prussia had started the conscious revulsion against things Germanic. Now Beethoven became the deliverer of the oppressed, of whatever nationality. He was, for some, the musician of socialism, as we find in one of the essays in Edgar Quinet's collection, *Ce que dit la musique*; for him the Ninth Symphony is a work dedicated to

The liberty that Beethoven celebrated, liberty as the just, the wise hero understands it . . . at last [comes] the hymn of deliverance, of resurgent liberty, of France born anew, the hymn of a republic which is unshakeable and unswerving if all Frenchmen unite in an immense patriotism—'All Men become Brethren' is 'the Marseillaise of humanity'.[2]

It was this kind of writing that dominated much criticism in the latter part of the nineteenth century, reaching its climax in the little book by Romain Rolland first published in 1903. Beethoven the socialist here comes very much to the fore in the selection of documents and letters that Rolland quotes at length. The extremely doubtful letter of Beethoven to Bettina von Arnim describing Beethoven's refusal to bow to the

[1] *Gazzetta Musicale di Milano*, 14 February 1886.
[2] Edgar Quinet, *Ce que dit la musique*, quoted in Leo Schrade, *Beethoven in France: the growth of an idea* (New Haven, 1942), p. 135.

Imperial family while in the presence of Goethe is given in full.[1] Still more does Rolland in his commentary on life and works stress Beethoven's 'message' of heroism and strength. Schrade[2] finds the whole of this early book an assault on the lack of self-confidence endemic in France after both the defeat in war and the Dreyfus affair. Whether this view is true or not, there can be no doubt that Rolland uses Beethoven to preach a message:

Beloved Beethoven! So many others have praised his artistic grandeur. But he is easily the first of musicians. He is the most heroic soul in modern art. He is the grandest and the best friend of those who suffer and struggle. When we are saddened by worldly miseries, it is he who comes near to us, as he used to go and play to a mother in grief, and without uttering a word thus console her by the song of his own plaintive resignation. And when we are utterly exhausted in the eternal battle uselessly waged against mediocrity, vice and virtue, it is an unspeakable boon to find fresh strength in this great ocean-torrent of strong will and faith. An atmosphere of courage emanates from his personality, a love of battle, the exultation of a conscious feeling of the *God within*. It seems that in his constant communion with nature he had ended by assimilating its deep and mighty powers. Grillparzer, who admired Beethoven with a kind of awe, said of him, 'He penetrated into regions where art melts away and unites with the wild and capricious elements.' Schumann wrote similarly of his *Symphony in C minor:* 'Every time it is performed it exercises an unvarying power on us, like natural phenomena which fill us with awe and amazement every time they occur.' And Schindler, his confidential friend, says, 'He possessed the spirit of nature.' It is true, 'Beethoven is a force of nature; and this battle of elemental power against the rest of nature is a spectacle of truly Homeric grandeur.'

His whole life is like a stormy day. At the beginning—a fresh clear morning, perhaps a languid breeze, scarcely a breath of air. But there is already in the still air a secret menace, a dark foreboding. Large shadows loom and pass; tragic rumblings; murmuring awesome silences; the furious gusts of the winds of the *Eroica*

[1] Romain Rolland, *Vie de Beethoven* (Paris, 1903), trans. B. Constance Hull (5th ed., London, 1924), p. 28.
[2] Op. cit., p. 159.

and the *C minor*. However, the freshness of the day is not yet gone. Joy remains joy; the brightness of the sky is not overcast; sadness is never without a ray of hope. But after 1810 the poise of the soul is disturbed. A strange light glows. Mists obscure his deepest thoughts; some of the clearer thoughts appear as vapour rising; they disappear, are dispelled, yet form anew; they obscure the heart with their melancholy and capricious gloom; often the musical idea seems to vanish entirely, to be submerged, but only to re-appear again at the end of a piece in a veritable storm of melody. Even joy has assumed a rough and riotous character. A bitter feeling becomes mingled in all his sentiments. Storms gather as evening comes on. Heavy clouds are big with tempests. Lightning flashes o'er the black of night. The climax of the hurricane is approaching. Suddenly, at the height of the tempest, the darkness is dispersed. Night is driven away and the clear, tranquil atmosphere is restored by a sheer act of will power. What a conquest was this! What Napoleonic battle can be likened to it? What was Austerlitz glory to the radiance of this superhuman effort, this victory, the most brilliant that has ever been won by an infirm and lonely spirit. Sorrow personified, to whom the world refused joy, created joy himself to give to the world. He forged it from his own misery, as he proudly said in reviewing his life. And indeed it was the motto of his whole heroic soul:

JOY THROUGH SUFFERING[1]

This is essentially a nineteenth-century view; or, more accurately, a pre-1914 one. After the First World War, such writing on Beethoven has diminished. Rolland's own later book on Beethoven, published in 1928, though not radically different in style, nevertheless gives a somewhat more balanced picture.

There had always been dissentient views, of course, even after the theorists had managed to assimilate Beethoven's novelties of technique. The very strength that was the attraction to the romantics was a stumbling-block to other observers. The Russian nobleman Alexandre Oulibicheff, writing in the light of the earliest biographies, especially the critical work of Wilhelm von Lenz, was inclined to see the later work as merely eccentric:

[1] Rolland, op. cit., pp. 52 ff.

515

A change took place in the great composer's character as a result of the malicious insinuations and smears that were put about in a deliberate and successful attempt to alienate him from his well-wishers; at the same time he was steadily losing his ability to sense certain harmonic and acoustic effects, which will be analysed in another chapter. The eccentricities and anomalies in his nature, which he had until then made efforts to restrain while he was composing, crept into his work, and the style of his second period disintegrated. Freakish bad temper gradually disrupted his inspiration and became audible in his ideas; he forgot important principles. From discovering unknown facets of beauty, in which his true originality lay, and which made great demands on his audiences, he had recourse by fits and starts to disagreeable and bizarre effects which constituted a facile originality, easily grasped by any casual hearer. Beethoven ceased to examine the validity of his ideas and became self-indulgent in their development and repetition; losing sight of the one essential principle of moderation, he failed to steer the middle course between overstatement and understatement which alone leads to success. In short, there are *longueurs* in the later works of Beethoven.[1]

He takes this still further when, after quoting a passage from the second movement of Beethoven's Quartet in F, Op. 135, he says:

If, after examining this fragment with the careful scrutiny it deserves, you think that Beethoven heard it in his mind as you can hear it with your ears, that he saw it on the paper with the same eyes as your own, and that he attached to it the sense, that is, the utter non-sense, that it conveys to every one of us, then it must be your opinion that Beethoven was not mad but an imbecile; for madmen reason like those who are not mad, their logic obeys the same laws as understanding and differs from the logic of ordinary men only in that they exercise it upon the delusions born of the hallucinations of their sick minds.[2]

But during most of the later nineteenth century such views should not always be taken too seriously: they often stem merely from the desire to

[1] Alexandre Oulibicheff, *Beethoven, ses critiques et ses glossateurs* (Leipzig and Paris, 1857), pp. 156 f.
[2] Ibid., p. 282.

dethrone a too acknowledged god. That professional debunker, George Bernard Shaw, although a firm supporter of Beethoven (as any Perfect Wagnerite had to be), could not resist an occasional throwing of a stone at something which seemed to be firmly accepted:

. . . Everybody acknowledges that the first movement of the Waldstein is a colossal piece of pianoforte music. I confess I have never been able to see it. It certainly was not colossal as Miss Zimmerman scampered through it, and for the life of me I do not know what else she could have done with a long, scrappy movement which is neither bravura nor tone poem, though it asserts itself occasionally in both directions. The allegretto, which is the really popular and interesting part of the sonata, was admirably played, the exposition of the theme being particularly happy. Miss Zimmerman got a double recall.[1]

The same desire to reduce to man-size, though not as naughtily as 'Corno di Bassetto', is evident in the review of Sir George Grove's eminently sensible book on the symphonies by an anonymous writer in the *Edinburgh Review* in 1896:

No great musical genius has suffered more lately from this kind of unreasoning adulation than Beethoven. To merely question the artistic propriety or perfection of anything which he wrote is to expose oneself to the charge of a kind of profanity. Why is a great composer, more than any other class of producer in art, to be exempt from all critical judgement as to his works? When J. Addington Symonds produced his admirable and thoughtful study on Michelangelo he did not hesitate, although the book originated in his great admiration for and interest in its subject, to endeavour to analyse and discriminate in regard to the productions of the artist, and to show where he was greatest and what were his limitations. Michelangelo was as great a genius as Beethoven—possibly greater, and most certainly a greater man; but no one thought of accusing Symonds of audacity for attempting a critical estimate of his genius. But any one who attempts to adopt the same attitude of critical consideration in regard to Beethoven excites among the ranks of professional musicians and musical critics

[1] G. B. Shaw, *London music in 1888–89 as heard by Corno di Bassetto (later known as Bernard Shaw)* (London, 1937), p. 68.

either anger or a kind of foolish surprise: 'he even criticises Beethoven', etc; as if the object of all art-criticism that is worth the name were not to get at the whole truth about art, and as if discriminating admiration were not a better homage to offer to any artist than mere blind prostration of the judgement before him. Those, we venture to think, who can judge in a dispassionate spirit the works of Beethoven, and who can realise when he was least successful, are also those who can appreciate most fully his highest and greatest works, though they may not be so ready to prate about them: the deepest and sincerest enthusiasm is not always the most loquacious.[1]

In the same review, the old opinion of the *Harmonicon* commentator[2] on the late works still finds an echo when its author turns to the Ninth Symphony:

In no composition, perhaps, has Beethoven shown such sustained grandeur and elevation of style, with the exception only of the rather eccentric and certainly not happy device of anticipating the real subject by the weak and uninteresting tentative passage, as it may be called, which mystifies the hearer at the opening. This is one of the eccentricities by which Beethoven sometimes vexes us unexpectedly in some of his greatest works. How far grander and more impressive would have been the immediate starting off with the broad and powerful unison passage which forms the real theme of the movement! And yet the modern Beethoven critics would persuade us that this preliminary passage is an added beauty, simply because it is there. But, with all the elevated style of the composition when it fairly commences, the earnest tone which pervades it, the breadth of phrasing (especially shown in the wide spaced intervals constantly employed in the bass), and the amount of interesting and highly finished detail in the orchestration, there seems to be a want of spontaneity and charm about it in comparison with many of the composer's earlier works; it has not that indefinable magic of beauty which we find in so many of its predecessors . . . As to the *adagio* . . . words can hardly do justice to its

[1] *Edinburgh Review*, No. 378 (July–October 1896), p. 455.
[2] See above. pp. 496–9.

beauty . . . It is with the *finale* that we have to drop into the questioning mood again. The theme to which the first verses of Schiller's ode are set is indeed a golden and immortal melody, such as once heard can never be forgotten. But in the prelude to it Beethoven has become materialistic again. The crashing discords which precede both the instrumental introduction and the subsequent vocal portion of the movement are obviously discords of set purpose, introduced in order to contrast with the 'joy' which is to follow, and the rebuke of the bass solo, 'Friends, not these tones', etc.; but this employment of music involves a perfectly false aesthetic. It is the employment of sounds which are literally and materially harsh, instead of the symbolising of harshness by the legitimate use of musical expression. The conversational recitative passages for the basses, in which they seem to comment on the themes offered to them, form a piquant piece of musical humour, but it has been much overrated; it is hardly a kind of device in keeping with a great and serious work of art, and it is, moreover, of a kind which becomes less effective the more one becomes familiarised with it. In the subsequent development of the music the composer seems to have lost his artistic balance altogether, and the expression of Fanny Mendelssohn when she first heard the symphony, which is quoted by Sir G. Grove, 'A gigantic tragedy with a conclusion meant to be dithyrambic, but falling from its height into the opposite extreme—into burlesque', is no more than the truth, however harsh the words may seem; and many people who hear it even now in their own hearts feel the same, if they would say the truth.

With this result we feel convinced that the composer's sad affliction of deafness had something to do . . . we are convinced that if Beethoven had still possessed his bodily faculty of hearing, he would not have written those 'crashes' at the commencement of the *finale*, nor the absurd grunts for the contrafagotto which introduce the march, nor the noisy and screaming passages through which the chorus have to scramble later on . . .

Nearly all this kind of criticism, however, seems directed less against the actual music than against the legend that had been created by the idolators. This is generally true of twentieth-century writing, which is less hostile than might be believed from the widespread changes in attitude to composition and aesthetics. At first sight, the ideals and aims of Debussy appear totally at odds with the Beethovenian tradition, and in Debussy's journalism there is an occasional hint of this, as in the following view of the Sixth Symphony, which only goes to show that a 'Back to Nature' movement is invariably eroded into seeming a 'Hymn to Convention' by the passage of time:

The popularity of the *Pastoral Symphony* is due to the widespread misunderstanding that exists between Man and Nature. Consider the scene on the banks of the stream: a stream to which it appears the oxen come to drink, so at least the bassoons would have us suppose; to say nothing of the wooden nightingale and the Swiss cuckoo-clock, more representative of the artistry of M. de Vaucanson than of genuine Nature. It is unnecessarily imitative, and the interpretation is entirely arbitrary.

How much more profound an interpretation of the beauty of a landscape do we find in other passages in the great Master, because, instead of an exact imitation, there is an emotional interpretation of what is invisible in Nature. Can the mystery of a forest be expressed by measuring the height of the trees? Is it not rather fathomless depths that stir the imagination?

In this symphony Beethoven inaugurates an epoch when Nature was seen only through the pages of books. This is proved by the storm, a part of this same symphony, where the terror of man and Nature is draped in the folds of the cloak of romanticism amid the rumblings of rather disarming thunder.

It would be absurd to imagine that I am wanting in respect for Beethoven; yet a musician of his genius may be deceived more completely than another. No man is bound to write nothing but masterpieces, and, if the *Pastoral Symphony* is so regarded, the expression must be weakened as a description of the other symphonies. That is all I mean.[1]

But Debussy's attitude to the Ninth Symphony, a field in which he was, as a composer, not in the slightest interested, reveals an understanding which previous commentaries often lacked:

[1] Claude Debussy, *M. Croche the dilettante hater*, trans. anon. (London, 1927), pp. 87 f.

A fog of verbiage and criticism surrounds the *Choral Symphony*. It is amazing that it has not been finally buried under the mass of prose which it has provoked. Wagner intended to complete the orchestration. Others fancied that they could explain and illustrate the theme by means of pictures. If we admit to a mystery in this Symphony we might clear it up; but is it worth while? There was not an ounce of literature in Beethoven, not at any rate in the accepted sense of the word. He had a great love of music, representing to him, as it did, the joy and passion piteously absent from his private life. Perhaps we ought in the *Choral Symphony* to look for nothing more than a magnificent gesture of musical pride. A little notebook with over two hundred different renderings of the dominant theme in the *Finale* of this symphony shows how persistently Beethoven pursued his search and how entirely musical his guiding motive was; Schiller's lines can have only been used for their appeal to the ear. Beethoven determined that his leading idea should be essentially self-developing, and, while it is of extraordinary beauty in itself, it becomes sublime because of its perfect response to his purpose. He is the most triumphant example of the moulding of an idea to the preconceived form; at each leap forward there is a new delight, without either effort or appearance of repetition; the magical blossoming, so to speak, of a tree whose leaves burst forth simultaneously. Nothing is superfluous in this stupendous work, not even the *Andante*, declared by modern aestheticism to be over long; is it not a subtly conceived pause between the persistent rhythm of the *Scherzo* and the instrumental flood that rolls the voices irresistibly onward to the glory of the *Finale*? Beethoven had already written eight symphonies and the figure nine seems to have had for him an almost mystic significance. He determined to surpass himself. I can scarcely see how his success can be questioned. The flood of human feeling which overflows the ordinary bounds of the symphony sprang from a soul drunk with liberty, which, by an ironical decree of fate, beat itself against the gilded bars within which the misdirected charity of the great had confined him. Beethoven must have suffered cruelly in his ardent longing that humanity should find utterance through him; hence the call of his thousand-voiced genius to the humblest and poorest of his brethren. Did they hear it? That is the question.[1]

Even more remarkable, perhaps, the ideas of the young men of the 1920s did not preclude acceptance of Beethoven's music, though now the reputations of the middle-period works are somewhat denigrated. Busoni, writing in 1916 to his pupil Egon Petri, remarks:

The Latin attitude to art, with its cool serenity and its insistence on outward form, is what refreshes me. It was only through Beethoven that music acquired that growling and frowning expression which was natural enough to him, but which perhaps ought to have remained his lonely path alone. Why are you in such a bad temper, one would often like to ask, especially in the second period.[2]

And the desire for a condensed rather than an expansive musical style led him to develop this idea in his more public writing:

. . . in the first of Beethoven's creative periods feeling overcomes helplessness, in the third period this same feeling, coming up from the depths, drowns the acquired mastery.

In the middle period, on the other hand, feeling withdraws before symphonic expansion and splendour of forms. The second period of Beethoven's is the exploitation of the strong ideas in the first period. The passionate defiance of the 'Pathétique' remained the basis for ideas in all similar moods of sound during the following periods, from the Fifth Symphony onwards, only more expanded, adorned, and underlined. But the expansion stands in bad relationship to the extensiveness of the melodic element which gets lost on a kind of—what shall I say?—plateau of modulatory and figurative eloquence.

I am thinking, for example, of the exposition in the first movement of the 'Appassionata' where the great rising and persistence in temperament takes the place of subject matter. It is the thrilling eloquence—his own—the infectious conviction of the orator, instead of his theme, which affects the listener here; it has an impact on larger masses of people and makes a more sudden impact. Temperament puts a mask of more physical uncontrol-

---

[1] Ibid., pp. 29 f.
[2] Edward J. Dent, *Ferruccio Busoni* (London, 1933), p. 230.

lability before thought and the emotion of feeling, that is without thought or feeling.[1]

Cecil Gray takes up the theme in his history of music, written presumably during the grand centenary jamboree of 1927, in which at least some of the old legends had been resurrected, even to the point of making Beethoven a Fleming, and thus making him an internationalist rather than a nationalist (as though this were not self-evident in the music). Gray seems rather snobbish: however sophisticated we may be, the freedoms for which Shelley and Beethoven fought in their different ways are hardly less desirable today, nor are we much nearer to achieving them:

. . . Professor Dent, for example, in his 'Terpander; or Music and the Future', questions whether Beethoven's music 'is still convincing to modern ears'. If by this the writer means the Beethoven of the middle period, the composer of the *Emperor Concerto*, the *Waldstein* and *Appassionata Sonatas*, the *Rasoumoffsky Quartets*, and the *Fifth* and *Sixth Symphonies*, he is unquestionably right. It is music that, with all its great qualities, is unmistakably dated. It belongs to a period, and speaks the same language and utters dogmatically in music the same order of ideas and emotions that Rousseau, Shelley and other literary men of his time expressed in words—the brotherhood and equality of man, the perfectibility of human nature, and all the rest of the outworn shibboleths of that age which have no longer any meaning for us, or when they have, repel us with their inadequacy and seeming falsity. But if Professor Dent means to include the music of the last period in his implied stricture, we must emphatically dissent. Indeed, it is probably true that, contrary to his supposition, the later music of Beethoven is about the only music that *is* still convincing to modern ears. All the *Sturm und Drang* of the music of the last century, all the restlessness and conflict of the music of our own time, seems to fade away into nothingness and silence before the unearthly beauty and serenity of such music as the slow movement of the A minor quartet, called in the score a *Song of thanksgiving offered up to the Divinity by a convalescent*. There is a symbolic significance for us in

[1] Ferruccio Busoni, *The Essence of music and other papers*, trans. Rosamund Ley (London, 1957), p. 31.

523

the description. We too are convalescents; the world is only just emerging from a paroxysm of madness, hatred, strife and disillusion, and it is this music, more than any other, that corresponds with our innermost experiences, expresses our most intimate thoughts, and satisfies our deepest and most heart-felt desires.[1]

By this time it was late Beethoven which had become fashionable among the intellectuals. In Aldous Huxley's novels, the aesthetes take their young ladies to recitals where Op. 132 is being played, or beguile them with talk about the *Arietta* of Op. 111 (it was the solidly bourgeois, as in E. M. Forster's *Howard's End*, who had found the message in the Fifth). And it is the last piano sonata which provokes a particularly moving passage in Thomas Mann's *Doctor Faustus*, where its meaning is expounded by the hero's teacher, Wendell Kretschmar, in a way that is meant to reveal its effect on the state of mind of the German avant-garde during the early part of this century.[2] Again it is more the significance than the actual music itself which seems important: take this significance away and we are left with Britten's views on the same music:

I'm not blind about them [Beethoven and Brahms]. Once I adored them. Between the ages of thirteen and sixteen I knew every note of Beethoven and Brahms. I remember receiving the full score of *Fidelio* for my fourteenth birthday. It was a red letter day in my life. But I think in a sense I never forgave them for having led me astray in my own particular musical thinking and natural inclinations. Only yesterday I was listening to the *Coriolanus Overture* by Beethoven. What a marvellous beginning, and how well the development in sequence is carried out! But what galled me was the crudity of the sound; the orchestral sounds seem often so haphazard. I certainly don't dislike all Beethoven, but sometimes I feel I have lost the point of what he's up to. I heard recently the piano sonata, Op. 111. The sound of the variations was so grotesque I just couldn't see what they were all about.[3]

Ernest Newman would have applauded Britten's insistence on musical values. His centennial tribute, *The Unconscious Beethoven*, begins with a diatribe against the interpretations of the past. His attempt at dethroning Beethoven involved a flimsy argument that the composer was

[1] Cecil Gray, *The History of music* (London, 1928), p. 189.

[2] Thomas Mann, *Doctor Faustus*, trans. H. T. Lowe-Porter (London, 1951), pp. 51 ff.

[3] Murray Schafer, *British composers in interview* (London, 1963), p. 119.

syphilitic; worse, he was possessed of a 'morbid sex-complex'. Yet perhaps Newman was right in sensing that Beethoven was in need of rescue from politics and conventional religion:

At a very early stage a Beethoven legend established itself, and the later biographers went zealously about the traditional business of polishing up this legend and eliminating from it everything that did not harmonize with it. This paralysis of the critical faculty extended, in time, to his music. Beethoven became, for the late nineteenth century, not a mere musician, the value of whose work should be judged by the purely aesthetic tests we would apply to that of any other composer, but a man with a message, a seer, an oracle whose plenary inspiration on all occasions it were blasphemy to doubt. His music was admired not simply in terms of music but as an achievement in morality. The humanitarian and democratic nineteenth century was so impressed by his choice of certain lofty literary subjects that it hardly occurred to it to look critically at his manner of treating these subjects in music. It was held, for example, to be the sign of a particularly virtuous nature that he should have chosen for the theme of his solitary opera a story of conjugal fidelity. There had been a regrettable tendency on the part of previous librettists and composers of operas to take an interest in characters, especially female characters, who would hardly have been asked to tea by the most broad-minded of Victorian rural deans; even in our own day English writers have been known to assure us solemnly that the subjects of *Don Giovanni* and *Figaro* are 'not edifying'. But the Leonora of *Fidelio* was respectable enough to be admitted into any Victorian drawing-room: she could show her marriage lines, she was not French, nothing was known against the family, and she clung to her lawful spouse with an adoring fidelity that especially appealed to Victorian male notions of the duty of woman. 'It' [*Fidelio*] 'remains to this day,' Sir Charles Stanford could write, 'the noblest, most ideal, most human, most touching opera in existence.' One already suspects that verdict to be founded on moral rather than purely musical considerations, great as *Fidelio* is in its best moments; and the suspicion becomes a certainty when we read on a little further. The libretto 'contained the germ of the finest quality in human nature, self-sacrifice, and provided him [Beethoven] with the means of preaching a great sermon upon a small but piquant text. A crust of bread has become in his hands the means of stirring the world's emotions for a century.' Even so acute and critical a musician as Stanford, we see, could allow his judgment of *Fidelio* to be affected by moral and humanitarian considerations that are quite outside the domain of aesthetics. Beethoven is praised not so much for the music he has written to the opera as for having chosen a subject that was unimpeachable on the ground of morals. First of all we have the somewhat dubious *obiter dictum* that self-sacrifice is 'the finest quality in human nature'—a sentiment of peculiar appeal to the comfort-loving nineteenth century, that dearly loved to read of self-sacrifice on the part of others—and then, in some queer way, it is held to be a point in Beethoven's favour as an artist that his morals were sound, at any rate theoretically. It is a doctrine that, pushed to its logical extreme, would justify any bad oratorio written to any good Bible text. As it happens, Beethoven's music to *Fidelio* is often fine enough to justify all the praise we can give it; but to regard a musical work as in any way worthy of admiration merely because its text is based on sound moral principles is to confuse aesthetics with morality. Many an eye has been blinded with tears during the Prisoners' Chorus, not because of any particular quality in the music but because the scene has struck home to the spectator's humanitarian feelings: for the time being every member of the audience has become a potential subscribing member of the Howard Association.[1]

Newman's views were supported even more forcibly by Edward Dent, in whose centennial non-tribute Beethoven becomes a positive hindrance to one man's appreciation of the moderns. Dent, it must be said, was fifty and the President of the International Society for Contemporary Music:

I can understand the feelings of the pious, and can even feel a certain weak-kneed sympathy with them, for I was brought up on Beethoven from infancy. Beethoven is the earliest musical impression that I can distinctly remember, and by the time I was twenty-

[1] Ernest Newman, *The Unconscious Beethoven* (London, 1927; rev. ed. 1968), pp. 5 ff.

five I had heard, or at least read and studied, practically the whole of his works, including many which are quite unknown to most musicians, let alone to the ordinary concert-goer. They were not forced upon me by teachers; I read them of my own free will, with the firm conviction that Beethoven represented the supreme height music had ever attained. I imagine that most musicians of my age were educated on similar lines; it was only later on that I came across younger musicians who had been brought up mainly on Bach and had but a sporadic acquaintance with Beethoven. I know that my whole musical outlook has been developed on the foundation of Beethoven, and I begin to see that my outlook might have been more broad-minded if I had in younger days been less whole-heartedly devoted to him. It is Beethoven, I fear, who stands perpetually in the way of my understanding modern music; it is Beethoven who perpetually hinders me from achieving a really sympathetic and intelligent contact with younger minds. Yet I know that if I am ever to enter into the spirit of contemporary music, I must revise my whole outlook on music in general. If so, I must revise my attitude to Beethoven; and however shocked and grieved my more elderly readers may be at so blasphemous an intention, I say plainly and definitely that I do so without hesitation, because my experience as a student of musical history has led me to the conviction that the music of the present day has a higher value for me, as an aesthetic experience, than the music of the past. I am not 'tired of Beethoven' because I was saturated with Beethoven from five to twenty-five and beyond; but I do not much want to hear any of his works again. I may now and then be interested to hear something of Beethoven in order to study the impression which he makes on someone else in whom I may happen to be interested, either as a performer or as a pupil; but for myself alone, Beethoven belongs to the experience of my past life. It is an experience which I absorbed once long ago, and I can never renew it. It is contemporary music that I want to hear now.[1]

Neither history nor most modern composers have endorsed such views. If it is impossible today to follow the Beethovenian paths to

[1] Dent, 'Beethoven and a younger generation', *Musical Quarterly*, XIII (1927), p. 321.

greatness, or for many people to think of him in symbolic terms, there has been a welcome return to the appreciation of the smaller-scale works, those with the less obvious message. Stravinsky sums up the view:

The Eighth Symphony is a miracle of growth and development and I am therefore reluctant to cite my particular admirations out of context. Nevertheless, the entrance of the trumpets and drum in F major in the last movement, after the F sharp minor episode, is the most wonderful moment. I actually had the temerity to imitate this in the March that is No. 6 of my Eight Instrumental Miniatures. For me, the Ninth Symphony contains no event of comparable force. But then, for me, nothing in the Ninth is as perennially surprising and delightful as the development section of the last movement of the Fourth Symphony, or the repeated B flat–A in the Trio of the Fourth, or the *tutti*, measures 50–54, in the *Adagio* of the Fourth.

What are my criticisms of the Ninth? Consider the *Adagio* without prejudice—or try to. The echo-dialogue of winds and strings lacks variation, and the *Andante moderato*, with the pedal A and the repeated octaves, sixths, thirds, is harmonically heavy. (The metronome markings must be in error here, incidentally, for the *Adagio molto* is 60 and the *Andante moderato* only 63.) I find the movement rhythmically monotonous, too—for Beethoven— except in its finest episode, the E flat *Adagio*, but the effect even of that beautiful passage is deadened by the rhythmic inanity of the subsequent $\frac{12}{8}$. Another weakness, or miscalculation, is the repetition, after only six measures, of the heroics at measure 121. What has happened to Beethoven's need for variation and development? The movement is the antithesis of true symphonic form.

The failure of the last movement must be attributed, in large measure, to its thumping theme. As the composer cannot develop it—who could?—he spreads it out like a military parade. I am ever surprised in this movement by the poverty of the *Allegro ma non tanto*, as well as by the riches of the *Allegro energico* (especially measures 76–90, which, oddly enough, anticipate Verdi). I am undoubtedly wrong to talk this way about 'The Ninth', of course, or to question 'what everyone knows'. 'The Ninth' is sacred, and it was already sacred when I first heard it in 1897. I have often wondered why. Can it actually have something to do with a 'message' or with so-called proletarian appeal?[1]

Yet in the end we may doubt whether Beethoven the musician can be divorced from Beethoven the political figure, or whether he himself would have wanted to be. It was a coincidence that it was the opening rhythm of the Fifth Symphony which was found during the Second World War to be a Morse Code 'V', and thus became a victory cry; it was certainly not a coincidence that his music expressed popular feeling against tyranny. So the final word may be left with a politician, Lenin, who, though aware of his own shortcomings as a music critic, none the less felt a general truth:

I know nothing which is greater than the *Appassionata*; I would like to listen to it every day. It is marvellous, superhuman music. I always think with pride—perhaps it is naive of me—what marvellous things human beings can do.[2]

[1] Igor Stravinsky and Robert Craft, *Dialogues and a diary* (London, 1968), pp. 112 f.

[2] Maxim Gorky, *Days with Lenin* (New York, 1932), p. 52.

INDEX

INDEX OF BEETHOVEN'S WORKS